1 CORINTHIANS

THE NIV
APPLICATION
COMMENTARY

From biblical text . . . to contemporary life

1 CORINTHIANS

THE NIV APPLICATION COMMENTARY

From biblical text . . . to contemporary life

CRAIG BLOMBERG

ZONDERVAN®

ZONDERVAN.com/
AUTHOR**TRACKER**
follow your favorite authors

In loving memory of

JOHN W. BLOMBERG (1918–93):

lifelong educator,

inspiring teacher,

faithful Christian,

dedicated father.

ZONDERVAN®

The NIV Application Commentary: 1 Corinthians
Copyright ©1994 by Craig L. Blomberg

Requests for information should be addressed to:

Zondervan, *Grand Rapids, MI* 49530

Library of Congress Cataloging-in-Publication Data

Blomberg, Craig
      1 Corinthians / Craig L. Blomberg.
          p. cm.—(NIV application commentary)
          Includes bibliographical references and index
          ISBN-10: 0-310-48490-1
          ISBN-13: 978-0-310-48490-5
          1. Bible. N.T. Corinthians, 1st—Commentaries. I. Title. II. Title: First Corinthians.
III. Series.
BS2675.3.B56 1995
227'.307—dc20   94–21472

This edition is printed on acid-free paper.

Edited by Jack Kuhatschek

Printed in the United States of America

16 /DCI/ 30 29 28 27

Table of Contents

The NIV Application Commentary Series

When complete, the NIV Application Commentary
will include the following volumes:

Old Testament Volumes

Genesis, John H. Walton
Exodus, Peter Enns
Leviticus/Numbers, Roy Gane
Deuteronomy, Daniel I. Block
Joshua, Robert L. Hubbard Jr.
Judges/Ruth, K. Lawson Younger
1-2 Samuel, Bill T. Arnold
1-2 Kings, Gus Konkel
1-2 Chronicles, Andrew E. Hill
Ezra/Nehemiah, Douglas J. Green
Esther, Karen H. Jobes
Job, Dennis R. Magary
Psalms Volume 1, Gerald H. Wilson
Psalms Volume 2, Jamie A. Grant
Proverbs, Paul Koptak
Ecclesiastes/Song of Songs, Iain Provan
Isaiah, John N. Oswalt
Jeremiah/Lamentations, J. Andrew Dearman
Ezekiel, Iain M. Duguid
Daniel, Tremper Longman III
Hosea/Amos/Micah, Gary V. Smith
Jonah/Nahum/Habakkuk/Zephaniah,
    James Bruckner
Joel/Obadiah/Malachi, David W. Baker
Haggai/Zechariah, Mark J. Boda

New Testament Volumes

Matthew, Michael J. Wilkins
Mark, David E. Garland
Luke, Darrell L. Bock
John, Gary M. Burge
Acts, Ajith Fernando
Romans, Douglas J. Moo
1 Corinthians, Craig Blomberg
2 Corinthians, Scott Hafemann
Galatians, Scot McKnight
Ephesians, Klyne Snodgrass
Philippians, Frank Thielman
Colossians/Philemon, David E. Garland
1-2 Thessalonians, Michael W. Holmes
1-2 Timothy/Titus, Walter L. Liefeld
Hebrews, George H. Guthrie
James, David P. Nystrom
1 Peter, Scot McKnight
2 Peter/Jude, Douglas J. Moo
Letters of John, Gary M. Burge
Revelation, Craig S. Keener

To see which titles are available,
visit our web site at http://www.zondervan.com

NIV Application Commentary
Series Introduction

THE NIV APPLICATION COMMENTARY SERIES is unique. Most commentaries help us make the journey from the twentieth century back to the first century. They enable us to cross the barriers of time, culture, language, and geography that separate us from the biblical world. Yet they only offer a one-way ticket to the past and assume that we can somehow make the return journey on our own. Once they have explained the *original meaning* of a book or passage, these commentaries give us little or no help in exploring its *contemporary significance.* The information they offer is valuable, but the job is only half done.

Recently, a few commentaries have included some contemporary application as *one* of their goals. Yet that application is often sketchy or moralistic, and some volumes sound more like printed sermons than commentaries.

The primary goal of The NIV Application Commentary Series is to help you with the difficult but vital task of bringing an ancient message into a modern context. The series not only focuses on application as a finished product but also helps you think through the *process* of moving from the original meaning of a passage to its contemporary significance. These are commentaries, not popular expositions. They are works of reference, not devotional literature.

The format of the series is designed to achieve the goals of the series. Each passage is treated in three sections: *Original Meaning, Bridging Contexts,* and *Contemporary Significance.*

THIS SECTION HELPS you understand the meaning of the biblical text in its first-century context. All of the elements of traditional exegesis—in concise form—are discussed here. These include the historical, literary, and cultural context of the passage. The authors discuss matters related to grammar and syntax, and the meaning of biblical words. They also seek to explore the main ideas of the passage and how the biblical author develops those ideas.

After reading this section, you will understand the problems, questions, and concerns of the *original audience* and how the biblical author addressed those issues. This understanding is foundational to any legitimate application of the text today.

THIS SECTION BUILDS a bridge between the world of the Bible and the world of today, between the original context and the contemporary context, by focusing on both the timely and timeless aspects of the text.

God's Word is *timely*. The authors of Scripture spoke to specific situations, problems, and questions. Paul warned the Galatians about the consequences of circumcision and the dangers of trying to be justified by law (Gal. 5:2–5). The author of Hebrews tried to convince his readers that Christ is superior to Moses, the Aaronic priests, and the Old Testament sacrifices. John urged his readers to "test the spirits" of those who taught a form of incipient Gnosticism (1 John 4:1–6). In each of these cases, the timely nature of Scripture enables us to hear God's Word in situations that were *concrete* rather than abstract.

Yet the timely nature of Scripture also creates problems. Our situations, difficulties, and questions are not always directly related to those faced by the people in the Bible. Therefore, God's word to them does not always seem relevant to us. For example, when was the last time someone urged you to be circumcised, claiming that it was a necessary part of justification? How many people today care whether Christ is superior to the Aaronic priests? And how can a "test" designed to expose incipient Gnosticism be of any value in a modern culture?

Fortunately, Scripture is not only timely but *timeless*. Just as God spoke to the original audience, so he still speaks to us through the pages of Scripture. Because we share a common humanity with the people of the Bible, we discover a *universal dimension* in the problems they faced and the solutions God gave them. The timeless nature of Scripture enables it to speak with power in every time and in every culture.

Those who fail to recognize that Scripture is both timely and timeless run into a host of problems. For example, those who are intimidated by timely books such as Hebrews or Galatians might avoid reading them because they seem meaningless today. At the other extreme, those who are convinced of the timeless nature of Scripture, but who fail to discern its timely element, may "wax eloquent" about the Melchizedekian priesthood to a sleeping congregation.

The purpose of this section, therefore, is to help you discern what is timeless in the timely pages of the New Testament—and what is not. For example, if Paul's primary concern is not circumcision (as he tells us in Gal. 5:6), what *is* he concerned about? If discussions about the Aaronic priesthood or Melchizedek seem irrelevant today, what is of abiding value in these passages? If people try to "test the spirits" today with a test designed for a specific first-century heresy, what other biblical test might be more appropriate?

Yet this section does not merely uncover that which is timeless in a passage but also helps you to see *how* it is uncovered. The author of the commentary seeks to take what is implicit in the text and make it explicit, to take a process that normally is intuitive and explain it in a logical, orderly fashion. How do we know that circumcision is not Paul's primary concern? What clues in the text or its context help us realize that Paul's real concern is at a deeper level?

Of course, those passages in which the historical distance between us and the original readers is greatest require a longer treatment. Conversely, those passages in which the historical distance is smaller or seemingly nonexistent require less attention.

One final clarification. Because this section prepares the way for discussing the contemporary significance of the passage, there is not always a sharp distinction or a clear break between this section and the one that follows. Yet when both sections are read together, you should have a strong sense of moving from the world of the Bible to the world of today.

THIS SECTION ALLOWS the biblical message to speak with as much power today as it did when it was first written. How can you apply what you learned about Jerusalem, Ephesus, or Corinth to our present-day needs in Chicago, Los Angeles, or London? How can you take a message originally spoken in Greek and Aramaic and communicate it clearly in our own language? How can you take the eternal truths originally spoken in a different time and culture and apply them to the similar-yet-different needs of our culture?

In order to achieve these goals, this section gives you help in several key areas.

First, it helps you identify contemporary situations, problems, or questions that are truly comparable to those faced by the original audience. Because contemporary situations are seldom identical to those faced in the first century, you must seek situations that are analogous if your applications are to be relevant.

Second, this section explores a variety of contexts in which the passage might be applied today. You will look at personal applications, but you will also be encouraged to think beyond private concerns to the society and culture at large.

Third, this section will alert you to any problems or difficulties you might encounter in seeking to apply the passage. And if there are several legitimate ways to apply a passage (areas in which Christians disagree), the author will bring these to your attention and help you think through the issues involved.

In seeking to achieve these goals, the contributors to this series attempt to avoid two extremes. They avoid making such specific applications that the commentary might quickly become dated. They also avoid discussing the significance of the passage in such a general way that it fails to engage contemporary life and culture.

Above all, contributors to this series have made a diligent effort not to sound moralistic or preachy. The NIV Application Commentary Series does not seek to provide ready-made sermon materials but rather tools, ideas, and insights that will help you communicate God's Word with power. If we help you to achieve that goal, then we have fulfilled the purpose for this series.

— *The Editors*

General Editor's Preface

Although separated by nearly two thousand years of history, there are many similarities between the church in Corinth and the world of today. As we read Paul's first letter to the Corinthians and Craig Blomberg's excellent commentary, one underlying similarity stands out: the Corinthian church was riveted by factions that threatened to tear it apart. Paul had to handle strong differences of opinion among the Christians on such topics as marriage, lawsuits, meat sacrificed to idols, worship, and Christian doctrine. Similarly, the world today—and all too often the church as well—is in danger of a terminal fragmentation, a new tribalism.

Is it possible that some of the solutions Paul suggests to the Corinthians can help our dilemma today? Absolutely! To Paul, fostering division was a worldly and immature method of operating. What the church at Corinth needed above all was a unifying wisdom—a wisdom that might seem foolish, weak, and naive to the world, but in reality found its source in the God of all grace.

In the course of his commentary on this magnificent letter, Professor Blomberg details the issues Paul raises and provides an expert analysis of each one of them. In each case the world's wisdom—human reason, unbridled freedom, litigation, no-fault divorce are modern equivalents—is contrasted with the values of God-given wisdom—purity, forgiveness, reconciliation, and mutual faithfulness. Believers then and now must learn that decisions should not be made according to some limited human ethical system but according to whether they will contribute to the building up of the kingdom of God.

Paul's general approach also produces less judgmentalism and more of a "we're in this together trying to solve this problem" approach. To him, if we would just acknowledge the ultimate source of our allegiances, then we would have a much better chance of getting along.

Perhaps no image better personifies the whole purpose of this book than the beautiful image Paul uses of "one body, many parts." We cannot deny we are different from other people in many ways. But Jesus Christ taught us that in the end we are all made and claimed by the same source. It is that source, that one body, to which we owe all that we are and can be. And that is what unifies us in the end.

— *Terry Muck*

Author's Preface

Paul's first letter to the Corinthians might well be entitled "Christian Hot Potatoes" in today's culture. So many of the controversies that divide the contemporary church are addressed in detail in this letter—most notably, sexual immorality, marriage and divorce, women in ministry, and spiritual gifts. Although most of my previously published work has focused on the Gospels, I have regularly taught Paul's two letters to the Corinthians at the seminary and college levels, as well as to laypersons in a variety of contexts. Passages from 1 Corinthians have formed the basis for several recent sermon series I have had the opportunity to preach. It was with great delight, therefore, that I accepted the invitation to contribute to the NIV Application Commentary Series by writing a commentary on one of my favorite biblical books. It is my hope that the format of this series will uniquely enhance the discussion of the relevance of this letter for today's world.

The Series Introduction lays out the overall goals of these commentaries and explains their distinctive format. Each individual author, however, will no doubt interpret the guidelines given there somewhat differently. I have tried to keep the discussion in the sections labeled Original Meaning to a bare minimum. There I include a brief overview of the structure of each unit of Paul's letter, discuss the narrative flow of the author's thought, give insights into significant words and expressions, and make paraphrases and summaries of the main points of the text. I also include remarks on the first-century setting of the passage and occasional, short comments on key interpretive or theological issues.

Under the Bridging Contexts sections, I include information I believe is necessary to help the reader move from first-century Corinth to a different time or culture. Depending on the particular text, I may talk about its interpretation at some other period in history, compare it to other biblical teaching on the topic, raise key interpretive issues that valid applications must take into account, or comment on the form of the passage and how that helps us understand what Paul is emphasizing. My main goal is to formulate the timeless principles that transcend the original situation of the given passage. This section encompasses any material that does not narrowly focus on first-century meaning or twentieth- (and twenty-first-) century application.

The final section, Contemporary Significance, comments on the relevance of the text for the church and our world at the end of the second millennium of the Christian era. I have tried to avoid narrowly parochial concerns in order to address issues that are relevant to a wide cross-section of the church of Jesus Christ, particularly in the Western world, but by no means limited to it. Nevertheless, any commentator's experience of the world is limited. So I do not doubt that readers will be able to reconstruct a lot of my life from my comments, recognize recurring themes of concern, and probably think of many important applications that I have not even considered.

In short, I have tried to follow Jack Kuhatschek's three-step model for applying the Bible: understanding the original situation, determining the broader principles that the biblical application reflects, and applying those general principles to situations we face.[1] Inevitably, there is overlap in the process. I am aware of a number of places where a good case could be made for placing certain comments in a different section, but for a variety of reasons I have felt they belong best where they are. Readers of the commentary should feel free to dip into it anywhere they like, but to get a complete understanding of a particular passage, they should at least consult all three of the sections on that passage. I have tried to provide ample footnotes to allow the reader to follow up numerous comments with more extensive treatments of the topics at hand, while not including so many as to appear cumbersome or overly "scholarly." But scholarly study does indeed lie behind the commentary, for I have worked through the entire text of 1 Corinthians in the Greek, translating and diagramming it, and engaging in an inductive study of my own reflections on each passage before turning in detail to read what others have had to say.

I am grateful to many people who have made this work better than it would have been without their help. Each person on my editorial committee read the entire manuscript and most of them commented on it in detail: Terry Muck, Jack Kuhatschek, Scot McKnight, Marianne Meye Thompson, and Klyne Snodgrass. The students of my July term class at the Southern Baptist Seminary in Louisville, Kentucky, where I taught 1 and 2 Corinthians as a visiting professor in 1993, interacted with much of the material in lecture and discussion form and sharpened my thinking in a variety of ways. Smaller portions of this material have been intensively reviewed by three years of "Tensions in Contemporary Exegesis" classes at Denver Seminary. I am grateful, too, to the faculty and Board of Trustees of the seminary for granting me a sabbatical term during the Winter Quarter of 1994 to help me to complete this project. At the last minute, I received Ben Witherington's manuscript on the Corinthian correspondence in prepublication form. As

---

1. Jack Kuhatschek, *Taking the Guesswork Out of Applying the Bible* (Downers Grove, Ill.: InterVarsity Press, 1990), 33.

my bibliography indicates, I believe this commentary will immediately become one of the most valuable on both of Paul's letters to the Corinthians. Unfortunately, I was unable to incorporate formal references to the work in the body of my text, but I was greatly encouraged to see how regularly we agree, with important, occasional exceptions, on difficult interpretive problems.

Two other works have crossed my desk more recently still. Again, I can commend them only by last-minute additions to my bibliography: Kevin Quast's short but reliable commentary and Duane Litfin's helpful study of ancient rhetoric with special reference to 1 Corinthians 1–4. Otherwise the books reflects literature known to me by May of 1994.

On Thanksgiving Day, 1993, my father, John W. Blomberg, suddenly passed away of a heart attack at age 75. His lifelong passion was education: a public school teacher for thirty-five years and a Christian day-school teacher for ten more, most of them spent in instructing high school students in Spanish. He was an avid fan of my own educational career and, in more recent years, looked forward to each new book of mine. He had read and commented in detail on my previous three manuscripts and would have doubtless done the same for this one. He epitomized the "educated layperson" that Christian publishers so regularly seek to attract for books that bridge the gap between weighty academic tomes and popular paperbacks. He kept me focused on the practical without ever playing down the importance of rigorous scholarship. I would like to think that this book reflects that balance more than anything else I have written. It is to my dad, therefore, that I dedicate this commentary. He is enjoying wonderful happiness with our Lord and the company of the redeemed. If this work can help others gain greater understanding and assurance of their own salvation and live the Christian life in such a way as to attract others to faith, it will prove a fitting tribute to his life. But to God be all the glory!

Abbreviations

ABR—Australian Biblical Review
Bib—Biblica
BibRev—Bible Review
BSac—Bibliotheca Sacra
BT—Bible Translator
BTB—Biblical Theology Bulletin
CBQ—Catholic Biblical Quarterly
CTM—Currents in Theology and Mission
CTR—Criswell Theological Review
EvQ—Evangelical Quarterly
GTJ—Grace Theological Journal
HTR—Harvard Theological Review
Int—Interpretation
JBL—Journal of Biblical Literature
JETS—Journal of the Evangelical Theological Society
JSNT—Journal for the Study of the New Testament
JTS—Journal of Theological Studies
LouvStud—Louvain Studies
Louw and Nida, *Lexicon*—Johannes P. Louw and Eugene A. Nida, *Greek-English Lexicon of the New Testament*, vol. 1 (New York: UBS, 1988)
Neot—Neotestamentica
NIDNTT—Colin Brown, ed., *The New International Dictionary of New Testament Theology*, 3 vols. (Grand Rapids: Zondervan, 1975–78)
NovT—Novum Testamentum
NTS—New Testament Studies
PRS—Perspectives in Religious Studies
RB—Revue Biblique
RevExp—Review and Expositor
RestQ—Restoration Quarterly
RSR—Revue de sciences religieuses
SJT—Scottish Journal of Theology
SWJT—Southwestern Journal of Theology
TrinJ—Trinity Journal
TynB—Tyndale Bulletin
VC—Vigilae Christianae
ZNW—Zeitschrift für die neutestamentliche Wissenschaft

Introduction

IMAGINE A CHURCH wracked by divisions. Powerful leaders promote themselves against each other, each with his band of loyal followers. One of them is having an affair with his stepmother, and, instead of disciplining him, many in the church boast of his freedom in Christ to behave in such a way. Believers sue each other in secular courts; some like to visit prostitutes. As a backlash against this rampant immorality, another faction in the church is promoting celibacy—complete sexual abstinence for all believers—as the Christian ideal. Still other debates rage about how decisively new Christians should break from their pagan past. Disagreements about men's and women's roles in the church add to the confusion. As if all this were not enough, alleged prophecies and speaking in tongues occur regularly, but not always in constructive fashion. A significant number of these immature Christians do not even believe in the bodily resurrection of Christ!

Does this sound like anything you have ever heard of? Probably no contemporary church faces this exact cluster of issues all at once. But all of the issues remain remarkably current. The description, of course, is not of any contemporary church but of the first-century church in Corinth. Yet if we can understand the nature of these problems and the nature of Paul's divinely inspired instruction in response to them, then we will gain great insights into numerous debates that threaten to divide today's church and keep it from having the world-transforming impact God intends it to have.

Yet understanding Paul's message to first-century Corinth is one thing; finding valid applications to communities in other parts of the world and periods of history is another. Paul condemns the disunity in Corinth, but must we condemn denominational divisions seemingly demanded by the heresy or apostasy of one church group? Perhaps the ideal is for believers never to sue one another, but what if they won't submit to Christian mediation? How can churches excommunicate people today when they may turn around and win a major lawsuit against those congregations? How do we apply Paul's apparent preference for the single life to a world in which virtually no one promotes celibacy as desirable for all believers? Should preachers today follow Paul's model of refusing money from the churches to which they are currently ministering?

Finding valid applications, however, is not the only difficulty. Inconsistent applications also seem to abound. Third-World Christians, having just heard and responded to the gospel for the first time, often question why

Western missionaries apparently find no contemporary relevance in 1 Corinthians 11:3–16 (on men's and women's hairstyles or head coverings) and yet earnestly stress the seriousness of the very next passage, verses 17–34 (on not profaning the Lord's Supper). Conversely, most Westerners seem to find all kinds of applications for Paul's teaching on eating meat sacrificed to idols, even though that is scarcely an issue in modern, secularized cultures. Yet Christian congregations are repeatedly pointed to this text as a source for instruction on the consumption of alcohol or the choice of viewing entertainment. Are such applications legitimate?

On the other hand, leaders in many of those same churches seem to feel free flagrantly to disobey Paul's very clear teaching on an issue that is regularly a concern in our world—the manifestation of charismatic gifts. Concluding his discussion of the topic, Paul declares decisively: "Be eager to prophesy, and do not forbid speaking in tongues" (14:39). But many conservative churches do precisely that as they forbid all of the so-called "sign-gifts," at least in public worship. Yet those churches that avoid this error often seem to repudiate Paul's next statement: "But everything should be done in a fitting and orderly way" (v. 40) which, in context, includes such commands as, "If anyone speaks in a tongue, two—or at the most three—should speak, one at a time, and someone must interpret" (v. 27). How can we account for such inconsistencies?

Hopefully no further examples are necessary to convince us of the relevance of 1 Corinthians and of the need for thinking carefully about how to apply it. But before we can begin our commentary on the letter's original meaning and contemporary significance, we need to sketch out the circumstances that led to Paul's writing it. The following comments do not form a comprehensive introduction; this is available in the more traditional commentaries such as those recommended in the bibliography (pp. 31–34). But they do represent the bare minimum of background information we need in order to understand the setting of the letter and to move on to the body of the commentary proper.

The City of Corinth

ANCIENT CORINTH[1] HAD become a prominent city-state in the southern Greek province known as Achaia several centuries before the time of Christ. Already in this era, it had eclipsed Athens in prominence. But the Roman mil-

---

1. Jerome Murphy-O'Connor, *St. Paul's Corinth: Texts and Archaeology* (Wilmington: Glazier, 1983) collects together and comments on the most relevant texts, inscriptions, and artifacts from the ancient Greco-Roman world germane to a study of Corinth during the period leading up to and including Paul's founding of the church there.

itary attacked and destroyed major sections of the city in 146 B.C., leaving it a relatively insignificant, small community until Julius Caesar rebuilt it and established it as a Roman colony in 44 B.C. Roman Corinth had roughly eighty thousand people with an additional twenty thousand in nearby rural areas.[2] Because of its strategic location near an isthmus, which enabled sailors to drag boats across a small strip of land rather than sailing a considerable extra distance around the dangerous coastline of southern Greece, it quickly regained its prominence. In Paul's day, it was probably the wealthiest city in Greece and a major, multicultural urban center. Every two years Corinth played host in its massive stadium to the Isthmian games, competition which was second only to the Olympics in prominence. A large theater seating eighteen thousand and a concert hall which could hold three thousand regularly brought drama and musical entertainment of many forms. Nearby farmers could find a large market for their produce in town, and the city in turn could provide necessary services for the countryside.

The massive hill overlooking the town, somewhat reminiscent of Stone Mountain outside Atlanta, or to a lesser extent Mount Rushmore in South Dakota, housed on its summit a temple to Aphrodite, goddess of love. The temple in Paul's day was smaller than it had been before Roman destruction, and even the earlier temple does not seem to have been big enough to house the one thousand cult prostitutes that the ancient Greek geographer Strabo claimed once worked there. But other writers attest to a sizable contingent within the city itself, so that it is understandable how the Greek word meaning "Corinthian girl" came to be a slang term for a loose woman. Corinth housed other religious shrines too, most notably a temple to Asclepius, the Greek god of healing, as well as sites for worshiping Isis, the Egyptian goddess of seafarers, and her Greek male counterpart Poseidon. Less directly religious in nature but even more pervasive were the Greek ideals of individualism, equality, freedom, and distrust of authority.

Ruins of a Jewish synagogue remain too, with a fragmentary inscription proving its identity. Although these finds probably do not date back quite to Paul's day,[3] there is no reason to doubt a small, earlier Jewish presence in Corinth in the mid-first century, as described in Acts 18:1–6. But the majority of the church, like the majority of the community, would have come from Gentile and pagan backgrounds of numerous cultures (cf. vv. 7–17). The majority too came not from the small, wealthy, and powerful segment of

---

2. Donald Engels, *Roman Corinth* (Chicago: University of Chicago Press, 1990), 84.

3. This is a point seldom observed in the major commentaries, but stressed by Richard E. Oster, Jr., "Misuse and Neglect of Archaeological Evidence in Some Modern Works on 1 Corinthians (1 Cor 7,1–5; 8, 10; 11, 2–16; 12, 14–26)," *ZNW* 83 (1992): 55–58.

ancient Roman society that tended to proliferate in Corinth but from the ranks of ordinary tradesmen and workers (1 Cor. 1:26). But the fact that Paul could command everyone in the church to give generously toward his collection for the needy in Jerusalem (16:1–2) suggests that not many were from the poorest classes either. Corinth may have been one of the few predominantly middle-class churches of the ancient world, but we must remember that "middle-class" was still a far lower standard of living than what we generally associate with that label today.

The few wealthy members of the Corinthian congregation, however, seemed to exercise an influence all out of proportion to their numbers. Corinth was well known for its many "patrons," a Roman designation for well-to-do, influential persons who took on individuals, families, and entire associations of people as their "clients." Patrons provided land, jobs, money, and legal protection for the less well-off, while their clients were expected to reciprocate with various services, including political support, and positive public relations, not too unlike the political nepotism of corrupt governments in many major cities of the world today. There is a fair amount of evidence to suggest that the divisions in the Corinthian church, the neglect of the poor by the rich in celebrating the Lord's Supper, the reaction to Paul's refusal to accept money for his ministry, and perhaps even the proliferation of litigation and sexual immorality had a lot to do with these patrons' reluctance to break from the social conventions of their community which well served their own interests and reputations.[4] Each local house church in Corinth may have been led by one or more of these patrons. Their competing allegiances to Christian leaders like Paul, Peter, and Apollos (1:12) may well have exacerbated the conflicts already present due to class division. At any rate, it is likely that the minority of social elite in the Corinthian church were behind a large percentage of the problems Paul addresses, whether or not they were formal patrons.[5] Little wonder, in light of the accumulation of worldliness in Corinth, that one commentator likens this city to "at once the New York, Los Angeles, and Las Vegas of the ancient world"![6] And another finds Paul's principles in addressing the Corinthian church as a paradigm for how to do urban ministry in the modern world.[7]

---

4. See esp. Gerd Theissen, *The Social Setting of Pauline Christianity: Essays on Corinth* (Philadelphia: Fortress, 1982); John K. Chow, *Patronage and Power: A Study of Social Networks in Corinth* (Sheffield: JSOT, 1992).

5. David W. J. Gill, "In Search of the Social Elite in the Corinthian Church," *TynB* 44 (1993): 323–37.

6. Gordon D. Fee, *The First Epistle to the Corinthians* (Grand Rapids: Eerdmans, 1987), 3.

7. William Baird, *The Corinthian Church: A Biblical Approach to Urban Culture* (Nashville: Abingdon, 1964).

The Circumstances of the Letter

PAUL PLANTED THE CHURCH in Corinth during his second missionary journey, soon after preaching up the coast a bit at Athens (Acts 18:1–17). To support himself he worked as a tentmaker, a trade he shared with fellow Jews Aquila and Priscilla, whom he had met in Corinth (vv. 2–3). As was his custom, he began by preaching Christ to local Jews in their synagogue, but upon receiving repeated rebuffs he moved to a nearby Gentile home and ministered predominantly to the non-Jewish peoples of the town (vv. 4–7). Still, the synagogue ruler (the lay leader who aided the rabbi in conducting services and functioned as a kind of "chairman of the elder board") was converted and joined the fledgling church with his family (v. 8).

One night the Lord spoke to Paul in a vision and encouraged him to stay on in Corinth, because many would come to the Lord. So Paul remained a year and a half, substantially longer than he had in any of the other communities he had evangelized to date (vv. 9–11). How many joined the church we do not know. Any given house church could probably accommodate a maximum of fifty people, but we do not know how many separate gatherings there may have been.

During this time, some of the Jews who had rejected Paul tried to get him imprisoned by Gallio, the Roman governor of the province. Gallio recognized that Paul and his message posed no legal threat to Rome and so refused to take action. Gentile anti-Semitism, never far from the surface in the ancient world, swelled up in response, as some in the crowds used Gallio's acquittal as a pretext to attack the Jewish authorities who had harassed Paul (vv. 12–17). Because Gallio served in this particular role only for about a year, most likely from summer of A.D. 51 to summer of A.D. 52, we can date Paul's stay in Corinth fairly precisely to include this time period. It is also possible that these dates should be reduced by one year, putting Gallio in Corinth from A.D. 50–51, but this seems less likely.[8]

First Corinthians was written approximately three years later, probably in the spring of A.D. 55 (or 54, if we date Gallio's stay a year earlier), since Paul's next major stopping point for any considerable period of time was Ephesus, near the outset of his third missionary journey. And Acts 19:10–22 suggests that Paul stayed there for between two and three years, while 1 Corinthians 16:5–9 reads as if Paul wrote to Corinth during the last few weeks or months of his time in Ephesus, prior to the Jewish festival of Pentecost, usually held in what we would call May. This makes 1 Corinthians the fourth letter Paul penned, after Galatians and 1 and 2 Thessalonians. But several important

---

8. For the most recent discussion, see Jerome Murphy-O'Connor, "Paul and Gallio," *JBL* 112 (1993): 315–17.

developments occurred between Paul's initial trip to Corinth and his writing of this letter.

To begin with, 1 Corinthians is not really the first letter Paul wrote to Corinth. First Corinthians 5:9 alludes to a previous letter which the Corinthians had misunderstood. We know nothing of its contents except that Paul must have told the church not to associate with immoral people. The Corinthians had taken him to be referring to non-Christians when in fact he had meant flagrantly immoral and unrepentant believers (vv. 10–11).

Why was this letter not preserved? Presumably it did not have sufficient instruction on enough topics of abiding significance to be sufficiently valuable to the broader Christian community. We must remember that the biblical writers were inspired only when they wrote what now forms Scripture and not in everything they ever spoke or wrote.

Second, Paul received an oral report from certain unnamed members of the household of a Corinthian woman named Chloe (1:11a). It is possible that these individuals were Stephanas, Fortunatus, and Achaicus, three men whom Paul says arrived with encouragement from the church in Corinth (16:17), but then again they may not have been. Either way Paul learned of several distressing aspects of life in that congregation, most notably the divisions within their fellowship (1:11b–12). Since these divisions included factions aligning themselves with both Paul and Apollos, and since Apollos had ministered in Corinth after Paul had (Acts 18:27–19:1), it is possible that the third Christian leader named—Cephas (or Peter)—had come to town too. Or perhaps some Judaizers, who preached that Gentile Christians still had to keep Jewish laws, had come to town claiming to represent Peter and the Jerusalem apostles. From his visitors, Paul presumably also learned of the problems of sexual immorality and litigation, which he addresses in chapters 5–6.

Third, Paul received a letter from some or all of the church asking questions about specific issues which were dividing that congregation. This too could have been brought by Stephanas and company, but again we have no way of knowing for sure. The way Paul introduces his reference to this letter suggests that chapters 7–16 deal, in turn, with each of the issues it raised ("Now for the matters you wrote about"—7:1).[9] It is likely that we can de-

---

9. Some commentators have assumed that only those topics subsequently introduced with the formula "now about . . ." (7:1, 8:1, 12:1, 16:1, 12) were actually in the letter Paul received and that intervening topics (head coverings, Lord's Supper, resurrection) must have resulted from Paul's personal informants. But it is not likely that the purpose of "now about" is to specify which items have come from the written letter; they merely form one of several ways of introducing a new topic. See esp. Margaret M. Mitchell, "Concerning PERI DE in 1 Corinthians," *NovT* 31 (1989): 229–56.

duce the positions of various groups within the Corinthian church on most of these issues, because Paul often begins by stating a perspective which he then substantially qualifies. This is why, for example, the NIV footnote offers alternative renderings of 7:1 and 8:1, which put part of Paul's words in quotations. Presumably he is quoting a Corinthian slogan and then proceeding to critique it. This strategy is even clearer in 6:12 and 13, in which Paul is responding to oral reports, and in which the NIV inserts the quotation marks into the text itself and not just the footnotes.[10]

The Heart of the Corinthians' Problems

AT FIRST GLANCE, it seems improbable that all of the Corinthians' disparate problems could have had one underlying cause. But a closer look suggests several ways in which their divisions probably sprang from a common source. Certainly their disunity was marked by a recurring arrogance and immaturity. As is so often the case, the most immature often think they are quite mature. In a passage dripping with sarcasm, Paul exclaims, "Already you have all you want! Already you have become rich! You have become kings— and that without us!" (4:8a). And lest anyone not catch the tone of his words, he goes on to add more sorrowfully, "How I wish that you really had become kings so that we might be kings with you!" (v. 8b). At the very least, then, we can say the Corinthians had a misguided view of their own maturity. "They simply considered themselves to have reached the heights of human potential."[11] Related to this is the natural tendency of humanity "to play down the challenge of the gospel and over-emphasize its comfort."[12]

This arrogance may have been tied in with the popularity of lofty and flowery rhetoric among Greek philosophers, especially those known as Sophists, who often valued form above content. Much of chapters 1–4 makes good sense as Paul's response to a church that had become overly impressed with the sophistry of its culture.[13] At other times, their rhetoric was

---

10. The most detailed reconstruction of the events that led up to 1 Corinthians, including suggestions as to the contents of all of these various prior communications, is John C. Hurd, *The Origin of 1 Corinthians* (New York: Seabury, 1965). Admittedly speculative in places, Hurd's overall approach is compelling, except for his idiosyncratic dating of the epistle in relation to the Jerusalem Council of Acts 15.

11. John M. G. Barclay, "Thessalonica and Corinth: Social Contrasts in Pauline Christianity," *JSNT* 47 (1992): 64.

12. Nigel Watson, *The First Epistle to the Corinthians* (London: Epworth, 1992), xxxiii.

13. D. A. Carson, Douglas J. Moo, and Leon Morris, *An Introduction to the New Testament* (Grand Rapids: Zondervan, 1992), 281–82. A major study of Greco-Roman rhetoric more generally, which stresses its difference from philosophy *per se*, and which reconstructs the

less lofty, but the Sophists still valued social status and privilege in ways that perpetuated class distinctions.

The role of patrons as the power-brokers of the Corinthian church points out another contributing factor to the cluster of its problems. Principles of secular leadership carried over into the church, as the wealthy continued to try to buy the friendship of the lower classes, enhance their reputation through litigation, and seek the acclamation of the non-Christian world around them. All of these and other practices relied on models that permeated Roman society but were inconsistent with a cross-centered gospel. Paul must thus avoid the entangling relationships of patronage and insist on models of servant leadership.[14]

In fact, fresh from their immersion in the many pagan religions of the community, most of the Corinthian Christians had not adequately broken in numerous ways from the immorality of the prevailing culture that surrounded them. And, although this culture and these religions reflected stunning diversity, certain perspectives predominated across the board in the Greco-Roman world.

Most noteworthy, perhaps, was a dualism between the material and spiritual worlds. Deeply embedded in Greek philosophy, particularly from the days of Plato on, and eventually culminating in the decades just after Paul's ministry in full-blown Gnosticism, this perspective drove a deep wedge between spirit and matter. Only the former was potentially good and redeemable; the latter was inherently evil. What then was to be done about bodily appetites and desires? A majority of the philosophers tried to deny them and became ascetic in their morality. A majority of the common people took the opposite tack and indulged them. If matter was by nature irredeemable, if religion was primarily or exclusively a matter of the spirit, then why not enjoy sensual pleasures while one could? Life after death, from this perspective, was limited to the immortality of the soul, not the resurrection of the body. Many commentators thus speak of the philosophical background to the Corinthians' problems as even more deeply rooted in Hellenistic and Hellenistic-Jewish wisdom than either sophistry or patronage alone might explain.[15]

---

historical context in Corinth in terms of a church enamored with position and social privilege, is Stephen M. Pogoloff, *Logos and Sophia: The Rhetorical Situation of 1 Corinthians* (Atlanta: Scholars, 1992).

14. For a detailed study, see Andrew D. Clarke, *Secular and Christian Leadership in Corinth: A Socio-Historical and Exegetical Study of 1 Corinthians 1–6* (Leiden: Brill, 1993).

15. See esp. James A. Davis, *Wisdom and Spirit: An Investigation of 1 Corinthians 1.18–3.20 Against the Background of Jewish Sapiential Traditions in the Greco-Roman Period* (Lanham, Md.: University Press of America, 1984).

All of the major problems in the Corinthian church can thus be viewed as stemming from one or the other of these two outworkings of dualistic thought—either asceticism or hedonism. In the latter category naturally appear sexual immorality (chap. 5; 6:12–20), eating food sacrificed to idols (chaps. 8–10), and drunkenness at the Lord's table (11:17–34), all of which indulge bodily appetites. Other alleged manifestations of freedom in Christ—asserting one's own rights with little regard for others—probably belong here as well: lawsuits (6:1–11), flaunting social convention with respect to head coverings (11:2–16), and competition and chaos in the exercise of spiritual gifts (chaps. 12–14). In the former category clearly appear the promotion of celibacy behind chapter 7 and the disbelief in the bodily resurrection behind chapter 15, which both deny the potential goodness of the body and its desires. Here too probably belong the inflated claims to knowledge and wisdom, as immaterial attributes, which exacerbated the divisions addressed in chapters 1–4.[16]

From a theological point of view, this cluster of errors may be labeled an "overly realized eschatology." "Realized eschatology" refers to the blessings of God's kingdom that are available to believers in this age. Overly realized eschatology thus implies that the Corinthians saw all of the blessings of the age to come as available to them immediately, without an adequate appreciation of the gap that still remained between what they were and what they would be only after Christ's return.[17] From a behavioral point of view, we may label this phenomenon overly "triumphalist."

Our introduction thus ends where it began, as we become bombarded with the relevance of this letter. The church of Jesus Christ today, particularly in the West, seems overly triumphalist in so many ways. It appears outwardly strong—and is, if the sole criteria are numbers of members and value of assets and material resources. But the church in the U.S. has been said to be three thousand miles wide and yet only one-half inch deep! So few Westerners have ever experienced the severity of persecution that the early church did, or that many Christians still do in certain parts of our world, that ultimately tests if their faith is genuine or not (cf. 1 Peter 1:6–7). Polls repeatedly claim that upwards of eighty percent of Americans claim to be

---

16. It is probably best to call the distinctively Corinthian manifestation of this dualism a proto- or incipient Gnosticism, rather than full-fledged Gnosticism on the one hand or purely Hellenistic wisdom speculation on the other. See esp. R. McL. Wilson, "Gnosis at Corinth" (pp. 102–14), and John Painter, "Paul and the πνευματικοί at Corinth" (pp. 237–50), both in *Paul and Paulinism*, eds. M. D. Hooker and S. G. Wilson (London: SPCK, 1982).

17. See esp. Anthony C. Thiselton, "Realized Eschatology at Corinth," *NTS* 24 (1977–78): 510–26.

Christian and that between thirty to forty percent claim to have had a "born-again" experience,[18] yet there is little evidence of many of the fruits of genuine conversions or of the practice of true spirituality. Instead we see much behavior that closely parallels the immorality and "I demand my rights" attitude that so characterized Corinth.

Secular standards of leadership also plague our churches. We can learn models of planning and efficiency from the business world. But we err when we leave no room for the Spirit to redirect us or when we fail to exhibit compassion and forgiveness in personal relationships. And when margins of profit or loss replace the demands of the gospel in determining our priorities of ministry, we have replaced Christianity with idolatry.

Quasi-Gnostic attitudes pervade our world today too, from their direct descendants in Christian Science, the Unity School of Christianity, and other "religious science" cults, to their pantheistic cousins, the Eastern religions of Hinduism and Buddhism, in which release from this body is the ultimate good. Still more subtle parallels emerge in a privatized form of Christianity that relegates faith to individual quiet times and insulated church activities but has little effect on the workplace, the public arena, or observable morality and holiness.

An ascetic backlash often reacts against the prevailing hedonism of our day by mandating absolute abstention from various practices and by setting up legalistic requirements as the key to a Christian lifestyle. Nor is it obvious that the average modern person, nor even the average Christian, anticipates a *bodily* resurrection. Popular expectation of life after death, on the upsurge in an era of numerous claims for out-of-the-body and near-death experiences, almost without exception imagines a disembodied afterlife and usually presents it as a relatively bland and unexciting prospect.

Triumphalism covers the waterfront. In some respects it has uniquely characterized the American Christian experience.[19] But today it gives rise to the "health and wealth" gospel with its "name it and claim it" heresy. It appears in the more materialistic branches of the church which, since the early 1980s, have more often than not been found in the evangelical rather than the liberal wing of Christianity. It emerges in the resurgence of postmillennial eschatology—the view that Christians with the help of the Spirit can usher in the completed kingdom of God on earth this side of the return of Christ—which in turn frequently spawns an overly optimistic timetable for

---

18. Cf., e.g., George Gallup, Jr. and Sarah Jones, *100 Questions and Answers: Religion in America* (Princeton: Princeton Religion Research Center, 1989), 68, 166.

19. See Martin E. Marty, *Protestantism in the United States: Righteous Empire* (London: Macmillan; New York: Charles Scribner's Sons, 1986).

fulfilling the Great Commission, often complete with target dates. It results too in the more extreme forms of Reconstructionism, whose adherents believe it is both possible and desirable to create truly Christian political entities this side of the Second Coming. Triumphalism even intrudes into church growth manuals and self-help guides for our therapeutic age, explicitly or implicitly promoting the notion that spiritual success or maturity can be guaranteed and problems eliminated if only we follow the correct formulas outlined for us. But it is time to turn to the antidote for such mentalities—Paul's first letter to the Corinthians itself. May God help us to interpret it properly so we can order our lives according to his priorities.

Outline

I. **Introduction: Greeting and Thanksgiving** (1:1–9)

II. **Letter Body** (1:10–16:4)

  A. **Paul Responds to Oral Reports About the Corinthian Church**
    (1:10–6:20)

    1. Divisions in the Church (1:10–4:21)
      a. The Problem: Rival Factions (1:10–17)
      b. The Cross as the Necessary Center of the Gospel
        (1:18–2:5)
      c. Christian Wisdom as the Necessary Growth (2:6–3:23)
        i. Spiritual People vs. Natural People (2:6–16)
        ii. Spiritual Christians vs. Carnal Christians (3:1–23)
      d. The Right Attitude Toward the Apostles (4:1–21)
    2. A Case of Incest (5:1–13)
    3. Lawsuits Between Believers (6:1–11)
    4. The Seriousness of Sexual Immorality in General (6:12–20)

  B. **Paul Responds to the Letter From the Corinthians** (7:1–16:4)

    1. Concerning Marriage (7:1–40)
      a. To Those Currently or Previously Married (7:1–16)
      b. Analogies With Circumcision and Slavery (7:17–24)
      c. To Those Never Married or Contemplating Marriage
        (7:25–40)
    2. Concerning Food Sacrificed to Idols (8:1–11:1)
      a. Introduction to the Problem and the Solution: Tempering
        Knowledge With Love (8:1–13)
      b. A Second Application: Money for Ministry (9:1–18)
      c. The Underlying Motive: Saving as Many as Possible
        (9:19–27)
      d. Examples of the Danger of License: The Idolatry of Israel
        and Idol Feasts in Corinth (10:1–22)
      e. Summary: Balancing Freedom and Restraint (10:23–11:1)
    3. Concerning Worship (11:2–14:40)
      a. Head-coverings (11:2–16)
      b. The Lord's Supper (11:17–34)

Annotated Bibliography of Commentaries

THE FOLLOWING IS a select list of commentaries and related works on 1 Corinthians, ranked roughly in descending order of overall value. Each is followed by a brief annotation about its scope, perspective, or contents. Works that appear on this list are cited by a full reference the first time they appear in this commentary's footnotes and by short references thereafter. All other works cited throughout the commentary are given a full reference the first time they appear *in any pericope* and short references thereafter in that pericope.

Commentaries on 1 Corinthians

Fee, Gordon D. *The First Epistle to the Corinthians.* New International Commentary on the New Testament, rev. Grand Rapids: Eerdmans, 1987—Solidly evangelical and massive in detail. Probably the single most important commentary on 1 Corinthians from any perspective.

Witherington, Ben III. *Conflict and Community in Corinth: A Socio-Rhetorical Commentary.* Grand Rapids: Eerdmans, 1994—An up-to-date treasure trove of historical background information for each part of 1 and 2 Corinthians, with particular sensitvity to sociological and literary structure.

Barrett, C. K. *A Commentary on the First Epistle to the Corinthians.* Harper's New Testament Commentary. New York: Harper, 1968—A moderate approach from one of Britain's best. The standard before Fee and Witherington came along.

Robertson, A. and Plummer, A. *A Critical and Exegetical Commentary on the First Epistle of St. Paul to the Corinthians.* International Critical Commentary. Edinburgh: T & T Clark, 1911—An enduring standard on the Greek text.

Morris, Leon. *The First Epistle of Paul to the Corinthians.* Tyndale New Testament Commentary. Grand Rapids: Eerdmans, 1985, rev.—Best shorter evangelical exposition, significantly enhanced in its revised form.

Annotated Bibliography of Commentaries

Bruce, F. F. *1 and 2 Corinthians*. New Century Bible. London: Marshall, Morgan & Scott, 1971—Much briefer than all of the above but with remarkable exegetical sense by this century's dean of evangelical scholarship.

Prior, David. *The Message of 1 Corinthians*. The Bible Speaks Today. Downers Grove, Ill.: InterVarsity Press, 1985—Single best volume of contemporary application by a scholar-pastor who reflects international and cross-cultural insights.

Watson, Nigel. *The First Epistle to the Corinthians*. [Epworth] London: Epworth, 1992—An up-to-date, brief, accurate exposition by a long-time Australian professor of note.

Kistemaker, Simon. *Exposition of the First Epistle to the Corinthians*. New Testament Commentary. Grand Rapids: Baker, 1993—Detailed study of text, with special sections on key interpretive issues, Greek words, and practical considerations. Breaks little new ground and tends to read in Reformed theology, but solidly evangelical and thorough.

Snyder, Graydon F. *First Corinthians: A Faith Community Commentary*. Macon, Ga.: Mercer, 1992—A new work by a Mennonite with helpful sections on biblical theology and historical significance in addition to original meaning.

Talbert, Charles H. *Reading Corinthians*. New York: Crossroad, 1987. An important short study focusing on Jewish and Greco-Roman backgrounds and literary structures.

Conzelmann, Hans. *1 Corinthians*. Hermeneia. Philadelphia: Fortress, 1975—Translation of the modern German critical standard. A wealth of historical detail not readily accessible elsewhere, but so consistently idiosyncratic in interpretive views as to make its value very uneven.

Ellingworth, Paul and Howard Hatton. *A Translator's Handbook on Paul's First Letter to the Corinthians*. New York: United Bible Societies, 1985—Particularly helpful for those without Greek; it compares and comments on the RSV and TEV with suggestions for alternate translations and clarifications.

Barclay, William. *The Letters to the Corinthians*. Daily Study Bible rev. Philadelphia: Westminster, 1975—Vintage exposition and application by one of Scotland's great preachers.

Murphy-O'Connor, Jerome. *1 Corinthians*. New Testament Message. Very brief but based on numerous detailed studies by one of this generation's foremost scholars of 1 Corinthians, a moderately conservative Roman Catholic.

Quast, Kevin. *Reading the Corinthian Correspondence: An Introduction*. New York: Paulist, 1994—Reliable, brief evangelical exposition from a predominantly Catholic publishing house!

Chafin, Kenneth L. *1, 2 Corinthians*. Communicator's Commentary. Waco: Word, 1985—Like Prior, very helpful on application. Less exegesis but some excellent homiletical illustrations.

Harrisville, Roy A. *1 Corinthians*. Augsburg. Minneapolis: Augsburg, 1987—Medium-level exposition by an important contemporary Lutheran scholar.

Ruef, John. *Paul's First Letter to Corinth*. Westminster Pelican Commentary. Philadelphia: Westminster, 1971—Concise, readable, but with selected comments rather than running prose in many places. Few exegetical distinctives.

Grosheide, F. W. *Commentary on the First Epistle to the Corinthians*. New International Commentary, orig. Grand Rapids: Eerdmans, 1953—Fee's predecessor before the series was revised. Frequently dated but still at times helpful.

Héring, Jean. *The First Epistle of Saint Paul to the Corinthians*. London: Epworth, 1962—Translation of important older French work, but now increasingly dated and less useful.

Orr, William F. and James A. Walther. *1 Corinthians*. Anchor Bible. Garden City: Doubleday, 1976—One of the less substantial volumes in an illustrious series but with occasionally useful insights.

Patterson, Paige. *The Troubled Triumphant Church*. Nashville: Thomas Nelson, 1983—Tends to overinterpret, but generally solid, popular-level exposition by an influential Southern Baptist.

Vines, Jerry. *God Speaks Today*. Grand Rapids: Zondervan, 1979—Another important Southern Baptist preacher expounds 1 Corinthians, but these are basically just sermons in printed form, and many of the illustrations are becoming quite dated.

Mare, W. Harold. "1 Corinthians." In *The Expositor's Bible Commentary*, ed. Frank E. Gaebelein, vol. 10. Grand Rapids: Zondervan, 1976. Pp. 173–297—One of the weaker contributions to an otherwise important series. At times simply wrong, Mare nevertheless brings his archaeological expertise to bear helpfully on certain passages.

MacArthur, John F. *1 Corinthians*. Chicago: Moody, 1984—Printed form of sermons by one of America's leading preachers, but his dispensationalism at times overwhelms sane exegesis.

Expositions of Parts of 1 Corinthians

Carson, D. A. *The Cross and Christian Ministry: An Exposition of Passages from 1 Corinthians*. Grand Rapids: Baker, 1993—Vintage exegesis and application of 1 Corinthians 1–4 and 9 by one of America's foremost evangelical New Testament scholars.

Carson, D. A. *Showing the Spirit: A Theological Exposition of 1 Corinthians 12–14*. Grand Rapids: Baker, 1984—Same as above on vexed questions of spiritual gifts; perhaps finest balance in interpretation available.

Liftin, Duane. *St. Paul's Theology of Proclamation*. Cambridge: University Press, 1994—A scholarly treatment of chapters 1–4 in light of ancient rhetoric.

Martin, Ralph P. *The Spirit and the Congregation: Studies in 1 Corinthians 12–15*. Grand Rapids: Eerdmans, 1984—Not quite the quality of Carson's second volume noted above, but close.

Studies of Key Themes in 1 Corinthians

Ellis, E. Earle. *Pauline Theology: Ministry and Society*. Grand Rapids: Eerdmans, 1989—Chapters include treatment of body of Christ, spiritual gifts, the "eschatological woman," and so on. By an extremely prolific and influential American evangelical.

Green, Michael. *To Corinth with Love*. London: Hodder & Stoughton, 1982—Thematic studies of most major topics in 1 and 2 Corinthians by an important Anglican pastor-scholar.

Grudem, Wayne A. *The Gift of Prophecy in 1 Corinthians*. Washington, D.C.: University Press of America, 1982—A revised Cambridge thesis, a comprehensive and balanced discussion of the topic.

Hemphill, Kenneth S. *Spiritual Gifts*. Nashville: Broadman, 1988—Solid scholarship, excellent balance, and eminently readable, by one of today's leading Southern Baptist pastor-scholars.

Hurley, James B. *Man and Woman in Biblical Perspective*. Grand Rapids: Zondervan, 1981—Growing out of a Cambridge thesis on 1 Corinthians, this remains the best treatment of the topic from a hierarchical perspective.

Keener, Craig S. *Paul, Women and Wives*. Peabody, Mass.: Hendrickson, 1992—The most exegetically sane and historically detailed discussion of the topic by an egalitarian. Keener is a rising star on the National Baptist horizon.

Schatzmann, Siegfried. *A Pauline Theology of Charismata*. Peabody, Mass.: Hendrickson, 1987—Excellent biblical theology from a mildly charismatic perspective.

1 Corinthians 1:1-9

P AUL, CALLED TO BE an apostle of Christ Jesus by the will of God, and our brother Sosthenes,

²To the church of God in Corinth, to those sanctified in Christ Jesus and called to be holy, together with all those everywhere who call on the name of our Lord Jesus Christ—their Lord and ours:

³Grace and peace to you from God our Father and the Lord Jesus Christ.

⁴I always thank God for you because of his grace given you in Christ Jesus. ⁵For in him you have been enriched in every way—in all your speaking and in all your knowledge—⁶because our testimony about Christ was confirmed in you. ⁷Therefore you do not lack any spiritual gift as you eagerly wait for our Lord Jesus Christ to be revealed. ⁸He will keep you strong to the end, so that you will be blameless on the day of our Lord Jesus Christ. ⁹God, who has called you into fellowship with his Son Jesus Christ our Lord, is faithful.

THE CONVENTIONAL LETTER in the ancient Greco-Roman world began with a salutation, in which the writer identified himself and his recipients and gave a brief greeting.[1] This letter is from Paul, the Pharisaic Jew converted to Christ (Acts 9:1–31), who became the first generation of Christianity's premier church-planter among the non-Jewish world (Acts 13–28).[2] He identifies himself as "called" (v. 1) or commissioned to be an "apostle," not in the sense Luke uses that term for one of the twelve disciples of Jesus (Acts 1:21–26), but as one divinely sent out on a mission of church-planting. Paul will later identify apostleship as a spiritual gift (1 Cor. 12:29). This calling was not of Paul's own choosing, as his Damascus road experience makes plain, but was due entirely to "the will of God." This letter is said also to come from "our brother," that is, fellow-Christian,

---

1. For an excellent analysis of ancient Greco-Roman letter writing and an assessment of the New Testament epistles in that light, see Stanley K. Stowers, *Letter-Writing in Greco-Roman Antiquity* (Philadelphia: Westminster, 1986).

2. An excellent brief overview is Richard N. Longenecker, *The Ministry and Message of Paul* (Grand Rapids: Zondervan, 1971).

Sosthenes, possibly the synagogue ruler of Acts 18:17, if he was later converted. He does not seem to have been involved in the actual writing of the letter but was merely accompanying Paul at the time of its composition.[3]

The recipients of the letter are the Corinthian Christians. They probably comprise several house-congregations, but Paul addresses them as a collective whole, "the church" or assembly of those God has saved. "Sanctified" in verse 2 does not mean *"made* holy," as often in Paul, but separated apart for God. It is virtually synonymous with the next phrase, *"called* to be holy." Paul is reminding the Corinthians of their overarching purpose in the Christian life. He then generalizes to include all Christians everywhere, though obviously not all would immediately read his letter for themselves. "Their Lord and ours" stresses the spiritual unity that all believers share in Jesus Christ.

"Grace" (v. 3) reflects the conventional Greco-Roman form of greeting; "peace," the typical Jewish salutation. But each suggests theological overtones too. Grace is a free gift; peace is wholeness in every aspect of life. Paul Christianizes these conventional greetings by adding a reference to the origin of grace and peace—the one, true, living God revealed in Jesus Christ.

The second section of an ancient Greco-Roman letter was a prayer or a word of thanks. One might typically thank God or the gods for learning that the recipient was in good health or that his or her family prospered. Paul adopts this convention in most of his letters as well but centers primarily on spiritual blessings.[4] When Paul says he "always" thanks God (v. 4a), he means either "repeatedly," or "whenever I pray." His thankfulness for God's "grace" (v. 4b; from the same root as "gift") prepares the way for his references to spiritual gifts in verses 5–7. Paul is grateful that the Corinthian Christians have been enriched or "made wealthy" (v. 5), specifically with reference to the spiritual gifts of speaking and knowledge—most prominently words of knowledge and wisdom, prophecy, and tongues (12:8–10). This occurred as they responded to his preaching with faith and repentance and thus received the Spirit, who began to distribute his gifts among them. The truth of Paul's message was thus confirmed (vv. 6–7). "You do not lack any spiritual gift" (v. 7) might also mean "you are not deficient in the exercise of any gift."

---

3. So most commentators, since Paul's use of the first person plural usually implies "I and other apostles" or "I and other Chrisitans" or is simply an editorial "we." Jerome Murphy-O'Connor, "Co-Authorship in the Corinthian Correspondence," *RB* 100 (1993): 562–79, finds Sosthenes' contribution behind the "we" forms in 1:18–31 and 2:6–16.

4. See esp. Peter T. O'Brien, *Introductory Thanksgivings in the Letters of Paul* (Leiden: Brill, 1977); for incisive, popular exposition, cf. D. A. Carson, *A Call to Spiritual Reformation: Priorities from Paul and His Prayers* (Grand Rapids: Baker, 1992).

How can Paul be so thankful and positive about a church rife with divisions and abuses even of these very gifts? Verses 8–9 supply the answer: God's character provides the guarantee. He will remain faithful to his promises ultimately to perfect his people, however immature they at times seem to be (vv. 8a, 9). When he returns, when the age of the fulfillment of all of the remaining biblical promises arrives, then believers will be made wholly blameless (v. 8b). Acquitted of their past sins, they will be fully prepared for the life to come. Even now, his people are in the process of being remolded, even if it is with fits and starts, as they enter into a personal relationship with Jesus.

 IN TRYING TO APPLY all of a biblical book, it is easy to milk relatively peripheral parts for more than they are worth. This temptation proves particularly strong at the beginning of a letter with preachers who want to start a series of sermons on a given letter with a "bang." The solution to this problem is to determine what a letter writer was stressing in a greeting and thanksgiving and what was merely conventional.

As we have already seen, the name of the author, recipients, and a brief salutation were conventional. So we must not read too much theology into "grace" and "peace" this early in the letter, any more than we assume today that people consciously mean "God be with you" when they say "goodbye," even though that is the etymology of the word. Nor should we make too much of Paul's greeting to "the church of God in Corinth," as if this demonstrated something about the completeness of the church in each of its local manifestations. Instead, we should look for ways in which Paul broke from convention and stress these aspects.

In doing this, we sense Paul's concern to stress his authority in verse 1, by the conjunction of the terms "called," "apostle," and "the will of God." It would not be conventional to add all these descriptions of an author's identity. But many of the Corinthians have rejected his authority (1:12), so immediately at the outset of his letter he begins to seek ways to reassert it. His use of the term "called" is relatively rare. Usually he applies it to what God does for all believers when they are saved—designating them as his own.[5] There is no biblical evidence that all Christians are given a unique calling or commissioning upon conversion which they must seek to discover, though some, like Paul, may be given one. Rather Paul will outline in chapter 12 how

---

5. See esp. William W. Klein, "Paul's Use of *Kalein*: A Proposal," *JETS* 27 (1984): 53–64; idem, *The New Chosen People* (Grand Rapids: Zondervan, 1990), 199–209.

every believer is given at least one spiritual gift. Discovering our gifts is the appropriate way to determine our unique avenues of service or "niches" in the kingdom. Paul's unique additions in verse 1 further stress his authority, but they do so gently, a strategy Paul follows with only occasional deviation throughout his letters.

Unusual in this greeting too are Paul's declarations of the spiritual state of the Corinthians and of God's purposes for them, particularly because when we learn more about them it will be clear that they seem far from holy or "sanctified" in the more traditional sense of that word. Paul hints here at part of the solution—recognizing that the church is "of God" (v. 2) and does not belong to a particular leader or congregation. The Corinthians must also recognize that they are not the center of their religious universe but merely one cog in a large wheel of "those everywhere who call on the name of our Lord." The same Lord is Lord over all, which should inspire Christians in all times and places to seek unity and not factionalism.

Paul's thanksgivings are typically lengthier and more theological than was customary in his day. They obviously provide an opportunity for him to praise God for his many blessings and to set the stage and tone for topics in the letter to come. As with his greetings, we must again look for the unconventional or unexpected to see where Paul's emphases lie to see what we should stress in contemporary application.

Surely the most striking feature of this thanksgiving is how positive Paul can be about a church torn with strife and abuses of the very gifts he thanks God for having given its members. The surprises extend to the very words Paul employs. Being "enriched" (v. 5) will reappear in 4:8 in a passage dripping with sarcasm: "Already you have become rich!" There Paul lambastes their misguided views of their own maturity, yet here he genuinely praises God for their manifold enrichment. Chapters 12–14 make plain that gifts of speaking and knowledge form a central part of the Corinthians' problem with spiritual gifts, but here he is grateful that they have received them. "Knowledge" is closely related to "wisdom," which is being defined by some in the church in an elitist, esoteric fashion, anticipating the development of full-blown Gnosticism. Yet Paul can give thanks because spiritual gifts are the sign of the presence of the Spirit. This is not nominal Christianity—profession without reality. Neither is it lifeless orthodoxy. The Spirit is active amid the Corinthians, even if they are employing their gifts in a somewhat chaotic way.

Verse 7b is crucial in three respects. First, the overly realized eschatology in Corinth (see Introduction, p. 25) probably meant that most were not "eagerly awaiting" Christ's return at all. Paul's statement either reflects what a minority were faithfully doing or refers to their objective state rather than their subjective behavior. So again Paul picks up on what they *should* be doing rather than what most *are* doing, to try to point them in a positive direction. Second, this clause strongly suggests that all the spiritual gifts will last until Jesus comes back. Faithful exercise of the gifts is what Christians are to be about until their Lord returns; they are believers' characteristic form of ministry for this age.[6] Third, by reminding them of Christ's second coming, he prepares the way for what verse 8 implies even more clearly: the church in general is not yet perfected, and this one in particular has a long way to go.

Our focus on God's strength rather than human frailty and on what's going right more than on what's going wrong should lead us to outbursts of praise to God for his grace and faithfulness. This praise should take place privately but also publicly, so that the people we thank God for can be encouraged by hearing us and knowing that we are speaking well of them before the Lord. "To delight in God for his working in the lives of others, even in the lives of those with whom we feel compelled to disagree, is sure evidence of our own awareness of being the recipients of God's mercies."[7] In so doing, we do not abdicate our responsibility to correct others gently (Gal. 6:1), particularly those over whom we are given positions of spiritual authority and responsibility. But we hopefully prepare the way for the best possible reception of our correction, though human freedom to reject our advances ensures that we can never be guaranteed success.

The primary cross-cultural principle that emerges from both Paul's greeting and his thanksgiving is to focus on what is going right in Christian circles before addressing problems that require attention. This is made possible by focusing on the faithfulness of God rather than the fickleness of humans, including Christians who still await perfection. Christian leaders in every age need to imitate Paul's combination of authority and tact (see his classic letter to Philemon), avoiding heavy-handed authoritarianism on the one hand and *laissez-faire* uninvolvement on the other.

THE THEOLOGICAL EMPHASES of Paul's greeting (vv. 1–3) all recur more explicitly and pointedly as his letter unfolds, so detailed application is best reserved for subsequent commentary. But

---

6. E. Earle Ellis, *Pauline Theology: Ministry and Society* (Grand Rapids: Eerdmans, 1989), 26–52.

7. Fee, *First Corinthians*, 37.

we can make some general remarks here and comment on a few specific applications of the thanksgiving (vv. 4–9).

Paul's words in verse 7 offer important insights into the current debate about spiritual gifts. To begin with, since even the most immature believers are gifted in some way, every Christian is immediately useful to Christ and his church with a unique opportunity for ministry. We do not need to seek additional gifts or experiences, as many do today, though we may need training in the use of the gifts we already have. And God may graciously choose to grant us additional ones as we grow. But our primary task is to act in faithful obedience to God and service to his people with what we have already been given.

Second, what is true individually is true corporately. On the one hand, "as far as knowledge is concerned, the church as a body has access to all the wisdom, insight, discernment and truth which it needs; it needs no special gurus to bring it to them."[8] On the other hand, if all the gifts are for the entire Christian age, serious questions must be asked of contemporary congregations that are closed to certain of the so-called sign gifts. It seems likely that they run the serious risk of missing out on blessings the Spirit would want to bring them. Such conclusions will, of course, remain controversial. Perhaps we can more readily agree that, charismatic or not, fellowships that err on the side of overexercise and misuse of their gifts and talents are less displeasing to God than those that err on the side of underuse. Immature but growing children delight their parents far more than those who simply refuse to mature in some area of their lives.[9]

At the same time we must vigilantly guard against false claims of maturity, of a sense of having arrived, or of achieving sinless perfection for any substantial length of time, as certain modern offspring of the Wesleyan and holiness movements periodically claim.[10] This will occur only when Christ returns (v. 8b). For most of us, this reminder should actually provide great comfort and encouragement. In our complex and pressure-filled world, most Christians more commonly struggle with the awareness of persistent sin in their lives, with feelings of inadequacy and immaturity. Yet God remains

---

8. David Prior, *The Message of 1 Corinthians* (Downers Grove, Ill.: InterVarsity Press, 1985), 24–25.

9. For a recent, reasonably well-balanced discussion of several of these themes, see Jack Deere, *Surprised by the Power of the Spirit* (Grand Rapids: Zondervan, 1993).

10. Indeed, such a claim virtually disproves itself, for as Dale Moody (*The Word of Truth* [Grand Rapids: Eerdmans, 1981], 324) puts it, "Perfect sanctification is good to pursue, but self-righteousness is sure to follow any claim that it has been achieved."

faithful: "He who began a good work in you will carry it on to completion until the day of Christ Jesus" (Phil. 1:6).

Verses 8–9 also have important implications for the so–called "eternal security" debate. Those whom the Spirit has genuinely indwelt will experience transformation. Those who begin this process can rest assured that God will be faithful to complete it. Of course, such verses provide no assurance for professing believers who have never shown any evidence of the gifts of the Spirit. Eternal security is not a doctrine to be applied glibly to all who have claimed to be Christian, however superficial their commitment has seemed to be.

It is also important to note that Paul speaks to the church collectively. In our day of so many "lone-ranger" Christians, it is important to recall that neither here nor elsewhere does Scripture envisage Christians apart from a local church. So God is also in the process of perfecting his people corporately as well as individually.

1 Corinthians 1:10–17

❦

I APPEAL TO YOU, BROTHERS, in the name of our Lord Jesus Christ, that all of you agree with one another so that there may be no divisions among you and that you may be perfectly united in mind and thought. ¹¹My brothers, some from Chloe's household have informed me that there are quarrels among you. ¹²What I mean is this: One of you says, "I follow Paul"; another, "I follow Apollos"; another, "I follow Cephas"; still another, "I follow Christ."

¹³Is Christ divided? Was Paul crucified for you? Were you baptized into the name of Paul? ¹⁴I am thankful that I did not baptize any of you except Crispus and Gaius, ¹⁵so no one can say that you were baptized into my name. ¹⁶(Yes, I also baptized the household of Stephanas; beyond that, I don't remember if I baptized anyone else.) ¹⁷For Christ did not send me to baptize, but to preach the gospel—not with words of human wisdom, lest the cross of Christ be emptied of its power.

 VERSE 10 BEGINS the actual body of the letter, which falls into two main parts—Paul's response to information about the Corinthians, which he has heard by word of mouth (1:10–6:20) and his reply to a letter the Corinthians sent him (7:1–16:4).

In the first half, Paul refers to four problems he has heard about that are plaguing the Corinthian church—factions (1:10–4:21), incest (5:1–13), lawsuits (6:1–11), and sexual immorality more generally (6:12–20). The members of Chloe's household, an otherwise anonymous but presumably Corinthian family, have brought him news of the first of these problems (1:11). These emissaries, possibly the same as Stephanas, Fortunatus, and Achaicus (16:17), probably also described the latter three problems, because in 7:1 Paul shifts to matters about which the Corinthians had written him.

Paul deals with the first of the four problems at greatest length, perhaps because the Corinthian divisiveness to varying degrees underlay all the other problems. First Corinthians 1:10–17 states the essential problem (rival factions) and Paul's essential solution (an appeal for unity). First Corinthians 1:18–4:21 will unpack why that unity is so crucial and how it can become possible. This section in essence gives four methods for achieving unity: focusing on the cross of Christ (1:18–2:5), understanding true spiritual wisdom (2:6–16), recognizing the fundamental equality of all believers (3:1–23), and treating Christian leaders appropriately (4:1–21).

Paul's basic appeal for unity (v. 10) involves several key expressions. He exhorts the church in the "name" (power or authority) of Jesus that all of them "agree," literally meaning that they all "say the same thing." They must abolish "divisions," a political term for rival parties or factions.[1] They should become "perfectly united," a verb probably better rendered "restored to unity,"[2] in "mind" and "thought," terms that include the ideas of counsel and choice. Together these two expressions embrace volition as well as cognition.

Verses 11–12 then elaborate the nature of the Corinthian factions: people are quarreling because they are aligning themselves with different Christian leaders. We do not know anything about Chloe except that it is a woman's name, often used among the well-to-do. It is natural to assume she was a member of the church in Corinth; those in her household could well have been her sons or slaves. Some have speculated that she was a leader of some kind in the church. But we do not even know for sure that she was a Christian, and it is just barely possible that she lived in Ephesus, and the messengers from her had traveled to Corinth and returned back to Paul with this news.

The reasons for the rival alignments are not much clearer. In light of the dispute between Peter and Paul in Antioch (Gal. 2:11–14), many have seen a theological debate here too between a more legalistic and a more law-free gospel. Apollos, we know from Acts 18:24–28, was a gifted orator. Perhaps those inclined to be impressed with lofty rhetoric and speculative wisdom rallied around him. But there is little evidence that Paul, Peter, and Apollos were themselves at odds with one another at this point. And the disparity between the "haves" and the "have-nots" at the Lord's Supper (11:17–34) suggests that a polarization along the lines of rich (with Apollos?) and poor (with one or more of the other party leaders?) may have been an even more fundamental factor in the divisions (see Introduction, p. 20).

Worth noting also is the fact that three of the four parties were *not* aligning themselves with Paul. His authority was seriously in jeopardy with a sizable number in the church. Was the Christ-party one that nobly refused to over-exalt any human leader, or had it too become factious? Its inclusion with the rest would suggest the latter. Similarly, Paul does not seem to be pleased that any are clinging to his name as a point of contention with the others. If

---

1. Margaret M. Mitchell, *Paul and the Rhetoric of Reconciliation* (Tübingen: Mohr, 1991), 75.
2. C. K. Barrett, *The First Epistle to the Corinthians* (New York: Harper & Row, 1968), 42.

the church in Corinth was comprised of multiple house-congregations meeting in different parts of town, the seeds of rivalry could have been sown by those geographical divisions as well.

Paul's initial reply to these reports consists of three rhetorical questions all implying the answer "no" (v. 13). Christ is not divided, so how can his people be? Neither Paul nor any other human leader was crucified for the world's sins, so how can these Christians so exalt merely mortal authorities? Christian baptism was into the "name" (again implying power or authority) of Jesus (Acts 2:38), not into the names of Paul, Peter, or Apollos. Verses 14–16 then expand on this last observation as Paul tries to recall how many people he baptized in Corinth. The answer is few.

Here is perhaps another clue to the nature of the rivalries: these young Christians may have been idolizing the particular leaders who first brought them to the Lord. We know Apollos preached in Corinth after Paul did (Acts 19:1), and it is quite possible that Peter or some of his disciples did as well. Crispus is most likely the synagogue ruler of Acts 18:8. Gaius is almost certainly the host of the church whom Paul praises in Romans 16:23 (and to be distinguished from the recipient of 3 John). Of Stephanas we know nothing else except that which is told in 1 Corinthians 16:15–17.

Baptism played a prominent role in the life of the early church, as the outward ritual signifying repentance from sin and initiation into the Christian community. Still, as throughout the New Testament, it takes a back seat here to the ministry of proclamation and the response of conversion. By saying Paul did not baptize many, he must mean that he delegated this responsibility to others. The reference to Stephanas' "household" (v. 16) recalls the household baptisms of Acts 16:15 and 32. Verse 17a must thus be taken as referring to relative priorities. Paul's primary calling was to preach rather than to baptize.

Verse 17b introduces the thought that will form the main idea of 1:18–2:5. The focus of Christian proclamation must remain clearly centered on the message of the crucifixion rather than baptism or any other doctrine, however important in its own right it may be. "Words of human wisdom" correctly interpret the more literal "wisdom of a word," with "human" being used to refer to that which is merely "human" and therefore separate from the divinely transforming message of the atonement.[3] Paul is surely stressing that

there can be no room for pyrotechnic displays of rhetorical virtuosity such as were offered by the traveling sophists who could be heard

---

3. See esp. Richard A. Horsley, "Wisdom of Word and Words of Wisdom in Corinth," *CBQ* 39 (1977): 224–39.

in the market places of any Mediterranean city. Such oratorical skill would leave his hearers gaping at his cleverness and rob the cross of its force.[4]

But even when Greco-Roman rhetoric was not this flowery, it still was based on a fundamentally anti-Christian worldview that Paul could not accept—enshrining the beautiful and powerful people of that day in a position of social power.

PRINCIPLES FOR DEALING with divisions emerge from several parts of this passage and can apply in many cultures. By beginning with an "appeal," Paul avoids the twin errors of demanding his way and not addressing the problems at all. Any authority he has comes solely from "our Lord Jesus Christ" (v. 10). First-century churches operated neither by autocratic decisions imposed by ecclesiastical authorities nor by a simple majority vote. Acts outlines the ideal with its repeated references to decisions the church made only when they were "in one accord" (Gk. *homothumadon*—cf. Acts 1:14; 4:24 [cf. v. 32]; 15:25).

Paul does not side with one particular faction; this would exacerbate the problem. Instead, he is after whatever it takes to dispel factiousness and create harmony. But he cannot be requesting unanimity of perspective on every issue nor requiring uniformity of action, inasmuch as his emphasis on the diversity of spiritual gifts in chapters 12–14 precludes demands for Christian "cloning." Cooperation, mutual concern, peaceful coexistence, edification in love—all these are the positive antidotes to divisiveness.

Paul most likely refrained from spelling out the nature of the factional alignments because his audience already knew what they were. But the omission was undoubtedly providential. By leaving unspecified the contents of the rival positions, we are enabled to generalize broadly when we come to apply the text. If we knew with certainty, for example, that the Cephas party were Judaizers, we might be tempted to apply Paul's teaching only to analogous groups today. As it stands, Paul remains committed to unity despite numerous brands of strife, and in applying this passage we need to see that his principles transcend the specific conflicts.[5]

But we may still highlight particularly close parallels to our best guesses at what each group represented. Legalism has quenched growth in many

---

4. Watson, *First Corinthians,* 8.

5. For an excellent example of such application, see D. A. Carson, *The Cross and Christian Ministry: An Exposition of Passages from I Corinthians* (Grand Rapids: Baker, 1993), on 1:18–4:21 and 9:19–27.

Christian circles down through the centuries. The temptation to elevate form over substance seems equally timeless. Always there will be faithful followers of a church's founder, but they may prove as divisive in clinging to tradition as the more avant-garde. Similarly, churches that reject the labels that link denominations with human founders (e.g., Lutheran, Wesleyan, Mennonite) have often become as denominational or even sectarian in their exclusive claims to serve Christ only (e.g., Disciples of Christ, Church of Christ, Church of Jesus Christ of Latter-Day Saints).

Paul's reminder of the uniqueness of the atonement in verse 13 remains beneficial against periodic rival claims. More specifically, given the amount of detail he devotes to it, we find throughout verses 13–17 a crucial warning against elevating baptism to the level of importance that only salvation should occupy.

On the one hand, baptism played a more central role in the early church than it often has in certain Protestant traditions. It closely followed on the heels of conversion (e.g. Acts 8:36), and biblical writers often used the word *baptism* as a metonymy (one object substituted for a closely related object) for repentance itself (e.g. Rom. 6:3–4). And even the most articulate exponents of infant baptism will admit that there is no clear biblical evidence for such a practice, that it is more a theological corollary from other doctrines, developed after the first generation of church life.[6] The one specific item we learn from Acts about household baptisms, for example, comes in the story of the Philippian jailer in which Luke implies that all were old enough to "believe" (Acts 16:34).

On the other hand, right here in 1 Corinthians Paul makes plain that baptism itself does not regenerate or guarantee salvation (1 Cor. 10:1–12). And when it becomes divisive, as it apparently had at Corinth, then it has been unduly stressed. The doctrine of baptismal regeneration (that one must be baptized to be saved) is unbiblical. So too is the establishment of rigid boundaries between baptists and paedobaptists that prevent loving, vibrant, cooperative ministry for kingdom causes.

Verse 17 paves the way for the discussion that ensues and sets up a contrast that will take two forms: (1) that which is obviously merely human versus that which is clearly from God; and (2) that which claims to be Christian—but is at best immature and at worst downright false because it is not cross-centered—versus genuine, mature Christianity with the crucifixion at its heart. What would have stunned the Corinthians, as it has many

---

6. See, for example, Geoffrey W. Bromiley, *Children of Promise* (Grand Rapids: Eerdmans, 1979).

would-be believers ever since, is Paul's claim that their brand of Christianity falls into the category of the immature and possibly even false.

In short, Paul introduces in verses 10–17 the key for promoting unity and avoiding divisiveness—focusing on Christ rather than exalting human leaders. In so doing, we are driven to the cross, which should also promote humility rather than arrogance and rivalry. When we recognize the cross and all it stands for—the atoning, substitutionary sacrifice of the God-man for sinners in need of salvation, vindicated by his bodily resurrection and exaltation—we have identified the cluster of complementary and fundamental truths that must forever form the core of Christian faith. We also recognize how most other doctrines recede into the periphery, most notably the external signs of inward truths, such as baptism. We should resolve not to let these less central matters erect barriers to fellowship and service among God's people in his world.

ONE CAN SCARCELY reflect at length on verses 10–17 without raising serious questions about the history of Christian denominationalism. There have no doubt been times when certain wings of the church have become so heretical or disobedient that faithful disciples of our Lord have had to distance themselves and start afresh. Protestants have often pointed to the Reformation as the classic example of this, although some church historians wonder what would have happened if Luther had worked more patiently within the Roman Catholic Church for another generation, given the winds of change heralded already by Erasmus and arguably stifled by Luther's tactical intransigence.

But surely the majority of Christian denominations, particularly the numerous subgroups into which most of the major branches of Protestantism have split, have been spawned at least as much by personal rivalry, animosity, and a spirit of intolerance, often along geographical or ethnic lines. As Snyder puts it, "Theological plurality has not been as much a problem as alienating behavior, a behavior which has developed a sense of uncompromising rectitude on the part of some people."[7]

The disunity of the church of Jesus Christ remains one of the greatest scandals which compromises its witness today. In John 17, Jesus prayed that his disciples might be united. In Ephesians 3, Paul expounds the unity of the church across the greatest sociological divisions of the ancient Middle East—Jew versus Gentile. The evangelistic potential of a united church

7. Graydon F. Snyder, *First Corinthians: A Faith Community Commentary* (Macon, Ga.: Mercer, 1992), 25.

extends to the most powerful anti-Christian forces in the universe (Eph. 3:9–10). The only way this unity can have an impact on a non-Christian world is for it to be visible.

Church should be a place where people who have no other natural reason for associating with each other come together in love, but instead it often remains the most segregated aspect of Western society today.[8] Whatever benefits homogeneous groupings have for certain kinds of outreach, a fully mature congregation should integrate people of disparate races, nationalities, socioeconomic strata, and societal status.[9] It should probably also strive to determine as little as possible by a fifty-one percent vote but utilize a consensus approach to crucial decisions, in which a substantial majority of members can agree and in which others can agree to subordinate their interests to the will of the majority.[10]

Whatever forces work within a given congregation to promote rivalries around human leaders, divisions over matters not fundamental to preserving the true gospel of Jesus must be lovingly but firmly dissipated. Today this may often mean that generation gaps and disputes over philosophies of ministry can be settled by having alternate services and programs for different groups within a congregation. Still, a far more powerful witness occurs when people agree to learn to sing music they don't naturally like and support activities that are not their highest priorities. Church leadership in return should seek a blend of ministries and experiences in worship that sooner or later addresses the needs of all in one unified body.

The Christian celebrity phenomenon presents great hazards as well, creating "groupies" who hang on every word (or song) of radio and television preachers or singers without testing their messages against the Scriptures as carefully as they do those of their own pastors and leaders.

The contemporary ecumenical movement, particularly within the World Council of Churches, has scared many evangelicals away from creating new visible, external structures to display Christian unity. Certainly Paul would never have tolerated the popular "lowest common denominator" form of ecumenism that promotes only what all professing Christians can accept. But

---

8. One of today's most articulate spokespersons against this segregation, who personally pastors a church currently modeling cross-cultural diversity, is Anthony T. Evans. See esp. his *America's Only Hope: Impacting Society in the '90s* (Chicago: Moody, 1990).

9. For a more balanced perspective from within the church growth movement, and against earlier paradigms, see Thom S. Rainer, *The Book of Church Growth: History, Theology, and Principles* (Nashville: Broadman, 1993).

10. Helpful suggestions for facilitating this unity, drawing on the examples of the early church, appear in Luke T. Johnson, *Decision-Making in the Church: A Biblical Model* (Philadelphia: Fortress, 1983).

this is not the *goal* of the WCC, and not a few evangelicals have participated in it.

What is more, conservative Christians have excelled at creating parachurch organizations with doctrinal statements that preserve the fundamentals of the faith while allowing full participation of some members of virtually every Protestant church. With renewal movements in Catholic and Orthodox circles, some parachurch organizations will also admit certain members of these branches of Christendom. But if we recognize this distinction between the fundamentals and the peripherals of the faith outside the institutional church, how much more ought we not to recognize it within the church?

Views on baptism, the Lord's Supper, the millennium or the rapture, women in ministry, spiritual gifts, and numerous other items should not stand in the way of intensive networking and cooperation among a wide variety of churches in a given community or region for the larger purposes of the kingdom.[11] Many new church plants, like older but growing congregations, are removing denominational labels from their buildings and advertising in favor of a "community church" identity. Interdenominational congregations frequently grow better than those that remain restricted by outmoded forms of ministry they have inherited from their denominations. Others remain affiliated but play down potentially divisive denominational allegiances. All these models need to be imitated and multiplied.[12]

Denominations should seriously consider the possible advantages of merging with their closest cousins and then ask the tougher questions about those issues that divide them from more distant kin. The Church of South India stands as a testimony from the twentieth century of how disparate denominations could formally merge without compromising the fundamentals of the faith. The indigenous church in China after the Communist Revolution demonstrated the necessity and vitality of obliterating most Western denominational distinctions, though not surprisingly they created some new ones of their own.

Missions organizations working in the least evangelized parts of the world regularly sense the need to cooperate and join forces. Recent efforts have even shared donor databases.

---

11. For excellent suggestions on the way baptists and paedobaptists could remove many of the obstacles which still separate them, see David Bridge and David Phypers, *The Water That Divides* (Downers Grove, Ill.: InterVarsity Press, 1977).

12. For an incisive treatment of many of the issues at stake, see Leith Anderson, *Dying for Change* (Minneapolis: Bethany, 1990).

When will the institutional church, and particularly the church in the individualized West, put away its petty squabbling and begin to demonstrate this biblically mandated unity more visibly? Not a few unbelievers ancient and modern have rejected the gospel on the grounds that a religion as visibly divided as Christianity could scarcely reflect the truth!

1 Corinthians 1:18–2:5

FOR THE MESSAGE of the cross is foolishness to those who are perishing, but to us who are being saved it is the power of God. ¹⁹For it is written:

"I will destroy the wisdom of the wise;
the intelligence of the intelligent I will frustrate."

²⁰Where is the wise man? Where is the scholar? Where is the philosopher of this age? Has not God made foolish the wisdom of the world? ²¹For since in the wisdom of God the world through its wisdom did not know him, God was pleased through the foolishness of what was preached to save those who believe. ²²Jews demand miraculous signs and Greeks look for wisdom, ²³but we preach Christ crucified: a stumbling block to Jews and foolishness to Gentiles, ²⁴but to those whom God has called, both Jews and Greeks, Christ the power of God and the wisdom of God. ²⁵For the foolishness of God is wiser than man's wisdom, and the weakness of God is stronger than man's strength.

²⁶Brothers, think of what you were when you were called. Not many of you were wise by human standards; not many were influential; not many were of noble birth. ²⁷But God chose the foolish things of the world to shame the wise; God chose the weak things of the world to shame the strong. ²⁸He chose the lowly things of this world and the despised things— and the things that are not—to nullify the things that are, ²⁹so that no one may boast before him. ³⁰It is because of him that you are in Christ Jesus, who has become for us wisdom from God—that is, our righteousness, holiness and redemption. ³¹Therefore, as it is written: "Let him who boasts boast in the Lord."

²:¹When I came to you, brothers, I did not come with eloquence or superior wisdom as I proclaimed to you the testimony about God. ²For I resolved to know nothing while I was with you except Jesus Christ and him crucified. ³I came to you in weakness and fear, and with much trembling. ⁴My message and my preaching were not with wise and persuasive words, but with a demonstration of the Spirit's power, ⁵so that your faith might not rest on men's wisdom, but on God's power.

FIRST CORINTHIANS 1:18–2:5 EXPLAINS verse 17b—how genuine, full-orbed Christianity stands opposed to the fundamental values of a fallen, sinful world but provides the necessary antidote to the self-centered factionalism of the Corinthians. First Corinthians 1:18–25 puts forth the essential contrast between God's wisdom and the wisdom of the world. First Corinthians 1:26–2:5 then defends Paul's claim that the true gospel is the message centered on the cross, by appealing to the Corinthians' own experience, both in their pre-Christian background (1:26–31) and in their reception of Paul's initial ministry among them (2:1–5).

First Corinthians 1:18 provides the thesis sentence which sums up the point of the first paragraph of this section (vv. 18–25). Verse 19 supplies scriptural support for Paul's thesis. Verses 20–25 then begin to explain why the world so roundly rejects the cross-centered gospel and why the Corinthians should nevertheless believe it.

Paul's thesis affirms that there are only two kinds of people in the world—those in the process of perishing and those in the process of being saved (v. 18). Each will respond to the gospel message in diametrically opposite ways. Verse 19 quotes Isaiah 29:14 for support, from a context in which the prophet is proclaiming God's intentions to judge Israel for her superficial and hypocritical religion. "Frustrate" in this verse comes from a word that means "reject, refuse, ignore, make invalid, set aside, break."[1] Verse 20a rebukes the seemingly learned. "Wise man," "scholar," and "philosopher" are intended to be roughly synonymous; the latter two are more literally "scribe," and "debater," respectively.[2] Paul may be intending to address both Greek and Jewish wise men with his labels.[3]

Verse 20b makes it clear that Paul is not disparaging *Christian* wisdom, intelligence, scholarship, or philosophy; indeed 2:6–16 will expound the appropriate wisdom for believers. Rather, he is predicting the ultimate demise

---

1. Barclay M. Newman, *A Concise Greek-English Dictionary of the New Testament* (London: United Bible Society, 1971), 4.

2. Markus Lautenschlager, "Abschied vom Disputierer: Zu Bedeutung von συζητητής in 1 Kor 1, 20," *ZNW* 83 (1992): 276–85, prefers "philosophical investigator" to "debater."

3. Less likely, but still possible, is the view that this triad of titles corresponds to the three leaders in a Pharisaic school (*bet midrash*): the sage (*hakam*), scribe (*soper*), and commentator (*darsan*). See Martin Hengel, *The Pre-Christian Paul* (Philadelphia: Trinity, 1991), 42.

of the sages, legal experts, and orators "of this age" or "of this world"—parallel expressions for sinful humanity apart from Christ.

Verse 21 explains how the state of affairs of verse 18 came about. People in their fallen, worldly wisdom rejected God, so God confirmed humanity in its rebellion with a plan of salvation that would seem foolish (cf. Rom. 1:18–32). But in his omniscience, he had anticipated this all along, so that the whole plan itself was "in the wisdom of God."

Verse 22 then specifies two key ways major ethnic groups of Paul's world found Christianity foolish. Many Jews looked for dramatic, miraculous confirmation of Jesus' claims, which he refused to give (e.g. Matt. 12:38–42). Many Greeks considered speculative philosophies the highest human ideals, with their concomitant emphasis on rhetoric, esoterica, and elitism. For such people, the cross was a stumbling-block (literally, "scandal") and foolishness (v. 23). Many Jews viewed the crucifixion as ultimate proof that Jesus had been cursed by God for some sin of his own (Deut. 21:23). Many Greeks found numerous aspects of the story of Christ's death foolish—a suffering God, the ideal of perfect order destroyed, a criminal Messiah, and a way to God not based on human speculation.

But those whom the Spirit of God touches and convicts, from whatever ethnic background, will find in the cross both godly wisdom and power to transform their lives (v. 24). That the gospel seems foolish by human standards should not count against it. Surely one should expect the ways of an omniscient and omnipotent God to be far above human ways. Hence, the NIV correctly fills in the ellipses of verse 25, which more literally reads, "for the foolishness of God is wiser than humans and the weakness of God is stronger than humans." That which is least clever or powerful of all about God still greatly surpasses the most stupendous achievement of humanity.

First Corinthians 1:26–31 contrasts the status of most of the Corinthians in their society when they were first saved ("called"). Not many were among the seemingly wise philosophers or rhetoricians; not many were powerful ("influential") in the government, military, or religious circles; not many were born into wealthy families (v. 26). Many slaves and freedmen had made their way to Corinth. Although the majority of people in the church were not from the most destitute strata of society (see Introduction, pp.19–20), they were outside the circle of the strong and mighty. Hence, Paul could term them "the foolish," "the weak," and "the lowly" (vv. 27–28), in direct opposition to the three attributes of verse 26.

Then Paul adds the perspective of the powerful on such people—they are "despised" and "things that are not." Yet these are the people God for the most part chose to be saved, to shame the wise and strong and to "reduce to nothing" (NRSV) people who claim to be something. In short, he removes any grounds for boasting in one's self-sufficiency (v. 29). And if the world deems people unfortunate who cannot boast about their own accomplishments, blessings in Christ far more than compensate. In him, believers receive true wisdom: the wisdom of the cross and all its benefits (v. 30)—right standing before God ("righteousness"), moral cleansing ("holiness"), and rescue from slavery to sin ("redemption"). Christians can properly boast, not in their own achievements, but in the Lord (v. 31), as in Jeremiah 9:24, the verse Paul quotes here. This quote interestingly follows a verse that declares, "Let not the wise man boast of his wisdom or the strong man boast of his strength or the rich man boast of his riches" (Jer. 9:23). And those are precisely the three categories Paul has enunciated in 1 Corinthians 1:26.[4]

Paul's references to boasting, both positive and negative, form an important motif throughout his letters. Boasting about oneself played a crucial role in Greco-Roman sophistry and in secular leadership more generally.[5] Some philosophers criticized its most self-serving forms; others applauded its rhetorical flourishes. Most all agreed that the one form of boasting that was usually justified was boasting in one's weaknesses. This theme takes on special prominence in Paul's correspondence with Corinth, especially in 2 Corinthians 10–13.[6]

First Corinthians 2:1–5 rounds out this section by reminding the Corinthians of the content and style of Paul's own ministry when he was with them. "Superior" in verse 1a probably modifies both "eloquence" and "wisdom." Paul does not deny that he tried to present his message in as compelling a form as possible, merely that by the world's standards he was at best ordinary. Second Corinthians 10:10 confirms this understanding, as Paul notes that some in Corinth claim that "in person he is unimpressive and his speaking amounts to nothing." Early manuscripts are fairly evenly divided between "the testimony" and "the mystery" in verse 1b. If the latter is what Paul wrote, then it paves the way for the term's reappearance in verse 6, but the former is perhaps slightly more likely original. Verse 2 cannot be taken absolutely as if the only doctrine Paul taught on was the crucifixion (cf. 1 Cor. 15:3–8, in which the resurrection proves equally crucial) but refers rather to its centrality in his preaching. At Corinth, in particular, the church

---

4. For an interesting study of the determinative role of the Jeremiah verses on this entire paragraph, see Gail R. O'Day, "Jeremiah 9:22–23 and 1 Corinthians 1:26–31: A Study in Intertextuality," *JBL* 109 (1990): 259–67.

5. Andrew D. Clarke, *Secular and Christian Leadership in Corinth* (Leiden: Brill, 1993), 95–99.

6. See esp. Christopher Forbes, "Comparison, Self-Praise, and Irony: Paul's Boasting and the Conventions of Hellenistic Rhetoric," *NTS* 32 (1986): 1–30.

needed to embrace more of the humility of the cross and tone down the triumphalism of the resurrection.[7]

Verse 3 underlines Paul's sense of personal inadequacy and dovetails with the Lord's reassurance to him not to be afraid (Acts 18:9–10). His "weakness" here may also allude to the thorn in his flesh (2 Cor. 12:7)—some persistent physical ailment. The "wise and persuasive words" of verse 4 must again refer to worldly wisdom and persuasion, since they are contrasted with "the Spirit's power." Verse 5 restates the rationale for his strategy, complementing the contrast between 1:29 and 31. We might paraphrase Paul's intent in verses 4–5 as follows:

> Though my speech and my proclamation persuaded you so that you have πίστις [faith], your πίστις is not a γνῶσις [knowledge] gained through rhetoric which swayed you on the basis of the opinions of those who are honored as possessing superior, wise eloquence. Rather, your faith is grounded on something far more sure than clever arguments based on opinion. Your faith is based on the most absolute form of proof—the sure proof of God's Spirit and power.[8]

In short, the Corinthians came to faith by focusing on the cross of Christ which seemed so foolish to every one else. They must now return to that focus rather than splitting the church by magnifying human leaders.

Bridging Contexts

THE PROBLEMS THAT Paul addresses in this passage recur in almost every society, because they reflect human nature and not merely conditions of specific cultures. The self-centeredness that is at the heart of rejecting "Paul's gospel" is the essence of human sin. As a result, numerous timeless principles emerge from this text. Paul raises three questions in particular, the answers to which must be balanced by Paul's further teaching in 2:6–3:23: (1) Should Christians seek to possess wisdom? (Answer: Only if it is cross-centered—cf. 1:18–2:5 with 2:6–16); (2) Do Christians with godly wisdom merit any special status? (Answer: no, but they will receive greater praise on Judgment Day—cf. 1:26–31 with 3:1–23); (3) Can we recognize true wisdom through our speech? (Answer: Yes, if it points people to the cross; no, if it revels in its own rhetoric—2:1–5).[9]

---

7. On Paul's theology of the cross more generally, see Charles B. Cousar, *A Theology of the Cross: The Death of Jesus in the Pauline Letters* (Minneapolis: Fortress, 1990).

8. Stephen M. Pogoloff, *Logos and Sophia* (Atlanta: Scholars, 1992), 140.

9. I owe the formulation of these questions to James A. Davis, "1 Corinthians 1–6" (Unpubished manuscript, 1993): s.v. 1:18–2:5, "Form/Structure/Setting," but the formulation of the answers is my own.

Verses 18–25 counterbalance the remarkable successes in Jerusalem at Pentecost (Acts 2:1–41) or in Thessalonica twenty years later (1 Thess. 1:4–10) and remind us that we cannot expect all or perhaps even a majority of people to respond positively to the gospel. Conversely, if Christianity becomes too popular, we had better check to make sure we have not so diluted it that the offense of the cross has been removed.

This paragraph puts apologetics in its proper place too. Compelling arguments for the faith must always be formulated, but only the convicting work of the Spirit will ever use them to bring people to Christ. In neither preaching nor apologetics is the scandal of the cross an excuse for putting unnecessary stumbling blocks, such as tactlessness or lovelessness, before people. But Murphy-O'Connor offers the salutary reminder that "any attempt to make the gospel palatable by bringing it into line with the tastes of those to whom it is preached distorts it, because in this case the criterion is made the expectations of *fallen* humanity."[10] In so doing, it loses its power.

Because the wisdom Paul rails against is "of the world" (v. 20), nothing in this paragraph may be taken as grounds for anti-intellectualism. Yet Paul surely stands staunchly against *godless* intellectualism. Verses 21–25 point out that such godlessness may take three different forms, each increasingly more subtle. People may simply reject God outright (v. 21). Or they may look for him in the wrong places, demanding miraculous signs or engaging in speculative philosophies (vv. 22–23). Or they may remake him in their own image, not recognizing the qualitative difference between God and humanity (v. 25). With respect to signs, God may choose to grant them in hopes that people will thereby believe (John 20:31), but he seldom if ever supplies them on demand, and he insists that people have enough evidence for belief without them (John 20:29).

Verse 21 presents an interesting triad of agents of salvation and damnation. To begin with, humans are directly accountable for their own destinies: "The world through its wisdom did not know him," while the saved are "those who believe." Next there is the intermediate agency of "what was preached" versus rival methods purporting to save or claiming salvation unnecessary. But ultimately all is ascribed to God ("since in the wisdom of God ... "). Consistently in Scripture the doctrine of election allows God to be sovereign without compromising human freedom or responsibility. Indeed, God's elective purposes are effected precisely through such free activity—in the proclamation of the word.

Overall 1:18–25 demonstrates a close congruence between the Corinthians' claims to religious wisdom and the wisdom that is in fact the domain of

---

10. Jerome Murphy-O'Connor, *1 Corinthians* (Wilmington: Glazier, 1979), 14.

fallen humanity.[11] False religion, especially that which masquerades as Christianity, is as vacuous as utter secularism and more dangerous because it hides its true colors. Paul stops short of making this equation complete, since the Spirit has taken up residence in these believers. But he offers a stern reminder that "the cross thus stands as the final negation of all human attempts to attain God. Its truth cannot be *achieved* through the best of human intellect and strength but must be *received* as a gift in the humble submission of faith and trust."[12]

The rich and powerful of every era in church history love to point out that the logical inference of verses 26–31 is that if not many were wise, influential or wealthy, then a few must have been. We have noted earlier (pp. 19–20) that more of the Corinthians might have been tolerably well off than in many of the early churches. But all this is the opposite of Paul's main thrust here. Of course, it is possible to be rich and Christian, but frequently at the times the church has been least compromised with culture and politics, the majority of believers have not come from the upper classes of the world.[13] From the pre-Constantinian era to the Radical Reformation, from religiously motivated immigration to America in past centuries to the rapid spread of Christianity in the Two-Thirds World today, this trend has proved surprisingly recurrent. For it is precisely the well-to-do who are often likely not to sense any need for God, because they believe they can buy or manipulate their way into meeting all their needs.[14]

Conversely, Scripture nowhere guarantees salvation for all people under a certain socioeconomic level. But it does consistently reflect God's special concern for the poor, oppressed, and marginalized people of the world. James 2:5 parallels 1 Corinthians 1:26–31 in pointing out the sociological makeup of much of early Christianity. But when God "chose the poor" they were also "those who loved him," who recognized their need for help and

---

11. Peter Lampe, "Theological Wisdom and the 'Word About the Cross'," *Int* 44 (1990): 117–31.

12. John B. Polhill, "The Wisdom of God and Factionalism: 1 Corinthians 1–4," *RevExp* 80 (1983): 330.

13. Cf., e.g., Bruce L. Shelley, *The Gospel and the American Dream* (Portland: Multnomah, 1989).

14. For a full history, see Robert G. Clouse, Richard V. Pierard, and Edwin M. Yamauchi, *The Two Kingdoms: The Church and Culture through the Ages* (Chicago: Moody, 1993). For additional implications, cf. L. L. Welborn, "On the Discord in Corinth: 1 Corinthians 1–4 and Ancient Politics," *JBL* 106 (1987): 110: "What *is* certain is that [Paul's] attempt to avoid any complicity in the affairs of this world, to separate religion as far as possible from practical politics, proved to be of historic significance. Its repercussion can be heard in Augustine's negative evaluation of the *civitas terrena* and in the political naturalism of Machiavelli and Rousseau."

their personal inadequacy and hence turned to the true and living God. One of the key Hebrew terms for "poor," the *anawim*, combines precisely these two elements—material poverty and spiritual piety.[15] Historically, Christians have had to guard against the twin errors of spiritualizing "the poor," as if they could include the materially wealthy, and of politicizing the term, as if salvation could be claimed apart from explicit faith in Christ.

First Corinthians 2:1–5 must be read in its larger context to avoid serious misrepresentations of Paul in particular and Christianity in general. Rhetorical criticism is increasingly demonstrating how well-trained in literary artistry Paul was. Verse 1 cannot be taken absolutely, because 1 Corinthians itself is very carefully crafted, using numerous devices designed to try to persuade Paul's readers of his message.[16] Paul is thus "willing to employ human eloquence, for this is intrinsically neutral, as long as it remains subservient to the message of the Gospel and the divine work of the Spirit." But even in this qualified use he distances himself from many of his contemporaries, as he argues "against that method of preaching which employs literary figures not as a means to convey better the message of the Gospel, but as ornamentations intended to please and amuse the congregation."[17] Nor does this paragraph give preachers the right not to prepare their messages thoughtfully. But it reminds us that homiletical techniques alone do not prepare us to preach with spiritual power. Only when the Spirit first convicts us from a given text do we then have the right to preach it to others.

First Corinthians 2:2 must not be taken as any kind of reversal of policy from Paul's frustrations with a poor reception in Athens, inasmuch as Acts 17:22–31 actually stands as a masterful model of the effective contextualization of the gospel. But urban philosophers are not normally a receptive audience for the Christian message, so only a few respond positively there. Verses 3–5 play a central role in formulating a theology of Paul's preaching. To "proclaim" is to act as a herald and authoritatively declare the news, in this case with the authority of the Lord. "But because God's authority is not obvious, as measured by human standards, the preacher as herald stands in a

---

15. Cf. Matthew 5:3 with Luke 6:20. The reason these verses do not contradict each other lies precisely in this twofold significance of the term *poor*.

16. On chapters 1–4 in particular, see esp. K. E. Bailey, "Recovering the Poetic Structure of 1 Cor. 1,17–2,2," *NovT* 17 (1975): 265–96 (more convincing on 1:18–30 than on the rest); J. Bradley Chance, "Paul's Apology to the Corinthians," *PRS* 9 (1982): 145–55 (on the function of 1:4–6:20 as a defense of Paul's apostleship); and Benjamin Fiore, "'Covert Allusion' in 1 Corinthians 1–4," *CBQ* 47 (1985): 85–102 (on the proliferation of figures of speech and their rhetorical functions in these chapters).

17. Timothy H. Lim, "'Not in Persuasive Words of Wisdom, but in the Demonstration of the Spirit and Power'," *NovT* 29 (1987): 149.

vulnerable position. Preaching is thus a weak medium both in content and form."[18] Still, it demonstrates its power as people are saved and churches established.

The contrasts in 1:18–2:5 may be summed up in terms of a theology of glory versus a theology of the cross. The former leads to equations between true Christianity and specific political parties or agendas, material wealth, or heavy-handed leadership. The latter seeks to bind up the broken-hearted, empower the disenfranchised, and love the unlovely of our world.[19] In short, 1:18–2:5 drives people to the level ground at the foot of the cross. If we really understand that Christ experienced the agony that we deserved to suffer, how can we possibly exalt ourselves or any other human leaders?

As we turn to apply this passage today, we must ask who in our world are the high and mighty, inside or outside the church, and stop to see if they are truly using their power for selfless purposes. We must also identify the downtrodden, again both Christian and non-Christian, and see if we are paying them ample and appropriate attention. Some poor, for example, are as self-centered as some rich. On the other hand, we must beware of seeking to help only "the worthy poor," since God never waits for any of us to be worthy before he helps us.[20] Above all, we should look for ways to communicate the centrality of Christ's atoning death in compelling fashion to contemporary cultures.

ONE WONDERS HOW much contemporary preaching is in fact cross-centered. Ours is an age of user-friendly, seeker-sensitive techniques for church growth. Some of these techniques affect only the form and not the substance of the gospel, but others are more suspect. Many people have rejected human sin and personal accountability for evil actions in favor of passing the blame onto corrupting societal influences. Such people have an acute need to hear the true meaning of the crucifixion of Christ. Positive thinking and possibility thinking perhaps have a limited place for people with an overly poor self-image,[21] but they do not adequately substitute for repentance and trust in Jesus.

---

18. J. W. Beaudean, *Paul's Theology of Preaching* (Macon, Ga.: Mercer, 1988), 118.

19. Cf. the particularly poignant exposition of these themes in Molly T. Marshall, "Forsaking a Theology of Glory: 1 Corinthians 1:18–31," *Ex Auditu* 7 (1991): 101–4.

20. See the challenging treatment of this theme in Robert Lupton, *Theirs is the Kingdom* (San Francisco: HarperCollins, 1989), 60–61.

21. This is the strength, for example, of the often maligned but stunningly successful ministries of people like Norman Vincent Peale and Robert Schuller.

Such counter-cultural attitudes will, of course, continue to be branded as foolish, even by some within the church. Secular and liberally minded religious scholars as well as self-taught philosophers and gurus stand at the forefront of the crowds that most consistently mock evangelical Christianity. They tolerate every bizarre and immoral ideology conceivable but refuse to include born-again Christians in their antidiscrimination campaigns. We should not be surprised, but we should avoid the constant peril of trying to imitate secular standards of wisdom in striving to make our Christian institutions closely resemble their secular counterparts. An overemphasis on professionalism in the pastorate, scholarship as the dominant criterion for jobs in higher education, purely market-driven strategies for church growth, and therapeutic models of Christian counseling that deliberately avoid prayer, Bible study, and confession of sin all illustrate the dangers of such imitation. In each case, something takes center stage away from a frank admission of our spiritual impotence apart from the crucified Christ working through us. [22]

The contemporary church also struggles to formulate a balanced theology of signs and wonders. Chapters 12–14 will expand on this theme, but the very least that must be said here is that we dare never try to put God in a box, either by demanding that he *must* work a miracle (or claiming that if he doesn't somebody obviously had inadequate faith) or by pretending to know that he no longer *does* work miracles![23] Parallels to the Greek lust after wisdom emerge directly in modern-day Gnosticism, reflected in various branches of the New Age movement,[24] and indirectly in our degree-hungry society, saturated also with self-help seminars and studies for those who want more informal education.

The same standards for popularity—wisdom, power, and money—remain in our culture. These determine who receives adulation from their peers in our schools. They form the heart of the lure of most advertising campaigns. And their inroads into the church must always be thwarted. Much Western Christianity has fallen to a "suburban captivity" which domesticates the gospel and loses the central focus of the Scriptures on the spiritually *and physically* poor and needy of this world. Healthy churches will combat this trend by expending significant portions of their budgets and personal attention on

---

22. Cf. the only slightly overstated critique by Os Guinness, *Dining with the Devil: The Megachurch Movement Flirts with Modernity* (Grand Rapids: Baker, 1993).

23. For a balanced perspective, see Lewis B. Smedes, ed., *Ministry and the Miraculous* (Pasadena: Fuller Theological Seminary, 1987).

24. See esp. Douglas Groothuis, *Revealing the New Age Jesus* (Downers Grove, Ill.: InterVarsity Press, 1990).

evangelism and social action, locally and globally, in balanced combinations.[25] And 1:30 directs our attention to another pair of priorities that cannot be divorced—correct knowledge and correct behavior. Too many today, both inside and outside of the church, more closely resemble the ancient Greek philosophers who drove a wedge between inward spirituality and outward morality.

First Corinthians 2:1–5 forces us to raise the question of styles of Christian preaching and leadership. Fundamental matters of the faith require forceful proclamation; peripheral ones, more tentative affirmation. The authority of the Word must not be supplanted by authoritarian styles of proclamation and administration. Highly polished turns of phrase must never overwhelm the clarity and correctness of the essential message. In many large and gifted congregations, we need more worship and less performance.

It is interesting to compare possibly the three greatest evangelists in North America during the last 150 years—D. L. Moody, Billy Sunday, and Billy Graham. Neither Moody nor Graham was known for impressing audiences with lofty rhetoric; frequently their sermons were deemed simplistic. Sunday was known for a flashy style, but he still preached a very basic gospel message. But all three centered on the cross and the need for personal conversion. As a result, they gave encouragement to millions of "down-and-outers," and countless came to the Lord through their preaching.

On the other hand, Western missions is still recovering from an imperialist, triumphalist perspective that often failed to treat indigenous Christians in other lands, or the poor and minorities in our own inner cities, as equals. But for those in every part of our world who feel deeply their own inadequacy, Paul gives great encouragement that God can use even them in powerful and mighty ways as they rely not on themselves but on his strength.[26]

---

25. For details, see Ronald J. Sider, *One-Sided Christianity* (San Francisco: HarperCollins; Grand Rapids: Zondervan, 1993).

26. For a more academic study of this theme, see David A. Black, *Paul: Apostle of Weakness* (New York: Lang, 1984). For challenging practical applications to the way Western Christians do ministry, see Alice F. Evans, Robert A. Evans, and William B. Kennedy, *Pedagogies for the Non-Poor* (Maryknoll, N.Y.: Orbis, 1987).

1 Corinthians 2:6–16

WE DO, HOWEVER, speak a message of wisdom among the mature, but not the wisdom of this age or of the rulers of this age, who are coming to nothing. ⁷No, we speak of God's secret wisdom, a wisdom that has been hidden and that God destined for our glory before time began. ⁸None of the rulers of this age understood it, for if they had, they would not have crucified the Lord of glory. ⁹However, as it is written:

> "No eye has seen,
>   no ear has heard,
> no mind has conceived
>   what God has prepared for those who love him"—

¹⁰but God has revealed it to us by his Spirit.

The Spirit searches all things, even the deep things of God. ¹¹For who among men knows the thoughts of a man except the man's spirit within him? In the same way no one knows the thoughts of God except the Spirit of God. ¹²We have not received the spirit of the world but the Spirit who is from God, that we may understand what God has freely given us. ¹³This is what we speak, not in words taught us by human wisdom but in words taught by the Spirit, expressing spiritual truths in spiritual words. ¹⁴The man without the Spirit does not accept the things that come from the Spirit of God, for they are foolishness to him, and he cannot understand them, because they are spiritually discerned. ¹⁵The spiritual man makes judgments about all things, but he himself is not subject to any man's judgment:

> ¹⁶"For who has known the mind of the Lord
>   that he may instruct him?"

But we have the mind of Christ.

THUS FAR IT might seem that Paul has little positive to say about "wisdom," introduced in 1:24. This section corrects this impression but clarifies that beneficial wisdom must be compatible with the truths of Christianity. He develops this point by contrasting two different pairs of people: Christians versus non-Christians (2:6–16) and spiritual Christians versus worldly Christians (3:1–23). There is a wisdom that all Christians have by the mere fact that they have the Spirit living in them, but it is appropriated only when they yield themselves to the Spirit rather than act in accordance with the desires of the flesh—their fallen human nature.

While there is a foolishness to the gospel (1:18–25), there is also a wisdom that the Corinthians must understand in order to overcome their divisiveness. The content of that wisdom remains a profoundly cross-centered Christianity (recall 1:23). First Corinthians 2:6–10a introduces the theme of this wisdom and its acceptance by believers and rejection by unbelievers (parallel to the contrasts of 1:18–25). Verses 10b–16 then elaborate those responses by contrasting those who have the Spirit with those who do not.

The "mature" of verse 6a are the opposite of "the rulers of this age" (v. 6b) just as Paul's "message of wisdom" (v. 6a) contrasts with the "wisdom of this age" (v. 6b). Because those who are not mature are unbelievers, the mature in this context must be all Christians, at least in principle, and not just some elite group of believers. But the irony is that the Corinthians are not living according to this reality but as if they were still unsaved and in the grip of the world's values.

The "rulers" refer at least to the religious and political authorities of the day, comparable to Caiaphas and Pilate, who crucified our glorious Lord (v. 8). But they may also refer to demonic powers behind the opposition to the gospel (cf. Eph. 2:2, in which Satan is the "ruler of the kingdom of the air").[1] "Coming to nothing" at the end of verse 6 thus refers to the ultimate transience of this age and its powers (cf. NRSV: "doomed to perish").

"God's secret wisdom" (v. 7a) is literally "wisdom in a mystery." But the word *mystery* in the New Testament most commonly refers to components of the gospel once hidden but now revealed.[2] The concept of a crucified

---

1. Wesley Carr, "The Rulers of this Age—1 Corinthians II.6–8," *NTS* 23 (1976–77): 20–35, strongly disputes this, noting that the plural of the noun is never so used in the New Testament. But he has to play down the possible influence of incipient Gnosticism (which regularly used ἄρχοντες for quasi-angelic or demonic beings) as well as the cluster of New Testament concepts surrounding "the powers of this age" or "this world," which often include demonic forces.

2. See esp. Raymond E. Brown, *The Semitic Background of the Term "Mystery" in the New*

Messiah was not clearly understood in Old Testament times and was still not grasped in Paul's day by those who rejected Jesus (v. 8). But this should not cause surprise; Isaiah himself had prophesied unexpected wonders surrounding God's coming salvation for his people (Isa. 64:4; 52:15, quoted and paraphrased in v. 9). And all along God had planned these wondrous events for the benefit of those who would respond positively (v. 7b). The Holy Spirit who brings people to Christ now reveals to them what once was unknown (v. 10a).

The contrast between those who possess the Spirit and those who do not (vv. 10b–16) begins with a syllogism—a three-part argument in which two premises, if true, logically entail a particular conclusion (vv. 10b–12). (1) The major premise observes that only a person's own spirit or mind knows that individual's thoughts unless he or she chooses to disclose them to someone else (v. 11a), an affirmation which is true for God as well as humanity (vv. 10b, 11b). "Search" (v. 10b) thus equals "knows the thoughts of" (v. 11b). (2) The minor premise reiterates that Christians have God's Spirit living in them (v. 12a). "The spirit of the world" (v. 12a) refers to fallen, human nature and ideologies, not to anything more directly demonic. (3) The conclusion logically follows then that Christians can know God's thoughts, at least to the extent that his Spirit graciously reveals them (v. 12b).

Verses 13–16 reiterate the fundamental contrast of 1:18–2:5. "Human" wisdom (v. 13a) must thus refer to that which is *merely* human, that is, unregenerate. Verse 13b is notoriously difficult to translate but the NIV has probably captured it. The margin gives the next most likely rendering: "interpreting spiritual truths to spiritual people."[3] Fortunately the overall sense remains intact on either reading (cf. 1 Thess. 4:9).

"The man without the Spirit" (v. 14) interprets the adjective *psychikos*, from the noun *psyche*, meaning "soul" or "life." The KJV is well-known for its translation, "the natural man." In other words, this is a person in his ordinary, unredeemed state of earthly existence, which he inherited from the Fall. Such a person "does not accept" Christian truths. This phrase makes it clear that

---

Testament (Philadelphia: Fortress, 1968). Chrys C. Caragounis, *The Ephesian "Mysterion"* (Lund: Gleerup, 1977), has made a convincing case that the term also refers to an element of inscrutability in God's ways.

3. The Greek reads *pneumatikois pneumatika sunkrinontes*. The second adjective is clearly neuter; the first could be either neuter (referring back to *logois*—"words"—in verse 13a) or masculine (referring to people and looking ahead to verse 14). A third possibility is to translate *sunkrino* as "compare," which could yield "comparing spiritual things with [other] spiritual things." Cf. Simon J. Kistemaker, *Exposition of the First Epistle to the Corinthians* (Grand Rapids: Baker, 1993), 90–91.

the "understanding" described in verse 14b is not primarily cognitive but volitional.

Conversely, the "spiritual man" (v. 15a) simply refers to the person *with* the Spirit, and, hence, to any Christian (cf. 12:13). "Makes judgments" comes from the same verb as "discerned" and helps to interpret it. Believers have the ability to bring God's perspective to bear on every aspect of life.[4] Verse 15b must be interpreted in light of the entire context: Christians are not subject to any *merely* human evaluation, that is, one that does not take God's perspective into account. But Paul may also be anticipating his argument in 4:3–5 that even evaluation by fellow believers is provisional; the only judge who ultimately counts is God. Verse 16 rounds out the passage by quoting Isaiah 40:13 on the inscrutability of God's ways, but it echoes the thought of verses 7 and 10–12 that some of this mystery has now been removed in the Messianic age, in which the Spirit brings Christ's thoughts to believers by living in them.

Bridging Contexts

HERE APPEARS PAUL'S third method for heeding his appeal to heal the wounds of divisiveness (1:10–17). In addition to the first two methods—Christians must concentrate on what is going right (1:1–9) and on Christ and him crucified (1:18–2:5)—now Paul advocates that they focus on true godly wisdom (2:6–16). In this section, Paul uses numerous technical terms that the Corinthians employed to justify their spiritual elitism ("wisdom," "mature," "secret," "spiritual") and redefines them so that they include that which is available to all believers.[5] Therefore, one of the keys to applying this section is to understand accurately how Paul himself reapplied these terms and then how they can be translated into today's world.

Clearly Paul wants to insist that "all Christians are potentially perfect or mature in Christ, though only some are actually what all ought to be."[6] Paul's redefinitions should therefore preclude a common misunderstanding of the text which affirms that he is establishing two categories of believers related to their knowledge or giftedness. In 3:1–4, he will introduce termi-

---

4. Harold Mare, "1 Corinthians," in *The Expositor's Bible Commentary*, ed. Frank E. Gaebelein (Grand Rapids: Zondervan, 1976), 10:203, helpfully defines *anakrino* in both of these uses as "to make intelligent spiritual decisions."

5. For how these terms would have been used in Hellenistic or Jewish circles influenced by pre-Gnostic tendencies, see esp. Birger A. Pearson, *The Pneumatikos-Psychikos Terminology in 1 Corinthians* (Missoula, Mont.: Scholars, 1973); Richard A. Horsley, "Pneumatikos vs. Psychikos: Distinctions of Spiritual Status Among the Corinthians," *HTR* 69 (1976): 269–88.

6. Barrett, *First Corinthians*, 69.

nology to distinguish two kinds of Christians, but the contrast there is between "carnal" and "spiritual," not "natural" and "spiritual." In other words, he will use the term *spiritual* more narrowly in chapter 3 than in chapter 2. Here we must avoid the hermeneutical error of interpreting a passage in light of what its author has not yet said and therefore may not yet be thinking. In 2:6–16 the spiritual (or mature) person is the one who accepts the crucified Christ as Savior, over against natural (and therefore immature) person who rejects him. Christians' behavior in any age needs to match their status; they must learn the truth that "we never . . . move on from the cross of Christ— only into a more profound understanding of the cross."[7]

If the rulers of this age include demonic forces, then verse 6 offers an important qualification of Romans 13:1–7. Government may be ordained by God, but non-Christian rulers can likewise do the devil's bidding. Hence, believers may be caught in the dilemma of having to obey God rather than human authorities (Acts 5:29; cf. Dan. 1, 3, 6). But Christians can take heart that even the most powerful of godless authorities will ultimately be eternally condemned and stripped of all their ability to harm God's people.

The secret of verses 7–8 is clearly an "open secret" for all believers. Verse 9 must be interpreted in light of verse 10: what once was inconceivable has now been revealed. Hence every use of these verses to justify the promotion of some esoteric knowledge not known to the church at large is wholly unjustified. So too verse 9 may not fairly be applied to Christ's second coming in order to support the latest, fanciful reconstruction of end-time events. Neither may it legitimately be attributed to support the latest *human* plans or proposals which seem to diverge from consensus wisdom in the church. Indeed, verse 10a warns against all attempts to reach God through human speculation.

Verses 10b–12 have often been held to teach more about the doctrines of human nature and the Holy Spirit than Paul intended. To be sure, there are valid inferences to be drawn here. A person's "spirit" (usually synonymous in the New Testament with one's "soul") is the invisible, immaterial part of a human being which survives the death of the body. But during life, and after being reunited with one's resurrection body, one's spirit is integrally related to the material aspect of human existence. Put simply, there is an ultimate dichotomy between body and spirit/soul in every human but a fundamental interrelatedness of both elements. Hellenistic philosophy often neglected the latter; contemporary psychology often ignores the former.[8]

---

7. Prior, *1 Corinthians*, 51.

8. On this anthropological dualism, see esp. John W. Cooper, *Body, Soul, and Life Everlasting* (Grand Rapids: Eerdmans, 1989).

That God's Spirit parallels human spirits in revealing thoughts demonstrates too that the Holy Spirit is an integral part of the Godhead, with characteristics of a person, and not simply a force. Yet all these anthropological and pneumatological observations are at best corollaries from what Paul teaches and not his primary focus. Still less is there any reference or legitimate inference to a doctrine of the inspiration of Scripture in these verses. In context, Paul's point is just that only an individual knows his or her own unexpressed thoughts, so that the only way we can commune with God and know his thoughts is through his indwelling Spirit. And even then, we may learn only what he chooses to disclose ("what God has freely given"— v. 12b).

The contrasts in verses 13–16 have received widespread abuse in the history of the church. As with 1:18–20, they cannot be used to legitimate anti-intellectualism, although they certainly oppose all forms of *godless* intellectualism. Nor do they justify attempts at interpreting God's will, including his revelation in the Scriptures, apart from standard, common-sense principles of hermeneutics.

These verses do remind us, however, that a sympathetic reading of Scripture or assessment of Christianity, namely, that which is at least open to the premises of the existence of God and of his salvation made available through faith in Christ, are necessary prerequisites for understanding biblical religion at its deepest levels.[9]

But the Spirit never teaches that which is contrary to the plain meaning of passages interpreted in their original historical and literary contexts. And this meaning is accessible to anyone—believer or unbeliever—willing and able to put in the necessary study time.[10] Many non-Christians, skilled in the biblical languages and in ancient history and literature, can tell us what specific passages of Scripture *mean* every bit as adequately as the best Christian commentators, and often better than some less competent Christian interpreters. The "understanding" these non-Christians do not possess is what the Bible consistently considers to be the fullest kind of understanding: a willingness *to act on and obey* the word of God (cf. v. 14a).

---

9. Cf. esp. Peter Stuhlmacher, "The Hermeneutical Significance of 1 Cor 2:6–16," in *Tradition and Interpretation in the New Testament*, ed. G. F. Hawthorne and O. Betz (Grand Rapids: Eerdmans, 1987), 328–47.

10. For an excellent layperson's introduction to the principles of biblical interpretation, see Gordon D. Fee and Douglas Stuart, *How to Read the Bible for All It's Worth* (Grand Rapids: Zondervan, rev. 1993). For a more detailed survey, cf. William W. Klein, Craig L. Blomberg, and Robert L. Hubbard, Jr., *Introduction to Biblical Interpretation* (Dallas: Word, 1993).

Verse 15 too is susceptible to severe misunderstanding. Even in this same letter, Paul will elsewhere command believers to judge the flagrantly disobedient in their midst (5:3–5), to evaluate those who claim to bring words from the Lord (14:29), and to examine themselves to see if they are behaving appropriately enough to take the Lord's Supper (11:27–32). Here, therefore, he is thinking primarily of being unjustly evaluated by non-Christians (or by Christians employing worldly standards), who have no authority to criticize believers for their misbehavior, since they themselves do not accept the standards they employ in making their judgments. Christians, on the other hand, may legitimately evaluate the truth or error of non-Christian beliefs and behavior, although their primary concern should be to keep their own house in order (5:12–13).

THIS SECTION OF Paul's letter "has endured a most unfortunate history of application in the church. . . . Almost every form of spiritual elitism, 'deeper life movement,' and 'second blessing' doctrine has appealed to this text," even though each of these is "nearly 180 degrees the opposite" of Paul's intent.[11] This sad trend continues, especially in sectarian circles which stress certain doctrines not widely accepted in Christianity as a whole (for example, Mormonism[12]) and in some charismatic circles that relate the secret wisdom of verses 6–10a to special experiences of certain spiritual gifts.

But attitudes of elitism are far more pervasive. In an age of specialization, we are bombarded by claims that the key to a happy, healthy Christianity, individually or corporately, is to be found in some new technique of evangelism, practice of certain spiritual disciplines, strategy for church growth, self-help therapy, Sunday-school curriculum, form of music or style of worship, and on and on. When these so-called "keys" pit their agendas against the majority of believers' beliefs and practices and move away from the humbling, central focus on the cross of Christ, they have become elitist and potentially divisive and must be rejected.

So too the church has become increasingly populated by single-issue people, analogous to single-issue voters in the political arena. One person constantly clamors for apologetics to be taught as the cure for all the church's ills; another repeatedly insists that foreign missions must overshadow every other commitment. A third is captivated by the writings of a famous Chris-

---

11. Fee, *First Corinthians*, 120.

12. Cf., e.g., Stephen E. Robinson, *Are Mormons Christians?* (Salt Lake City: Bookcraft, 1991), 96–97.

tian celebrity and promotes them as if they never erred. A fourth harps on nothing but social activism.

This list could be extended indefinitely, but it illustrates how factions and ultimately heresies begin—when one aspect of God's agenda for humanity is so emphasized that other crucial, balancing aspects are ignored. That so many Christians today tolerate such imbalance is an indictment of the lack of effective, comprehensive, week-in and week-out teaching ministries of our local congregations, a lack which leaves believers feeling that they need seminars and specialists to teach them what they have become convinced they could not otherwise learn on their own.[13]

Verses 10b–16 call us to walk the narrow path between the equally dangerous swamps of hyper-intellectualism and anti-intellectualism. In general, the evangelical church continues to fall off more often into the latter; the liberal church, more often into the former. But key exceptions cut across both major traditions. In scholarly circles, academic study of Scripture has often replaced faith, even in more conservative arenas. Or at least we compartmentalize religious truth and forget "to stress that Christ is the principle of coherence in every department of life."[14]

On the other hand, at the grass roots level, many laypeople even in liberal churches continue to read the Scriptures without a grasp of sensible hermeneutics. Overall, anti-intellectualism is probably the more prevalent danger: "too often in discussions that affect us all, the church has played the role of the frightened, insecure institution and not that of the people who gather weekly to worship the God of all true wisdom."[15]

William Barclay's definition of the person without the Spirit (*psychikos*) remains both timeless and timely. This kind of individual "lives as if there was nothing beyond the physical life and there were no needs other than material needs." Such a person "thinks that nothing is more important than the satisfaction of the sex urge" and thus "cannot understand the meaning of chastity." One "who ranks the amassing of material things as the supreme end of life cannot understand generosity," and one "who has never a thought beyond this world cannot understand the things of God."[16] Surely sexual immorality, materialism, and atheism prevail even more pervasively in our Western world today than in mid-twentieth-century Scotland where Barclay first penned these words.

---

13. A simple, introductory manual with constructive advice for discerning Christian truth from error is Robert M. Bowman, Jr., *Orthodoxy and Heresy* (Grand Rapids: Baker, 1992).

14. Michael Green, *To Corinth with Love* (London: Hodder & Stoughton, 1982), 90.

15. Kenneth L. Chafin, *1, 2 Corinthians* (Waco: Word, 1985), 47.

16. William Barclay, *The Letters to the Corinthians* (Philadelphia: Westminster, 1956, rev. 1975), 28.

Verses 14–16 also call us to steer a central course between two extremes. The first is a form of evangelism and missions that believes that if only we use the right methods and arguments, people will have to respond in faith. The second is a naive individualism that claims to have "hot-lines" to heaven apart from what has been consensus truth throughout the history of the church.

The constant use of the first-person plural throughout this passage is deliberate. Paul shares with the most immature Corinthian that which all Christians today therefore share: an ability to commune with God, understand his will, and make sense of the foundational truths of Scripture.[17] It is deeply ironic that the generation with the greatest number of accurate, understandable translations of the Bible, replete with study helps from brief annotations to massive commentaries, should be one of the most biblically illiterate societies in the history of the church. When we are dependent on a handful of prominent leaders, we then become unable to reject false teaching or to discipline immoral behavior by our favorite authorities.

If Christians form an interdependent community, then we must admit that much of the wisdom that most closely approximates what Paul commended is found today in the Two-Thirds World. Here the humble circumstances of impoverished and marginalized Christians often leave them little option but to center on the crucified Christ. Affluent believers would do well to read and listen to their poorer brothers and sisters and to learn from their perspectives on biblical wisdom, which are often obscure to those who fall, by global standards, into the categories of the rich and powerful (recall 1:27).

The Spencers' words emerge out of just such a dialogue and merit careful consideration: "The spiritual person is one who lives out Christ crucified," which includes "turning away from a life of excessive wealth and being ready to be despised or thought irrelevant if necessary to promote God's reign." Hence, "the oppressed Christians of this world in South and North America and elsewhere may well be more 'spiritual' than those Christians considered successful by the world because they are already nearer to imitating Paul's example." What is more, "true oppression will not lead to the pitfall of arrogance, another deception of the world. To hear God's Spirit we must live a prophetic life, always ready to follow our crucified Lord; and we must always listen to others who live such lives."[18]

---

17. Wendell Willis, "The 'Mind of Christ' in 1 Corinthians 2,16," *Bib* 70 (1989): 110–22, rightly stresses that verse 16 is an implicit appeal for appropriate *community* life.

18. Aída B. Spencer and William D. Spencer, "The Truly Spiritual in Paul: Biblical Background Paper on 1 Corinthians 2:6–16," in *Conflict and Context: Hermeneutics in the Americas*, ed. Mark L. Branson and C. René Padilla (Grand Rapids: Eerdmans, 1986), 247–48.

1 Corinthians 3:1–23

BROTHERS, I could not address you as spiritual but as worldly—mere infants in Christ. [2]I gave you milk, not solid food, for you were not yet ready for it. Indeed, you are still not ready. [3]You are still worldly. For since there is jealousy and quarreling among you, are you not worldly? Are you not acting like mere men? [4]For when one says, "I follow Paul," and another, "I follow Apollos," are you not mere men?

[5]What, after all, is Apollos? And what is Paul? Only servants, through whom you came to believe—as the Lord has assigned to each his task. [6]I planted the seed, Apollos watered it, but God made it grow. [7]So neither he who plants nor he who waters is anything, but only God, who makes things grow. [8]The man who plants and the man who waters have one purpose, and each will be rewarded according to his own labor. [9]For we are God's fellow workers; you are God's field, God's building.

[10]By the grace God has given me, I laid a foundation as an expert builder, and someone else is building on it. But each one should be careful how he builds. [11]For no one can lay any foundation other than the one already laid, which is Jesus Christ. [12]If any man builds on this foundation using gold, silver, costly stones, wood, hay or straw, [13]his work will be shown for what it is, because the Day will bring it to light. It will be revealed with fire, and the fire will test the quality of each man's work. [14]If what he has built survives, he will receive his reward. [15]If it is burned up, he will suffer loss; he himself will be saved, but only as one escaping through the flames.

[16]Don't you know that you yourselves are God's temple and that God's Spirit lives in you? [17]If anyone destroys God's temple, God will destroy him; for God's temple is sacred, and you are that temple.

[18]Do not deceive yourselves. If any one of you thinks he is wise by the standards of this age, he should become a "fool" so that he may become wise. [19]For the wisdom of this world is foolishness in God's sight. As it is written: "He catches the wise in their craftiness"; [20]and again, "The Lord knows that the thoughts of the wise are futile." [21]So then, no more boasting

about men! All things are yours, ²²whether Paul or Apollos or Cephas or the world or life or death or the present or the future—all are yours, ²³and you are of Christ, and Christ is of God.

IN THIS PASSAGE Paul continues the theme of godly wisdom as the key to growth in the Christian faith, which 2:6–16 introduced. But now he shifts from contrasting Christians (those with the Spirit) and non-Christians (those without the Spirit) to comparing two kinds of Christians—those who are being controlled by the Spirit and those who are not.

The latter are described in 3:1–4 as factious. Their quarreling not only mocks the cross-centered gospel (1:18–2:5) but fails to recognize the fundamental equality of all believers when measured against the attributes and character of God. Paul illustrates this equality with the metaphors of farmers in a field (3:5–9a) and construction workers on a building, specifically one as valuable and holy as the temple (3:9b–17). First Corinthians 3:18–23 forms an *inclusio* (a repetition that marks off the beginning and end of a section of text) with verses 1–4, as verses 4 and 22 both refer back to the Corinthians' aligning themselves with rival leaders. Verses 18–23 thus round off chapter 3 by stressing believers' access to all spiritual blessings, making such rivalry unnecessary and inappropriate.

The contrast between "spiritual" and "worldly" in 3:1–4 thus differs from the contrasts in 2:6–16. "Worldly" in verse 1 is a slightly different Greek word than in verse 3, but both are pejorative.[1] The KJV translates both as "carnal," that is, "fleshly" or dominated by one's sinful nature, in this context manifested by jealousy and quarreling. "Spiritual" must therefore mean not merely having the Spirit but having the Spirit *in charge*. Even at the end of Paul's one-and-one-half-year stay in Corinth, he had expected these young Christians to be more transformed in their behavior. Now, a full three years later, their squabbling is that much more inexcusable. Their immaturity resembles that of adults acting like infants by still eating only baby food (v. 2). Or, to change the comparison, they are acting like unregenerate people ("mere men"—v. 3b) rather than those in whom the Spirit has come to reside. Verse 4 reminds us of the specific problem at hand and reiterates two of the slogans of 1:12.

---

1. In verse 1, the term is *sarkinos* ("belonging to the flesh," or "having the characteristics of the flesh"); in verse 3, *sarkikos* ("composed of flesh," or "full of fleshly activities")—Mare, "1 Corinthians," 206.

Verses 5–9a clarify another problem with the Corinthians' divisiveness. Not only is their behavior diametrically opposed to a focus on Christ crucified (the point of 1:18–2:5), but it also ignores the fact that all Christian leaders are merely "servants" (v. 5) with relatively equal and insignificant roles to play compared to the role God plays in causing his church to grow.

Verse 5b confirms our suspicions from 1:13–17 that part of the factionalism involved allegiance to those individuals who had personally led different groups of the Corinthians to the Lord.

Verses 6–7 compare the church to a field and its leaders to workers in that field. Particularly in the first century, farmers were keenly aware that their own contribution to a successful harvest in any given year was rather minimal compared to the vagaries of nature, which were seen to be directly in the hand of God or the gods. Verse 7a is thus not an absolute statement but a relative one: compared to God's role, humans' roles are nothing of consequence. And although there is diversity of function (vv. 5b, 6a, 8b), all godly leaders have a common purpose (literally "are one"—v. 8a), which is the growth of the church.

Verse 9a must thus be interpreted not as teaching that Paul and Apollos were on a par with God but that they are fellow workers in God's service and hence on a par with each other.[2] Indeed, the emphatic position of the word *theos* in all three of its occurrences in the Greek of verse 9 makes it clear that Paul is stressing *God* as the one to whom the "fellow workers," "field," and "building" belong.

The end of verse 9 belongs with verses 10–15 as the start of a new paragraph. The NIV omits the Greek "you are" which prefaces "God's building." Just as Paul has described the church and its leaders with an agricultural metaphor in verses 6–9a, he now does so by turning to the world of construction (vv. 9b–17). Here again God's sovereign guidance comes to the fore (v. 10). Paul likens himself to an "expert builder," literally a "wise mastercraftsman" or "chief-engineer." Paul deliberately chooses the word for "wise" to contrast his godly wisdom with the Corinthians' misguided claims to wisdom. The word for "builder" is the word from which the English "architect" derives, but in Greek it referred not so much to the one who drew up a blue-

---

2. W. H. Ollrog, "συνεργός, συνεργέω," in *Exegetical Dictionary of the New Testament*, ed. Horst Balz and Gerhard Schneider (Grand Rapids: Eerdmans, 1993), 3:304, defines συνεργός here as "a person who is active with and like Paul a representative of God in the mission 'work' of proclamation . . . not synergistically God's fellow 'workers,' as the context clearly shows."

print as to the on-site supervisor.[3] The foundation of any truly Christian edifice must, of course, be the cross-centered gospel of Jesus Christ (v. 11).

There remain, however, two quite different ways of building on that foundation. Gold, silver, and costly stones reflect valuable materials that do not easily burn. Wood, hay, and stubble cost less and are quickly consumed by fire (v. 12). In the ancient world, people would have built a temple out of the former and an ordinary home out of the latter. Verse 13 likens "the Day" (i.e., the Day of the Lord or Judgment Day) to just such a fire. "It will be revealed" (v. 13b) probably refers to "the Day" and not to "the work." When Christ returns, all believers will have to appear before him, "that each one may receive what is due him for the things done while in the body, whether good or bad" (2 Cor. 5:10).[4]

"What he has built" (v. 14a) is more literally "the work which he built." Paul is not teaching salvation by works but is referring instead to Christ's assessment of the way Christians have lived their lives subsequent to salvation (elaborating the theme of v. 8b). These works flow from faith and include everything that pleases God, aligns itself with kingdom priorities, and advances his purposes in the world.[5]

The nature of believers' rewards remains unspecified here (v. 14b), but in 4:5 it will be described as "praise from God." One naturally thinks, for example, of the master's words to the faithful stewards in the parable of the talents: "Well done, good and faithful servant" (Matt. 25:21, 23) or of the imagery of Revelation 14:13 in which the good deeds of those who die in the Lord follow them.[6] Such people receive the reward of knowing that they spent substantial time building relationships that would last into eternity.

The "it" with which the NIV begins verse 15 is spelled out in the Greek as a person's "work." This work thus becomes the nearest and most natural antecedent for the unexpressed object of "suffer loss." As Prior puts it, "No doubt every Christian's work is mixed in quality; no doubt we all shall have

---

3. For this meaning, and for the significance of related terms in this paragraph, see Jay Shanor, "Paul as Master Builder: Construction Terms in First Corinthians," *NTS* 34 (1988): 461–67.

4. Harm W. Hollander ("The Testing by Fire of the Builders' Works: 1 Corinthians 3.10–15," *NTS* 40 [1994]: 89–104) believes that Paul has derived his imagery from the *Testament of Abraham* 13, but has reapplied language about the judgment of the righteous and wicked to two kinds of believers.

5. Commentators often try to limit this work to doctrine or teaching, to working specifically for the church, or to aspects of Christian character. Paul does not suggest any such limitations. More helpful, therefore, is Leon Morris, *The First Epistle of Paul to the Corinthians* (Grand Rapids: Eerdmans, 1985), 65: "Probably none [of these interpretations] is completely out of mind, and it is best to see the reference as quite general."

6. Cf. Gaston Deluz, *A Companion to 1 Corinthians* (London: Darton, Longman & Todd, 1963), 40.

the awesome sadness of seeing much of our work burned up."[7] But it may be that Paul has in mind also the loss of the reward, that is, diminished praise and increased shame as we stand before Christ's judgment seat (cf. 1 John 2:28, in which avoidance of shame before the Lord is one of the motives for faithful living now) and as we realize how much of our lives were spent in activity of no eternal value.[8] Such believers are still saved, but by the skin of their teeth or, to use Paul's metaphor, like escaping from a burning house (v. 15b).

If the temple imagery is implicit in the metaphor of building with costly stones and metal (vv. 9b–15), Paul makes it explicit in verses 16–17. The church is not just any building; it is the most holy and valuable of edifices. Of course, Paul does not mean a literal place of residence, but the body of Corinthian believers. All the "you's" of these two verses are plural; corporately these Christians form one temple. "In you" at the end of verse 16 would be better translated "among you." Just as Jewish and pagan temples were believed to be the dwelling place of God (or the gods), so also the Christian fellowship is the special place of the Spirit's presence. That is why the threat of verse 17a is so harsh. Here Paul warns against any who would try to destroy[9] the church. These are clearly different people (potentially some of the patrons or local leaders of the Corinthian factions) from those who used poor building materials in the previous paragraph. Here people are trying to tear down the structure! Understandably, God's response will significantly differ as well: he "will destroy" (i.e., eternally condemn) them.

Verses 18–23 close the chapter with Paul repeating his appeal to banish divisiveness. The quarrelsome Corinthians are deceiving themselves into thinking they are wise by following society's standards of self-promotion, when in fact they must become foolish by the world's standards and embrace the godly wisdom which Paul has been expounding (vv. 18–19a).

The futile end of those who fail to take this corrective action is again underlined by two Scriptures: Job 5:13 and Psalm 94:11, quoted in verses 19b–20. In both Old Testament contexts, sinful, godless behavior is in view, so again it is clear that Paul is not condemning all wise people, merely those who think they can be wise without God.[10]

---

7. Prior, *1 Corinthians*, 60. Cf. TEV: "But if anyone's work is burnt up, then he will lose it."

8. Cf. esp. William F. Orr and James A. Walther, *1 Corinthians* (Garden City: Doubleday, 1976), 173.

9. The present tense may well be conative (referring to attempted action), as suggested by Barrett, *First Corinthians*, 91. *Phtheiro* could also be translated "corrupt" in its first usage, but it must be rendered "destroy" in its second.

10. The psalmist actually says, "the thoughts of [sinful] *man*." Paul makes the observation all the more pointed by substituting "wise" to indicate the subgroup in Corinth that most needed to learn this lesson.

Verses 21–23 highlight a final reason for the futility of such attitudes: the Corinthians have everything they could legitimately need or want in Jesus. Indeed, Paul turns their slogans upside down. They do not belong to human leaders; those leaders, as servants (v. 5), belong to them, as does everything else in creation, present and future, inasmuch as they are in Christ who shares in all the Father's sovereignty (cf. Rom. 8:38–39).

THE OVERARCHING THEME of chapter 3 suggests a fourth way to overcome divisiveness: recognize the fundamental equality and humble position of all Christians when compared against God's infinitely holy and perfect standards (for the first three methods, see above, p. 67). To be sure, 3:1–4 is sometimes kept with 2:16–26, as it continues the theme of "spiritual" people. Similarly, 4:1–5 is sometimes tacked on to 3:5–23 because of its reference to judgment. But despite these thematic overlaps, the inclusion of 3:4 and 22, coupled with the pervasive contrasts between right and wrong ways to live out one's Christian life, mark chapter three out as a self-contained unit.[11]

The major issue we must resolve in order to apply 3:1–4 today is the question of who in contemporary Christianity corresponds to the "carnal" Christians in Corinth. There are in fact two ever-present dangers to avoid in coming to grips with the identity of these carnal Christians. The first is to deny the category altogether, in flat contradiction to Paul. There are those who seem to claim that there is no such thing as a carnal Christian.[12] This is an unfortunate way of putting things, since the term *carnal* comes straight out of the Bible here.

The second danger is to define carnality in much broader terms than Paul does, so that anyone who has ever made a profession of faith, however superficial, can be counted as a true (but carnal) Christian, irrespective of his or her subsequent lifestyle.[13] We must remember that Paul is not talking

---

11. Cf. esp. Brendan Byrne, "Ministry and Maturity in 1 Corinthians 3," *ABR* 35 (1987): 83–87.

12. John F. MacArthur, Jr. has often been associated with this view. What he says, in *The Gospel According to Jesus* (Grand Rapids: Zondervan, 1988), 97, n. 2, is that 1 Corinthians 3:3 was "not meant [to] establish a special class of Christianity." It is easy to see why he has been interpreted as he has, but the rest of his footnote explains simply that "these were not people living in static disobedience." He does add, however, "Paul does not suggest that carnality and rebellion were the rule in their lives." True, but neither does he deny it.

13. Charles C. Ryrie, *So Great Salvation* (Wheaton: Victor, 1989), 59–66, is not as extreme as some but still defends the possibility of a prolonged period of carnality on the basis of

about such people here. These Corinthians have received the Spirit, exercised his gifts, and grown in wisdom and knowledge (1:7; 12:13) but are now using what they have learned and experienced in a destructive rather than constructive fashion. What is more, spirituality in Paul's world was much more bound up with group behavior than with individual piety.[14] The New Testament knows of no Christians who are not associated with a fellowship of believers. This does not mean that a person cannot be saved if he or she never goes to church, merely that Paul is not likely to have had such people in mind when he spoke of carnal Christians.

A subordinate issue is whether or not Paul imagines carnality (or worldliness or immature behavior) as acceptable for those who are new Christians but not for those who have had time to mature. Although this approach is widely touted, it is probably invalid.[15] It often results from reading Paul's contrast between milk and solid food in verse 2 in light of Hebrews 5:12 or 1 Peter 2:2, in which milk takes on more positive connotations. But neither of these letters was yet written when Paul penned 1 Corinthians. And if "spiritual" in verse 1 means being controlled by the Spirit, exhibiting the fruit of love, joy, peace, patience, and so on (Gal. 5:22–23), then such spirituality is possible for every believer from the moment of conversion on and in every subsequent stage of life. So, too, is carnality, whenever a person rebels against the Spirit's guidance.[16]

The view that denies carnality altogether does rightly stress that many Christians have interpreted this concept out of context. Carnal or worldly Christianity is nothing more or less than being controlled by one's sinful nature, performing what Galatians 5:19–21 calls "the acts of the sinful nature"—sexual immorality, impurity, debauchery, idolatry, witchcraft, hatred, discord, jealousy, fits of rage, selfish ambition, dissensions, factions, and on and on (cf. the vice lists of Rom. 1:29–31 and 1 Cor. 6:9–10).

---

the four-to-five years that these Corinthians had been Christians. But that is based on an assumption that goes well beyond the text—that these believers were in an uninterrupted state of carnality for all these years.

14. A definitive treatment of this topic appears in Bruce J. Malina, *The New Testament World: Insights from Cultural Anthropology* (Atlanta: John Knox, 1981).

15. See esp. Fee, *First Corinthians*, 124–27.

16. Cf. James Francis, "'As Babes in Christ'—Some Proposals Regarding 1 Corinthians 3.1–3," *JSNT* 7 (1980): 57: "Maturity is possible for every Christian who has received the Spirit, and Paul is urging the Corinthians to grow in the sense of realising afresh what they have received." Conversely, "Paul chides his readers not for failure to advance their understanding (some were exceedingly proud of their knowledge), but for failing to allow what they had known and realised to be true to inform their ongoing Christian life."

Those who deny that Christians still have a sinful nature run afoul of the twin emphases of Romans 6–8, in which Christians are promised substantial victory over sin but repeatedly commanded to put to death the old self which continues to compete with the Spirit for an individual's allegiance. But a person who seems never to submit to God's will is more likely the "natural" person of 2:14 than a carnal Christian, regardless of what professions he or she has made at some time in the past. Again, we must remember 1:6–7, where Paul states that these Corinthians had seen remarkable transformation in their lives and spiritual empowerment but were now abandoning these victories in favor of petty infighting.

Fee concisely captures the correct balance: "There is no question that Paul considers his Corinthian friends believers and that they are in fact acting otherwise. But Paul's whole concern is to get them to change, not to allow that such behavior is permissible since not all Christians are yet mature." Again, "spiritual people are to walk in the Spirit. If they do otherwise, they are 'worldly' and are called upon to desist. *Remaining* worldly is not one of the options."[17]

The major interpretive debate that affects our application of the rest of chapter 3 is the controversy over whether Paul teaches degrees of reward in heaven. Otherwise, Paul's metaphors remain quite universal. People in most all times and places understand the basic concepts of planting and harvesting. And temples continue to stand and be viewed as holy places by people in many cultures.

The theme in verses 5–9a of the fundamental equality of Christians, including Christian leaders in particular, must be stressed in order to make sense of Paul's teaching about judgment in verses 8 and 12–15. From a human perspective, it is natural to imagine that the great evangelists and faithful sufferers among God's people deserve much more than the convicted criminal who converts on death-row. But to demand what we deserve is to wind up defeated from the outset. Compared to the perfection God requires, the differences among his people are like the differences in elevation between Mt. Everest in the Himalayas and the Mariana Trench in the West Pacific—seemingly vast from an earth-bound perspective yet negligible when viewed from another planet! There is diversity of performance to be sure (vv. 5b, 8b) but not at expense of this ultimate leveling factor (v. 7).

Why are only Paul and Apollos named in verse 5? Some think the reference to building on another foundation in verse 11 implicitly reproaches those who were overly exalting Peter, perhaps in light of Christ's promise that he would be the rock on which the church would be built (Matt.

---

17. Fee, *First Corinthians*, 128.

16:18). But this seems overly subtle. Others suggest that the Apollos party was the most troublesome because of its apparent attachment to (false) wisdom. Although this may be more likely, we must take care not to read in too much. Perhaps Paul and Apollos were the only two rival leaders who had personally evangelized Corinth. More probable still, based on the observation that Cephas does reappear in verse 22, is the interpretation that Paul is giving just a representative rather than an exhaustive list of the factions.

Because Paul applies his metaphors of farm and construction workers to church leaders, some are tempted to limit the application of this imagery to a minority of believers. Once this is done, it is possible even to identify the judgment of verses 13–15 as separate from the final judgment of all humanity.[18] But "the Day" is not easily turned into anything other than the universal, public reckoning which all people must face on Christ's return (cf. Matt. 25:31–46, in which pronouncements of salvation and condemnation are combined with an assessment of the works that demonstrate the presence or absence of faith). Given that all believers are potentially leaders in some small sphere of ministry, and that all ultimately contribute in one way or another to the growth or stagnation of the church, it seems far too restrictive to limit the judgment of these verses to any select group of Christians.

At first glance, verse 11 seems flatly to contradict Ephesians 2:20, in which the apostles and prophets are the foundation of the church. This tension is one of several reasons many have denied the Pauline authorship of Ephesians. Such protests completely overlook the fluidity of metaphorical language. If Christ is the ultimate foundation, from a human perspective those who plant churches and proclaim the gospel also form a necessary base for the growth of any new congregation (cf. 1 Cor. 12:28). For the hypercritical, there is potential tension even between verses 10 and 11 here: does Paul lay the foundation (the preaching of the gospel) or was it already laid (in the completed work of Jesus)? Clearly both are true, depending on which aspect of church planting one wishes to stress.[19]

Interpreters of verse 12 must guard against allegorizing the six individual building materials. Their significance is collectively to contrast three relatively fireproof elements with three that quickly burn up. Nor may this fire be interpreted literally. The "as" of verse 15b makes plain that Paul is still writing at the metaphorical level. Historically, this passage has been the single most important New Testament text used by traditional Roman Catholic

---

18. E.g., Craig A. Evans, "How Are the Apostles Judged? A Note on 1 Corinthians 3:10–15," *JETS* 27 (1984): 149–50.

19. Archibald Robertson and Alfred Plummer, *A Critical and Exegetical Commentary on the First Epistle of St. Paul to the Corinthians* (Edinburgh: T & T Clark, 1929), 61–62.

theology to support the doctrine of purgatory. But modern Catholic scholars are increasingly recognizing the illegitimacy of this interpretation. Nothing in the text refers to any *process* of purgation that would last beyond Judgment Day. But this very observation renders equally suspect the common Protestant doctrine of varying degrees of status or hierarchies in heaven.[20] Doubtless all will have varying degrees of praise and blame from Christ on Judgment Day, but nothing in this passage even remotely suggests that such differing responses are somehow perpetuated throughout all eternity. Other New Testament texts that have been taken as teaching eternal rewards refer, on closer inspection, either to this same temporary differentiation before Christ's judgment seat, to heavenly bliss without degrees of distinction, or to varying privileges in this life. The idea that our eternal happiness is at all contingent on performance in this life should be fundamentally depressing for all who are honest about their level of maturity or growth in the faith.[21]

A misinterpretation of the judgment seat of Christ is often bound up with a misrepresentation of carnality. The apparent injustice of being able to profess faith but never show any fruit of it and still be saved seems to be ameliorated by assuming that such a person will in some sense not get as much out of heaven. If one recognizes that neither verses 1–4 nor 13–15 admit such a person to be a Christian at all, then the tension is relieved by stressing that such people are not even saved.

We must exercise great care, therefore, not to use the category of carnal Christian to give false hope to people that perpetual "backsliddenness" is a viable option for those who want to spend eternity with the Lord. It is important to stress too that this conclusion does not favor either perspective in the Calvinist-Arminian controversy. Both sides recognize that those who die in unbelief and rebellion are lost. They merely differ as to what that proves about whether or not such people once were saved.

---

20. Indeed, this notion developed in part as an attempt to salvage something of the Catholic concept of purgatory—see Emma Disley, "Degrees of Glory: Protestant Doctrine and the Concept of Rewards Hereafter," *JTS* 42 (1991): 77–105.

21. See further Craig L. Blomberg, "Degrees of Reward in the Kingdom of Heaven?" *JETS* 35 (1992): 159–72. Cf. John B. Polhill, "The Wisdom of God and Factionalism: 1 Corinthians 1–4," *RevExp* 80 (1983): 335: "Rewards are difficult to square with a doctrine of salvation by grace and can easily become the back door for a theology of works." Again, "it is best to avoid seeing this in terms of graduation [*sic*] in heavenly rank or in materialistic terms such as various types of heavenly real estate. It is more likely that both Paul and Jesus had something in mind like the Lord's commendation, 'Well done, good and faithful servant' (Lk 19:17)"; and Watson, *First Corinthians*, 33: "Perhaps the reward will simply be the satisfaction of seeing one's work survive, the penalty the mortification of seeing it dissolve in the flames."

The major error to avoid in verses 16–17 is the individualistic interpretation. Later, 6:19 will teach that believers are each little temples of the Holy Spirit. But this passage speaks only of the church, corporately, as the residence of God.

A subordinate error equates the people trying to destroy God's temple with the poor builders of the previous paragraph. Even shoddy construction is at least *erecting* a building of some kind, but those Paul warns in verses 16–17 are trying to *demolish* it.

The transition between verses 9b–15 and 16–17 seems to be as follows: God will indeed respond differently to different kinds of believers on Judgment Day, but the real danger to fear is the eternal destruction of those who would divide and tear down the church now. Paul never says that any of the Corinthians have crossed over this line, but he clearly warns against the activity in which some are engaging as having the potential to lead to this extreme. Once again, this does not necessarily imply that true Christians can lose their salvation. It remains possible that Paul would agree with John that those who split the church demonstrate by their behavior that they were never truly born again, no matter what previous professions they may have made (1 John 2:19). What is important is that Paul does not take for granted that every church member is a true disciple of Jesus, particularly when someone's behavior remains fundamentally contrary to the spirit of unity that the gospel promotes.

The term for "destroy" (v. 17) must not be watered down to refer merely to temporal judgment nor taken as support for any doctrine of annihilation, in light of the consistent testimony of Paul elsewhere, the rest of the New Testament, first-century Judaism, and the Apostolic Fathers.[22] The reason Paul chose this term, over against more common terms for eternal condemnation, is to show that the punishment fits the crime. They who would do away with God's sacred enterprise will themselves perish. Overall these two verses form the strongest warning in all the New Testament "against those who would take the church lightly and destroy it by worldly wisdom and division."[23]

Verses 18–23 climax Paul's discussion on a more positive note. Divisiveness and fear of judgment both prove unnecessary for true believers because of their present, partial, and future full access to all spiritual blessings in the universe. This enables Christians to persevere in faith and obedience even

---

22. See esp. William V. Crockett, "The Metaphorical View," in *Four Views on Hell*, ed. William Crockett (Grand Rapids: Zondervan, 1992), 43–81; and his "Response to Clark H. Pinnock," pp. 171–74.

23. Fee, *First Corinthians*, 146.

when others ridicule both their beliefs and their behavior (vv. 18–19a). They can relax, knowing that those who exalt themselves against God will eventually come to ruin (vv. 19b–20).

The Job 5:13 quotation ("he catches the wise in their craftiness"), comes from one of Eliphaz's speeches. Like Job's other "friends," Eliphaz is not always a reliable interpreter of God's perspective. But this particular statement proves true as a generalization, even if Eliphaz seems to have misapplied it to Job.

Verses 21–23 then give the ultimate rationale as to why believers should not quarrel with each other—there is no spiritual blessing someone else has which they cannot have access to as well, either now or in the future. Paul generalizes beyond the various Christian leaders who unwittingly triggered these rivalries to include all of the cosmic forces people tend to fear, most notably the uncertainty of the future and the inevitability of death. In short, judgment for the true believer functions in a consistently positive fashion in this chapter, as compensation for present, often inglorious labor, and as a threat only for the person not genuinely related to Christ.[24]

 CAMPUS CRUSADE FOR Christ has popularized the concepts of 1 Corinthians 2:6–3:4 with its well-known circle diagrams for the natural, carnal, and spiritual persons. The natural person does not have the cross of Christ anywhere in his or her life; ego is on that person's throne. The carnal Christian has the cross inside the circle of his or her life, but ego still remains on the throne. The spiritual Christian has the cross central and ego dethroned.[25] These diagrams are both helpful and misleading. They correctly remind us that believers do not automatically have Christ in charge of every area of their lives. Christians are free to take back a certain measure of control and in essence do so every time they consciously sin. The diagrams also correctly capture the fundamental difference between Christian and non-Christian, though it is perhaps worth noting that ego is not always on the throne of an unbeliever's life. More noble, family-centered or humanitarian concerns may be central, but the point remains that God is not.

---

24. This is the central theme of the very helpful, detailed study by David W. Kuck (*Judgment and Community Conflict* [Leiden: Brill, 1992]), subtitled *Paul's Use of Apocalyptic Judgment Language in 1 Cor. 3:5–4:5.*

25. See, e.g., *Sharing the Abundant Life on Campus* (San Bernardino: Campus Crusade for Christ International, 1972), 209–17, which reproduces the widely used tract, "Have You Made the Wonderful Discovery of the Spirit-Filled Life?"

The diagrams tend to mislead, however, when they are interpreted as meaning that a room full of Christians could be divided into carnal and spiritual. If carnality, or worldliness, means yielding to one's sinful nature, while spirituality means yielding to the indwelling Spirit, then genuine believers may often be spiritual at one moment and carnal not long afterwards, or vice-versa. Some perhaps stay in one state longer than another. Many mature believers have been *transformed* by God's Spirit over time (cf. Rom. 12:1–2) so that they sin much less than they once did, while many immature believers have experienced significantly less transformation. But to *remain* worldly, in rebellion against God's Spirit, for too long a period of time calls into question one's salvation, while to claim not to have sinned for some equally long interval trivializes the amount of conscious and unconscious violations of God's perfect standards which all humans regularly commit.

The current debate over "lordship salvation" presents similar pitfalls.[26] On the one hand, there is no biblical justification for a two-stage process in which one accepts Christ as Savior at one point in life but acknowledges him as Lord only at another point. No one may come to Christ who does not surrender his or her entire self in allegiance to a new master. On the other hand, this call must not be presented in such a way that it appears as if one must understand or be able to anticipate everything that will be involved in following Jesus. Similarly, inability to conquer sin in certain, specific areas must not automatically call one's salvation into question. The seemingly paradoxical statement that encapsulates the biblical balance is that salvation is absolutely free but it costs people their entire lives.[27]

The view that one can be carnal for long stretches of time and still sneak into heaven with lesser rewards continues to remain prominent in certain conservative circles. These circles also tend to spawn sharp differentiations between the many biblical pictures of judgment. So, for example, the judgment seat of Christ is often separated off from the judgment of all humanity at Christ's return. But, as already noted, the language of verse 13 renders this unlikely. Questions of how our experience with Christ during "the intermediate state" relates to coming resurrection, judgment, and the fullness of the kingdom tantalize us because of the lack of clear biblical answers, but we must resist the temptation to separate that which Scripture does not.

Presumably, for believers, final judgment is simply a public vindication and declaration of what they already knew about their destiny from death

---

26. As especially in the contrast between MacArthur, *Gospel According to Jesus*, and Ryrie, *So Great Salvation*.

27. For a well-balanced assessment and mediation of this debate, see Darrell L. Bock, "A Review of *The Gospel According to Jesus*," *BSac* 146 (1989): 21–40.

onwards. This further reinforces the idea that Judgment Day for Christians is not designed to separate believers into various ranks or hierarchies for all eternity. Ironically, those who most want to preserve the biblical doctrine of grace often unwittingly allow works a greater prominence in determining believers' destinies than do those who stress lordship salvation.[28] As one of my students once put it, much conservative Christianity reminded him of an exclusive country club trying to attract a broader clientele. The club, therefore, advertised that membership for the first year would be absolutely free. But after that, you paid through the nose!

Much of the application of Paul's warnings against factionalism in 3:5–23 has already been highlighted in our discussion of chapters 1–2. Verse 5 anticipates a key definition of ministry—servanthood—which our discussion of chapter 4 will elaborate. The key distinction of 3:5–23, namely, the fundamental importance and relative equality of all believers' contributions to God's work in this world, requires further exploration here.

The metaphors of field and building anticipate Paul's more developed metaphor of the body, in chapters 12–14, with all Christians exercising their spiritual gifts for the edification of the church (cf. Eph. 4:11–13). This vision of every-member ministry is being increasingly recaptured in growing churches today,[29] but it still tends to empower only a minority of congregations and a minority of members within a given congregation. The image of Christ as the church's one foundation (v. 11) functions much like Galatians 1:6–9 to warn us against following the proliferation of pseudo-Christian sects and organizations that profess allegiance to Jesus but lack fundamental orthodox tenets of the faith, most notably, the true Jesus of the Scriptures.

The positive function of Christ's judgment seat in verses 13–15, parallel to the doxology in verses 22–23, should relieve the fear of death and of life after death that continues to haunt many Christians. No one should want to displease God or look forward to hearing his censure, but if there are no eternal hierarchies in heaven, then motivation by guilt should recede in importance in Christian ministry. In fact, there are good signs that this is happening increasingly.[30]

---

28. As most notably in Zane C. Hodges, *Grace in Eclipse: A Study on Eternal Rewards* (Dallas: Redención Viva, 1985); and Joe L. Wall, *Going for the Gold: Reward and Loss at the Judgment of Believers* (Chicago: Moody, 1991).

29. For good suggestions on implementation, see Frank R. Tillapaugh, *Unleashing Your Potential* (Ventura: Regal, 1988).

30. An outstanding example is S. Bruce Narramore, *No Condemnation* (Grand Rapids: Zondervan, 1984), though at times he may swing the pendulum too far in the opposite direction.

On the other hand, verses 16–17 preserve a crucial warning which is not adequately being heeded—that the powerful, dynamic church leaders who consistently split congregations, engage in "witch hunts" and heresy trials against fellow Christians, and in general seek to build their own kingdoms in opposition to, rather than in cooperation with, fellow ministers may be headed down the road to outright apostasy themselves. Like the Corinthian faction leaders and their "groupies," such people and their followers are not usually thought of as Paul's primary candidates for carnality or even eternal condemnation, but in many ways they are the closest modern equivalents to those who went about quarreling and destroying the Corinthian church from within.[31] Even in less extreme instances, Jerry Vines' pointed remark rings true: "Many people in America today . . . are building crowds but are not willing to pay the price to build a church."[32]

Freedom from fear of judgment should have profound effects on true believers in other ways. Our culture grows ever more performance-centered with each passing year. Competition infects our play, school, sports, and work. Adults face longer hours on the job with less security and more performance-based evaluation than was ever anticipated a generation ago when labor-saving devices were being heralded as ushering in the thirty-hour work week with vastly increased leisure and recreation time. Not surprisingly, but nevertheless tragically, the spirit of competition, comparison with one another, and rewards based on merit have overwhelmed many aspects of Christian living as well, both corporately and personally. Too many Christians continue to think that God relates to them just like the taskmasters they have known in their families and jobs, as they expect daily blessings or punishments according to their level of faithfulness and obedience. How liberating it can be when the church decides instead to model a counter-cultural lifestyle, loving people unconditionally, as Christ did.[33]

We need to recover too the foundational Reformation (and especially Lutheran) emphasis on gratitude as the primary motivation for living the Christian life. A person needs little added incentive for being friends with someone who has rescued him or her from drowning. Christ's death for us

---

31. Cf. Paige Patterson, *The Troubled Triumphant Church* (Nashville: Thomas Nelson, 1983), 55: "In a sense, the tendency to identify more strongly with Christian leaders than with Jesus, the founder of Christianity, is another sure insight into one's stature as a babe in Christ."

32. Jerry Vines, *God Speaks Today* (Grand Rapids: Zondervan, 1979), 73.

33. For elaboration of the ideas in this paragraph, see the outstanding discussion and practical suggestions in Chap Clark, *The Performance Illusion* (Colorado Springs: NavPress, 1993).

on the cross should provide all the motivation we need to serve him. If we need more incentive, we have failed to grasp the most foundational logic of the gospel (cf. Rom. 6:1) and perhaps have not really appropriated God's forgiveness at all. In that case, fear of not making it to heaven, not merely loss of reward, should provide ample motivation![34]

The doctrine of grace is arguably the watershed that separates Christianity from all other world religions. It should cause no surprise, then, that the church has a difficult time warding off the persistent intrusion of works-righteousness. It is central to fallen, human nature to say that grace is unfair and we should get what we deserve. But no one honest about his or her own sinfulness could ever really want that. What makes God's grace-filled gospel "good news" is that we *don't* have to get what we deserve. Verses 12–15 remind a society preoccupied with statistics that God desires quality as well as quantity as his church grows. But true progress occurs when believers obey him in joyful response to the salvation Christ has already provided, rather than in the hopes of gaining greater reward (cf. Luke 14:12–14; 17:7–10).

Thus we receive "all things" (v. 21), and the way Paul defines "all things" in verses 21b–22 leaves little room for some believers to have certain blessings excluded. Such promises can enable ostracized, marginalized, and suffering disciples, who form perhaps a majority of all Christians worldwide today, to endure the pain of this world.

All too often we try to accumulate more and more possessions without finding lasting satisfaction in them. But we should not compete for limited goods at others' expense when we realize the eternal compensation that will make present affliction pale into insignificance (cf. 2 Cor. 4:17; Rom. 8:18). The "baby busters" are increasingly recognizing what the rest of the world long since knew—that there is not enough material wealth for everyone to "have it all" in this life. Yet spiritually that is precisely what Christ promises. It is indeed worth becoming a "fool" (v. 18) to gain eternity!

---

34. An important international symposium on this and related topics is *Right with God: Justification in the Bible and the World*, ed. D. A. Carson (Grand Rapids: Baker, 1992). Paul, in his own way as much as James, teaches that good works necessarily flow from saving faith. P. T. O'Brien helpfully surveys recent approaches to justification by faith and judgment by works in Paul in his article in this volume entitled, "Justification in Paul and Some Crucial Issues in the Last Two Decades" (pp. 69–95; see esp. pp. 89–95), correctly concluding that they "are two poles of the same matter" (p. 94).

1 Corinthians 4:1–21

🌿

So then, men ought to regard us as servants of Christ and as those entrusted with the secret things of God. ²Now it is required that those who have been given a trust must prove faithful. ³I care very little if I am judged by you or by any human court; indeed, I do not even judge myself. ⁴My conscience is clear, but that does not make me innocent. It is the Lord who judges me. ⁵Therefore judge nothing before the appointed time; wait till the Lord comes. He will bring to light what is hidden in darkness and will expose the motives of men's hearts. At that time each will receive his praise from God.

⁶Now, brothers, I have applied these things to myself and Apollos for your benefit, so that you may learn from us the meaning of the saying, "Do not go beyond what is written." Then you will not take pride in one man over against another. ⁷For who makes you different from anyone else? What do you have that you did not receive? And if you did receive it, why do you boast as though you did not?

⁸Already you have all you want! Already you have become rich! You have become kings—and that without us! How I wish that you really had become kings so that we might be kings with you! ⁹For it seems to me that God has put us apostles on display at the end of the procession, like men condemned to die in the arena. We have been made a spectacle to the whole universe, to angels as well as to men. ¹⁰We are fools for Christ, but you are so wise in Christ! We are weak, but you are strong! You are honored, we are dishonored! ¹¹To this very hour we go hungry and thirsty, we are in rags, we are brutally treated, we are homeless. ¹²We work hard with our own hands. When we are cursed, we bless; when we are persecuted, we endure it; ¹³when we are slandered, we answer kindly. Up to this moment we have become the scum of the earth, the refuse of the world.

¹⁴I am not writing this to shame you, but to warn you, as my dear children. ¹⁵Even though you have ten thousand guardians in Christ, you do not have many fathers, for in Christ Jesus I became your father through the gospel. ¹⁶There-

fore I urge you to imitate me. [17]For this reason I am sending to you Timothy, my son whom I love, who is faithful in the Lord. He will remind you of my way of life in Christ Jesus, which agrees with what I teach everywhere in every church.

[18]Some of you have become arrogant, as if I were not coming to you. [19]But I will come to you very soon, if the Lord is willing, and then I will find out not only how these arrogant people are talking, but what power they have. [20]For the kingdom of God is not a matter of talk but of power. [21]What do you prefer? Shall I come to you with a whip, or in love and with a gentle spirit?

WITH THIS CHAPTER Paul concludes his appeal for unity among the Corinthian factions. He brings the discussion full circle: having begun with the wrong way to treat the apostles (overly exalting them), he now elaborates the right ways to consider them. They are faithful servants (vv. 1–5), to be judged by Scripture (vv. 6–7), unjustly suffering (vv. 8–13), even though specially related (vv. 14–21).

Verse 1 picks up one of the themes of 3:5–23 with two key terms to describe the nature of the apostles' servanthood. Instead of seeing Christian preachers as rival leaders, the Corinthians should recognize them as helpers and overseers. "Servant" (v. 1) is not the general term used previously (3:5) but a word that referred to "an assistant to someone in an official position."[1] "Those who have been given a trust" (v. 2) reflects the Greek noun *oikonomos* ("steward")—the highest ranking servant of a wealthy landowner, who was in charge of the entire estate in his master's absence. Together, both words compare Paul, Apollos, Peter, and their peers to servants answerable primarily to God but with authority over their charges. "The secret things" (v. 1b) are "the mysteries," as in 2:7—those aspects of the gospel once hidden but now revealed, and centering on the cross of Christ.

The key task of a steward is faithfulness to his master, not kowtowing to every demand of his underlings (v. 2). Verse 3 must thus be kept in context. The Corinthians' view of Paul matters little *relative to* God's view of him. Even his own self-estimation pales against this divine assessment. "My con-

---

1. Paul Ellingworth and Howard Hatton, *A Translator's Handbook on Paul's First Letter to the Corinthians* (New York: United Bible Societies, 1985), 75. Many commentaries commit the fallacy of defining this word (*huperetes*) according to its etymology (as "under-rower"), but there are no known uses of this word in ancient Greek literature with this meaning. See D. A. Carson, *Exegetical Fallacies* (Grand Rapids: Baker, 1984), 27–28.

science is clear" (v. 4) loosely translates "I am aware of nothing against my-self." The verb "to be aware" comes from the same root as "conscience"—an everyday Greek word "which in general had the morally bad negative sense of the pain that we feel when we do something wrong."[2]

All human judgments not only lack God's omniscient perspective but also remain premature (v. 5). The "appointed time" is defined as when "the Lord comes," that is, Judgment Day. Only then will all facts be known and all the thoughts and intentions of human hearts disclosed (cf. Matt. 10:26), enabling a wholly fair evaluation of Christians' behavior. These things are not only hidden from human judges, leading to error and bias, but "there is a positive darkness which poisons and misdirects the mind," as in the Corinthians' evaluation of Paul. "If it were only a matter of revealing facts of which his ac-cusers were ignorant, that could soon be put right."[3]

Again Paul singles out himself and Apollos for special mention (cf. 3:5 and the previous comments, p. 73). They have tried to model a principle ap-parently well-known to the Corinthians, which Paul wishes the whole church would follow (v. 6).[4] For Paul, "what is written" usually refers to his Scripture, our Old Testament. But there is no specific verse that states, "Do not go beyond what is written," so probably he is referring more generally to the need to remain within biblical standards and hence not become puffed up (NIV "take pride"). Or Paul may be quoting a popular proverb of the day, with "what is written" referring to the rules of arbitration between warring factions or to children carefully tracing letters as they learn to write.[5] In each case, however, the general sense would remain the same: ob-serve proper behavior and put an end to rivalries. Verse 7 underlines this ap-peal with three rhetorical questions anticipating the answers, "no one,"

---

2. Colin Brown, "Conscience," in *New International Dictionary of New Testament Theology*, vol. 1 (Grand Rapids: Zondervan, 1975), 351.

3. Nigel Turner, *Grammatical Insights into the New Testament* (Edinburgh: T & T Clark, 1965), 132.

4. The word translated "applied" in v. 6 normally means "transformed." This has sug-gested to a few writers that Paul is really talking about the local leaders of the Corinthian factions but "transforms" his references to himself and Apollos to be less direct. See esp. David R. Hall, "A Disguise for the Wise μετασχηματισμός in 1 Corinthians 4.6," *NTS* 40 (1994): 143–49.

5. For each of these three views, see, respectively, Morna D. Hooker, "'Beyond the Things Which Are Written': An Examination of 1 Cor. IV.6," *NTS* 10 (1963–64): 127–32; L. L. Welborn, "A Conciliatory Principle in 1 Cor. 4:6," *NovT* 29 (1987): 320–46; C. H. Tal-bert, *Reading Corinthians* (New York: Crossroad, 1987), 8. Verse 6b is admittedly quite dif-ficult, because it reads literally, "In order that you might learn in us the not beyond what is written." Conjectural emendations of the text, while clever, lack all textual evidence and therefore fail to persuade.

"nothing," and "no good reason." The first of these conveys the sense of "Who made you superior to others?" (TEV). Together, the three questions remind the Corinthians that all their spiritual gifts and natural blessings came from God and therefore give them no grounds for boasting.

With verse 8 Paul shifts tone abruptly and unleashes a bitter invective, dripping with irony and sarcasm. The three questions of verse 7 give way to three exclamations. Verse 8b makes it clear that verse 8a is not to be taken literally. Most of the Corinthians were neither wealthy nor royal. Rather, Paul is reflecting the Corinthians' own arrogant and misguided views of their maturity. Perhaps true on a material level of a minority of the church (but of a majority of the factious leaders),[6] Paul's description of the Corinthians as rich and regal is more directly related to their spiritual self-appraisals.

Here is one of the key texts that discloses the prevailing "overly realized eschatology" (the idea that all of the blessings of the messianic age had already arrived) that afflicted the church at Corinth. "You have all you want" translates a verb which means "satiated," as in the result of overeating. "Become kings" reads, more literally, "reigned." If all the blessings of the messianic age had really come all at once, then Paul and his companions would have been experiencing the same freedom from imperfection that these Corinthians claimed.

Instead, verses 9–13 provide a poignant catalogue of the apostles' suffering. "It seems to me" alerts the reader to Paul's use of two metaphors throughout verse 9. First, he imagines himself and his companions as prisoners of war in a victory procession by the opposing army (cf. 2 Cor. 2:14–15). Second, he envisions the frequent outcome of such capture—thrown to the gladiators or wild animals in the sporting arena, with death as the most common result. The Greek of verse 9 actually leaves out numerous words that the NIV supplies (literally, "For it seems God has exhibited us apostles as last, as condemned to die, because we have become a spectacle . . . "), but the insertions seem likely to reflect Paul's intentions. In verse 10, Paul returns to using irony to mock the way the Corinthians are viewing him as quite different from themselves. At one level, of course, his statements are true: by the world's standards, he is foolish, weak, and dishonored (recall 1:26). But spiritually, he is the exact opposite, and it is the church in Corinth which is ailing, impoverished, and inglorious.

Verses 11–12a provide a more straightforward list of Paul's hardships. Some of these result from hostility to the gospel, some from the arduous lifestyle of an itinerant minister in antiquity (cf. 2 Cor. 11:23b–29). Verse 12a

---

6. On which, see esp. Peter Marshall, *Enmity in Corinth: Social Conventions in Paul's Relations with the Corinthians* (Tübingen: Mohr, 1987), 209.

anticipates a criticism of Paul's ministry which chapter 9 will unpack. Verses 12b–13a give a remarkable model of how to respond in godly fashion to ungodly treatment and echo several sayings of Jesus from the Sermon on the Mount (cf. Matt. 5:38–48 and esp. Luke 6:28).

Verse 13b introduces a measure of hyperbole. Ironically, the Corinthians' view of Paul too frequently matches that of the non-Christian world. "Scum" and "refuse" both refer to that which is removed by a process of cleaning—dirt, filth, garbage. Some have tried to see allusions to sacrificial language of the Old Testament here but these are not demonstrable. "Up to this time" comes at the end of the sentence in Greek and closes this paragraph by implying that the fullness of the kingdom has not yet arrived, contrary to the claims of many in Corinth. In short, whereas the Corinthians think that their relatively prosperous conditions reflect God's blessing, Paul points to his sufferings for the sake of the gospel as a more accurate measure of Christian faithfulness.[7]

As abruptly as Paul's sarcasm began, it now equally abruptly gives way to tender tones (vv. 14–17). The right way for Corinth to view its apostles in general, and Paul in particular, is as special relatives. Their local leaders are only "guardians" (literally, "pedagogues"—Greek slaves in charge of seeing that children got from home to school and back again safely), but Paul is their spiritual father (v. 15). This parental imagery unites all of verses 14–21 and accounts for Paul's concern and strong warnings. "Ten thousand" in verse 15 translates the Greek word *murios* ("myriad"), the highest named number and is equivalent to the old RSV's "countless." "Not many" is equally figurative. In fact, they have only one father, Paul (unless he is also thinking of other evangelists who have ministered in Corinth after him).

Verse 16 introduces Paul's call to imitate him, just as a father in the ancient world regularly taught his sons a trade by modeling it as they studied under him as apprentices. Paul will repeat this call in 11:1 and qualify it: "as I follow the example of Christ." Because of his unique relationship to this congregation as their church planter and the one responsible for leading many of its members to the Lord, Paul has a unique responsibility and authority to oversee their spiritual growth. He would like to be personally present again to model correct Christian living, but he believes the Lord wants him to stay on in Ephesus a little while longer (1 Cor. 16:8–9). So he has sent

---

7. For an excellent articulation of Paul's theology of persecution, taking 1 Cor. 4:10–13 as its starting point, see Anthony T. Hanson, *The Paradox of the Cross in the Thought of St. Paul* (Sheffield: JSOT, 1987). Cf. also John S. Pobee, *Persecution and Martyrdom in the Theology of Paul* (Sheffield: JSOT, 1985).

Timothy as his personal surrogate (cf. 16:10–11; Acts 19:22), who will hopefully overcome his timidity and arrive soon.

Timothy, one of Paul's specially beloved travel companions and disciples, first appeared in Acts 16:1–4, was sent out on similar missions elsewhere (1 Thess. 3:2; Phil. 2:19), and ultimately became pastor of the church in Ephesus (1 and 2 Timothy). Timothy will thus remind the Corinthians, through his exemplary behavior, of the appropriate Christian walk, which Paul describes as his "way of life" (v. 17).[8]

With verses 18–21, Paul closes this four-chapter section of his letter with a final warning. He is coming soon, Lord willing (cf. 1 Cor. 16:5–7), even though some in Corinth are claiming that he is not (vv. 18–19a). He agrees with them that talk is cheap but disputes their claim that "his letters are weighty and forceful, but in person he is unimpressive and his speaking amounts to nothing" (2 Cor. 10:10). If he speaks gently to them in person, it is out of love (v. 21b). But if necessary he will come, metaphorically speaking, with a rod (NIV "whip"), just as faithful fathers in Paul's day made guarded use of corporal punishment as a disciplinary tool for their children.

What ultimately counts, however, is the presence of genuine spiritual power, as befits the presence of God's reign (vv. 19b–20). This kingly power must not be narrowly conceived. It consists of the edifying manifestation of spiritual gifts, of winning people to Christ and discipling them, of moral living, and of appropriate humble self-assessment, all in striking contrast to the regal roles the Corinthians thought they were playing (v. 8).

WITH CHAPTER 4, Paul offers the fifth and final method for combating divisiveness and promoting unity: a correct understanding of church leaders as servants of their congregations under God. They are not to be overly exalted but should be respected as his designated authorities for pastoral care in their midst. (For the first four reasons, see above, pp. 67 and 76.)

The key to applying this chapter lies in recognizing how Paul is correcting an imbalance in the Corinthians' approach to leaders. Taken by itself, Paul's corrective could lead to an equal but opposite imbalance. But in light of the entirety of Scripture, we can see church leaders as *servants* who nevertheless have authority (vv. 1–5), as *examples* who deserve to be followed but not placed on a pedestal (vv. 6–7), and as *sufferers* who also receive relief from

---

8. See further Boykin Sanders, "Imitating Paul: 1 Cor 4:16," *HTR* 74 (1981): 353–63.

affliction (vv. 8–13). The parental balance between toughness and tenderness is already amply illustrated within this chapter (vv. 14–21).

The two terms for "servant" in verse 1 are in fact aptly suited for conveying an appropriate balance between the authority and submission of church leaders, even if Paul focuses more on the latter here. On the one hand, congregations must not tie the hands of their pastors by so carefully monitoring every small decision that vision, passion, leadership, and growth are squelched. On the other hand, leaders must remain accountable to the cross-centered standards of the gospel, not neglecting the desires of the majority under their care so long as they are compatible with that gospel. The idea of "servant ministry" is variously defined, but the antiauthoritarian core of the concept is profoundly biblical and acutely needed in every area of church life.[9] Andrew Clarke sums it up as a *task*-oriented perception of leadership, avoiding the emphasis in secular society on the status of the *persons* in leadership.[10]

Verse 2 underlines another crucial criterion for ministry—faithfulness. God does not require us to be successful, certainly not by worldly standards, and often he does not supply success even on a spiritual level as much as we might desire. Rather he calls us to constant faithfulness regardless of external results. Verse 3 contrasts sharply with 2:15 and, like that verse, must be kept in context.[11]

As noted under 2:15, 1 Corinthians itself includes numerous references to appropriate forms of judgment which the Christian community must exercise (see above, p. 68). The next two chapters will illustrate two major examples of such judgment: church discipline (5:1–13) and Christian arbitration of legal disputes among church members (6:1–11). But here Paul is stressing that human judgment is *relatively* insignificant compared with God's opinion of a person's behavior. The balance resembles that of Matthew 7:1 compared with verses 2–6. We must not be unfairly or hypocritically judgmental, but when we are prepared to deal with our own problems it is

---

9. One of the most balanced treatments of this theme is James E. Means, *Leadership in Christian Ministry* (Grand Rapids: Baker, 1989). On p. 58 he defines spiritual leadership as "the development of relationships with the people of a Christian institution or body in such a way that individuals and the group are enabled to formulate and achieve biblically compatible goals that meet real needs. By their ethical influence, spiritual leaders serve to motivate and enable others to achieve what otherwise would never be achieved."

10. Andrew D. Clarke, *Secular and Christian Leadership in Corinth* (Leiden: Brill, 1993), 119.

11. Robertson and Plummer, *First Corinthians*, 76, quote T. C. Edwards (1885) as explaining the difference between these verses: "Self-knowledge is more difficult than revealed truth."

appropriate and essential to deal, however gently, with others' sins as well (cf. Gal. 6:1).

Similar qualifications apply to verses 3b–4a. Conscience or moral awareness can play a very positive role in convicting individuals of sin and leading them to repentance. But consciences, like all other parts of the human person, have been corrupted by sin. A clear conscience may simply be the product of a faulty memory or, worse, a denial or suppression of moral failure. Conversely, some people's consciences accuse them falsely (cf. 1 John 3:20), burdening them with undue guilt.

The implicit qualifications of verses 3–4 carry over to verse 5 as well. Preliminary assessments of human behavior, inside and outside the church, are regularly required, but they must always remain subject to correction by information that at times may not be disclosed until Judgment Day. A classic example involves the question of who will ultimately be saved. To paraphrase C. S. Lewis, there will be three surprises in heaven—who's there, who's not there, and that you're there! As in chapter 3, Paul here highlights the positive role of judgment for believers, even though some of the things hidden in darkness will inevitably be negative. Nevertheless, each will receive "praise from God." "The implication may be that the Lord in his omniscience will find cause for approval where another judge will find none."[12]

Given the uncertain meaning of verse 6a, one must beware of drawing any overly dogmatic applications from this half-verse. But the purpose of the saying remains clear from verse 6b. The presumption implied in going "beyond what is written" naturally leads to the ingratitude implicit in verse 7. This verse proved crucial for Augustine in his battle with Pelagius and in his development of the concepts of human depravity, irresistible grace, and predestination. But although these were broadly legitimate theological inferences, they go far beyond Paul's immediate point of dealing with the Corinthians' arrogance. Verse 7 does, however, provide further support for the understanding of chapter 3 that sees all believers as fundamentally equal before God, since nothing they possess or have done even after conversion merits reward.

Verses 8–13 starkly highlight the irony of affliction. The New Testament never commands believers to seek suffering or martyrdom; indeed Jesus and Paul often fled from it. And Christ specifically ordered his disciples to escape persecution when they could (Matt. 10:23). Neither does Scripture ever assign any atoning value to Christian suffering. Christ's cross-work was utterly unique in that respect. Paul's statement in Colossians 1:24, "I fill up in my flesh what is still lacking in regard to Christ's afflictions," most likely refers

---

12. F. F. Bruce, *1 and 2 Corinthians* (London: Marshall, Morgan & Scott, 1971), 48.

to a fixed amount of suffering which believers must endure in Christ, not to any inadequacy in the atonement.

On the other hand, Scripture consistently points out the positive value of affliction. Paul's very next letter to the Corinthians supplies a veritable catalogue of reasons why God allows his people to suffer: to enable them to comfort others with divinely given comfort (2 Cor. 1:4), to help a watching world recognize a supernatural origin in our ability to cope (4:7–12), because of the glorious compensation that one day awaits them (4:17; 5:1–10), and because God's power is often perfected in human weakness (12:9).

In the Sermon on the Mount, Christ declared, "Blessed are those who are persecuted because of righteousness, for theirs is the kingdom of heaven" (Matt. 5:10). The phrase "because of righteousness" reminds us that God's blessing does not extend to those who are persecuted for wrongdoing, false teaching, or lack of tact (cf. 1 Peter 3:13–17). We must avoid the fallacy of assuming that religious persecution automatically proves our cause right!

On the other hand, given Paul's remarks about his "thorn in the flesh" (2 Cor. 12:7–10), almost certainly a reference to some physical affliction, it probably *is* legitimate to extend Paul's principles about suffering to natural disaster, disease, and disability, to the extent that they are not brought on by our own sin or negligence. And even then, God can graciously override our mistakes to help us learn from them and grow.[13]

Here in 1 Corinthians 4:11, three of the four maladies Paul mentions do not stem from his preaching *per se* ("brutally treated" would be the one exception) but from the dangers of itinerant ministry in the ancient world more generally, when a person entrusted himself to the provisions of others. In parts of our world where ministry is less itinerant, where travel is less dangerous, and where people are less impoverished, we need not anticipate as much hunger, thirst, homelessness, or hard manual labor. But in many parts of our world, these conditions do continue to prevail. There pastors may expect to be bivocational, to be poorly paid, and to travel long distances to small, scattered outposts of believers, ministering in poor conditions with few material resources.

Sooner or later, though, all faithful believers who witness boldly will encounter opposition and hostility to their testimony (2 Tim. 3:12). Sharing in Christ's sufferings thus becomes a prerequisite to sharing in his glory (Rom. 8:17). The nature of that opposition will vary widely and may at times be less physically severe than what Paul encountered (and for others it may be worse). But common features will doubtless include being thought foolish,

---

13. For an outstanding introductory treatment of several of these themes, see D. A. Carson, *How Long, O Lord? Reflections on Suffering and Evil* (Grand Rapids: Baker, 1990).

weak and dishonorable (v. 10) and being reviled and slandered (vv. 12–13). Ministers and others prominent in Christian leadership should expect to receive the brunt of such opposition and must model appropriately gracious responses. This is all the more reason why status, power, prestige, or wealth simply cannot be valid motives for entering full-time ministry.

Parental concern, in sharp contrast, probably does form the most foundational and legitimate motive for Christian work. The paternal imagery of verses 14–21 reappears in 1 Thessalonians 2:11 but is balanced in that context by corresponding maternal imagery (v. 7). So the point of Paul's "fathering" the Corinthians has little to do with his gender but much to do with the authority and love exercised over their children by godly *parents* of either gender.[14]

More striking is the image of parental modeling, to be imitated by the children. To command the Corinthians to "imitate me" (v. 16) either represents the height of presumption or reflects one of the most profound and challenging insights of all time on how to reproduce Christian disciples. In light of the rest of Paul's life and teaching, the latter is more probable. Progress along the road to sanctification demands that new believers have consistent, positive, mature Christian models to imitate in all aspects of daily life. This, in turn, implies that more mature Christians must make themselves accessible and transparent to younger believers around them. The ideal, as with Jesus and the Twelve and with Paul and his traveling companions, is for one believer to work with and even live with those he or she is discipling to such an extent that they can truly observe a godly lifestyle. This does not imply that such believers manifest perfection. How to deal with one's sin—in repenting and seeking forgiveness—is as crucial to model as virtuous behavior.

Parental love earns the right to discipline—hence verses 18–21. Paul warns us that our behavior ought to match our words. If not, then corrective action is required. Yet this corrective action must have the proper balance.

---

14. This point is often obscured in our contemporary milieu, which has been particularly sensitized to gender issues. Hence, e.g., Eva M. Lassen ("The Use of the Father Image in Imperial Propaganda and 1 Corinthians 4:14–21," *TynB* 42 [1991]: 127–36) correctly stresses the hierarchical, paternalistic emphasis in Roman Corinth against its more democratic Greek background. But when she concludes that Paul's invocation of a father figure thus stresses his authoritative relationship over his congregation, she loses sight of the fact that it is parental rather than male authority which he is invoking. Conversely, Prior (*1 Corinthians*, 67–68) throws the baby out with the bathwater when he vehemently insists that Paul's role as father carried with it *no* overtones of authority and that to claim otherwise represents "false teaching" which "is arguably the strongest barrier to the growth and health of the church in our day"!

All love without discipline produces a pampering permissiveness that leaves its recipients spoiled and still in their sins. Yet discipline untempered by love produces a harsh authoritarianism that drives people away from the church, and often from God, the minute they have the chance to escape.

THE PERFECT BALANCE between the two extremes of authoritarianism and servility among Christian ministers (v. 1) remains a rare commodity today. Many churches seem enslaved to powerful leaders; others fail to let their pastors lead by retaining the real decision-making power in the hands of other official or unofficial church authorities. The refusal of prominent, "fallen" leaders to submit to sufficient church discipline well illustrates the former malady. The rapid turnover rate among church staff, particularly at the associate level, often indicates the latter ailment.

Secular standards of success continue to overshadow biblical ones. Almost any criterion imaginable seems to be exalted above the faithfulness Paul highlights in verse 2—budget, income, size and appearance of church buildings, the presence of Christian celebrities, or the numbers of programs. Even at the more "spiritual" level, we often deceive ourselves into thinking that counting conversions, baptisms, or additions to church membership demonstrates the presence of mature, obedient ministry. Only when we take note with equal care of the number of people turned away from the gospel through our lack of tact or taste and the number of people leaving the church through "the back door" can we determine if the first group of statistics amounts to much.

Churches that are growing numerically may not be as healthy spiritually as some smaller churches in which members are personally and corporately maturing in holiness. Sometimes external forces beyond their control account for the lack of numerical growth. As a classic example, one thinks of the long waits for extensive spiritual fruit encountered by William Carey and Adoniram Judson in India and Burma, and one wonders if some modern church-growth gurus would ever have permitted them to remain faithful long enough to see that fruit ripen.[15]

It is also difficult to maintain the delicate balance between not judging individuals and congregations at all, even in biblical ways, and judging every minute detail of their lives, often by secular criteria. So too we must walk the tightrope between never dealing with sin in our midst and becoming overly

---

15. Cf. the opposite results John predicts for the equally faithful Christians in Smyrna (Rev. 2:9–10) and Philadelphia (3:8–10).

harsh or judgmental in constantly trying to purge it (vv. 3–5). Matthew 7:1 ("Do not judge, or you too will be judged") seems to have replaced John 3:16 as the most well-known Bible verse by non-Christians, and it is almost always taken out of context and misapplied. For example, protesters supporting a homosexual lifestyle picketed a convention of Christian men trying to recover biblical values for their families, and they paraded this verse on their posters without any awareness of Matthew 7:5 ("First take the plank out of your own eye, and then you will see clearly *to remove the speck from your brother's eye* ").

In our radically individualistic, highly democratic society, "Let your conscience be your guide" sounds akin to biblical truth. Verse 4 makes plain that it is not. The theological concepts of the "priesthood of all believers" and of "soul competency" have often been applied far more widely than their Reformation-era framers ever intended. The Bible does teach the ability of each individual to relate directly to God, to understand enough of Scripture to come to salvation, and to be valued in God's eyes as much any other human being. But these themes have increasingly been distorted to support idiosyncratic, personal interpretations of the Bible and to challenge the right of Christian institutions to uphold standards by exercising discipline and removing unrepentant offenders.[16]

If verse 6 does refer to following scriptural standards, then we must surely comment on our modern world's appalling biblical illiteracy, an ignorance which leaves many even in Christian churches unable to cite a majority of the Ten Commandments, name the four Gospels, or identify who delivered the Sermon on the Mount.[17] Little wonder that disobedience to the Bible runs even more rampant! Yet Christian education in many churches seems to be on the decline, not on the rise as it should be. Pulpit ministries need to include major biblical teaching components; so must adults' and children's Sunday-school classes, home fellowship groups, one-on-one discipleship programs, and so on.[18]

Most of society works against our learning not to boast about ourselves (v. 7). We grow up learning to take credit for and even advertise our ac-

---

16. Cf. esp. Timothy George, "The Priesthood of All Believers and the Quest for Theological Integrity," *CTR* 3 (1989): 283–94.

17. George Gallup, Jr. and Sarah Jones, *100 Questions and Answers; Religion in America* (Princeton: Princeton Religion Research Center, 1989), 42: Only 42% of Americans polled could name five commandments; only 46% could name all four Gospels, and only 42% knew who delivered the Sermon on the Mount.

18. For implementation, see, e.g., Lawrence O. Richards, *Creative Bible Teaching* (Chicago: Moody, 1970); Howard G. Hendricks, *Teaching to Change Lives* (Portland: Multnomah, 1987).

complishments in education and employment via resumes and job evaluations. Not surprisingly, such advertisement carries over, consciously and unconsciously, to the Christian life, as we take pride in the statistics of which our ministries and churches can boast. It seems that professional church and parachurch workers are particularly prone to workaholism.

Instead of succumbing to these temptations, we need daily reminders that we accomplish nothing of eternal value apart from God's empowerment and guidance. This makes all boasting about our successes hypocritical and all hyperactivity overly presumptuous about our indispensability. Consider too the number of Americans who think they are in some way better than foreigners because of the wealth and ease of their lives, without ever significantly reflecting on the fact that they had absolutely nothing to do with the choice of their birthplace!

There are numerous contemporary counterparts to the triumphalism lurking behind Paul's description of the Corinthians in verse 8 (in addition to our discussion here, see the Introduction, pp. 25–27). Overestimation of our spiritual health and, indeed, of the extent to which we can progress spiritually (and physically, morally, and technologically) is endemic to Western society.

Conversely, we who experience the most widespread affluence of any culture in the history of the world have a poor understanding of the positive value of affliction (vv. 9–13). Like the Corinthians, we often fail to grasp how regularly suffering must precede glory. Michael Green provocatively predicts that "the church in the West will probably remain flaccid and effete until it is called upon to suffer. We ourselves are likely to learn the most significant lessons of our lives through suffering." What is more, "if Jesus had to tread this path, there can hardly be another way for us. But that is something that we, like the Corinthians, are most reluctant to accept."[19] Given the increased hostility to evangelical Christianity in the public sectors of education, media, and the like, it is not improbable that the American church will increasingly be purged of its dross and learn to tread this path.

At the moment, however, we create uniquely Western heresies such as the so-called "health-and-wealth gospel," replete with its "name-it and-claim-it" policies for prayer. Those who have immersed themselves in poverty-and sickness-laden Third World cultures and their Christian communities find it almost incomprehensible how any one could believe such wholesale distortion of the Scriptures.[20] Mission strategies would also be significantly inverted

---

19. Green, *Corinth*, 127.

20. For an extremely sympathetic yet adequate critique, see Bruce Barron, *The Health and Wealth Gospel* (Downers Grove, Ill.: InterVarsity Press, 1987).

if 4:1–13 were taken seriously, for less money would be devoted to maintaining Western standards of living in impoverished communities and much more on meeting the desperate spiritual and physical needs of others.[21]

To be sure, a depressive defeatism which does not believe God can work miracles today, or at least acts as if he could not, is equally unwarranted. Prayer for healing is an entirely appropriate response to a diagnosis of cancer—much more appropriate than immediately making funeral arrangements! God can and does bring miraculous healing from all sorts of afflictions, but such miracles by definition remain the exception and not the rule. More pervasive (or at least more in the limelight) than lack of prayer for healing are the preachers and televangelists who attribute all sickness to sin and blame people for their lack of faith when they pray for healing but do not receive it. Karl Plank succinctly outlines the necessary balance:

> Neither the word of enthusiasm nor futility lies open to a theology of affliction. But between the naiveté of cheap confidence and the arrogance of despair spans a more generous irony. The world which hosts the intimacy of life and death demands theology to speak through paradox and allows it to do so in good faith.[22]

Plank adds that theology must neither condemn nor glorify affliction. It remains an enemy and yet "may bear a preciousness."

Neither do we handle persecution well. A small minority, particularly in sectarian, separatist circles, glorifies rejection by the world and other Christian groups as if it confirmed their faithfulness. The silent majority so fears rejection that it barely even witnesses to its faith. A correct, mediating position will recognize that Christians are called to stand boldly but lovingly for God's truth in all walks of life, in speech and in behavior, and accept whatever consequences result. As political and social factors favorable to the gospel continue to deteriorate, even a little light shines brightly in the growing darkness. There is intense irony in the fact that our society speaks out strongly against discrimination directed toward just about every conceivable subgroup of our culture except evangelical Christians.[23] Such inconsistency is itself a backhanded testimony to the unique claims and power of Christianity over against all other ideologies.

---

21. See esp. Jonathan J. Bonk, "Doing Mission out of Affluence: Reflections on Recruiting 'End of the Procession' Missionaries from 'Front of the Procession' Churches (1 Corinthians 4:1–13)," *Missiology* 17 (1989): 427–52.

22. Karl A. Plank, *Paul and the Irony of Affliction* (Atlanta: Scholars, 1987), 93.

23. Contrast Stephen L. Carter, *The Culture of Disbelief* (New York: Basic Books, 1993), who calls for preserving a special role for religious communities as consistent with the First Amendment and the enhancement of our democratic traditions.

Even more ironic and misguided are Christian calls to fight back with the weapons of the world. One of the very reasons more militant blacks, Jews, women, gays, and other diverse minorities have at times been able to sensitize society so highly to discrimination against them is because of the aggressive political and legal tactics they have often adopted, tactics that would be inappropriate for Christians purporting to promote a cross-centered gospel to imitate. We may win certain battles—with boycotts against advertisers, asserting our rights to public prayer and Bible study, or overcoming the straightjackets of certain mandates for "politically correct" speech. A limited amount of such protest, when a larger consensus in society is likely to be forged, may at times prove helpful. But in many instances, we go overboard and lose the war, so alienating those with whom we do battle that we may lose them forever as potential citizens of the kingdom.[24]

The theme of parent-like modeling of Christian behavior that pervades verses 14–21 presents profound possibilities for discipleship in a transient, fragmented, event-oriented society. Again, however, trends in Christian circles seem almost uniformly to follow the patterns of our culture rather than of the gospel. Where academic institutions increasingly compartmentalize knowledge and limit teaching to the classroom, seminaries must create better models of church-assisted education.[25] Where the average-length pastorate continues to decrease, we need people prepared to commit themselves to one community of believers for the long haul, through thick and thin. Where Christian leaders tend increasingly toward performance- or entertainment-based ministries, we need more who will make themselves accessible and transparent—and have enough maturity to make the lifestyle then visible worth imitating. Where leadership tends to retain all significant power in its own hands, it needs to recover the model of growth by multiplication—pouring out one's life into a handful of followers who will in turn each reproduce his or her own followers in like fashion (cf. 2 Tim. 2:2). Where hurting people are increasingly referred to counselors who restrict contact with "clients" to certain hours for which they receive pay, we need sensitive Christians, including those with counseling skills, to be available

---

24. A study of Paul's behavior in Acts proves particularly instructive. Paul asserts his legal rights as a Roman citizen *when and only when* the benefit of others and the advance of the gospel more generally are at stake. Cf. Acts 16:37 (he could have appealed *before* being imprisoned but did not), 22:25–29 (he knew the primary debate was with the Jewish, not the Roman leaders), and 25:10–11 (he already knew God wanted him to go to Rome [23:11]). The dominant pattern of Acts finds Paul simply leaving a given region without protest once persecution begins.

25. Cf. Michael Green's provocative suggestions in *Acts for Today* (London: Hodder and Stoughton, 1993), 174.

freely to come alongside fellow believers inside and outside an office. They need to show them by example what mature Christian living involves in numerous walks of life. The more believers can live in genuine community, the more likely much of this will occur. Some of the current resurgence of the house-church movement holds the potential for recovering these strengths of discipleship by imitation.[26]

Above all, modeling Christian living will include embracing suffering when it is inevitable: "We must incarnate our teachings in a life of service that may invite or at least will not avoid suffering for the faith and the faithful. If we merely talk, we are no better than the false apostles"[27] (cf. vv. 19–20).

Verses 18–21 also remind us of the necessary balance between tolerance and discipline, which chapter 5 will elaborate at greater length. If Christian parents are recovering from the permissiveness of the 1960s in order to "dare to discipline,"[28] churches need to embark on a parallel recovery of exercising kind but firm resistance against arrogant powermongers who would split congregations today the way factions did in first-century Corinth.

---

26. See, e.g., Christian Smith, *Going to the Root: 9 Proposals for Radical Church Renewal* (Scottdale, Pa.: Herald, 1992).

27. William D. Spencer, "The Power in Paul's Teaching (1 Cor 4:9–20)," *JETS* 32 (1989): 61.

28. The title of the immensely popular book by James Dobson, originally published by Tyndale House, Wheaton, in 1970, and frequently reprinted and revised.

1 Corinthians 5:1–13

It is actually reported that there is sexual immorality among you, and of a kind that does not occur even among pagans: A man has his father's wife. ²And you are proud! Shouldn't you rather have been filled with grief and have put out of your fellowship the man who did this? ³Even though I am not physically present, I am with you in spirit. And I have already passed judgment on the one who did this, just as if I were present. ⁴When you are assembled in the name of our Lord Jesus and I am with you in spirit, and the power of our Lord Jesus is present, ⁵hand this man over to Satan, so that the sinful nature may be destroyed and his spirit saved on the day of the Lord.

⁶Your boasting is not good. Don't you know that a little yeast works through the whole batch of dough? ⁷Get rid of the old yeast that you may be a new batch without yeast—as you really are. For Christ, our Passover lamb, has been sacrificed. ⁸Therefore let us keep the Festival, not with the old yeast, the yeast of malice and wickedness, but with bread without yeast, the bread of sincerity and truth.

⁹I have written you in my letter not to associate with sexually immoral people—¹⁰not at all meaning the people of this world who are immoral, or the greedy and swindlers, or idolaters. In that case you would have to leave this world. ¹¹But now I am writing you that you must not associate with anyone who calls himself a brother but is sexually immoral or greedy, an idolater or a slanderer, a drunkard or a swindler. With such a man do not even eat.

¹²What business is it of mine to judge those outside the church? Are you not to judge those inside? ¹³God will judge those outside. "Expel the wicked man from among you."

HERE BEGINS THE second major topic Paul addresses in response to the oral reports he has received about the Corinthian church. He deals with this problem more briefly than the overarching problem of divisions in the church (1:10–4:21). Still, chapters 5–6 may be seen as a larger, loosely connected unit structured in an ABA pattern that discusses sexual sin (5:1–13), lawsuits (6:1–11) and sexual sin again (6:12–20).

Common to all three of these sections is the manifestation of the libertine or hedonistic wing of the church which is flaunting its freedom in Christ. This group depreciates the significance of the physical world and exaggerates the arrival of all of the blessings of the coming age. Worse still, the church refuses properly to monitor and judge its most sinful members. As such, chapter 5 ties back in with the end of chapter 4 with its repeated references to the Corinthians' arrogance (cf. 4:18–19 with 5:2). Paul's discussion falls naturally into three parts: a judgment pronounced (vv. 1–5), a rationale explained (vv. 6–8) and a misunderstanding corrected (vv. 9–13).

A horrible state of affairs in the Corinthian church has captured Paul's attention. "Reported" in verse 1 is literally "heard." We do not know how widely the news had traveled, but it had at least reached Paul. "Sexual immorality" translates the Greek *porneia*, the most general of all terms for sexual sin. In this context, however, it is clear that the sin is a matter of incest. If the man involved were one of the faction leaders or patrons in the church, one might well understand why people were reluctant to take action against him, and why Paul was so upset.

"Has" suggests an ongoing sexual relationship; "father's wife," that the woman is not the man's mother but his stepmother. She may have been considerably younger than her husband and hence attractive to his son. If the son was a patron, then he was wealthy, and the liaison could have led to significant financial benefit for the woman. It may well be that the father had died, and that his estate had passed to his son rather than his wife. Whether or not the son had legally married the woman is impossible to determine.[1] This kind of incest was strictly forbidden in Jewish law (Lev. 18:8). Despite the general moral laxity of the Greco-Roman world, this kind of incest remained one form of sexual sin that was relatively rare and widely condemned there too.[2]

The church's reaction to this affair was as bad or worse than the affair itself. Instead of grieving over sin in their midst,[3] they were actually smug over

---

1. On all of these details, cf. further Andrew D. Clarke, *Secular and Christian Leadership in Corinth* (Leiden: Brill, 1993), 74–85.

2. Many commentators cite Cicero's slightly exaggerated outrage at the marriage of a woman to her son-in-law: "Oh! to think of the woman's sin, unbelievable, unheard of in all experience save for this single instance!" (*Pro Cluentio* 15). Talbert, *Corinthians*, 13–14, supplies a good catalog of other relevant Jewish and Greco-Roman perspectives on the topic.

3. Brian S. Rosner, "'ΟΥΧΙ ΜΑΛΛΟΝ ΕΠΕΝΘΗΣΑΤΕ': Corporate Responsibility in 1 Corinthians 5," *NTS* 38 (1992): 470–73, makes a plausible case for viewing Paul's words against a Hebrew background of corporate responsibility, in which the church should have mourned in the sense of "confessing the sin of the erring brother as if it was their own" (p. 472).

their newfound, "enlightened" tolerance as Christians (v. 2). Paul recoils in horror. They must rather remove this man from their midst ("fellowship"). That no mention is made of removing the woman suggests she was not a church member to begin with.

In verses 3–4, Paul asserts his authority to pronounce judgment on the situation and in so doing to reflect the power and authority of Christ Jesus himself. Although physically absent, his thoughts were ever with them, and by means of this letter they knew his intentions and desires. "In the name of the Lord Jesus" begins verse 4 in the Greek and could also modify either "passed judgment" or "the one who did this" in verse 3. If the last of these is accepted, the problem in Corinth takes on even more horrifying proportions: the man has justified his sin by appealing to the authority of Jesus, presumably referring to his freedom in Christ. But the sentence is too convoluted in the Greek to know for sure.[4]

Precisely what Paul commands the Corinthians to do in verse 5 remains hotly disputed. All agree that it *at least* involves excommunication or disfellowshipping. A dominant modern view has seen Paul envisioning the physical death of the man. Perhaps he had some severe sexually transmitted disease, or perhaps Paul assumed that God would punish him more directly as he had other Corinthians (cf. 11:30) and Ananias and Sapphira (Acts 5:1–11). "Hand over to Satan" would thus refer to the death of his body (cf. NIV margin) and would explain why Paul then jumps ahead to Judgment Day: the severe discipline is to prevent the man from committing full-fledged apostasy and to ensure that he still will be saved in eternity.

On the other hand, the dominant perspective in the early church, now being revived in a number of recent studies of this passage, seems preferable. The Greek reads literally, "so that his *flesh* may be destroyed." But when Paul contrasts flesh and spirit, he usually does not refer to body versus soul but to the old versus new natures of a believer (or to the individual as oriented toward sin versus oriented toward God).[5] In 1 Timothy 1:20, Paul describes

---

4. A woodenly literal translation of verses 3–4 might read, "For I, absent in the body but present in the spirit, have already judged, as present, the one who has done this thing, in the name of the (our) Lord Jesus, when you have gathered together, and my spirit, with the power of the Lord Jesus. . . ."

5. Anthony C. Thiselton, "The Meaning of ΣΑΡΞ in 1 Corinthians 5.5: A Fresh Approach in the Light of Logical and Semantic Factors," *SJT* 26 (1973): 204–28, helpfully speaks of the "flesh" as referring here to the man's professed "self-sufficiency" or "self-satisfaction." For a good overview of the main arguments in favor of the NIV rendering, see Fee, *First Corinthians*, 210–13; cf. also N. George Joy, "Is the Body Really to Be Destroyed? (1 Corinthians 5.5)," *BT* 39 (1988): 429–36; and James T. South, "A Critique of the 'Curse/Death' Interpretation of 1 Corinthians 5.1–8," *NTS* 39 (1993): 539–61.

how he handed two believers over to Satan to be taught not to blaspheme, so presumably they did not die. And a good case can be made for seeing the repentant sinner of 2 Corinthians 2:5–11; 7:8–13 as this same individual addressed in 1 Corinthians 5.[6] In either event, Paul's purpose clearly remains remedial.[7]

Verses 6–8 appeal to the Jews' practice of purifying their homes and their temple from all leavened bread prior to the Passover feast (Ex. 12:15). Paul applies this imagery to the *moral* purity God requires of his new house/temple—the church.[8] Citing in verse 6 what may have been a popular proverb (cf. Gal. 5:9), he makes it clear that serious sin can infect the whole congregation. Thinking of Passover reminds him of Christ as our perfect sacrifice (v. 7), imagery which the writer to the Hebrews will later elaborate. Jesus' atonement was not intended to free us *to* sin but to liberate us *from* sin. As he likes to do in many of his letters, Paul thus calls his audience to "become what they are"—to act according to the way God has already chosen to consider them in Christ (cf. esp. Rom. 6–8). This means putting away all forms of evil ("malice" and "wickedness" are both general terms covering the waterfront of sin) and behaving in ways that genuinely conform to God's true standards (v. 8).

Verses 9–13 close this section by clarifying an apparent misunderstanding, or possibly even a deliberate misrepresentation, of Paul's previous letter (on which, see Introduction, p. 22). The verbs beginning verses 9 and 11 are simple past tense and should probably both be translated "I wrote," referring to the contents of that letter. When Paul had told them not to associate (literally, "mix up together with") flagrantly immoral people (v. 9), he was referring to professing Christians, not avowed unbelievers.

---

6. It is often objected that the man in 2 Corinthians must be someone else, because there it is a matter of personal affront to Paul. But in light of the intervening events between 1 and 2 Corinthians, it is entirely conceivable that Paul and this man had a personal "run-in" which accounts for his language in his second letter. See esp. Colin Kruse, *The Second Epistle of Paul to the Corinthians* (Grand Rapids: Eerdmans, 1987), 41–45, 81–84.

7. Barth Campbell ("Flesh and Spirit in 1 Cor 5:5: An Exercise in Rhetorical Criticism of the New Testament," *JETS* 36 [1993]: 331–42) believes, in the light of the corporate references in verses 6–11, that the flesh refers to the sinful element in the church and that saving the spirit is the restoration of corporate spirituality. There may be secondary implications along these lines, but it is hard to see such definitions as primary.

8. Brian S. Rosner, "Temple and Holiness in 1 Corinthians 5," *TynB* 42 (1991): 132–45, argues that 1 Corinthians 3:16–17 forms the theological framework for understanding Paul's commands: the incestuous man has defiled God's holy temple and must be put out of the assembly just as ritually defiled persons were excluded from the Old Testament congregations of God's people.

To drive home this point, Paul generalizes and lists several serious sins in addition to sexual immorality (vv. 10–11). "The greedy and swindlers" should be taken together to refer to those who were seizing "someone else's property by force,"[9] perhaps anticipating the problem of 6:1–11. "Idolaters" is Paul's general term for all who worship false gods. "Slanderer" should be translated "reviler" and may refer particularly to those who oppose and mock God's duly ordained authorities. "Drunkard," like the other terms in these lists, implies one whose lifestyle is consistently characterized by such behavior. Not only must the Corinthians remove from their fellowship people who repeatedly refuse to repent of their sins, they must not even associate with them in intimate social gatherings outside the church, such as table fellowship.

Verses 12–13 explain the logic of the commands of verses 9–11. The church's jurisdiction is restricted to its own membership. God will take care of unbelievers' sins; indeed, their fate will be bad enough that Christians ought not add to their agony but seek instead to lead them to Christ. So Paul concludes where he began, reminding the Corinthians to expel the incestuous offender. "Man," however, does not appear in the Greek, so Paul may be generalizing here to call them to cast out from their lives anyone or anything that is notoriously and persistently wicked.

Bridging Contexts

THE DOMINANT QUESTION that emerges from this chapter is the issue of how and when to practice church discipline in settings other than first-century Corinth.[10] Matthew 18:15–18 outlines the preliminary steps: private conversation, discussion in the presence of witnesses, and public confrontation by the entire church. As here in 1 Corinthians, the final action must never be taken unilaterally by a handful of church leaders but in agreement with the church body as a whole. In each case, the goal is to resolve the problem without having to proceed further. But if nothing else works, excommunication is the last step that Jesus commands. Has Paul assumed that everything else has already been tried in Corinth? Or, perhaps more plausibly, does he realize in view of the entire congregation's attitude that such preliminary steps will prove impossible and/or unsuccessful? On any view of verse 5, however, the rehabilitative purpose of the discipline remains unquestioned.

---

9. Ellingworth and Hatton, *First Corinthians*, 103.

10. Two particularly helpful studies are J. Carl Laney, *A Guide to Church Discipline* (Minneapolis: Bethany, 1985); and John White and Ken Blue, *Healing the Wounded: The Costly Love of Church Discipline* (Downers Grove, Ill.: InterVarsity Press, 1985).

If the man's death is not in view, then how is he subsequently to be handled? Jesus says "treat him as you would a pagan or a tax collector" (Matt. 18:17). Although Jesus socialized with such people, orthodox Jews did not, and in context Jesus' remark clearly refers to ostracism. But even other Jews did seek to win such people over to their points of view. The Christian equivalent would seem to be to treat an excommunicant as an unbeliever (while not claiming that he or she necessarily is). In other words, such people should not be permitted to take the Lord's Supper or participate in any other Christian gatherings that are reserved for believers only. But they presumably could be allowed to sit in a service in which unbelievers are welcome, so long as they are not treated as if nothing had happened.

Friends and fellow church members should continue to reach out and urge repentance just as they do in evangelizing non-Christians. But intimate social intercourse cannot continue unchanged. Interpersonal relationships will inevitably be strained so long as the individual refuses to acknowledge any wrongdoing (cf. the balance enjoined in 2 Thess. 3:14–15). The whole point in disfellowshipping is to so shock the persons involved by the severity of the church's disapproval that they are stimulated to change their behavior, after less radical action has left them unaffected. If excommunication in certain cultures is not likely to have this effect, then alternate forms of discipline may have to be sought.[11]

For what sins should such potentially severe measures of discipline be initiated? Incest was clearly an extreme example in first-century Corinth. Verses 10–11 are similarly characterized by very serious offenses for those claiming to be Christians. In 2 Thessalonians 3:6, 14–15, Paul warns us to shun the idle who refuse to work but disrupt believers' lives instead. In Titus 3:10 and Romans 16:17, the factious are to be avoided. It is as if Paul says of those who would try to split the church that they should "split" instead! First Corinthians 5:6–8 offers some implicit guidelines: church discipline is needed when a given sin carries with it the serious possibility of corrupting the entire congregation. Notwithstanding all of the biblical ideals for church unity, including those Paul has put forward in chapters 1–4, purity retains an even higher priority.[12] But "purity" has too often been the alleged basis for churches splitting over much lesser matters. Chapters 1–4 surely caution us against appealing to this rationale except in the most serious of situations.

---

11. Cf., e.g., Walter A. Trobisch, "Church Discipline in Africa," *Practical Anthropology* 8 (1961): 200–206.

12. See esp. Adela Y. Collins, "The Function of 'Excommunication' in Paul," *HTR* 73 (1980): 251–63.

Turning now to a look at some of the specific details of this chapter in sequence, we see first in verse 1 a concern for the reputation of the church in its society. If even the pagans of Paul's day usually found incest so offensive, then to tolerate it among Christians would seriously compromise the church's witness. If the offender was a leader in the church, then additional questions about the discipline and restoration of fallen pastors or elders are raised. Because of their prominent roles of influence, a good case can be made for saying that the discipline of such leaders should be more firm and the period of testing prior to restoration more lengthy than for other church members.[13]

Paul's commands to exercise judgment (vv. 2–5, 7, 13b) offer important qualifications of his instruction in 2:15 and 4:3, on which see comments there (pp. 68, 93–94). Regardless of the nature of this judgment, however, it remains consistent with the rest of early Christian teaching and practice. Church discipline was always originally intended (though never guaranteed) to be remedial, and not merely or even primarily punitive.[14] Contact, therefore, cannot be entirely broken with the offending individuals, even if "business as usual" cannot continue either.

The positive moral antidote to sin is purity, described in verse 8 as "sincerity and truth." These are not broad, all-encompassing terms for Christian virtue in quite the same way as "malice and wickedness" are for vice. Rather they remind us that hypocrisy damages the credibility of the gospel (hence the need for sincerity), but that sincerity alone is inadequate to save a person if one's trust is placed in that which is unreliable (hence the need for truth). Yet in Philippians 1:15–18, Paul rejoices that the gospel is preached even by those with wrong motives, whereas in Philippians 3:2–11 he lambastes those who sincerely promote heresy. In other words, sincerity and truth are not of equal value. If only one can be preserved, then we must cling to the truth.

The inversion of the Corinthians' standards in verses 9–13 has profound implications for the church's role in society. Its first responsibility is always to model God's countercultural standards before a watching world rather than trying to impose those standards on society as a whole. In the Roman empire, Christians had little opportunity to influence the laws of the land. In democracies, believers have both the right and the responsibility *as citizens* to promote their ideological and ethical convictions through legal

---

13. On which, see esp. Jack W. Hayford, *Restoring Fallen Church Leaders* (Ventura: Regal, 1988).

14. On which, see esp. G. W. H. Lampe, "Church Discipline and the Interpretation of the Epistle to the Corinthians," in *Christian History and Interpretation*, ed. W. R. Farmer, C. F. D. Moule and R. R. Niebuhr (Cambridge: Cambridge University Press, 1967), 337–61.

processes. But they have no unique mandate *as the church* to try to "Christianize" nations, though they may and ought to speak prophetically to society about the moral issues of their day. On the other hand, Paul's words caution strongly against those forms of separatism that leave the church unable to function as "salt" and "light" in the surrounding world.[15]

Verse 11 leaves open the question of the reality of the professions of faith of persistently immoral people. Doubtless some are true believers in serious rebellion against their Lord, but Paul probably suspects that many may merely be masquerading as Christians, especially in view of 6:9–10, on which see our comments below (p. 121). The specific sins mentioned particularly characterized pagan Corinth in the mid-first century, so evidence for a transformed lifestyle was significantly missing among those who consistently practiced such vice.

Many will continue to view the whole notion of church discipline, and certainly excommunication, as repulsive and unloving. Yet such people fail to grasp God's utter repugnance to sin and his infinitely perfect standards for holiness. Further, we must avoid a cheap grace that refuses to force professing believers to face up to the destructive consequences of grossly immoral behavior. They are not only damaging themselves by allowing sin to go unchecked but also destroying the church.

Not surprisingly, the church has regularly grown the fastest and become the healthiest where loving but firm church discipline has been implemented. A chain of quotations from William Barclay rings true in almost every society and captures the balance of Paul's teaching in this chapter: "To shut our eyes to offenses is not always a kind thing to do; it may be damaging;" "it has been said that our one security against sin lies in our being shocked at it;" yet "discipline should never be exercised for the satisfaction of the person who exercises it, but always for the mending of the person who has sinned and for the sake of the Church."[16]

LARGE SECTIONS OF the contemporary church virtually ignore 1 Corinthians 5 altogether. Doubtless this is a reaction against the horrible excesses and abuse of this chapter in past eras, such as in the Roman Catholics' Spanish Inquisition, in Luther's and Zwingli's excommunication of Anabaptists, or in recent Protestant funda-

---

15. For balanced approaches, cf. Alan Storkey, *A Christian Social Perspective* (Leicester: InterVarsity Press, 1979); with John Gladwin, *God's People in God's World* (Leicester: InterVarsity Press, 1979).

16. Barclay, *Corinthians*, 44–46.

mentalist legalism against all kinds of morally neutral practices. But to refuse to engage in church discipline, including excommunication if necessary, is to overreact so wildly as to jeopardize seriously the health of the church.

Ours is an age, tragically, in which even church leaders commit sexual sin or defraud their congregations, at times with virtual impunity. And if a period of discipline and restoration is established, they may refuse to agree to their church's terms. In still other cases, such a period of time seems woefully inadequate to demonstrate a genuine and lasting change of heart and behavior. Some Christian leaders even endorse a philosophy of restoring fallen leaders to ministry as soon as possible in the name of grace and forgiveness! But forgiveness and restoration to fellowship do not automatically carry with them the privilege of pastoring or leading a congregation. The criteria for overseers and deacons in 1 Timothy 3:1–13, including marital faithfulness and wholesome family life, are best understood as attributes which *currently* characterize one's life and *have done so over a long enough period of time* that they may be assumed to be enduring character traits (cf. esp. verse 10).[17]

The biggest problem, of course, with replicating the effect of biblical disfellowshipping today lies with the element of ostracism originally involved. The few churches that do excommunicate the defiantly immoral usually watch those individuals go down the road, or move to a new town, and join another church that pays little or no attention to the reasons they left their previous congregation. Churches even hire pastoral staff who have been let go from other ministries for unethical or illegal behavior without ever asking enough questions of the right people to find out that such behavior had occurred. Becoming a church or staff member should require that the church involved learn enough about an individual's past to determine if he or she is running away from problems left unaddressed. Sensitive but frank cooperation and networking between congregations becomes crucial if the original impact of "shunning" is to have any possibility of being reproduced in our transient world.[18]

Conversely, for people who simply want to be left alone by Christian friends and acquaintances, so that they are not forced to own up to their sins, loving but persistent personal contacts may be necessary to confront them with their inappropriate behavior.[19] One pastor has found that "temporary

---

17. See, e.g., Thomas D. Lea and Hayne P. Griffin, Jr., *1, 2 Timothy, Titus* (Nashville: Broadman, 1992), 109–10; C. H. Dodd, "New Testament Translation Problems II," BT 28 (1977): 112–16.

18. Good, practical suggestions for implementing this are found in Jay E. Adams, *Handbook of Church Discipline* (Grand Rapids: Zondervan, 1986), 99–118.

19. One thinks of the examples of "tough love" of parents for children outlined in Bill Milliken, *Tough Love* (Old Tappan, N.J.: Fleming Revell, 1968). But for these models to be

suspensions" from certain activities with required service in other facets of church life have proved a more effective form of discipline.[20]

At this point, important legal questions immediately clamor for attention. Ours is an age of rampant litigation, and church members who have been excluded from congregations, or even disciplined to lesser degrees, often turn around and sue those churches, compounding their prior sin with flagrant defiance of 1 Corinthians 6:1–11. In an age when many social forces discriminate against evangelical Christians, judges and juries are all too eager to award substantial sums of money to individuals who sue their former churches, often leaving those congregations in severe financial straits.[21]

Still, there are legal ways in which churches can and must practice biblically mandated discipline.[22] Constitutions or bylaws must clearly state the procedures of discipline, potential members must read and agree to them, a condition for membership may include signing forms waiving the right to sue the church, and then the congregation must carefully and consistently implement its policies. The laws in any given state must be carefully studied and followed to determine clergy's privileges of confidentiality as well as their responsibilities to disclose illegal behavior to local authorities.

The specific problem of incest that first stimulated chapter 5 has once again emerged as a scandal in Christian circles today. In some places its frequency inside the church rivals its commonness outside. It scarcely remains the one social taboo that almost no one practices, though in many non-Western cultures that is still true. Nevertheless, even our relativistic secular world often finds incest offensive in ways it does not with other sexual sin, particularly when minors are involved. The incongruity of it occurring in Christian circles and the serious need for loving but firm discipline when it occurs thus remain great.[23]

For many moderns, the word *immoral* is a synonym for sexually sinful. We need Paul's reminder of verses 10–11, therefore, that the biblical definition of the term covers the full range of humanity's sinful behavior, and that disciplinary action is equally incumbent in situations of financial mismanage-

---

practical in Christian fellowship more generally, strong bonds of friendship will have to be developed before problems arise.

20. Michael E. Phillips, "Creative Church Discipline," *Leadership* 7, no. 4 (1986): 46–50.

21. As described, e.g., in Karl F. Pansler, "Church Discipline and the Right of Privacy," in *Christian Ministries and the Law*, ed. H. Wayne House (Grand Rapids: Baker, 1992), 65–78.

22. See the helpful discussions by Jay A. Quine, "Court Involvement in Church Discipline," *BSac* 149 (1992): 60–73, 223–36; Laney, *Discipline*, 136–38; and Pansler, "Church Discipline."

23. For help for both offenders and victims, see Earl D. Wilson, *A Silence to be Broken* (Portland: Multnomah, 1986).

ment and fraud, flagrant heresy, repeated abusive and addictive behaviors, prolonged rebellion against authority, and a variety of other serious social sins. That Paul can lump all these together in his various "vice lists" should caution us against elevating sexual sin to a level of severity higher than these others, as we often do, or against overlooking the nonsexual sins listed as somehow more trivial.

That "greedy" makes it to the list in verse 11, separate from "swindlers" (contrast v. 10), provides an abrupt reminder of how far removed from biblical ideals our modern world often is. "Mammon" (money and all other material resources) remains the biggest competitor with God for human allegiance (cf. Matt. 6:19–34; Luke 16:1–13; 1 Tim. 6:3–10). What a perversion of God's priorities when wealthy Westerners spend exorbitant sums weekly to service personal and church debts, lavishing millions of dollars on buildings, utilities, food, and largely inward-looking ministries, while millions of people are dying of physical and spiritual malnutrition around the globe! This is not to say that every mortgage or church building program is sinful. But there are numerous creative alternatives that are both less costly and more responsible which should at least be considered much more than they are.[24] As Prior points out, "if we were to ask virtually any Third World Christian what is the most common and destructive sin in the Western church, the answer would invariably be 'covetousness'." Again, "from the perspective of Third World Christians the church in the West today is equally guilty, not just of moral laxity, but of smugness. There is a culpable blindness about the seriousness of certain sins, coupled with a perverse refusal to recognize the close link between this sinful compromise and ineffectiveness with the gospel."[25]

The idolatries of our age extend beyond materialism, however (vv. 10–11). New Age syncretism, wholesale alliance with secular models of business and management, aberrant church growth or counseling techniques, extreme forms of "power religion" (requiring miraculous signs and wonders), trusting in government to do what the church should be doing, and a host of other misplaced allegiances sap our congregations of genuine, Bible-based spiritual vitality.[26] As for "slanderers" (v. 11), Christian circles are rife with rebellion against authority, misrepresentation of opponents' views, and character assassination or defamation.

---

24. See Tom Sine, *Wild Hope* (Dallas: Word, 1991), 282–84, and throughout.

25. Prior, *1 Corinthians*, 80, 83.

26. For incisive surveys and only slightly overstated critiques of these idolatries, see Os Guinness and John Steel, *No God but God* (Chicago: Moody, 1992); and Michael Horton, ed., *Power Religion* (Chicago: Moody, 1992).

Paul's overall contrast between association with non-Christian sinners and nonassociation with unrepentant Christian sinners has been almost exactly inverted in massive segments of the contemporary church. We promote all kinds of separatism via Christian alternatives to secular institutions and activities. Thus we can comfortably spend most all of our lives in Christian schools, church meetings, Christian sporting leagues, church-based aerobics; in short, in fellowship groups for virtually any significant human activity, so that we need not interact in any intimate way at all with non-Christians![27] Indeed, most American adults who convert to Christianity are so overwhelmed with new acquaintances and activities that within a few years they know virtually no non-Christians well enough to engage in any meaningful kind of friendship evangelism.[28]

In sharp contrast stands Tony Campolo's more biblical vision of God's kingdom as a birthday-party for prostitutes thrown in an all-night diner at 3:00 A.M.[29] So too numerous inner-city ministries around our country and world are seeking to house the homeless, find jobs for the unemployed, offer affordable health care to the indigent, provide alternative recreation for kids in gang-ridden neighborhoods, all in the name of Jesus, with a view to bringing the light of the gospel to the most visibly sin-filled parts of our society. But of course the suburbs and rural areas contain their full range of problems as well, with equally needy and unsaved persons. No matter where we live then, Christian fellowship should be a periodic retreat from and revitalization of our regular involvement with the immoral and unbelieving in our world, and not vice versa. And those with the extra obstacle of working full time in Christian organizations must redouble their efforts at spending time away from work with non-Christian neighbors, volunteering in public schools and civic organizations, and the like.

Verses 12–13 also contrast sharply with the prevailing political agenda of the so-called religious right. We have tried, largely unsuccessfully, to Christianize society through antiabortion legislation, campaigning for prayer in the public schools, electing politicians who most closely match our evangelically correct political scorecards, often at the expense of devoting the bulk of our energies to modeling Christian ethics and countercultural lifestyles in our personal lives and in our local churches.

---

27. Cf. Prior, *1 Corinthians*, 83: There is a "desperate need for Christians to excise innumerable church meetings in order to free their diaries for proper meeting with unbelievers."

28. On which, see esp. Joseph C. Aldrich, *Life-Style Evangelism* (Portland: Multnomah, 1981).

29. Anthony Campolo, *The Kingdom of God Is a Party* (Dallas: Word, 1990), 3–9. There are conflicting reports as to whether this story which Campolo describes ever actually occurred; be that as it may, the vision remains on target.

Ephesians 3:4–11 reminds us of the enormous evangelistic potential of a Christian community that integrates people who have little or no human reason for getting together, much less getting along with each other, completely apart from any overt political or social activism. A holy congregation, which graciously cleans its own house to preserve its purity but which does not expect the same standards of obedience from the unregenerate, can profoundly impact an unholy world. To quote Prior once more, "The world is waiting to see such a church, a church which takes sin seriously, which enjoys forgiveness fully, which in its time of gathering together combines joyful celebration with an awesome sense of God's immediacy and authority." But "that will never happen if we refuse to come into costly, compassionate contact with men and women of the world."[30]

---

30. Prior, *1 Corinthians*, 79. The alternatives are frightening. One possible scenario is sketched in William Pannell, *The Coming Race Wars?* (Grand Rapids: Zondervan, 1993).

1 Corinthians 6:1-11

I F ANY OF YOU has a dispute with another, dare he take it before the ungodly for judgment instead of before the saints? ²Do you not know that the saints will judge the world? And if you are to judge the world, are you not competent to judge trivial cases? ³Do you not know that we will judge angels? How much more the things of this life! ⁴Therefore, if you have disputes about such matters, appoint as judges even men of little account in the church! ⁵I say this to shame you. Is it possible that there is nobody among you wise enough to judge a dispute between believers? ⁶But instead, one brother goes to law against another—and this in front of unbelievers!

⁷The very fact that you have lawsuits among you means you have been completely defeated already. Why not rather be wronged? Why not rather be cheated? ⁸Instead, you yourselves cheat and do wrong, and you do this to your brothers.

⁹Do you not know that the wicked will not inherit the kingdom of God? Do not be deceived: Neither the sexually immoral nor idolaters nor adulterers nor male prostitutes nor homosexual offenders ¹⁰nor thieves nor the greedy nor drunkards nor slanderers nor swindlers will inherit the kingdom of God. ¹¹And that is what some of you were. But you were washed, you were sanctified, you were justified in the name of the Lord Jesus Christ and by the Spirit of our God.

Original Meaning

PAUL TURNS TO a second example of how the judicial process should work *within* the church rather than outside it. The sin of the libertine group that he addresses here involves the practice of suing fellow Christians in secular courts. In short, he makes two main points: (1) if disputes require intervention, it should occur within the Christian community; and (2) it is even better to accept being wronged than to demand recompense in either a secular or a Christian context.

This section begins with Paul's disgust over what is going on. Verse 5 demonstrates that the "any of you" and "another" of verse 1 refer to fellow believers. "Dispute" is literally a "matter, practice, or thing," but in context obviously implies a legal complaint. Most common Hellenistic litigation involved property disputes. The verb "cheat" in verse 8 means to "defraud," so some sort of complaint concerning property or business dealings seems to have been the problem.[1] If this is what was going on at Corinth, then the disputants were among the minority of well-to-do believers in the congregation (and, again, possibly among its patrons), since the vast majority of people didn't own land or homes in those days.[2] "Saints" refers to Christians, not to particularly moral believers, so "the ungodly" must refer to non-Christians in general. Thus there is no particular criticism of corruption in the Roman courts implied here, common though such corruption was. Paul, in fact, probably recalled with thanks the fair treatment he had received from Gallio, the Roman proconsul, when he had been in Corinth (Acts 18:12-17).

Verses 2–3 present parallel examples of the logic of arguing "from the greater to the lesser." Drawing on Daniel 7:22, Paul reminds the Corinthians that they will help Jesus exercise judgment over the non-Christian world (both people and angels). Surely, therefore, they must be competent to handle earthly disputes in their own midst. "Trivial cases" (v. 2) does not mean that the Corinthian litigation did not involve serious offenses, merely that *all* human litigation is trivial when viewed in the light of Judgment Day.

The NIV translation of verse 4 is not nearly as likely as the alternative reading in the NIV footnote, "Do you appoint as judges men of little account in the church?" (cf. NASB, RSV, NEB). If the translation were correct, it would mean that even the least competent Christian is preferable to a non-Christian as judge between believers' disputes. But more probably Paul has constructed a parallel question to verse 2b, in which he formulates an "if . . . then" clause, culminating in a rhetorical question. The reading in the NIV footnote would refer to the non-Christian judges. "Of little account" is literally "despised" and would then refer to the Corinthians' normal attitude to the non-Christian judicial system, except, ironically, when they can get financial gain out of using it.[3]

Verse 5 contrasts with 4:14. Now Paul *is* prepared to shame the Corinthians. Their litigation incenses him even more than their factiousness, because

---

1. A less likely option is that the "dispute" of verse 1 refers back to the problem of chapter 5: the immorality there had occasioned the lawsuit here. For this suggestion, see Peter Richardson, "Judgment in Sexual Matters in 1 Corinthians 6:1–11," *NovT* 25 (1983): 37–58.

2. See esp. Alan C. Mitchell, "Rich and Poor in the Courts of Corinth: Litigiousness and Status in 1 Corinthians 6.1–11," *NTS* 39 (1993): 562–86.

3. Cf. the paraphrase by Reginald H. Fuller, "First Corinthians 6:1–11: An Exegetical Paper," *Ex Auditu* 2 (1986): 100: "Are you actually appointing to adjudicate your cases the very people whom as church people you otherwise hold in contempt?"

it so fundamentally compromises their witness before a watching world quick to ridicule and reject the church on such occasions. "Is it possible that there is nobody among you wise enough . . . ?" drips with irony, since the Corinthians had been claiming to be so wise (4:10). But Paul probably also believes quite seriously that among the godly (minority?) in the church, some bear the marks of true Christian wisdom (2:6) and perhaps also legal training, so that they might intervene constructively. "Believer" in verse 5 is literally "brother," as in verse 6.

Verses 7–8 proceed to the more radical of Paul's two points. "Have lawsuits" (v. 7) might better be rendered "get judgments" and is not limited to litigation in a secular context. Whether inside or outside the church, the attitude of demanding one's rights remains diametrically opposed to Christ's teaching (Matt. 5:39–42) and example (1 Peter 2:23). If two Christians cannot resolve their disagreements short of both secular litigation and Christian arbitration, something is fundamentally amiss. Better to suffer wrong—God will one day vindicate all injustices—than to alienate a fellow believer by requiring redress.

The fraud and injustice that trigger lawsuits, and which can even be exacerbated by them, lead Paul naturally to think about those who are "wicked" more generally (v. 9; from the same Greek root as "be wronged" and "do wrong" in vv. 7–8). So, as in 5:10–11, he warns against being sucked into the vortex of behavior that eventually calls into question one's very salvation.

Another vice list appears, uniquely tailored to the most common and offensive of Corinthian perversions. The same items that Paul mentions in chapter 5 reappear, along with four new ones. If they have anything in common, "it would seem to be that all represent some form of ruthless self-gratification, reckless of other people's rights."[4] "Thieves" cause no surprise in a list stimulated by the thought of lawsuits. "Adulterers" follow naturally after a reference to the "sexually immoral" in general. So too do "male prostitutes" and "homosexual offenders," though these two terms are better understood as referring to the more passive and more active partners, respectively, in any male homosexual act.[5] By using nouns that become labels for individuals only after persistent sin in particular areas, Paul makes plain that temporary lapses do not cause an individual to forfeit salvation. As Prior explains, "Paul is not talking about isolated acts of unrighteousness, but about a whole way of life pursued persistently by those who thus indicate that they would be aliens in the kingdom of truth and light"[6] (cf. 1 John 3:4–10).

---

4. Watson, *First Corinthians*, 56.

5. See, e.g., David E. Malick, "The Condemnation of Homosexuality in 1 Corinthians 6:9," *BSac* 150 (1993): 479–92.

6. Prior, *1 Corinthians*, 89.

Paul concludes on a more hopeful note (v. 11). Such behavior characterized the pre-Christian lives of many of the Corinthians, but they have now generally abandoned such practices. Therefore, they ought to be able to give up suing each other also! To stress the new holiness of character God has imputed to them, and in which they are progressively but fitfully growing, Paul ends this section with a reminder that they have been washed (inwardly, but possibly thinking of the external rite of baptism as well), made holy ("sanctified") and declared righteous ("justified"). The agency of Jesus and God's Spirit provides an important implicit Trinitarian reference to round out the paragraph.

AT THE OUTSET, it is crucial to observe both the contextual limitations and the lack of limitations that appear in this passage. On the one hand, nothing arises explicitly to solve questions about whether or not Christians may sue non-Christians or secular institutions such as corporations or the government. Verses 6–8, however, surely imply broader principles that may be brought to bear, particularly with respect to the potential discredit lawsuits may bring to Christianity in the eyes of unbelievers.

The key question to ask is whether or not the gospel is promoted by any contemplated litigation, as Paul's use and non-use of Roman courts throughout the book of Acts consistently demonstrates (see above, p. 101, n.24). There is also a key difference between seeking justice for others who have been disenfranchised and trying to avenge wrongs done against ourselves.[7] On the other hand, there is no restriction on Paul's prohibition within *Christian* circles. In other words, it would be invalid to say that, because my complaint is not property-related, then Paul's principles do not apply to my case. The disgrace described in verses 6–7 would still remain.

The criteria employed in determining whether or not to sue a non-Christian suggest parallel criteria for deciding whether or not to seek redress within the Christian community for an offense caused by a fellow believer. At times, such grievances prove legitimate and solutions must be sought— but within the church. Paul's Jewish heritage provided him with ready-made models of such conciliation, from Moses appointing judges during the wilderness wanderings to recent rabbinic use of the synagogue and its elders to function as a courtroom. The Greco-Roman world was rife with litigation, but Jews were forbidden to use heathen courts.

---

7. Fee, *First Corinthians*, 238, helpfully observes that litigation should hopefully be the last resort even with non-Christians. Only "if it is out of concern for the one defrauded and for all others who might be so taken in" is it fully justified.

Historically, among Christians, medieval Catholicism implemented parallel models with greatest frequency, creating a labyrinth of ecclesiastical courts and tribunals. But since the Reformation, Protestants, and increasingly Roman Catholics too, have used the church just to solve overtly religious squabbles and have allowed their members to use the state for everything else. The Alternative Dispute Resolution movement in both secular and Christian communities has only recently begun to turn this trend slightly around. Here is one place, however (contrast our comments on 5:9–13), where Christian alternatives are not only desirable but mandatory.

Paul's points in verses 2a and 3 (on believers judging both the world and angels) are subordinate to his contrasting questions in verses 2b and 4 (on being competent to provide judges for the church). But they do remind us that Matthew 19:28, with its reference to the twelve disciples judging the twelve tribes of Israel, offers no special privilege to the apostles. All believers will be involved in judging all of unredeemed humanity.

Verses 1–6 in general offer an important illustration of 5:12b (a Christian must judge insiders not outsiders) and again remind us that 2:15 and 4:3 cannot be taken as absolute prohibitions against all forms of judging (see above, pp. 68, 93–94). The alleged contradiction between 6:2 (the saints will judge the world) and 5:12a (Christians should not judge those outside the church) disappears once it is seen that the former verse refers to what believers will do at Christ's return; the latter, to what they are not to do prior to his return. Motivation by guilt (v. 5) is tricky to apply in cultures not as dominated by shame as the ancient Mediterranean world. Christian self-esteem is important, and false guilt can be destructive. But when a person is indeed objectively guilty, limited amounts of shame—helping the person recognize that a sin has been committed—should and can lead that person to appropriate repentance.[8]

Verses 7–8 stress a cardinal component of Christian living more generally—the voluntary relinquishing of one's rights to serve others (cf. Phil. 2:1–11). Chapters 8–10 will develop this theme in great detail. Verse 8 reminds us that the plaintiffs even in seemingly legitimate litigation often wind up demanding more than adequate compensation. Secular legal theory too has at times recognized that the very process of bringing suit almost inevitably dehumanizes all the parties involved.[9]

---

8. Cf. S. Bruce Narramore, *No Condemnation* (Grand Rapids: Zondervan, 1984), 26–34; Paul Tournier, *Guilt and Grace* (New York: Harper and Row, 1962), 63–71.

9. Robert D. Taylor, "Toward a Biblical Theology of Litigation: A Law Professor Looks at 1 Cor. 6:1–11," *Ex Auditu* 2 (1986): 105–16, esp. 110–13.

Like 3:16–17, verses 9–11 must be seen as a real and not merely hypothetical warning. Verse 11 suggests that Paul does think a majority of the Corinthian church is really saved, but there would be no point in his twofold affirmation that the wicked will not inherit the kingdom (vv. 9–10) if he did not fear that at least a few in his congregation might be masquerading as believers. Of course the Calvinist-Arminian controversy over "eternal security" cannot be solved by either of these passages, and interpretations consistent with both of those traditions can fit equally well here.

By far the biggest controversy surrounding the vice list of verses 9–10 has to do with the two words for homosexual offenders. As in Romans 1:24–27, homo- and heterosexual sins are paired in a way that suggests that neither is any better or any worse than the other. One can scarcely use these verses to claim that no one can simultaneously be a Christian and engage in homosexual actions unless one is prepared to say the same thing of one who commits adultery or exhibits greed! But in each of these instances true Christians should acknowledge their behavior as sinful and try to change it. *Persistent* rebellion increasingly calls into question any prior profession of faith. The Romans 1 passage also makes plain that Paul treats male and female homosexual offenders alike, even if only men are mentioned here.

What is more, it is important to stress that actions rather than orientations predominate throughout this list. While it is false to claim that the ancient world knew nothing of apparent homosexual *orientation* but only actions,[10] it is true that one's predisposition need not lead to actual sin. Celibacy remains the biblically mandated alternative to heterosexual marriage for people of any orientation unable to find a permanent partner of the opposite sex. It is also linguistically invalid to limit the type of homosexual behavior Paul describes either to pederasty (adult men with underage boys) or to homosexual prostitution (casual sex for profit between individuals not committed to a lasting relationship with each other).[11]

All the sins enumerated in verses 9–10 share the common traits of being self-indulgent and self-serving. From a spiritual perspective, they also become self-destructive. Hence, Christians should make sure they remain part of one's distant past (v. 11). Paul knows, of course, that they do not always do so, but he appeals again to his favorite, "Become what you really are" logic.

---

10. As demonstrated by James B. De Young, "The Source and New Testament Meaning of ΑΡΣΕΝΟΚΟΙΤΑΙ, with Implications for Christian Ethics and Ministry," *Master's Seminary Journal* 3 (1992): 191–215.

11. See esp. David F. Wright, "Homosexuals or Prostitutes? The Meaning of Arsenokoitai (1 Cor. 6:9, 1 Tim. 1:10)," *VC* 38 (1984): 125–53; cf. Talbert, *Corinthians*, 23–25.

AS WITH CHAPTER 5, 1 Corinthians 6 includes teaching that is not as well-known or obeyed in Christian circles as it should be. Our society rivals and possibly even surpasses ancient Corinth in its passion for suing people. Christians greedily join in the fray, taking fellow believers to court, and even more commonly suing churches and parachurch organizations whose insurance companies have "deeper pockets." Juries almost invariably award plaintiffs against such organizations substantial sums, at times leaving the defeated parties in dire financial straits.

On a broader level, the whole concept of relinquishing one's rights seems anathema to a culture immersed in asserting them. Women's rights, civil rights, gay rights, liberation theology, even the so-called "inalienable rights" of the American constitution, all contain important Christian components but also owe their existence to significant secular and even anti-Christian influences.[12]

Nevertheless, there are promising signs with the Alternative Dispute Resolution movement, a growing campaign in the secular arena to settle litigation out of court and to use innovative legal methods for avoiding formal lawsuits altogether. In Christian circles numerous conciliation services and societies have sprung up, some on a national level, and others as local ministries.[13]

Churches must go further:

> The faith community not only trains its members in the art of reconciliation, but it makes available the process of reconciliation to the world at large. Such projects as conflict management seminars, victim-offender reconciliation programs, and college and university peace departments witness to the life of the new age as well as offer a new way for those caught in the old.[14]

And there remain many unheralded Christian individuals who continue to obey Paul's words by not filing suit even when they have legitimate complaints and are encouraged by fellow Christians to get even. Certainly the

---

12. Cf. Mark A. Noll, *One Nation Under God?* (San Francisco: Harper and Row, 1988); with Richard A. Fowler and H. Wayne House, *Civilization in Crisis* (Grand Rapids: Baker, 1988).

13. See esp. H. Wayne House, "Reconciling Disputes Among Christians," in *Christian Ministries and the Law*, ed. H. Wayne House (Grand Rapids: Baker, 1992), 79–88, for a description of the Christian conciliation process, and "Appendix D," 219–20, for a sampling of some of the Christian conciliation ministries of North America.

14. Snyder, *First Corinthians*, 77.

media today love to pounce on every racy story of Christians fighting, while they simultaneously fail to cover numerous events and ministries that would portray believers in a more positive light.[15] The concern not to wash our dirty linen in public certainly remains valid.

Verses 9–11 raise afresh all the questions of right and wrong definitions of carnality discussed under 3:1–4. Deserving special comment again is the issue of homosexuality. Under no conceivable circumstances can the Bible be made to defend the often-heard allegation that God created homosexuals that way. What genetic component may contribute to homosexual predispositions remains to be determined but, like inherent predispositions to alcoholism, violence, or various diseases, such a component, if demonstrated, would be an offshoot of the Fall, not of creation.[16] Equally crucially, genetic predispositions never exempt humans from biblical standards and accountability before God for moral or immoral behavior. Those predisposed to alcoholism may have to impose more severe restrictions on themselves, such as teetotaling, than others might. But that does not mean that drunkenness for them becomes morally acceptable. Those predisposed to homosexual practices may have to monitor themselves more carefully too, but that scarcely turns sin into a divinely ordained lifestyle.

The strikingly consistent social factors that spawn "coming out of the closet" suggest, moreover, that the "nurture" component in the nature-nurture controversy has probably too often been underestimated.[17] After all, since the vast majority of homosexuals do not procreate, the simple laws of mathematics lead to the inexorable conclusion that homosexuality would have substantially died out over the centuries if there was a purely or even predominantly genetic component.

None of this is to deny that conservative Christians have often treated homosexuals far more abusively than they have other sinners. There is real discrimination against the gay community that must be fought—for example, restricted employment opportunities for jobs in which sexual behavior is irrelevant. There is genuine homophobia (fear of association with homosexuals, not merely opinions about their moral condition), especially in our churches. But the "politically correct" movement has often grossly exagger-

---

15. This is part of the broader polarization of public discourse ably documented in James D. Hunter, *Culture Wars* (New York: Basic Books, 1991).

16. For a balanced treatment of the theology of homosexuality more generally, see Richard F. Lovelace, *Homosexuality and the Church* (Old Tappan, N.J.: Fleming Revell, 1978).

17. For male homosexuals, absence of a positive adult male role model is particularly common. See esp. Elizabeth Moberley, *Psychogenesis: The Early Development of Gender-Identity* (London: Routledge, Kegan, and Paul, 1983); idem, *Homosexuality: A New Christian Ethic* (Greenwood, S.C.: Attic Press, 1983).

ated the extent of that homophobia and incorrectly applied that label to believers who are lovingly and compassionately trying to uphold biblical standards.

Verse 11 recalls another crucial point in this discussion: homosexuality can be abandoned with God's help. Both the Corinthians' and contemporary experiences demonstrate that gays can become "straight" and have loving, fulfilling heterosexual marriages, even though it is often a long process and difficult struggle.[18] As with conciliation services, there are a growing number of national and local ministries that facilitate these conversions.[19] These ministries should be greatly welcomed and enthusiastically supported by all Christians.

The same principles often apply to individuals and organizations working with AIDS victims. Here too Christians have tended to polarize along one of two unbiblical extremes. Some attribute the epidemic to God's direct judgment against sin and therefore find little reason to intervene with love or medical research. But this unfairly condemns innocent hemophiliacs and others infected with the disease through no sin of their own. It also assumes a more direct correlation between disease and God's agency than is usually present in Scripture. God generally saves his retribution for Judgment Day.

On the other hand, here is one plague that could be almost entirely wiped off the face of the earth if biblical sexual ethics were widely followed and appropriate testing for the virus practiced prior to marriage. How tragic, in a culture highly committed to sex education and bodily health, that promoting sexual abstinence outside of heterosexual marriage continues to be scorned and rejected! Totally apart from its religious underpinnings, it would bring the desired results our secular society craves, but of course at the "impossible" cost of restricting human freedom to indulge oneself.

---

18. Cf., e.g., William Consiglio, *Homosexual No More* (Wheaton: Victor, 1991); Darlene Bogle, *Strangers in a Christian Land* (Old Tappan, N.J.: Fleming Revell, 1990); and Gerard van der Aardweg, *Homosexuality and Hope* (Ann Arbor, Mich.: Servant, 1985).

19. One thinks especially of the nationwide network of organizations under the umbrella of Exodus International. For a good anthology of approaches to helping the church "promote hope and healing for gays and lesbians," see J. Isamu Yamamoto, *The Crisis of Homosexuality* (Wheaton: Victor, 1990).

1 Corinthians 6:12–20

"EVERYTHING IS PERMISSIBLE for me"—but not everything is beneficial. "Everything is permissible for me"—but I will not be mastered by anything. ¹³"Food for the stomach and the stomach for food"—but God will destroy them both. The body is not meant for sexual immorality, but for the Lord, and the Lord for the body. ¹⁴By his power God raised the Lord from the dead, and he will raise us also. ¹⁵Do you not know that your bodies are members of Christ himself? Shall I then take the members of Christ and unite them with a prostitute? Never! ¹⁶Do you not know that he who unites himself with a prostitute is one with her in body? For it is said, "The two will become one flesh." ¹⁷But he who unites himself with the Lord is one with him in spirit.

¹⁸Flee from sexual immorality. All other sins a man commits are outside his body, but he who sins sexually sins against his own body. ¹⁹Do you not know that your body is a temple of the Holy Spirit, who is in you, whom you have received from God? You are not your own; ²⁰you were bought at a price. Therefore honor God with your body.

Original Meaning

VERSES 9–11 HAVE provided a natural transition back into the broad area of sexual ethics, the theme that verses 12–20 now take up. Here appears the third error of the libertines in chapters 5–6. After the problems of the incestuous man (5:1–13) and of lawsuits against believers (6:1–11), Paul now turns to treat sexual immorality in general, but particularly manifested in prostitution, for which Corinth was infamous.

With verse 12 Paul begins a pattern that will frequently recur throughout the rest of the letter—quoting a Corinthian slogan, and thereby giving it a limited endorsement, but then at once substantially qualifying it. These Corinthian slogans (here the three sayings of verses 12–13 which the NIV encloses with quotation marks) all share four characteristics: (a) they are short, pithy, and proverbial; (b) they reflect the libertine wing of the church; (c) Paul himself could have conceivably uttered them in some specific context; and (d) apart from that context they were so misleading that abuse was almost inevitable.

Verse 12 quotes the first slogan twice (cf. also 10:23): "Everything is permissible for me." Paul might have spoken this in the context of Christian freedom from the law. The slogan of verse 13 ("Food for the stomach and the stomach for food") could reflect his more specific reference to freedom from the Jewish dietary laws. But apart from these contexts the slogans virtually invite people to sin, as the Corinthians apparently were doing. Hence Paul explains that Christians still must submit to moral principles—not because they obey all 613 commandments of the Mosaic Law but because many things simply are not beneficial and not truly liberating. Verse 12b reflects a Greek word play that could be approximated in English by translating, "All things are in my power, but I shall not be overpowered by anything."[1]

It is not clear if the next Corinthian slogan (v. 13) read as the NIV prints it or included in addition, "but God will destroy them both." The NIV omits another "but" with which the next sentence begins—"But the body"—which could be Paul's response to a longer slogan. Either way, the Corinthians were apparently inferring from the relatively accurate observation that food and stomach were made for each other that the body and sexual release were identically related. After all, both eating and having sex seem to be limited to this life. Not so, declares Paul! There may be no need for stomachs in resurrection bodies that do not need to eat, but there most certainly will be resurrection bodies! And sexual immorality affects one's entire body in a way that overeating cannot, as verse 18 will explain. Hence, that body is to be dedicated to the Lord in holiness and not to sexual impurity (vv. 13b–14).

Verses 15–17 form a syllogism (a three-part argument with two premises and a conclusion that necessarily follows): (1) The bodies of Christians are members of Christ himself. (2) Sexual intercourse unites two human beings (as taught already in Gen. 2:24). (3) Sexual intercourse with a prostitute, therefore, unites the members of Christ with that prostitute.

Clearly this does not mean that such a person becomes saved. Rather Paul expresses his utter repugnance to associating something as impure as prostitution with Christ's perfect holiness. Prostitution also creates the grotesque connection of the One who represents ultimate commitment with the act that represents the most casual of sexual relationships. Worse still, this sex is for hire, epitomizing the abuse of human beings by those with absolutely no commitment to their greater good.

Paul understandably reacts to this monstrous mismatch with a strong present tense command (suggesting ongoing action) to "flee" *porneia*. This is the broadest term for sexual sin in the Greek language, embracing any form of intercourse between two individuals who are not united in heterosexual

---

1. Morris, *First Corinthians*, 96.

marriage (v. 18a). At first glance, however, his next reason for this command seems patently false (v. 18b). Surely gluttony and drunkenness, self-mutilation, and suicide also sin against one's own body. The solution to this problem lies with the term "body" (*soma*), which can often carry the connotation of an individual in bodily, interpersonal communion. As Brendan Byrne explains:

> The immoral person perverts precisely that faculty within himself that is meant to be the instrument of the most intimate bodily communication between persons. He sins against his unique power of bodily communication and in this sense sins in a particular way 'against his own body.' All other sins are in this respect by comparison 'outside' the body—with 'body' having in this verse the strong sexual overtones that appear to cling to it throughout the passage as a whole. No other sin engages one's power of bodily personal communication in precisely so intimate a way.[2]

Verses 19–20 reapply the temple imagery, with its connotations of holiness, to the bodies of individual believers. As in 3:16–17, Paul writes literally "your [pl.] body [sg.]." But given the context of verses 12–17 it is more likely that he is still talking about individual bodies here, using what grammarians call a "distributive singular" construction. Verse 20 alludes to Jesus' costly atonement, which should cause believers to want to glorify God out of gratitude for the salvation he has purchased for them.

Bridging Contexts

PAUL CERTAINLY BELIEVES that moral absolutes remain in the Christian era (cf. Gal. 5:19–23). But the fundamental contrast between the age of the Law and the age of the Spirit has to do with living by long lists of external standards versus loving from internal attitudes birthed by a correct relationship to God in Christ. The sense in which the Corinthian slogans remain valid is later captured by St. Augustine in his famous proverb, "Love God and do as you please." But that proverb can equally easily be abused! Christians who operate out of heartfelt concern for their own and others' well-being will recognize many things as inherently harmful or even addictive. "The great fact of the Christian faith is, not that it makes a man free to sin, but that it makes a man free *not* to sin."[3] Further-

---

2. Brendan Byrne, "Sinning Against One's Own Body: Paul's Understanding of the Sexual Relationship in 1 Corinthians 6:18," *CBQ* 45 (1983): 613.

3. Barclay, *Corinthians*, 56–57.

more, "the man who has to express his freedom is actually in bondage to the need to show he is a free man. The genuinely free man has nothing to prove."[4]

Paul's affirmation of the body counteracts those forms of dualism which allege that the material world, including human bodies, is irredeemable. Here Paul counters the hedonistic outgrowth of such philosophy; in chapter 7 he will combat its ascetic counterpart. Christians must always guard against a truncated gospel that seeks to save souls but not bodies or that is unconcerned for the stewardship of the earth. To the extent that the kingdom is inaugurated, we must begin to model even in this life the priorities of care for our bodies and our planet that we will be able to perfect in the life to come.

Sexual immorality, and prostitution in particular, certainly have remained problems in almost every time and culture. But verse 20 closes Paul's discussion with a generalization that suggests other applications. Any kind of bodily abuse dishonors God. On the other hand, we dare not lose sight of the unique seriousness of sexual sin that verse 18 upholds. The effects of gluttony are usually reversible by an increase in sweat and a decrease in calories. Some effects of illicit sex can never be undone (though of course they can be forgiven). Memories, emotions, and attachments stay with us for life, although excessive promiscuity can eventually dull or numb our senses in certain ways.

Paul's theology of sexuality is profoundly humanizing, in that it treats people with the care and dignity that creatures made in God's image deserve. Paul understands that sex has unique effects on a person's psyche. Because sex reflects the most intimate of interpersonal relations among humans, it should be reserved for the most permanent of interpersonal commitments.[5] God established the principle of lifelong monogamy as a creation ordinance, transcending all cultures and periods of human history (v. 16). The quotation from Genesis must be read in context as affirming the intimacy and commitment that sexual intercourse should imply. It does not offer any justification for claiming that sex by itself constitutes a marriage. That requires the first half of Genesis 2:24 as well: "A man will leave his father and mother and be united to his wife"—the transference of ultimate human allegiance from parents to spouse.

---

4. Prior, *1 Corinthians*, 96.

5. Bruce, *1 and 2 Corinthians*, 64, quotes D. S. Bailey: Verse 16 "displays a psychological insight into human sexuality which is altogether exceptional by first-century standards . . . he insists that it is an act which, by reason of its very nature, engages and expresses the whole personality in such a way as to constitute an unique mode of self-disclosure and self-commitment."

The strong command to keep on fleeing *porneia* (v. 18) may need to be reenacted literally, as with Joseph fleeing from Potiphar's wife (Gen. 39:12). But it may also require refusing intimate friendships with people to whom one is improperly attracted, refraining in dating relationships from bodily contact that prematurely arouses too strong a sexual desire, or avoiding places that make pornography available in print or on television and film. It applies also at the mental level, whenever we dwell on that which is not true, noble, right, pure, lovely, admirable, excellent or praiseworthy (Phil. 4:8).

MUCH OF WHAT was said in applying 5:1–13 fits here too. Drastically countercultural themes persist in these verses. Ever since the sexual revolution of the 1960s, large segments of our modern world have subscribed to the "if it feels good do it" mentality. Yet when people adopt this ethic, families are destroyed and sexual addictions overwhelm many. We also overeat, particularly in the West, while our brothers and sisters around the globe starve. Other prevalent abuse of our bodies includes drunkenness, chain smoking, drug abuse, lack of proper exercise or diet, and workaholism.

The Christian view of sex—abstinence except in heterosexual marriage—makes good sense in our world, completely apart from Paul's primary rationale. The AIDS epidemic has now infected the subculture of the heterosexually promiscuous, particularly prostitutes and their companions. Other sexually transmitted diseases remain widespread. The dangers of unwanted pregnancies and potential abortions only compound the problem. But the most central Christian reason for limiting sex to husbands and wives deals with the permanent commitment that should be implied by interpersonal relations this intimate. In countless ways, women and men defy God and confidently proclaim that they can have sex without that commitment and without any destructive side-effects. Time and time again, they regret those choices. But this is not a sin we can test and then back off from; we must trust that God knows best. Once a person yields to temptation, in little or big ways, there are mental and emotional scars that may never entirely disappear, even though God's grace can bring substantial healing.[6]

---

6. Two excellent treatments of a Christian theology of sexuality are Tim Stafford, *The Sexual Christian* (Wheaton: Victor, 1989); and Randy C. Alcorn, *Christians in the Wake of the Sexual Revolution: Recovering Our Sexual Sanity* (Portland: Multnomah, 1985). On pp. 163–72, Alcorn discusses the backlash against the permissiveness of the sixties in certain more recent secular circles. For help in "healing and preventing affairs in Christian marriages," see esp. Henry A. Virkler, *Broken Promises* (Dallas: Word, 1992).

But what of people who, for whatever reasons, never have the opportunity to marry? How can they find appropriate sexual release for one of the body's strongest drives? Though still controversial and seldom talked about in public Christian discourse, a limited use of masturbation would appear to be the most appropriate answer. No biblical text directly addresses this practice, but if the one thing sexual sins have in common is the misuse of another human being to whom a person is not fully committed, then self-stimulation would seem to be exempt from this abuse. To be sure, it too can become addictive or lustful, but it need not, and it may in fact prevent improper interpersonal sexuality by periodically calming intense urges.[7]

---

7. A significant number of contemporary Christian writers concur. See, e.g., Jack O. Balswick and Judith K. Balswick, *The Family: A Christian Perspective on the Contemporary Home* (Grand Rapids: Baker, 1989), 184–87; Clifford and Joyce Penner, *The Gift of Sex* (Waco: Word, 1981), 230–36; Lewis B. Smedes, *Sex for Christians* (Grand Rapids: Eerdmans, 1976), 160–64, 243–46.

1 Corinthians 7:1–16

NOW FOR THE MATTERS you wrote about: It is good for a man not to marry. ²But since there is so much immorality, each man should have his own wife, and each woman her own husband. ³The husband should fulfill his marital duty to his wife, and likewise the wife to her husband. ⁴The wife's body does not belong to her alone but also to her husband. In the same way, the husband's body does not belong to him alone but also to his wife. ⁵Do not deprive each other except by mutual consent and for a time, so that you may devote yourselves to prayer. Then come together again so that Satan will not tempt you because of your lack of self-control. ⁶I say this as a concession, not as a command. ⁷I wish that all men were as I am. But each man has his own gift from God; one has this gift, another has that.

⁸Now to the unmarried and the widows I say: It is good for them to stay unmarried, as I am. ⁹But if they cannot control themselves, they should marry, for it is better to marry than to burn with passion.

¹⁰To the married I give this command (not I, but the Lord): A wife must not separate from her husband. ¹¹But if she does, she must remain unmarried or else be reconciled to her husband. And a husband must not divorce his wife.

¹²To the rest I say this (I, not the Lord): If any brother has a wife who is not a believer and she is willing to live with him, he must not divorce her. ¹³And if a woman has a husband who is not a believer and he is willing to live with her, she must not divorce him. ¹⁴For the unbelieving husband has been sanctified through his wife, and the unbelieving wife has been sanctified through her believing husband. Otherwise your children would be unclean, but as it is, they are holy.

¹⁵But if the unbeliever leaves, let him do so. A believing man or woman is not bound in such circumstances; God has called us to live in peace. ¹⁶How do you know, wife, whether you will save your husband? Or, how do you know, husband, whether you will save your wife?

HERE BEGINS THE second half of the body of this letter, as Paul turns to take up the issues about which the Corinthians had written to him. These include marriage (chap. 7), food sacrificed to idols (8:1–11:1), problems in public worship (11:2–14:40), the resurrection (chap. 15), and the collection for the Judean Christians (16:1–4). The Corinthians' concerns may have been phrased as questions or as challenges, but either way Paul recognizes substantial problems that need correcting.

The apostle may simply be responding to the Corinthian issues in the order in which they raised them. But he may also be deliberately placing the concerns about marriage immediately after the sexual topics addressed in chapters 5–6. Either way, he must now address the opposite error from the problem of promiscuity discussed there. Here the ascetic wing of the church (see p. 25) is advocating the virtue of celibacy.[1]

The key to a correct understanding of this chapter is the recognition that 7:1 is Paul's reluctant and qualified endorsement of a Corinthian slogan or position, just as he did in 6:12 and 13, a point recognized already by Origen around A.D. 200.[2] Verses 1–16, 17–24, and 25–40 seem to form an ABA structure, with two sections of explicit response to the proponents of celibacy sandwiched around a discussion of analogous situations in life in which it is good for Christians to "remain as they are." Applied to the issues of singleness and marriage, Paul's central point stresses that believers should not be in a hurry to change their marital status. More specifically, in every walk of life there is a place for asceticism, though at times it is often limited. In marriage, regular sexual relations should prevail. Paul's balance between extremes of indulging in and refraining from sex produces a sensitive, mediating position between the tendency in Jewish circles to overemphasize marriage and the Greek (and especially Gnostic) trend to idealize asceticism.

---

1. Some writers have thought they could discern reasons for associating this pro-celibacy movement more with one particular gender. Margaret Y. MacDonald, "Women Holy in Body and Spirit: The Social Setting of 1 Corinthians 7," *NTS* 36 (1990): 161–81, finds in these words of verse 34, as with later Greco-Roman Christian asceticism, evidence for women being the ones most inclined to refrain from sex. Jerome Murphy-O'Connor, "The Divorced Woman in 1 Cor. 7:10–11," *JBL* 100 (1981): 601–6, on the other hand, believes ascetic husbands to be a key problem, at least behind verses 10–11 on divorce.

2. See esp. Fee, *First Corinthians*, 266–357. Cf. more briefly, W. E. Phipps, "Is Paul's Attitude Toward Sexual Relations Contained in 1 Cor. 7.1?" *NTS* 28 (1982): 125–31. For a good, brief exposition of the whole chapter along the lines advocated here, see David E. Garland, "The Christian's Posture Toward Marriage and Celibacy: 1 Corinthians 7," *RevExp* 80 (1983): 351–62.

Paul uses a "Yes, but" logic as his thesis for the entire chapter. The NIV footnote ("It is good for a man not to have sexual relations with a woman") gives the most likely meaning of verse 1b on two grounds. First, it recognizes verse 1 as a Corinthian saying. Second, it better renders the Greek euphemism, "touch," as referring to sexual intercourse, not to marriage. Verse 2 offers Paul's qualification: sexual abstinence is, for the most part, inappropriate for wedded couples. To "have" a spouse probably does not mean to "acquire" one but to "engage in sexual relations." "Each man" and "each woman" must then refer to "each married person." With prostitutes and mistresses abundantly available (recall 6:12–20), Corinthian men unable to have sex with their wives would often look elsewhere.

Verses 3–7 unpack this first application of Paul's response to the pro-celibacy faction in Corinth. They advocated completely refraining from sex within marriage, but Paul can imagine only a very limited role for such abstinence. A husband and wife should have sex often enough so that neither is frustrated or tempted to cheat on the other.

"Fulfill his marital duty" (v. 3) reads literally "give back that which is owed." One's "body" (v. 4) probably carries the broader sense of an instrument of interpersonal communication, as in 6:18. "Does not belong to" should be rendered "does not have authority over." Married persons no longer control their own bodies but must surrender authority over them to their spouses. "Do not deprive" (v. 5) should probably read "Stop defrauding" (cf. KJV)—that is, cheating someone else out of what is properly his or hers. The only exception Paul will tolerate is if both partners agree that for a very limited time they will abstain from sex for the sake of some unusually concentrated period of communion with the Lord. But even this Paul says only by way of concession (v. 6); he never *insists* that married people abstain at all from sex with each other.[3]

Verse 7 offers the first hint of what verse 8 will make explicit: Paul is currently single, and he likes it that way. He wishes all could share his enjoyment of singleness but realizes that only some have that gift, while others are gifted for marriage.

In verses 8–9 Paul turns from the currently married to the previously married. "Unmarried" is a masculine plural, just as "widows" is a feminine plural (v. 8). Given that verses 25–38 will address those who have never married,

---

3. Some take verse 6 as referring back to verse 2 or to all of verses 2–5, in which case marriage becomes the concession to Paul's preference for singleness. But on our interpretation of verse 2 this is impossible, and even on more traditional understandings of verse 2 it is still less likely, inasmuch as verse 5 forms the nearest antecedent for verse 6 and contains within it an explicit concession.

and given that the more explicit Greek word for "widower" was falling into disuse in the first century, we should probably understand the unmarried here to refer to men whose wives had died.

The ascetics would of course be telling widowers and widows never to re-marry. Paul again affirms that this may be a good course of action but not if it leads to sexual immorality. "Cannot" (v. 9a) is absent from the Greek and somewhat misleading. The text actually reads, "If they *are* not controlling themselves, they should marry." "With passion" (v. 9b) is the NIV's attempt to interpret the Greek verb *puroomai* ("burn") and is probably correct (cf. Paul's burning with indignation in 2 Cor. 11:29). But it could just possibly mean "burn in hell" and be parallel to 1 Corinthians 6:9–10.

Verses 8–9 also make it clear that Paul is single. If his words here are lim-ited to widows and widowers, then perhaps his wife has also died. Rabbis were almost always married, and members of the Sanhedrin had to be. Acts 22:3 refers to Paul's rabbinic training under Gamaliel, but we do not know if he ever completed it. In Acts 26:10, Paul speaks of "casting my vote" with the Sanhedrin, but the language could be idiomatic for being in agreement with them. It is therefore perhaps likely that Paul was once married, but we sim-ply cannot be sure.

In verses 10–16 Paul returns to address those who are married, but this time in light of a different proposal by the ascetics. The pro-celibacy faction encouraged people to get divorced if they could not live with a spouse with-out engaging in sex. At this point Paul's ability to side with this faction is dras-tically curtailed. Only when an unbelieving partner walks out on a Christian spouse can Paul permit such a rupture (vv. 15–16). Verses 10–11, therefore, seem to be directed to marriages in which both partners are believers.

Paul's parenthesis, "not I, but the Lord" (v. 10), alludes to words of the earthly Jesus widely known in early Christian tradition (cf. Mark 10:11–12). Those already divorced must not remarry, in order to leave the door open for possible reconciliation with their estranged partners. The words translated "separate," "divorce," and "leave" throughout verses 10–16 are used inter-changeably. This is demonstrated by the close synonymous parallelism be-tween verses 10a ("A wife must not separate from her husband") and 11b ("A husband must not divorce his wife") and the antithetical parallelism between verses 12–13 (unbelievers willing to stay must not be divorced) and 15 (un-believers wishing to leave may do so). Many spouses in antiquity left marriage without legal divorce proceedings, but the end result was the same. If there is any difference between the wife "separating" in verse 10 and the husband "divorcing" in verse 11, it may be that the man was legally entitled to divorce his wife, whereas the woman often had no recourse but to move out.

In verses 12–16, however, Paul addresses the members of mixed marriages. With all the new converts in Corinth, there were no doubt many couples in which only one of the two had become a Christian. Some believers seem to have feared that sexual relations with an unbeliever would defile them. Paul disagrees and insists that if the unbelieving partner is content to stay, the believer must not initiate divorce (vv. 12–13). Here he can cite no word of the earthly Jesus but relies directly on his own sense of how God is guiding or inspiring him (cf. vv. 25, 40).[4] Verse 14 supplies the rationale for Paul's insistence on preserving the marriage: there are spin-off blessings for the non-Christian spouse and children that come from having even one member of the family follow the Lord. "Sanctified" and "holy" cannot here mean "saved," as verse 16 proves. Rather they refer to "the moral and spiritual impact of the life of the believer" on the rest of the family, making those other family members "set apart in a very special place . . . as God's object of devotion."[5]

But the tension introduced by one partner in a marriage suddenly having a new allegiance to Christ at times proved intolerable to the non-Christian partner. If such a person chose to divorce (or simply leave) his or her spouse, the Christian partner was not compelled to try to prevent the separation (v. 15a).[6] Often there would be nothing he or she could do anyway. "God has called us to live in peace" (v. 15b) offers another reason for Paul's permission to let the unbeliever depart. There is no guarantee that the non-Christian partner will ever be saved by staying, and the constant tension introduced by divergent loyalties may even exacerbate the unbeliever's alienation from both spouse and God (v. 16).[7]

---

4. So most commentators. For Peter Richardson, "'I Say, Not the Lord': Personal Opinion, Apostolic Authority, and the Development of Early Christian Halakah," *TynB* 31 (1980): 65–86, the distinction is between previous oral tradition (of Jesus' teaching) and Christian "halakah" (quasi-legal decisions required by new circumstances). But either way, attempts to distinguish levels of the authority of the two kinds of statements fail.

5. Patterson, *Troubled, Triumphant Church*, 118, 119–20.

6. See esp. R. L. Roberts, "The Meaning of *Chorizo* and *Douloo* in 1 Corinthians 7:10–17," *RestQ* 8 (1965): 179–84.

7. It is also possible to take verse 15b as supplying further rationale for verses 12–14, with verse 15a as parenthetical. Then God would be calling people to the peace of preserving marriages. Verse 16 can then be translated more hopefully than in the NIV, as, e.g., in the NRSV: "Wife, for all you know you might save your husband. Husband, for all you know, you might save your wife." But this makes the "nevertheless" in verse 17 almost unintelligible. One has to take it as contrasting not with the immediately preceding verse 16 but with verse 15a. Far more straightforward and plausible is the rendering we have given. The *de* with which verse 15b begins (not reflected in the NIV) need not be translated as "but," but as a looser connective: "and," "now," or "indeed." For help on all these issues, see esp. Sakae Kubo, "1 Corinthians VII.16: Optimistic or Pessimistic?" *NTS* 24 (1978): 539–44.

Bridging
Contexts

FEW PASSAGES OF Scripture have been more abused and ripped from their historical moorings than 1 Corinthians 7. Without understanding the context of the ascetic wing of the Corinthian church, one easily attributes to Paul an overly negative view of marriage and sexual intercourse. We must never lose sight of the fact that Ephesians 5:21–33 presents, in contrast, a very sublime and positive picture of marriage in the context of a much less "occasional" document (i.e., less tied to the immediate circumstances of the church addressed). The genius of Paul's reply to the Corinthians is that he avoids the extremes of asceticism and hedonism and refuses to prize too highly either single or married life. Even when he does give qualified assent to celibacy, as when he advocates remaining single, it is with an entirely different rationale than that used by the Corinthians (Paul primarily gives practical rather than theological reasons).

Paul demonstrates his pastoral genius by walking so delicate a tightrope. Given his personal preference for the single life, it would have been easy for him to cave in to the pro-celibacy faction and insist that all people become as he was. Given his "pro-marriage" upbringing in Judaism and the lures of easy sex in Corinth, it might have been equally tempting for him to issue a wholesale condemnation of the proponents of celibacy as legalistic, opposed to the goodness of God's creation, and placing an impossible burden on fellow-Christians' shoulders. But he takes neither of these tacks. Instead, he charts a central course, recognizing the strengths and weaknesses of both sides. Modern theological and ethical controversies regularly require Christian leaders to do the same.

Once we view verse 2 as Paul's qualification of the Corinthian slogan in verse 1, we become less likely to accuse Paul of taking a dim view of marriage and sex. Even if verse 2 is taken as a reason for *getting* married, it is not the only or even primary reason for doing so mentioned in this chapter (cf. vv. 26–35). But as noted above, verse 2 more likely prepares the way for verses 3–7 by commanding those already married not to withhold sexual privileges from their partners. Notable here too is the first of numerous statements in this chapter about the mutuality of marriage: husbands and wives have equal privileges and equal responsibilities (cf. vv. 3–5, 8–9, 10a/11b, 12–16, 28, 32–34). This strongly suggests that such mutuality is implied in other statements even when it is not made explicit (e.g. 10b–11a) and that other gender-specific references should in fact be treated generically—that is, applying equally to husband and wife (vv. 1, 7, 25, 29, 36–38, 39–40).

Against the highly patriarchal societies of antiquity, this mutuality stands out in sharp relief. Most non-Christian husbands would have been horrified at the notion that their bodies belonged to their wives (v. 4). These verses do not prove that Paul could not have envisioned any role differentiation— other texts will have to determine the outcome of that debate (e.g. Eph. 5:21–33). But the emphasis surely rests with his strong affirmation that both partners are essentially equal in God's eyes and must treat each other with the mutual respect such equality merits.

Verses 3–5 prove crucial in understanding the role of sex in marriage. It is something each partner "owes" to the other. So it should never be used as a bribe or reward for good behavior or as something to be withheld as a threat or punishment. Husband and wife alike must be sensitive to the emotional and physical states of each other and not insist on sex on demand. But neither should one partner consistently try to get out of satisfying his or her spouse's conjugal needs. The mutual agreement and submission Paul commands here should in fact apply to most all areas of marriage (cf. Eph. 5:21). The exceptional situation in which Paul permits temporary abstinence highlights, in passing, the central role spiritual disciplines (prayer, meditation, Bible study, etc.) should play in believers' lives. As with fasting, limited asceticism can free up time and energy for particularly focused prayer. But as with fasting, the New Testament nowhere commands sexual asceticism as a practice required of all believers and, indeed, seriously questions its overall religious value (see esp. Col. 2:20–23; 1 Tim. 4:1–5).

Paul's wish in verse 7 that all were like him resembles God's desire for everyone to be saved (2 Peter 3:9), in that simply wishing it does not mean that it will happen. But in the case of salvation, the alternative is undesirable. Here Paul quickly concedes that God gives gifts to different believers that result in equally desirable options. The word for "gift" (*charisma*) matches that used in 1:7 and reminds us that spiritual gifts are not to be limited to the representative lists of chapters 12–14. The capacities for celibacy or marriage are abilities God graciously bestows on us for the edification of his church, just as much as teaching, giving, or speaking in tongues (cf. also Matt. 19:10–12). Like other gifts, the gift of singleness may last only for a time. On the other hand, we may seek after the gift of marriage but not obtain it. Yet singleness and marriage are not quite the same as some of the other gifts because they also include obligations on believers that are not optional. No one, for example, may excuse premarital sex by claiming not to have the gift of celibacy! If people are unmarried, they must refrain from sexual intercourse whether they feel like it or not.

If our interpretation of verse 9 is correct, that Paul is speaking of those who are not controlling themselves, then again Paul seems far less negative about marriage than is often alleged. But even if "cannot" is inserted, as in the NIV's "cannot control themselves," verse 9 still remains only one valid reason for marriage among others yet to come. Still, avoiding unnecessary lust is an important consideration. Humans were created as sexual beings, and God did not intend for most of them to remain alone (Gen. 2:18; cf. 1:27–28). Sexual pleasures should be enjoyed, but within the proper constraints of a marriage relationship. Paul's recognition that widows and widowers often should remarry, notwithstanding his personal preferences, matches his counsel to younger widows in 1 Timothy 5:14, which is phrased somewhat more positively ("So I counsel younger widows to marry, to have children, to manage their homes and to give the enemy no opportunity for slander").

Applying the New Testament teaching about divorce requires an examination not only of verses 10–16 here but also of Jesus' teaching in the Gospels, especially in Matthew 5:31–32 and 19:1–12. Jesus clearly permits divorce in the case of *porneia* (Matt. 5:32; 19:9), though he never commands it. And by far the most common and contextually appropriate meaning of *porneia* is "sexual immorality," which among married people we refer to as adultery. Although the grammar of these two texts is less clear, Jesus probably permits remarriage in this instance as well.[8]

Why does Paul make no mention of Jesus' "exception clause"? Does he know Jesus' teaching only in the form that came to be incorporated into Mark's Gospel (Mark 10:11–12)? Or is he presupposing it, because Jews, Greeks, and Romans alike all agreed that divorce and remarriage were permitted in the case of adultery? We cannot be sure. But one little-noted hermeneutical observation remains clear. Paul cannot have interpreted Jesus' pronouncements on divorce and remarriage as intending to cover every possible scenario or he could not have felt free to add a second exception. Indeed, it is plain, especially from Matthew 19:1–2, that Jesus' words addressed distinctively Jewish debates and did not envision the situation, largely unique to the Hellenistic world, of a Christian (or Jew) marrying a pagan. But Paul's context is equally occasional, as evidenced by his lack of reference to adultery. And the discussion below suggests that it is the desertion, not the "mixed marriage," which legitimates divorce in verse 15, so that Paul's counsel should probably apply equally to desertion by a believer. The

---

8. For a detailed elaboration of the perspective adopted in this and the next two paragraphs, see Craig L. Blomberg, "Marriage, Divorce, Remarriage, and Celibacy: An Exegesis of Matthew 19:3–12," *TrinJ* 11 n.s. (1990): 161–96; on 1 Corinthians 7:10–16 in particular, see pp. 186–94.

question remains open as to whether or not there are other situations in which divorce and remarriage might be permitted.

A promising approach to answering this question arises when we ask what adultery and desertion have in common that makes divorce permissible even in those two instances. If we recall the foundational biblical definition of marriage (leaving/cleaving and becoming one flesh; recall 6:16), then it is noteworthy that adultery undermines the unique one-flesh relationship, and desertion makes it impossible to continue cleaving to one's spouse (as well as to have sex). This suggests that what these two behaviors share is that each *de facto* dissolves a marriage even before a legal divorce has occurred. To determine if divorce is ever otherwise permitted, we must ask if any other circumstances prove equally so damaging that for all intents and purposes a marriage is already destroyed, and a divorce does nothing but acknowledge legally what has in fact already occurred.

Rather than trying to create lists of such circumstances (some, for example, would include physical abuse, prolonged alcohol or drug abuse, insanity, advanced Alzheimer's disease, etc.), each situation should be considered on a case-by-case basis, including cases of adultery or desertion, since even then reconciliation remains the ideal if it is at all possible. Of course to open the door even to the possibility of other circumstances legitimating divorce is to run the risk of greatly abusing that freedom. But to refuse legalistically ever to countenance such exceptions may do even more physical and emotional damage to an individual.

Other items emerge from the details of verses 12–16. Paul's parenthesis in verse 12 ("I, not the Lord") reflects "the sovereign application of the necessarily restricted Jesus-tradition to the new and altered circumstances on the part of the apostle and charismatic, Paul. The *I* [of v. 12] and the *not I, but the Lord* [of v. 10] are a single authority."[9] In other words, neither is any more or less binding than the other. Too often, readers have inappropriately questioned the inspiration or authority of Paul's instructions in verses 12–16 on the grounds that these are merely Paul's fallible, spur-of-the-moment opinions. Paul's ironic conclusion to this chapter in verse 40 is actually a strong avowal of inspiration by the Holy Spirit for his entire letter.

Verse 14 has a curious history of application by certain Christians to support infant baptism, but nothing remotely related to baptism appears in the text itself. On the other hand, supporters of believers' baptism have often treated children of Christian parents as little different than outright pagans. At the very least, this text suggests that God looks on family units in which

---

9. Roy A. Harrisville, *1 Corinthians* (Minneapolis: Augsburg, 1987), 110.

at least one adult member is a believer as special recipients of his blessings. They have opportunities to learn God's word, see Christian living modeled, and make decisions for Christ. Even as children should be encouraged to internalize their own faith as they reach an age of accountability, so also they should be reared in a Christian environment at church and at home that makes them feel like insiders rather than outsiders.[10] More broadly, "there is an infection about Christianity which involves all those who come into contact with it." And "in a partnership between a believer and an unbeliever, it is not so much that the believer is brought into contact with the realm of sin, as that the unbeliever is brought into contact with the realm of grace."[11]

A major question surrounds verse 15a. If a believer is not bound to try to preserve a marriage in cases of permissible divorce, is he or she then free to remarry? Verse 39 uses similar language in addressing the widow. Once her husband dies, she is no longer "bound" to that marriage and is free to find another partner. The verb for binding is different in that context, but seemingly synonymous. If remarriage was universally granted to the legally divorced in both Jewish and Greco-Roman circles, it would seem that Paul would have been much more explicit in forbidding it if that was his intention. Verse 11a should then be understood as referring to the illegitimately divorced. But we must admit that no unequivocal answers emerge from the text.

Similar controversies surround verse 15b. If the statement "God has called us to live in peace" refers to preserving the marriage, then it obviously cannot be used as a criterion for legitimate divorce. But if, as we have suggested, it refers to not trying to prevent a desertion when one partner is unwilling to stay, then it raises the possibility of application to other contexts. But all kinds of trivial disputes could be said to disrupt the peace of a home without being grounds for divorce, so this criterion must be applied only in extreme instances.

FEW CHRISTIANS TODAY advocate total abstinence from sex as an ideal for all believers. Our problems parallel those of the hedonistic wing of the Corinthian church far more than those of the ascetic wing. So any application of 1 Corinthians 7 must proceed with the caution that these changed circumstances dictate. Perhaps the closest analogies to this sexual asceticism remain in traditional Roman Catholic cir-

---

10. Particularly helpful on both the exegesis and application of verse 14 is Paul K. Jewett, *Infant Baptism and the Covenant of Grace* (Grand Rapids: Eerdmans, 1978), 122–37.

11. Barclay, *Corinthians*, 63–64.

cles, which still insist on celibacy as a requirement for priests and various religious orders. Neither Paul nor any other biblical writer justifies this across-the-board requirement. Protestants, however, often continue to overreact against this extreme by inappropriately denigrating the single life. Some churches will not hire pastors if they are *not* married! Even single lay adults regularly testify to feeling like second class citizens in the church. The recent boom in singles groups has helped to allay much of their loneliness, but it is questionable if these groups have succeeded in integrating singles into the larger world of married adults and families in the church.[12]

The specific problem of advocating celibacy within marriage (vv. 2–7) also seems quite foreign to our modern experience. Yet some Christians continue to view sex as inherently dirty, and others use it in inappropriate ways in marriage (as a reward or punishment). Studies consistently suggest that married couples engage in sex much less frequently (usually about once a week or less often) than the three-to-four day cycle of peak desire, which at least younger and middle-aged adult men and women regularly experience.[13] Given the numerous opportunities in our modern world to gratify sexual desires illicitly, Paul's concern to guard against temptation (vv. 2, 5) remains equally appropriate. The option of temporary abstinence for the sake of spiritual devotion provides yet another example of how different Paul's world seems. Yet moves are afoot to recover an emphasis on the spiritual disciplines, particularly prayer,[14] and places need to be made for this option of unusually intense communion as well.

Verses 8–9 reflect a crucially needed balance among Christian singles who have been previously married. Sadly, it is common to hear attitudes voiced these days, particularly among divorced people, which insist on sex as a right but refuse ever again to consider marriage. Given the option of limited self-stimulation as an appropriate outlet for sexual drives (see above, p. 130), no one can ever legitimately claim that sex outside of marriage is either *a* right or *is* right. Still, remarriage can be good, even crucial, and not just for enjoying interpersonal sexual intimacy. Increasing numbers of single parents need help with rearing children, earning additional income, and over-

---

12. For a historical and sociological survey of Christian singles in America, see Carolyn A. Koons and Michael J. Anthony, *Single Adult Passages: Uncharted Territories* (Grand Rapids: Baker, 1991). For practical suggestions on balanced Christian living as singles, see Rhena Taylor, *Single and Whole* (Downers Grove: InterVarsity Press, 1984).

13. Cf., e.g., Herbert J. Miles, *Sexual Understanding Before Marriage* (Grand Rapids: Zondervan, 1971), 72.

14. Most notably in the works of Richard J. Foster, of which the most recent is particularly valuable—*Prayer: Finding the Heart's True Home* (San Francisco: HarperCollins, 1992).

coming loneliness. Yet none of these reasons alone or together is sufficient for justifying remarriage, since each views the new spouse as a means for meeting *my* needs. Only whole-hearted commitment to the other's well-being (v. 4) can lay the adequate groundwork for a healthy marriage.

The divorce and remarriage statistics, of course, continue to grow and stagger the imagination.[15] Attempts to synthesize biblical teaching on these topics quickly divide Christians today into at least four camps: those who believe neither divorce nor remarriage is ever permitted, those who believe divorce is at times permitted but never remarriage, those who permit both divorce and remarriage in the cases of adultery and desertion (or desertion by an unbeliever), and those who permit both divorce and remarriage for a wide variety of reasons.[16] There are in turn subdivisions of and mediating positions among these four primary positions. Since the days of the Reformation, however, the third of these positions has dominated in Protestant circles and, as we have suggested above, is probably the most correct. Many Christian workers committed to solid biblical principles insist that the views that prohibit all remarriage after divorce (or which prohibit all divorce as well) are simply unworkable, pastorally speaking, in the modern world.[17]

But proponents of divorce as a legitimate last resort in various instances must admit that this "way out" is adopted far more often than God could ever desire. Those contemplating divorce often feel that they have exhausted all alternatives long before they have really done so. Supportive Christian friends, fellowship groups, and churches need to come alongside couples well before they reach the point of no return to encourage, nurture, confront, and suggest options that the couples themselves may not have considered. Those couples, in turn, must be open to exploring such options, not least of which is individual and joint counseling from qualified Christian therapists. We need far more marriage enrichment experiences in our churches than divorce recovery workshops, though obviously the latter are necessary.

In spite of our best efforts, people will divorce even when biblical wisdom suggests they should not. In such instances, the Christian community needs to avoid the twin errors of easy acceptance and total lack of forgiveness that

---

15. Andrew Cornes, *Divorce and Remarriage: Biblical Principles and Pastoral Practice* (Grand Rapids: Eerdmans, 1993), 7–48, provides an up-to-date survey.

16. See esp. H. Wayne House, ed., *Divorce and Remarriage: Four Christian Views* (Downers Grove: InterVarsity Press, 1990).

17. See esp. Craig S. Keener, *. . . And Marries Another* (Peabody, Mass.: Hendrickson, 1991), whose exegetical and pastoral skills make this volume the single best book-length work on the topic of divorce and remarriage.

tend to polarize it today. The presence or absence of a genuinely repentant attitude on the part of those at fault will go a long way toward deciding which end of the spectrum Christian response should approximate. We need to ask hard questions of candidates for church membership that determine if they have inappropriately divorced or remarried and, if so, whether they are genuinely repentant.

We must be prepared to help those long since divorced to work through nagging personal problems that remain, even while continuing to confront (or eventually disfellowship) those who arrogantly insist they never did any wrong. Surely singles of all ages, including the never married, should be cautioned against marrying too quickly or for wrong motives. It is sad to hear how in older singles groups, the widowed and divorced often propose remarriage extremely early in the dating process, and how difficult it is for many singles to find unmarried friends of the opposite sex who will "just be friends." It is even more sad to hear the same reports from younger singles groups comprised primarily of the never married.[18]

Verses 12–14 remind us of another reason for doing everything in our power to preserve marriage—the effect of divorce on children. Although it goes beyond the specific issues Paul had in mind when he used the language of "unclean" and "holy," surely the prolonged, detrimental effects, particularly on younger children, of losing regular interaction with their father or mother, falls into the category of that which is not wholesome and therefore unholy.

New marriages and blended families may be better than single parenting. But statistics demonstrate they are increasingly not the solution, as they break up even more frequently than the original nuclear families.[19] The rationale that it is better to live happily divorced than unhappily married, while increasingly common, is fallacious on several grounds: (1) most who think they will be happy divorced are not; (2) even those who are happy themselves often do not take adequate account of the effect on their children or their ex–spouse; (3) the premise of the entire argument is ultimately self-centered and flies directly in the face of the fundamentally selfless nature of Christian living.

Verses 15–16 bear on modern dating practices and debates. While no biblical text clearly bans all Christians from marrying non-Christians (2 Cor. 6:14–7:1 more likely refers to the unequal yokes of legalism or pagan

---

18. Cornes, *Divorce and Remarriage*, 313–49, gives excellent pastoral applications of these themes, though his interpretation of Paul differs in places from ours.

19. These situations can, of course, be redeemed. For excellent guidelines, see, e.g., Beth E. Brown, *When You're Mom #2* (Ann Arbor: Servant, 1991).

worship), verse 39 places such restrictions on widowed Christians contemplating remarriage. And verse 16 reminds us that an evangelistic motive is not adequate for dating or marrying, because there is no guarantee that it will succeed. Certainly Christians need to have close non-Christian friends, if for no other reason than to make their witness credible, and there may be a limited place for fairly informal dating in this context. But a successful marriage demands shared commitments that can be extremely difficult for a believer committed to serving Christ wholeheartedly and a non-Christian unwilling to convert.

1 Corinthians 7:17–24

❧

NEVERTHELESS, each one should retain the place in life that the Lord assigned to him and to which God has called him. This is the rule I lay down in all the churches. ¹⁸Was a man already circumcised when he was called? He should not become uncircumcised. Was a man uncircumcised when he was called? He should not be circumcised. ¹⁹Circumcision is nothing and uncircumcision is nothing. Keeping God's commands is what counts. ²⁰Each one should remain in the situation which he was in when God called him. ²¹Were you a slave when you were called? Don't let it trouble you—although if you can gain your freedom, do so. ²²For he who was a slave when he was called by the Lord is the Lord's freedman; similarly, he who was a free man when he was called is Christ's slave. ²³You were bought at a price; do not become slaves of men. ²⁴Brothers, each man, as responsible to God, should remain in the situation God called him to.

VERSES 17–24 FORM a preliminary summary of Paul's argument in chapter 7 thus far and apply it to two analogous situations. If this chapter does form an ABA pattern (see p. 132), then this paragraph provides not only a summary but also the central focus (part B) of his argument. The main point is stated at the beginning (v. 17), middle (v. 20), and end (v. 24) of the paragraph and can be paraphrased as, "Do not be in a hurry to change the external circumstances of your life simply because you have become a Christian."

"Retain" (v. 17) is "walk about." "The place in life that the Lord assigned" refers to one's marital, socioeconomic, or physical circumstances. "To which God has called him," is a misleading translation; the Greek actually reads, "as God called him." In other words, the entire verse implies that in whatever state we are when we come to the Lord, we should function faithfully in that state without immediately seeking to change it.

Verses 18–19 illustrate this principle with the example of circumcision versus uncircumcision. Judaizers sought to force Gentile Christians to be circumcised (Acts 15:1), while many Jews who sought acceptance in the Greco-Roman world underwent a minor surgical procedure to make themselves appear to be uncircumcised.[1] Although it was one of the most funda-mental ritual requirements of Judaism, circumcision is now a matter of moral indifference for believers (cf. Acts 15:1–21). The New Testament counterpart to circumcision is salvation, symbolized by baptism (Col. 2:11–15).

"Keeping God's commandments" (v. 19) for Christians does not mean ob-serving all 613 pieces of Mosaic legislation, at least not literally, though all do have relevance in one way or another for believers (2 Tim. 3:16). Rather Paul refers to the reinterpretations and applications of the Law for a new age, in light of the words and works of Jesus and the apostles.[2]

Verses 21–23 give a second illustration of the theme "remain as you are." Here Paul contrasts the experiences of Roman slaves and freedmen. Neither state makes serving the Lord inherently easier than the other, and there are spiritual senses in which literal slaves are free in Christ and literal freedmen slaves to Christ. Yet Paul does add an exception here which he did not in the case of circumcision: "If you can gain your freedom, do so."[3] Physical slavery is a form of oppression that displeases God, so when an opportunity for free-dom arises, it should be seized.

It is worth recalling that slavery in ancient Rome did not always resemble the institution we know from the history of the Southern United States in the 1800s. To be sure there were cruel masters, but at times some slaves lived more like the indentured servants of wealthy families in medieval Europe. Others were government officials, teachers, traders, or artists. Unlike slaves in the American South, many were able to buy their own freedom; and many who could, chose not to, preferring instead the security of their patrons to the

---

1. For a description of the motivation for and nature of this procedure, see Robert G. Hall, "Epispasm: Circumcision in Reverse," *BibRev* 8.4 (1992): 52–57. Roman gymnasia were centers of athletic competition, and Roman baths (much like "hot tubs" in our recreational centers) were regularly used for discussing business and politics. Men remained nude in both settings, and Jews would be immediately recognizable. The operation of epispasm in-volved pulling the loose skin of the shaft of the penis up over the tip and suturing the wounds so that it would attach itself as a kind of substitute foreskin.

2. For a survey of Christian perspectives on the role of the Old Testament law in the New Testament age, see Wayne G. Strickland, ed., *The Law, the Gospel, and the Modern Chris-tian* (Grand Rapids: Zondervan, 1993). Of the five views presented, the most convincing is Douglas J. Moo, "The Law of Christ as the Fulfillment of Moses: A Modified Lutheran View," 319–76. Cf. William W. Klein, Craig L. Blomberg, and Robert L. Hubbard, Jr., *In-troduction to Biblical Interpretation* (Dallas: Word, 1993), 279–83.

3. The Greek could actually be translated, "Even if you can become free, use [your cur-rent condition of slavery] instead." But S. Scott Bartchy, *ΜΑΛΛΟΝ ΧΡΗΣΑΙ: First-Century Slavery and 1 Corinthians 7:21* (Missoula, Mont.: Scholars, 1973) has decisively demonstrated on both grammatical and historical grounds that this view is highly improbable. Slaves could not refuse manumission if an owner was determined to grant it, and *ei kai* is much more naturally translated "if indeed," than "even if."

vagaries of freedom.[4] Still, Paul knows that owning humans as property fundamentally contradicts their status in Christ (cf. Philem. 10–16), and he reminds all believers not to revert to physical or spiritual slavery, from which Christ's atonement was intended to save them (v. 23).

Bridging Contexts

IN GENERALIZING BEYOND the specific issues of sex and marriage, Paul indicates that we ought to range quite broadly in looking for applications of verses 17–24. The proverb, "Bloom where you are planted" can fit into a wide variety of contexts. Again, we must admire Paul's pastoral flexibility in relating to a host of people in different situations in life and in minimizing the status symbols that the society around him overly stressed.

Verse 21b ("If you can gain your freedom, do so") indicates that the call to remain as you are in verses 17, 20 and 24 may not be absolutized. But, as throughout the entire chapter, Paul is trying to discourage new Christians from taking sudden, drastic actions to change their lives, as if altering their external circumstances were the key to pleasing God. Acts 16:3 reminds us that Paul felt free to circumcise Timothy, a half-Jew, to keep from offending his contemporaries in his outreach to the Jewish community. But when Judaizers insisted on imposing their agenda as a prerequisite for salvation, Paul stood firmly against them (Acts 15:1; Gal. 2:11–14).

Verse 19 here would have stood out so starkly for anyone from a Jewish background (surely circumcision *was* one of the central commandments of God!), that it highlights just how far removed from Judaizing Paul is. While we must not lose sight of the presence of moral absolutes in Paul, his understanding of God's will is fundamentally rooted in the Spirit's guidance, not the letter of externally imposed laws (cf. esp. 2 Cor. 3:6–18).[5]

Verse 21 has a long history of abuse by pro-slavery advocates.[6] Parallels are often drawn with Colossians 3:22–25 and Ephesians 6:5–8. If Paul were pro-abolition, why did he not come out and say so more directly? Part of the answer is because he, like Jesus, was concerned primarily with fashioning a countercultural community of disciples who did not directly challenge the state but modeled better lifestyles for a watching world. Another part of the

---

4. A balanced, brief description of slavery in New Testament times appears in Carolyn Osiek, "Slavery in the Second Testament World," *BTB* 22 (1992): 174–79. For a detailed discussion with primary sources, see Thomas Wiedemann, *Greek and Roman Slavery* (Baltimore: Johns Hopkins, 1981).

5. Cf. further Stephen Westerholm, "'Letter' and 'Spirit': The Foundation of Pauline Ethics," *NTS* 30 (1984): 229–48.

6. See esp. Willard M. Swartley, *Slavery, Sabbath, War and Women* (Scottdale, Pa.: Herald, 1983), 31–64, on the Bible and slavery in the debate over abolition.

answer is probably because Christianity was such a tiny institution and slavery such a big one in the ancient Roman empire. Attempts to oppose slavery in more wholesale fashion would have proved so counterproductive as to threaten Christianity's very existence. But Paul sowed the seeds for a revolutionary alternative in Christ which in time could only but threaten social institutions of oppression.[7]

It is significant that throughout history, antislavery movements have often received their greatest impetus from Christians, even though the Bible takes only a low-key position against such mistreatment of human beings, and even though certain wings of the church have often impeded emancipation as well.[8] At the most fundamental level, however, Scripture's cautious approach stems from the fact that spiritual rather than physical freedom is what ultimately determines how a person will live in the age to come, a life that makes the circumstances of this age pale into insignificance by comparison (2 Cor. 4:17; Rom. 8:18). From Philippians 4:10–19, we may also apply these principles to the level of wealth or poverty in which we find ourselves.

The example of slavery versus freedom actually corresponds to the questions about celibacy versus marriage more closely than does circumcision versus uncircumcision. For the former two are matters of fundamental morality, and Paul does indicate that under certain circumstances one state is preferable to the other. But all three contrasts reinforce Paul's central theme that "status of any kind is ultimately irrelevant with God." Instead, "precisely because our lives are determined by God's call, not by our situation, we must learn to continue there as those who are 'before God' . . . and let the call of God sanctify to oneself the situation, whether it be mixed marriage, singleness, blue- or white-collar work, or socioeconomic condition."[9]

SNYDER SUCCINCTLY SUMMARIZES the central tension we experience in trying to apply this passage to modern society: "Paul's thought stands in sharp contrast to the autonomous thinking of the western world. For Paul there is no freedom except in peace with one's social network."[10]

These verses directly challenge our contemporary individualism, which teaches people never to rest content with the status they have already attained

---

7. Cf. esp. F. F. Bruce, *Paul: Apostle of the Heart Set Free* (Grand Rapids: Eerdmans, 1977), 401, on the impact of the letter to Philemon on slavery: "What this letter does is to bring us into an atmosphere in which the institution could only wilt and die."

8. For a full history, see David B. Davis, *Slavery and Human Progress* (Oxford: Oxford University Press, 1984).

9. Fee, *First Corinthians*, 322.

10. Snyder, *First Corinthians*, 109.

but always to seek more money, power, influence, and control over their lives. The results include a highly transient, upwardly mobile population, among the more affluent, who generally fail to notice that the numbers of poor and dispossessed often grow precisely as they climb their ladders and push others down.

The opposite danger is passivity. Verse 21a encourages us to try to improve our lot in this world, so long as we do not do it at others' expense or imagine that the key to happiness and a rewarding Christian life demands change in our current status. Certainly we must avoid the tendency to suggest to new Christians that leaving a secular job for full-time Christian work is somehow *by definition* the desirable thing to do.

About the only jobs that Christians cannot honorably and productively continue in after conversion are those which are inherently immoral—prostitution, pimping, racketeering, organized crime, drug dealing, and the like. Of course, there are some which are border-line, for example, operating a gambling casino or manufacturing nuclear weapons. Christians will continue to disagree on what to do about such jobs, and it is not clear that Paul's teaching here will end those debates.

On the other hand, it is entirely appropriate for Christians to seek to liberate *others* from oppressive social institutions in the name of Christ, so long as they do not transform the gospel into one that is exclusively this-worldly in focus. Here lie the errors of certain branches of radical liberationist theologies. But the errors of extremists do not invalidate the causes they support.[11] Slavery still does exist in parts of the Third World and is even experiencing a resurgence in other places, particularly as young women are sold into prostitution. Addictions to alcohol, drugs, sex, even religion, keep many Westerners in their grip. More subtle idolatries and ideologies captivate even greater numbers. Against all of these, Paul's words ring true even today: "You were bought at a price; do not become slaves of men" (v. 23). And people suffering under oppressive governments and impoverished by unjust economic structures need to hear that the gospel holds out hope for their physical as well as spiritual circumstances. But Christians who struggle to liberate them may need to work slowly, "over the long haul," rather than attempting the kind of violent intervention that may actually prove counterproductive to their efforts.[12]

---

11. For a biblically balanced liberationist study, see Orlando E. Costas, *Liberating News: A Theology of Contextual Evangelization* (Grand Rapids: Eerdmans, 1989). Generally helpful, too, is Thomas D. Hanks, *God So Loved the Third World* (Maryknoll, N.Y.: Orbis, 1984).

12. Cf. the generally helpful reflections of Andrew Kirk, *The Good News of the Kingdom Coming* (Downers Grove, Ill.: InterVarsity Press, 1983); and John M. Perkins, *Beyond Charity: The Call to Christian Community Development* (Grand Rapids: Baker, 1993).

1 Corinthians 7:25–40

NOW ABOUT VIRGINS: I have no command from the Lord, but I give a judgment as one who by the Lord's mercy is trustworthy. ²⁶Because of the present crisis, I think that it is good for you to remain as you are. ²⁷Are you married? Do not seek a divorce. Are you unmarried? Do not look for a wife. ²⁸But if you do marry, you have not sinned; and if a virgin marries, she has not sinned. But those who marry will face many troubles in this life, and I want to spare you this.

²⁹What I mean, brothers, is that the time is short. From now on those who have wives should live as if they had none; ³⁰those who mourn, as if they did not; those who are happy, as if they were not; those who buy something, as if it were not theirs to keep; ³¹those who use the things of the world, as if not engrossed in them. For this world in its present form is passing away.

³²I would like you to be free from concern. An unmarried man is concerned about the Lord's affairs—how he can please the Lord. ³³But a married man is concerned about the affairs of this world—how he can please his wife—³⁴and his interests are divided. An unmarried woman or virgin is concerned about the Lord's affairs: Her aim is to be devoted to the Lord in both body and spirit. But a married woman is concerned about the affairs of this world—how she can please her husband. ³⁵I am saying this for your own good, not to restrict you, but that you may live in a right way in undivided devotion to the Lord.

³⁶If anyone thinks he is acting improperly toward the virgin he is engaged to, and if she is getting along in years and he feels he ought to marry, he should do as he wants. He is not sinning. They should get married. ³⁷But the man who has settled the matter in his own mind, who is under no compulsion but has control over his own will, and who has made up his mind not to marry the virgin—this man also does the right thing. ³⁸So then, he who marries the virgin does right, but he who does not marry her does even better.

³⁹A woman is bound to her husband as long as he lives. But if her husband dies, she is free to marry anyone she wishes, but

he must belong to the Lord. ⁴⁰In my judgment, she is happier if
she stays as she is—and I think that I too have the Spirit of
God.

VERSES 25–40 RETURN TO the topic of sex and
marriage in response to the pro-celibacy faction
in Corinth. With the exception of Paul's words to
the widows in verses 39–40, this part of the
chapter focuses wholly on those who have never married. Verse 25 introduces this new category. "Virgins" here refer to young people of marriage-
able age, not necessarily to those who have never had intercourse. Verse 25b
parallels the parenthesis in verse 12. In each case, Paul cannot cite a word
from the earthly Jesus but believes God is inspiring him to offer reliable
counsel.

Verses 26b and 27b repeat the theme of "remain as you are." Because these
young people are single, like the widows and widowers of verses 8–9, Paul
can be more enthusiastic about celibacy. But he quickly reminds them that
his enthusiasm for abstinence does not carry over to the married (v. 27a) and,
against those in Corinth teaching that sex and marriage were inherently sinful, he affirms that "if you do marry, you have not sinned" (v. 28a). This "you"
is probably addressed to young men. The "virgin" in verse 28b is feminine
and provides the same reassurance for young women.

Verses 25–28 also introduce two new reasons for Paul's advice. The first
deals with "the present crisis" (v. 26a), which is further explained in verses
29–31. The second has to do with "many troubles in this life" (v. 28c) and is
elaborated in verses 32–35. Some have thought that the present crisis must
refer to some unique historical circumstances of famine or persecution in
Corinth.[1] But as far as we can tell, the city in the mid-50s was as prosperous
as any in the Roman world. And there is no indication that Corinthian
Christians were persecuted much, at least not more than most first-century
Christians. So it is better to understand verses 29–31 as explaining verse 26a,
in which case the NRSV reading, "impending crisis," is more helpful. Paul
knows that after Christ's first coming, his second coming could take place
very soon ("the time is short"—v. 29a). This does not mean that Paul had set
any dates or necessarily expected the Lord to return within his lifetime.

---

1. See esp. Bruce W. Winter, "Secular and Christian Responses to Corinthian Famines,"
TynB 40 (1989): 86–106. It is hard to determine how significant some lingering effects of
earlier famines were, and the fit with verses 29–31 makes it unlikely that we should look
for some other referent for verse 26 here.

Rather he, like the rest of the New Testament writers, recognized what C. E. B. Cranfield has phrased so aptly, that

> the Parousia is near . . . not in the sense that it must necessarily occur within a few months or years, but in the sense that it may occur at any moment and in the sense that, since *the* decisive event of history has already taken place in the ministry, death, resurrection and ascension of Christ, all subsequent history is a kind of epilogue, necessarily in a real sense short, even though it may last a very long time.[2]

All Christians should therefore sense an urgency to serving the Lord, caused by the uncertainty of the time of the end, after which point it will no longer be possible to win any more people to Christ or to disciple them to maturity. Paul is well aware that distractions of marriage may temper this urgency. So those who choose to wed must not become so preoccupied with their families that they can no longer effectively serve Christ (v. 29b). The same is true with other normal human activities—celebrations and wakes, commerce and shopping (vv. 30–31). All are legitimate endeavors, but all remain fleeting. The Christian should therefore be less involved in the affairs of this world than the non-Christian. The balance Paul seeks to achieve leads one writer to label him a "worldly ascetic."[3]

Verses 32–35 unpack Paul's second rationale for encouraging those who have never married to stay single. Even if Christ does not come back right away, attending to the concerns of spouse and children takes time away from ministering to the needs of others in both church and world (vv. 32–34). Yet once again Paul refuses to absolutize his preferences or endorse without qualification the stance of the pro-celibacy faction. Verse 35 supplies the most crucial clue in the whole chapter for determining when marriage is or is not appropriate. Whichever state enables one to "live in a right way in undivided devotion to the Lord" is preferable. Paul does not wish to "restrict" his audience (literally, "throw a noose around" them), one way or the other.

Verses 36–38 focus on one specific kind of unmarried person. But as the NIV footnote demonstrates, the language is vague enough to be taken in two quite different ways.[4] The early church almost without exception inter-

---

2. C. E. B. Cranfield, "The Parable of the Unjust Judge and the Eschatology of Luke-Acts," *SJT* 16 (1963): 300–301. On the eschatology of 1 Corinthians 7 in particular, cf. Jeremy Moiser, "A Reassessment of Paul's View of Marriage with Reference to 1 Cor. 7," *JSNT* 18 (1983): 103–22; Guy Greenfield, "Paul and the Eschatological Remarriage," *SWJT* 26 (1983): 32–48.

3. Vincent L. Wimbush, *Paul: The Worldly Ascetic* (Macon, Ga.: Mercer, 1987).

4. The footnote reads, "If anyone thinks he is not treating his daughter properly, and if she is getting along in years, and he feels she ought to marry, he should do as he wants. He

preted these verses, as in the footnote, to refer to a father considering whether or not to give his daughter's hand in marriage. The term for "marry" in verse 38 (*gamizo*) is different from that used elsewhere in this chapter (*gameo*—vv. 9, 10, 28, 33, 34, 36, 39), and in its other, relatively rare biblical occurrences it means "to give in marriage" (Matt. 22:30 [par. Mark 12:25; Luke 20:35]; Matt. 24:38 [par. Luke 17:27]). But it is rare in extra-biblical Greek too, and other verbs with the same suffix (*-izo*) were losing their causative force in the New Testament period.

To "act improperly" (v. 36) translates a word that suggests sexual innuendoes that would be inappropriate for a father-daughter relationship. All of the language in verse 37 about the man settling the matter, not being under compulsion, and being in control over his own will, sounds strange if the practice of arranged marriages is in view, for the father would not normally have vacillated in these ways.

It is probably better, therefore, to follow the NIV text and take the two people involved to refer to fiancé and fiancée.[5] The trend in Greco-Roman society was decidedly away from arranged marriages in the first century. But even then ambiguities remain. Some have seen these verses as implying the contemplation of a "spiritual" marriage, in which two people of the opposite sex would agree to live together without sexual relations. The word translated "getting along in years" might actually mean "oversexed" and refer to the young man rather than the woman. But all in all, the NIV has probably got it right. Engaged couples should not feel compelled to heed the pro-celibacy faction and refrain from marriage, but if they choose to do so, that is acceptable as well. Indeed, as in verses 7–8, 26, and 40, Paul reiterates his preference for the single life (v. 38), but he refuses to legislate it.

Verses 39–40 round out the chapter by reaffirming monogamy as a life-long commitment. These verses also contain the only explicit reference to remarriage in this chapter. Christian widows and, by implication, widowers are free to remarry, so long as they marry fellow believers. As in verse 8, Paul reiterates his preference for the single life but will not absolutize it. "I think that I too have the Spirit of God" (v. 40b) does not reflect any doubt on Paul's

---

is not sinning. He should let her get married. But the man who has settled the matter in his own mind, who is under no compulsion but has control over his own will, and who has made up his mind to keep the virgin unmarried—this man also does the right thing. So then, he who gives his virgin in marriage does right, but he who does not give her in marriage does even better."

5. The most thoroughgoing defense of this view is Werner G. Kümmel, "Verlobung und Heirat bei Paulus (1. Cor 7, 36–38)," in *Neutestamentliche Studien für Rudolf Bultmann*, ed. Walther Eltester (Berlin: Töpelmann, 1954), 275–95. No comparable English language treatment of any substantial length exists.

part but represents a slightly sarcastic aside to the Corinthians, who felt that only they had attained true spiritual insight.

PAUL CONTINUES to chart his careful course between the hedonists and the ascetics in Corinth. Most of what we said under verses 1–16 about the overall method of moving from original meaning to contemporary significance applies here too. In addition, various other specifics clamor for attention.

First, as with verse 12, verses 25–26 and 40 must not be viewed as any less inspired than the rest of Paul's writing. He is simply admitting that he cannot cite any previous Christian authority but must rely on his own sense of God's guidance. Second, if "the present crisis" of verse 26 is taken to reflect some unique historical problem in first-century Corinth, then Paul's subsequent remarks will of course be relativized. But if we are correct in seeing verses 29–31 as disclosing the crisis to be nothing more than the characteristic tension believers experience between the two advents of Christ, then Paul's counsel remains equally valid for any time and place throughout church history. Third, verse 27 contains two further examples of "remain as you are," but it is significant that verse 28 qualifies only one of them. In other words, even though Paul stresses that those who choose to marry do not sin, he could never have written, "But if you do divorce, you have not sinned," except under the very limited circumstances previously discussed (see above, pp. 138–39).

Verses 29–31 should not be made to promote the very asceticism Paul was trying to play down. But they do suggest that the cares of this world must take a significant back seat to kingdom priorities. Vincent Wimbush helpfully characterizes this balance as a "middle-of-the-road ethic" that

> remains both as baggage and challenge for every subsequent model of Christian spirituality. For those for whom Christian faith demands and is synonymous with a worldly agenda for aggressive social change, the way of Paul and the Pauline Christians will appear embarrassingly weak and irrelevant. For those for whom Christian faith demands the development of interior piety first and foremost, the way of Paul and the Pauline Christians will appear to be substandard, a worldly compromise.[6]

---

6. Wimbush, *Paul*, 97.

Those concerned to obey God's word, however, will strive for precisely Paul's balance between being in the world but not of it.

Verses 32–35 offer crucial guidance for people in any time and culture trying to decide whether or not to marry. Instead of adopting the countless other criteria society suggests, Christians should ask themselves in which state, single or married, they can best serve the Lord. Michael Green recommends asking the following question, "Could I be equally useful to the Lord if married, or would it inevitably curtail my usefulness to him?" He then comments, "The quantity of time available for Christian involvement may be reduced once we are married, but its quality may be enhanced. At all events, I have no right to marry unless I have honestly faced the question of the impact marriage will have on my Christian life and service."[7]

The identical cluster of issues surrounds the decision whether or not to have children (or how many children to have)—to the extent that we are permitted such choices. Voluntary childlessness for the sake of the kingdom is an option not many married couples choose, but it is an option that is surely worth prayerful consideration.[8] Both spouses and children can influence Christians to become reluctant to obey Jesus in such areas as sacrificial financial giving and keeping oneself free from worldly pursuits, but they can also greatly enhance one's personal life, strengthening one's ability to minister to families and offering innumerable opportunities for discipleship right within one's own family.

Part of the application of verses 36–38 clearly hinges on which translation is adopted. If this is a father contemplating whether or not to "marry off" his daughter, the application to societies without arranged marriages will be minimal. If this is an engaged couple, then we learn that Paul did not consider engagement nearly as binding as did the Jews (who required a divorce to break it off). If "she is getting along in years" is a correct translation, then verse 36 may suggest that older engaged couples may often require a shorter period of betrothal than younger ones. Whatever translation is adopted, Paul's "Yes, but" logic is again clear.

Rounding out the chapter, verses 39–40 stress that marriage involves a lifelong commitment. That is another reason why it is not to be entered or dissolved lightly (particularly for the sake of avoiding sex). First Timothy 5:11–15 sounds a bit more positive toward remarriage precisely because Paul is not dealing with quite the same problem as in Corinth.

---

7. Green, *Corinth*, 116.

8. See esp. Diane Payette-Bucci, "Voluntary Childlessness," *Direction* 17.2 (1988): 26–41.

It is worth noting in passing that if Paul allowed for and at times even encouraged widows and widowers to remarry, then it is not likely that the criterion of church leadership usually translated "husband of one wife" (1 Tim. 3:2, 12) was intended to exclude the remarried. But there is no linguistic or contextual justification in 1 Timothy 3 for allowing this expression to include those remarried after the death of a spouse while excluding those who are remarried after a biblically legitimate divorce. Better, therefore, to understand "husband of one wife" as equivalent to "currently characterized by marital fidelity, if married."[9]

NOT MANY WESTERN CHRISTIANS give adequate consideration to the possibility of remaining unmarried for the sake of wholehearted devotion to the Lord's work. More need to do so. Examples such as the internationally influential Anglican pastor, John Stott, or the widely heralded Southern Baptist missionary, Lottie Moon, have demonstrated how much one life can accomplish when freed from the demands of family. Many Christian preachers, from John Wesley to contemporary workaholics, would have been better off unmarried rather than going through the agony of watching their marriages fall apart after years of neglect. William Carey's marvelous missionary career remains somewhat tarnished because of the sacrifices he demanded of his wife, Dorothy, who eventually lost her mind.[10] Some of this heartache could surely have been avoided if couples unprepared to count the cost simply had not married in the first place.

For all of us, single or married, if the end of the world truly could come in our lifetime, we should have an urgency about the Lord's work that contemporary Christians seldom reflect. And even if the Lord delays his coming, sudden death claims too many lives for any of us ever to assume complacently that we have a certain number of years or decades left to serve God more leisurely.

Verses 29–31 were followed more closely when evangelicalism as a movement in this country was poorer and more marginalized. Now with our great numbers and affluence, many Christians seem to be very "engrossed" in "the things of the world" (v. 31) and buy material possessions precisely as if they were "theirs to keep" (v. 30). Third-World Christians, of course, can

---

9. See esp. C. H. Dodd, "New Testament Translation Problems II.," *BT* 28 (1977): 112–16.

10. On which, see esp. James R. Beck, *Dorothy Carey* (Grand Rapids: Baker, 1992).

often teach us profound lessons concerning obedience to Paul's commands in these areas, because they are less tempted by such materialism. We must keep verse 31b ever before us, reminding ourselves, against every message society sends, that this life is an infinitesimal drop in the bucket compared to eternity. It is only worth investing our lives and our resources in that which will outlive this world.[11]

Many couples today can honestly attest that by the criterion of verse 35 they are better off married. Spouses can engage in team ministry, bring complementary gifts to a mutual task, and support and encourage one another (cf. Eccl. 4:12). But in growing numbers of Christian families, husbands and wives are torn in different directions and grow increasingly apart, especially when the daily responsibilities of each allow for little or no family time. Many spouses of seminarians these days seem uncommitted to their partners' present and future ministries, asserting instead their independence in other careers. If this is true for those preparing for full-time Christian service, how much more may it apply to the layperson?

Throw in children and the problems are exacerbated still further. We desperately need role models of entire families engaging in ministry together. For those who want children but are unable to have them, adoption could become a major form of Christian commitment and service. Almost every major American city has its long line of biracial, ethnic, abused, or physically challenged children whom no one wants to adopt. Meanwhile, white middle-class, childless couples themselves form long waiting lists, willing to consider only healthy white infants as prospective family members. But whether adopted or biological, rearing godly children can itself be a ministry, though, as with non-Christian spouses (v. 16), there is no guarantee that children of Christian parents will accept the Lord. The notion that Christians *ought* to have large families to help Christianize the world is refuted both by Paul's concerns in verses 25–35 and by the sad testimony of many who have attempted such a task and then grieved to watch their children give allegiance to other gods.

Verses 36–38 surely speak to contemporary dating patterns. By international standards, Americans tend to have relatively short engagement periods, often following prolonged periods of serious relationships with multiple partners in succession. Many other cultures have prolonged engagements, beginning early in a serious relationship, often preceded only by much more casual friendships with the opposite sex. Paul's commands necessarily favor neither of these approaches, but they do suggest that betrothal is a serious

---

11. For all kinds of practical suggestions for implementing these principles, see Ronald J. Sider, ed., *Living More Simply* (Downers Grove: InterVarsity Press, 1980).

matter, not to be entered rapidly. Yet once entered it is not the binding covenant marriage is. Careful thought and prayer should continue as to whether the marriage should be consummated. A balance must be struck between not prolonging engagement to such an extent that it leads to sexual frustration or sin and not making it so short that couples enter married life unsure if God's will has been done. The recent upsurgence of premarital and even pre-engagement counseling can be a good step in the direction of achieving this balance.[12]

Contemporary application of verses 39–40 in most aspects repeats what we have said under verses 8–9. These verses also underline the consistent biblical call to lifelong faithfulness which wedding vows normally promise. There are numerous reasons for a preserving marriage even when we don't feel like it, but one that modern people often ignore is that of keeping our promises. "Falling in love" does not constitute adequate grounds for marriage. "Falling out of love" does not grant a person the right to divorce. Warren Wiersbe suggests five questions to be answered when considering marriage, which aptly sum up Paul's concerns in this chapter: "What is my gift from God? Am I marrying a believer? Are the circumstances such that marriage is right? How will marriage affect my service for Christ? Am I prepared to enter into this union for life?"[13] These questions demand far more attention in contemporary Christian families, youth groups, and singles gatherings than they usually receive.

---

12. For an introduction to the process, see, e.g., H. Norman Wright, *Premarital Counseling* (Chicago: Moody, 1981).

13. Warren W. Wiersbe, *Be Wise* (Wheaton: Victor, 1983), 85.

1 Corinthians 8:1–13

🌿

NOW ABOUT FOOD sacrificed to idols: We know that we all possess knowledge. Knowledge puffs up, but love builds up. ²The man who thinks he knows something does not yet know as he ought to know. ³But the man who loves God is known by God.

⁴So then, about eating food sacrificed to idols: We know that an idol is nothing at all in the world and that there is no God but one. ⁵For even if there are so-called gods, whether in heaven or on earth (as indeed there are many "gods" and many "lords"), ⁶yet for us there is but one God, the Father, from whom all things came and for whom we live; and there is but one Lord, Jesus Christ, through whom all things came and through whom we live.

⁷But not everyone knows this. Some people are still so accustomed to idols that when they eat such food they think of it as having been sacrificed to an idol, and since their conscience is weak, it is defiled. ⁸But food does not bring us near to God; we are no worse if we do not eat, and no better if we do.

⁹Be careful, however, that the exercise of your freedom does not become a stumbling block to the weak. ¹⁰For if anyone with a weak conscience sees you who have this knowledge eating in an idol's temple, won't he be emboldened to eat what has been sacrificed to idols? ¹¹So this weak brother, for whom Christ died, is destroyed by your knowledge. ¹²When you sin against your brothers in this way and wound their weak conscience, you sin against Christ. ¹³Therefore, if what I eat causes my brother to fall into sin, I will never eat meat again, so that I will not cause him to fall.

PAUL NOW ADDRESSES the second issue raised by the Corinthians in their letter to him (see 7:1). Most meat sold in the town marketplace came from sacrificial animals that had been slaughtered at pagan temple ceremonies. Did these rituals somehow automatically taint the food? Could Christians buy it? Could they eat it if it was offered to them at friends' homes? What about the various social events—weddings, parties, clubs, and so on—which often used the temple dining halls for their festivities? Could Christians participate and eat meat at these events? What about more overtly religious rites in those temples? The issue clearly was not as simple or innocuous at it might at first glance seem to Westerners today.[1]

First Corinthians 8:1–13 and 10:14–11:1 clearly address this topic. At first glance, 9:1–10:13 does not appear to do so; but on closer inspection, these verses form an integral part of Paul's argument after all. First Corinthians 8:1–13 introduces the problem and its two-pronged solution: freedom in principle to eat when there are no inherently anti-Christian implications involved, but voluntary abstention when other Christians might be damaged by one's freedom. First Corinthians 9:1–18 then gives a second application of the principle of freedom tempered by love in morally neutral areas by discussing the issue of accepting money for ministry. First Corinthians 9:19–27 generalizes further by enunciating Paul's underlying principle for all of his behavior in these "gray areas of life"—what is most likely to bring more people to Christ. First Corinthians 10:1–13 prepares for Paul's absolute prohibition in the coming section by warning against using one's freedom as a license for immorality. First Corinthians 10:14–22 then lays down Paul's one unbending requirement on the topic of idol meat: It should never be eaten in overtly pagan religious rituals. First Corinthians 10:23–11:1 brings the discussion full circle by repeating the two key principles of 8:1–13 but ultimately tips the balance of the scales in favor of freedom.[2]

The present section divides into three discrete sections. Verses 1–3 offer Paul's "Yes, but" thesis, analogous to his approach in 6:12–13 and 7:1–2. Verses 4–6 expand on the "yes": the theme of freedom based on Christian knowledge (cf. v. 1a). Verses 7–13 then elaborate the theme of voluntary restraint based on Christian love (cf. vv. 1b–3). Given Paul's explicit references both to the marketplace and to private dining in 10:25–30, it is reasonable to assume that he has the widest range of contexts in view right from the outset. Given his explicit reference to eating in the temple in 8:10, in the context of that which is in principle acceptable for believers, it seems clear that he also has in mind those social gatherings in the temple precincts that were not overtly religious in nature.[3]

---

1. The most detailed and helpful background information and exegetical discussion appears in Wendell L. Willis, *Idol Meat in Corinth* (Chico, Calif.: Scholars, 1985).

2. H. Probst (*Paulus und der Brief* [Tübingen: Mohr, 1991]) observes that 8:1–11:1 form an integral unity, almost an epistle in miniature, by following the standard sequence of Greco-Roman epistolary rhetoric: 8:1–13 forms the introduction; 9:1–18, the narrative discussion; 9:19–10:17, the argumentation; and 10:18–11:1, the consequent commands.

3. The reconstruction of events adopted here closely follows Bruce N. Fisk, "Eating Meat Offered to Idols: Corinthian Behavior And Pauline Response in 1 Corinthians 8–10," *TrinJ*

Verse 1 introduces the issue. "Food" should be understood to refer to "meat," lest verse 13 be seen as narrowing the topic. Part of the meat of each sacrificial animal was burned on the temple altar, part was eaten in temple ceremonies, and part was sold in the Corinthian marketplace for consumption at home.

"We know that we all possess knowledge" (v. 1a) probably represents another Corinthian slogan, as the NIV footnote suggests ("'We all possess knowledge,' as you say"). Verse 7 will observe that such knowledge is more limited among those Paul calls the weaker brothers. So this slogan more likely reflects the position of the "stronger" Corinthians, who probably overlapped with the more indulgent rather than the more ascetic wing of the church there.

"Knowledge" translates *gnosis* and must be interpreted as in chapters 1–4 to refer to prideful human religious speculation. As with the previous slogans, there is a sense in which Paul can agree but not without immediate qualification (vv. 1b–3). Love, not knowledge, must form the foundation of Christian behavior. "The man who thinks he knows something" (v. 2) resembles our idiom, "Someone who thinks he or she *is* something." The force of the verb tenses in verse 2 suggests a paraphrase: "If a person thinks that he has attained to some degree of knowledge, he has not yet reached the stage when he has any knowledge at all in the real sense of the word."[4] True Christian knowledge is inseparable from *agape* love, which can be produced only by God's prior choice to love us (v. 3).

Verses 4–6 provide the basis for Christian freedom to eat this sacrificial food—the idols to which the meat is dedicated have no objective spiritual existence. Steeped in his Jewish understanding of monotheism and the sovereignty of God (e.g., Deut. 6:4; 10:17) and knowing well the Old Testament's scorn for idolatry (e.g., Deut. 32:15–17; Isa. 44:6–20), Paul forthrightly declares that there is only one true God in the universe (v. 4). The stronger Corinthian Christians would have agreed and were perhaps

---

10 n.s. (1989): 49–70. Traditionally, commentators have often limited chapter 8 to the contexts of the marketplace and eating in private homes, without adequately accounting for verse 10. Gordon D. Fee, " Εἰδωλόθυτα Once Again: An Interpretation of 1 Corinthians 8–10," *Bib* 61 (1980): 172–97, argues that illicit temple activity is exclusively in view right from the beginning. Both perspectives seem inappropriately truncated. Talbert, *Corinthians*, 56, sees an ABBA structure in 8:1–13; 10:14–11:1 (A = marketplace meat [8:1, 4; 10:23–11:1]; B = temple activity [8:10; 10:14–22]), which lends support to our approach. Ben Witherington, "Not So Idle Thought About *Eidolothuton*," *TynB* 44 (1993): 237–54, has recently marshalled additional support for Fee's view but without interacting with Fisk. Supporting Fisk, see Kistemaker, *First Corinthians*, 269–74.

4. Ellingworth and Hatton, *First Corinthians*, 160.

using this very logic to support their freedom to eat. Paul goes on to acknowledge that not everyone believes as he does. Many mythological deities and lords of mystery cults were fervently worshiped. Gnosticism believed in divine "emanations," and emperors were beginning to call themselves divine and demand sacrifice (v. 5). But in reality, none of these alleged gods or lords had anything to do with the creation, sustenance, or redemption of the world, as the God of Israel and the Father of the Lord Jesus did (v. 6).

Verses 7–13 unpack Paul's qualification of the exercise of Christian freedom: it may corrupt the weak consciences of certain fellow believers. Love must therefore limit freedom. Some of the Corinthian Christians could not eat idol meat, even in private homes, and almost certainly not in temple dining halls, without recalling the past religious associations that the meat had for them. This would have been a special concern for some of the poorer members of the church, who probably would not have had regular access to eating meat except at temple rituals. For them, meat still had inherently religious connotations. Their "weak conscience" was not a poorly developed sense of morality or propriety, as modern use of the expression might often imply, but rather the overscrupulous restrictions they placed on believers' freedom in Christ. Their inner thoughts unnecessarily accused them and led to feelings of guilt or defilement (v. 7).[5] Because they felt compelled to do that which did not proceed from faith, for them it *was* sinful (Rom. 14:23).

Verse 8 continues Paul's qualification; the introductory "but" should probably be translated "and." Here is the first of three reasons Paul gives for voluntarily abstaining from idol meat in the presence of those unable to "handle" the practice. Precisely because it is a morally neutral issue, there is no inherent spiritual advantage in eating the meat or disadvantage in avoiding it. Therefore concern for one's fellow Christian should take precedence.[6]

The "however" in verse 9 should again be taken as a mild continuative (e.g., "moreover"). Verses 9–12 combine to make the point that the Corinthians should not behave in ways that lead each other into sin. Verse 9 provides the thesis statement for the paragraph. "Stumbling block" and that which "causes [one] to fall into sin" (v. 13) are synonyms and help to explain each other. "The exercise of your freedom" reads more literally "your

---

5. See esp. Paul W. Gooch, "'Conscience' in 1 Corinthians 8 and 10," *NTS* 33 (1987): 244–54.

6. Part or all of verse 8 has often been seen as another slogan of the Corinthian "stronger brothers," but presumably they *did* think that eating commended themselves to God. It is possible, though not demonstrable, that they claimed that "we are worse off if we do not eat and better off if we do," and that Paul alludes to their saying but negates both clauses (Willis, *Idol Meat*, 98).

authority" or "your right." In short, verse 9 urges Christians not to demand their rights in ways that cause fellow Christians to sin.

Verse 10 is often understood to mean that while the "stronger" Corinthians could draw appropriate boundaries and eat meat from the marketplace without being tempted to go to the temple, the "weaker" Christians could not. Hence that which was morally neutral led the latter to go on to do that which was inherently sinful. More likely, however, the principle of Romans 14:23 ("Everything that does not come from faith is sin") again comes into play. What the strong were lawfully practicing (eating either in home or temple without religious ritual), the weak could not do in good conscience, so that for them the eating *was* sin. "Emboldened" reflects an unusual use of the verb "edify." Quite likely what the strong felt would build up the weak was actually daring them to do something destructive.

Verse 11 thus spells out the second reason for voluntary abstinence. Flaunting one's freedom was actually damaging the spiritual lives of the weak. "Is destroyed" is probably better rendered "is in the process of being ruined." It is doubtful if Paul could imagine that these inherently amoral issues could actually jeopardize a Christian's salvation. Rather he saw the strong believers' behavior as "an obstacle to Christian sanctification"[7] (cf. Rom. 14:15). Such damage stands diametrically opposed to the purpose of the atonement. Verse 12a elaborates and confirms the type of ruin described here as wounding others' weak consciences.

Verse 12b gives the third reason for abstinence: to avoid sinning against Christ. As in Matthew 10:42 and 25:40, treatment of fellow Christians equals treatment of their Lord. Paul concludes the chapter, therefore, with a conditional absolute. When there is good reason to believe that exercising one's freedom in amoral areas will actually lead a fellow Christian into sin, restraint is always right. Paul models this principle by his own example and states it with an emphasis worthy of Mark 9:42: "If anyone causes one of these little ones who believe in me to sin, it would be better for him to be thrown into the sea with a large millstone tied around his neck."

 A FULL UNDERSTANDING of the principles and applications of chapter 8 must await the completion of Paul's argument in chapters 9–10. By then it will be clear that an evangelistic principle of behaving in ways most likely to lead to others' salvation (see esp. 9:19–23)

---

7. Judith M. Gundry Volf, *Paul and Perseverance: Staying in and Falling Away* (Louisville: Westminster/Knox, 1990), 97.

is foundational to all that Paul says in these three chapters. But substantial initial progress can be made here. Three timeless principles dominate this chapter: what is safe for one Christian may not be for another; true discernment always requires love as well as knowledge; and believers have no right to demand certain freedoms if they in turn prove detrimental to those around them.[8]

Possible applications range far beyond the specific issue of idol meat, but they do not include that which is inherently good or bad. Rather 1 Corinthians 8 speaks to the gray areas of Christian living. Sometimes Scripture makes plain whether an issue is fundamentally immoral or amoral. Adultery, for example, is always wrong, but consumption of alcohol is wrong only if it leads to drunkenness or hurts a weaker brother.

In other cases, no passage speaks directly to the issue at hand. Christians must then ask if the practice in question has any inherently pagan religious (or anti-Christian) elements or if it is necessarily destructive and hurtful to the individuals involved. More positively, if the practice in question seems acceptable in light of both of these tests, might our participation enhance our outreach to the non-Christian world by cultivating friendships and social activities that unbelievers enjoy (cf. 9:19–23)? Two dangers remain ever-present: a separatism that prevents Christians from being the salt of the earth and the light of the world (Matt. 5:13–16) and a syncretism (a mixture of religions) that adopts pagan practices with damaging consequences.

As in 1:18–2:5, Paul's statements about knowledge (vv. 1–3) must not be construed as anti-intellectual. *Gnosis* ("knowledge") in this context is that which stresses freedom and human autonomy at the expense of concern for others, especially other Christians. Love rather than knowledge remains the center of Paul's ethics (cf. Gal. 5:14) and the highest of human virtues,[9] without which all spiritual gifts prove worthless (1 Cor. 13). This kind of love is sacrificial self-giving, centered around and imitating Christ's cross-work, not primarily a nice feeling, familial friendship, or mere altruism. The more believers mature, the more they understand how little they measure up to God's standards and how much depends on him and not themselves (v. 3).

A correct understanding of verses 4–6 must leave room for Paul's absolute prohibition of idolatrous eating and for his belief in the reality of the demonic world (10:18–22). But demons are the spiritual entities worshiped, usually unwittingly, in pagan religious ritual; they do not inherently reside in either statues or food. Mere possession of idols or consumption of food

---

8. Cf. Barclay, *Corinthians*, 76.
9. Cf. esp. Victor P. Furnish, *Theology and Ethics in Paul* (Nashville: Abingdon, 1968); idem, *The Love Command in the New Testament* (Nashville: Abingdon, 1972).

sacrificed to them cannot be detrimental unless one adds acts of religious devotion to the mix.

Verses 4–6 also form a strong defense of monotheism against all forms of animism, polytheism, or henotheism.[10] The contrast between verses 5 and 6 is not between two subjective perceptions of reality, as the "for us" of verse 6 might suggest, but between one false and one true perception. "For us" is explained by "we know" in verse 1. Believers know what pagans do not—that there is only one God over the universe. Verse 6 also contains a strong link between the Father and the Son, with crucial doctrine about each. The Father is Creator and the ultimate subject of adoration by Christians (cf. 10:26); the Son is the agent of creation and our daily sustenance (cf. 10:31).

The key issue in applying verses 7–13 involves recognizing those who truly have weak consciences. Nothing in the context justifies an association of "weaker brothers" with those who are merely offended by a particular practice, notwithstanding the misleading translation of verse 13 in the KJV ("if meat make my brother *to offend*"). Even less justified is the application of these principles to the "professional weaker brother"[11]—the Christian legalist eager to forbid morally neutral activities even though he or she would never personally indulge in those activities. Rather, the weaker brother or sister is the Christian who is likely to imitate a stronger believer in some morally neutral practice but feel guilty about doing so or, worse still, be led into that which is inherently sinful or destructive. The stronger believer's freedom thus actually has damaging consequences for the spiritual growth and maturation of the weaker sibling. Jack Kuhatschek points out that an adequate analogy to 1 Corinthians 8 must have three elements: (a) a threat to Christian freedom; (b) a potential stumbling block; and (c) a Christian brother or sister who might actually be led into sin.[12]

Application of verses 7–13 must also leave room for 10:25–30, in which Paul will stress the freedom of the "strong" more pointedly than he does here. If the strong should not hurt the weak, neither should the weak accuse the strong of sin. Romans 14:1–15:13, Paul's other major teaching passage on the

---

10. For a detailed elaboration, in view of the religious scene in first-century Corinth, see Bruce W. Winter, "Theological and Ethical Responses to Religious Pluralism—1 Corinthians 8–10," *TynB* 41 (1990): 209–26.

11. The term is used by Joseph C. Aldrich, *Life-Style Evangelism* (Portland: Multnomah, 1981), in an excellent discussion of the application of the principles of 1 Corinthians 8 (pp. 39–76).

12. Jack Kuhatschek, *Taking the Guesswork out of Applying the Bible* (Downers Grove, Ill.: InterVarsity Press, 1990), 68–70. Kuhatschek notes, e.g., that those who object to Christians wearing beards never consider wearing ones themselves, so that the third element on this list is lacking and the "weaker brother" principle does not apply.

topic, carefully balances these two commands. In fact, there is a probable sequence to the exhortational material that comprises the second major section of Romans (12:1–15:13). First come the necessary transformations of body and mind required of all believers (12:1–2). Then each must discover her or his spiritual gifts and employ them faithfully (12:3–8). But, just as in 1 Corinthians 12–13, spiritual gifts must be exercised in love (12:9–13:14). That love should in turn foster mutual tolerance of Christian diversity on amoral issues (14:1–15:13).[13] In the context of 1 Corinthians 8:7–13, this means that the converse of verse 8 is as true as the text itself: "Abstaining from food does not bring us near to God; we are no worse if we eat, and no better if we do not," except where our behavior leads others into sin. Paul further emphasizes the matters of freedom and tolerance in Galatians 5 and Colossians 2:18–23.

This crucial balance between permissiveness and legalism always proves far more difficult to maintain than either of the extremes. It requires much less thought and care simply to create a blanket prohibition of a certain practice or to tolerate it indiscriminately. But Paul's way rings much truer to reality and to revelation.

> Through fear the Weak would have forced the community into a self-imposed ghetto. Through a destructive use of freedom the Strong would have committed the church to a pattern of behaviour indistinguishable from that of its environment. If either group had prevailed, the identity and mission of the church would have been gravely compromised. Paul's response was to focus the vision of the Corinthians on their roots in Christ and on their responsibility to each other and to a wider world. His passionate prudence is a perfect illustration of *he agape oikodomei* [love builds up] (VIII,1).[14]

At the same time, Paul's principles of moderation may not be applied to murder, theft, extra-marital sex, gluttony, homosexuality, or a host of other sins that the Bible makes clear are always wrong. Nor may they be applied, for example, to the use of certain narcotics that are immediately addictive and therefore destructive. And even when Christian freedom leaves the door open to certain practices, and even when no one will be hurt by them, that does not mean Christians should necessarily get involved, unless there is some way in which that behavior glorifies God (10:31) or benefits oneself

---

13. See the particularly helpful book-length discussion of this theme in Robert Jewett, *Christian Tolerance: Paul's Message to the Modern Church* (Philadelphia: Westminster, 1982).

14. Jerome Murphy-O'Connor, "Freedom or the Ghetto (*1 Cor.*, VII, 1–13; X, 23–XI,1)," *RB* 85 (1978): 573–74.

or others (10:33). We should never ask, "How far can I go?" but "What are my motives in the first place?" "The key seems to be maintaining a balance between the believer's radical difference and his radical identification. Our radical difference is holiness (wholeness)—not legalism or externalism. Only holiness makes radical identification a legitimate option for the Christian."[15]

It is interesting to compare Paul's teaching in 1 Corinthians 8 with two other key New Testament passages. On the one hand, Paul betrays no awareness here of the Jerusalem council's "decree" of Acts 15:1–29, which concludes with the decision to request Gentile Christians in Antioch, Syria, and Cilicia to refrain from food sacrificed to idols for the sake of Jewish scruples. This decision, which was delivered about six years earlier (A.D. 49), was not of course addressed to Achaia (or to any province outside of those with large Jewish populations). Paul apparently felt no need to apply it in Corinth, perhaps because he sensed it still made too many concessions to legalism in a context where its positive gains—paving the way for Jewish evangelism—were no longer major concerns.

The other relevant passage is Galatians 1–2, in which Paul lambastes a more serious form of legalism that was putting people's salvation in jeopardy. When weak consciences become so warped that they require certain works, or forbid others, as prerequisites for salvation, Paul can no longer remain as subdued as he did in 1 Corinthians but has to condemn such teaching in the strongest of terms.

FOOD SACRIFICED TO IDOLS remains a pressing concern for Christians in various African, Latin American, and Asian cultures. As people in these cultures increasingly migrate to Western countries, they bring those issues with them. Others are closely analogous: whether or not to participate in various rites of ancestor veneration, whether or not to worship in ways reminiscent of other religions (for example, prostrate on prayer mats facing East), and the like. Yet for most readers of this commentary, idol meat and its analogues in other world religions will not rank among their top one hundred moral dilemmas in life! Still, when one realizes the overarching principles involved, applications clamor for attention at every turn.

Some contemporary analogies involve the overt religious associations that eating meat in idol's temples could at times have. Freemasonry, for example, has distinctively non-Christian religious rituals at its core, yet much superficial involvement with the organization can be maintained at a purely

---

15. Aldrich, *Evangelism*, 63.

secular level, and the organization does good with many charitable and humanitarian activities. Christians, therefore, continue to disagree as to whether believers may be involved, and at what levels, with this kind of organization. Room must be left for that disagreement to continue,[16] so long as Christians agree on the larger principles at stake.

Similar debate should be allowed to continue to surround participation by Protestants in the Eucharists of Roman Catholic and Eastern Orthodox congregations and vice-versa. In an age of ecumenism, not every church means what its predecessors have meant by Holy Communion. Each Christian must judge each context to see if he or she can partake in good conscience, in light of what that particular ceremony is believed to accomplish.

Where are the boundaries that differentiate Christian meditation, secular meditation, and Hindu or Buddhist (including transcendental) meditation? To what extent if any can one participate in a game like Dungeons and Dragons, which in at least some circles, but by no means all, can lead to the practice of witchcraft or the occult? The answers will vary from one context to another.[17]

The most common contemporary applications of 1 Corinthians 8, however, usually do not involve activities that could lead to overtly anti-Christian beliefs or rituals. Rather they have to do with involvement in activities that can lead to excess and sin but do not have to. These include drinking alcohol; wearing potentially suggestive forms of dress; listening to certain kinds of music; smoking or chewing tobacco; playing games that sometimes but not necessarily involve gambling; buying lottery tickets that support government, education, state parks, and the like; engaging in premarital physical contact of a variety of kinds; and on and on.[18]

Others deal with Sabbatarian regulations concerning what may or may not be done on Sunday, notwithstanding the fact that Sunday is not a Christian Sabbath or day of rest but a time for worship and honoring Christ's resurrection (see esp. Col. 2:16–17, which links the Sabbath with the ritual laws that Christians no longer literally obey).[19] A larger segment of Western

---

16. Contrast, e.g, Forrest D. Haggard, *The Clergy and the Craft* (N.p.: Missouri Lodge of Research, 1970); with John Ankerberg and John Weldon, *The Secret Teachings of the Masonic Lodge* (Chicago: Moody, 1989).

17. For guidance as to the dangers of this and other fantasy role-paying games, see John Weldon and James Bjornstad, *Playing with Fire* (Chicago: Moody, 1984).

18. Garry Friesen with J. Robin Maxson, *Decision-Making and the Will of God* (Portland: Multnomah, 1980), 382–83, gives a long and sadly humorous list of such activities he has personally experienced in twentieth-century American contexts.

19. Cf. Craig L. Blomberg, "The Sabbath as Fulfilled in Christ," in *The Sabbath in Jewish and Christian Traditions*, ed. Tamara Eskenazi, Daniel Harrington, and William Shea (Denver: Denver University Center for Judaic Studies, 1991), 196–206.

Christianity, however, resembles the "strong" at Corinth on this issue, as they flaunt their freedom and do not even take seriously the need to assemble regularly for extended times of worship, fellowship, and Christian education.

Cross-cultural experiences disclose that many of the traditions we once thought were biblical are not, even as we take care not to mock others' foibles in parallel contexts. Thus in many parts of the world, American evangelical discomfort with alcohol is almost unintelligible. Yet in the former Soviet Union, it is scandalous to most evangelicals for women to wear makeup or jewelry and common for men to insist on greeting one another with holy kisses—on the lips! In some parts of Africa and India, thanks to Western missionaries, it is considered sinful for a preacher to appear in church, even on sweltering days, without a white shirt and tie. In cultures where polygamy is still practiced, debates rage among missionaries about how to deal with a man who has several wives and then becomes a Christian.

In Western liberalism, the "strong" who choose to drink, smoke, and even swear often mock the poor "weak" fundamentalists who refuse to engage in these practices. While legalism is usually associated with the extremes of conservative Christianity, there is an equally rigid legalism of the left. This legalism is seen most clearly in those who are "politically correct" or who hold an approach to social action or ecological concerns that leaves no room for dissent in disputed areas.

Some Christians nevertheless insist on a kind of legalism that forbids morally neutral practices on the grounds that one never knows when someone else might be hurt. First Corinthians 10:25–30 addresses these concerns more directly, but here it is worth pointing out that such legalism itself often has damaging consequences. Jerry Vines, for example, encourages teetotaling, even in the privacy of one's home, on the grounds that children may be taught that drinking in moderation is acceptable when in fact they might turn out to be among the small minority of persons who have alcoholic propensities.[20] What Vines fails to consider, however, is the far more common pattern of children from legalistic homes and churches who rebel in behavior and belief against their upbringing precisely because of such rigidity. In general, educating children and adults to responsible behavior and moderation in morally neutral matters proves much more successful than absolute prohibitions or indulgent permissiveness in producing mature Christians.[21]

Knowledge without love (v. 1) seems especially prevalent in academic and clerical circles in which biblical and theological specialists easily look down on uneducated laity. But the criteria for hiring or honoring scholars and

20. Vines, *God Speaks Today*, 133.

21. Cf. further Donald E. Sloat, *The Dangers of Growing Up in a Christian Home* (Nashville: Thomas Nelson, 1986).

clergy continue to encourage such abuse. Millard Erickson seems highly countercultural yet faithful to verses 2–3 when he writes, "If in voting on a faculty appointment I ever have to choose between a brilliant but spiritually naive scholar, and one who meets only the minimum requirements academically but has a warm, mature commitment to Christ, I will unhesitatingly choose the latter."[22] Churches might consider applying the identical criteria to their pastoral searches.

Verses 4–6 prove equally countercultural in an age in which the only absolute at times is the requirement to tolerate pluralism. Yet the Bible consistently denounces idolatry, which in its broadest sense refers to giving ultimate allegiance to anyone or anything but the God and Father of Jesus Christ. Lesslie Newbigin offers a helpful model for constructive dialogue between Christians and adherents of other religions or ideologies, but he remains equally clear that we dare not surrender our conviction that Christianity contains unique, salvific truth unavailable elsewhere.[23]

Because idols are not living, spiritual beings, we should also guard against giving Satan too much credit for that which is merely human sleight of hand, as particular wings of the contemporary spiritual warfare movement often do.[24] First Corinthians 10:20–21, however, warns us against the more prevalent danger that characterizes modern secularism—denying the existence of demons and their influence in pagan religion altogether.

Verses 7–13 also cut against the grain of prevailing trends. Society bombards us with a myriad of signals urging us to demand rather than to relinquish our rights. Yet "insisting on one's rights, even insisting on one's rights as a Christian, is a sign that something else other than the true God is being worshipped."[25] First Corinthians 10:25–30 clarifies that there is a place for the "strong" to exercise their freedom, but here Paul, surely one of the "strong," models the behavior of what Aldrich calls the "nonparticipating mature brother."[26] Somewhat similar is the position that supports teetotaling as a social statement against the rampant, contemporary abuse of alcohol.[27]

Yet Paul refuses to absolutize this perspective and try to foist it on all Christians, and so must we. Sadly, the church today seems to be increasingly

---

22. Millard J. Erickson, *The Evangelical Mind and Heart* (Grand Rapids: Baker, 1993), 48.

23. Lesslie Newbigin, *The Gospel in a Pluralist Society* (Grand Rapids: Eerdmans, 1989).

24. A trend ironically inspired by Frank Peretti's works, which were by design intended to be fictional not doctrinal! For a balanced perspective on the topic, see Clinton E. Arnold, *Powers of Darkness* (Downers Grove: InterVarsity Press, 1992).

25. N. T. Wright, "One God, One Lord, One People: Incarnational Christology for a Church in a Pagan Environment," *Ex Auditu* 7 (1991): 45–56.

26. Aldrich, *Evangelism*, 43.

27. E.g., Norman L. Geisler, "A Christian Perspective on Wine-Drinking," *BSac* 139 (1982): 46–56.

polarized on the issue of permissiveness versus legalism. Clearly immoral behavior is tolerated on the one hand, and clearly amoral behavior is prohibited on the other. We need to educate people and to provide models of responsible choice on a case-by-case basis. Our teaching and our example should be grounded in the Christian ethic of love and should put others' well-being before our own, yet without allowing good to be called evil (Rom. 14:16).

1 Corinthians 9:1–18

❧

A
M I NOT FREE? Am I not an apostle? Have I not seen
Jesus our Lord? Are you not the result of my work in
the Lord? ²Even though I may not be an apostle to
others, surely I am to you! For you are the seal of my apostleship in the Lord.

³This is my defense to those who sit in judgment on me.
⁴Don't we have the right to food and drink? ⁵Don't we have the
right to take a believing wife along with us, as do the other
apostles and the Lord's brothers and Cephas? ⁶Or is it only I
and Barnabas who must work for a living?

⁷Who serves as a soldier at his own expense? Who plants a
vineyard and does not eat of its grapes? Who tends a flock
and does not drink of the milk? ⁸Do I say this merely from a
human point of view? Doesn't the Law say the same thing?
⁹For it is written in the Law of Moses: "Do not muzzle an ox
while it is treading out the grain." Is it about oxen that God is
concerned? ¹⁰Surely he says this for us, doesn't he? Yes, this
was written for us, because when the plowman plows and the
thresher threshes, they ought to do so in the hope of sharing
in the harvest. ¹¹If we have sown spiritual seed among you, is
it too much if we reap a material harvest from you? ¹²If others
have this right of support from you, shouldn't we have it all
the more?

But we did not use this right. On the contrary, we put up
with anything rather than hinder the gospel of Christ. ¹³Don't
you know that those who work in the temple get their food
from the temple, and those who serve at the altar share in
what is offered on the altar? ¹⁴In the same way, the Lord has
commanded that those who preach the gospel should receive
their living from the gospel.

¹⁵But I have not used any of these rights. And I am not
writing this in the hope that you will do such things for me. I
would rather die than have anyone deprive me of this boast.
¹⁶Yet when I preach the gospel, I cannot boast, for I am compelled to preach. Woe to me if I do not preach the gospel! ¹⁷If
I preach voluntarily, I have a reward; if not voluntarily, I am
simply discharging the trust committed to me. ¹⁸What then is

my reward? Just this: that in preaching the gospel I may offer it free of charge, and so not make use of my rights in preaching it.

PAUL TURNS NOW to a second illustration of the principle that Christian freedom should be tempered by voluntary relinquishing one's rights. But the illustration is scarcely arbitrary; it reflects one of the primary ways the Corinthians are challenging Paul. They have come to doubt his apostolic authority (vv. 2–3), precisely because he is not charging them for his ministry (cf. 2 Cor. 11:7). Itinerant Greco-Roman philosophers and religious teachers supported themselves in one of four ways: charging fees, staying in well-to-do households, begging, or working at a trade. The last of these was least common but generally acknowledged to give the philosopher the greatest freedom to teach however he liked.[1]

The powerful patrons in the Corinthian church doubtless would have preferred to have Paul accept their money but give them deference and political support in return. When he refused and continued to rely on tent-making instead (cf. Acts 18:1–4), they charged that his unwillingness to go along with their patronage demonstrated that he did not have the same authority as other itinerant apostles or preachers.[2]

Verses 1–12a therefore present the case in some detail for Paul's right to charge for his services. Yet in keeping with his "yes, but" logic, and in defense of his actual behavior, verses 12b–18 then explain why Paul has in fact renounced this right. Verses 19–27 generalize to the even broader principle that lies behind Paul's behavior on the issues in both 8:1–13 and 9:1–18. But these verses also tie in closely with the beginning of chapter nine by completing a chiasm (an ABBA pattern). In verse 1a, Paul raises two questions: "Am I not free?" (A) and "Am I not an apostle?" (B). Verses 1b–18 then defend the answer to the second question—of course he is an apostle (B); while verses 19–27 elaborate on the nature of his freedom, in response to the first question (A).

The four questions of verse 1 are all interconnected. If the answer to any proves negative, then all Paul's claims are in jeopardy. But in fact Paul is free, he is an apostle, he has seen Jesus, and he has spiritually fathered the Corinthians. The last two questions provide support for his apostolic claims.

---

1. See Ronald F. Hock, *The Social Context of Paul's Ministry* (Philadelphia: Fortress, 1980). On 1 Corinthians 9:1–19 in particular, see pp. 59–62.

2. For a detailed reconstruction of the charges against Paul, see Marshall, *Enmity*, 282–340.

He has seen the risen Lord (cf. 15:7–8, fulfilling the criterion of Acts 1:22b), and he has received a specific commission to preach to Jews and Gentiles (Acts 9:15–16). Thus verse 2 follows logically. No matter anyone else's opinion of Paul; for the Corinthians to question his apostolicity calls into question their own spiritual existence!

Verses 3–12a supply Paul's formal defense, via a barrage of further rhetorical questions. The answers to each of them are intended to be unambiguous. First, Paul reasserts his right to receive material provision for his ministry, by means of three questions in verses 4–6. The "food" of verse 4 no longer refers to idol meat, since it is combined with "drink," but has to do instead with physical nourishment and sustenance—one of the primary ways early Christians provided for itinerant preachers in their midst (cf. Luke 10:7a). Verse 5 implies that most of these men were married and brought their wives along on their travels. Again it was only natural and appropriate that the local Christians should take care of the wives' needs as well. On the Lord's brothers (probably the natural children of Joseph and Mary), see Mark 6:3. Mark 1:30 confirms that Peter (Cephas) was married. He is mentioned separately from the "other apostles" because of his association with one of the Corinthian factions (recall 1:12), not because Paul questions his apostolicity. The way Paul phrases the question of verse 5 ("Don't *we* have the right to take a believing wife?") makes one wonder if Paul had been married (recall the discussion under 7:8) when he first began his itinerant ministry, and if his wife had subsequently died.[3] Verse 6 then gets to the heart of Paul's complaint. More literally, it reads, "Or do only Barnabas and I *not* have the right *not* to work?"

In verses 7–12a, Paul begins accumulating a series of reasons why in fact he *does* have the right to request payment for his services. These continue into verses 13–14 as well. All told, there are five lines of argument: "common practice, scriptural precept, intrinsic justice, Jewish custom and Christ's command."[4] Verse 7 presents three analogies from the common practice of human experience in the areas of warfare, farming, and shepherding. Few in Paul's day would have disputed the logic of these examples.

Verses 8–11 argue from Deut. 25:4, which verse 9 explicitly quotes. "Merely" is a correct interpolation in verse 8 and could easily be added in verse 9b as well ("Is it merely about oxen that God is concerned?"). Verse 10a should then read, "Surely he says this [also] for us." Paul is not claiming that this quotation from the Mosaic Law never had anything to do with oxen,

---

3. So Snyder, *First Corinthians*, 132.
4. Prior, *1 Corinthians*, 153.

only that its application cannot be limited to animals. Verses 10–11 clarify, using imagery favored by Jesus in his parables of seed and sowing, that preaching the gospel is like planting a crop; and making disciples, like harvesting. So if oxen should not be muzzled as they plow, neither should preachers be prevented from eating due to lack of support from those among whom they minister (cf. Gal. 6:6; Rom. 15:27).

Verse 12a rounds out the formal part of Paul's defense with a third kind of argument. The Corinthians have already conceded the logic of everything Paul has said thus far with respect to their other leaders and itinerating Christian workers. It is the height of irony and injustice that they would refuse these same rights to the one who was most of all responsible for their spiritual rebirth.

Verse 12b begins as if Paul is ready to move to the "but" of his "Yes, but" argument. Verses 13–14, however, continue by providing the final two arguments in defense of Paul's right to receive remuneration: the analogy of priests and Levites in the Jewish temple (cf. Num. 18:8–31) and the express words of Jesus during his lifetime (Luke 10:7b). Yet these two examples also set the stage for verses 15–18 by hinting at a spiritual reward for ministry as well as a purely material one.[5] The temple example would have made good sense to ex-pagans also, since Greco-Roman cults likewise gave priests a portion of the meat they sacrificed. This illustration turns back to the topic of chapter 8 and sets the stage for the discussion of 10:14–22.

After the "interruption" of verses 13–14, Paul restates the theme of verse 12b ("I have not used any of these rights"—v. 15a) and goes on to explain why he has refused to charge for his ministry. Verse 12b has already given the essential reason: he wants to avoid all possible charges of impure motives or misuse of funds (cf. 2 Cor. 2:17). Verse 15b clarifies that his "defense" has not been a subtle hint that he wishes to reverse his policy now. Verse 15c forms an emotional outburst in the form of an anacoluthon (a grammatically incomplete sentence) in the Greek, literally, "For it would be better for me to die than—no one will empty me of my boast!" "Boast" here carries the sense of an appropriate pride in what the Lord has done in spite of Paul's weakness (cf. 1:31; 2 Cor. 10:12–12:10).

But Paul cannot legitimately boast merely in his ministry of preaching (v. 16). God has placed an irresistible call on his life to preach (cf. Jer. 20:9). Verse 17a ("if I preach voluntarily") is thus merely hypothetical; verse 17b ("if not voluntarily") expresses what in fact is true in Paul's case (cf. Luke

---

5. Harry P. Nasuti, "The Woes of the Prophets and the Rights of the Apostles: The Internal Dynamics of 1 Corinthians 9," *CBQ* 50 (1968): 251–54. In other words, the analogies of verses 7–11 are purely secular; those of verses 13–14 are sacred.

17:7–10). Verse 18a probably belongs with verse 17 to create tighter parallelism; together they may be helpfully rendered, "For if I do this voluntarily I have a reward, but if involuntarily I receive a commission from God, what then is my reward?"[6]

The rest of verse 18 answers this question. Paul's pay "turns out to be his total freedom from all merely human impositions on his ministry," which the acceptance of payment would have invariably brought.[7] The word for "use" in this verse (*katachraomai*) is a stronger term than the standard Greek word (*chraomai*) and is better rendered "full use" or even "abuse." Paul did at times accept money from churches to whom he was not currently ministering (cf. Phil. 4:10–19), but even then he never demanded it.

Bridging Contexts

THE REASONS WHY Paul does or does not encourage receiving money for ministry speak volumes to our contemporary materialistic world, if we are willing to listen. Sadly, this is one area, perhaps even more so than with sexual morality, where many Christians are unwilling to obey Paul's instruction. The underlying principles transcend his culture, even if his actual choice in any given instance is guided by the specifics of that situation. Again his "evangelistic principle" is not hard to detect (v. 12b), along with his concern not to lead believers into sin by linking Christian work with financial rewards.

Believers who individually and corporately benefit from the ministries of full-time Christian workers need carefully to examine and heed Paul's call in verses 1–12a. Such ministers should not have to be so preoccupied with providing for their basic needs that they cannot devote themselves wholeheartedly to their work. Congregations should not think of their giving as providing a salary, however, in ways that tempt them to demand satisfaction of their personal whims. "The church does not pay its ministers; rather, it provides them with resources so that they are able to serve freely."[8]

Those called to full-time Christian work, on the other hand, should always consider verses 12b–18. Whenever requesting or even accepting payment could hinder the spread of the gospel, "tentmaking" must always take precedence. Bivocational ministry has numerous advantages—freedom from human "strings," not imposing a financial burden on any group of believers, and exemption from charges of mismanaging funds or ministering primarily for financial gain.

---

6. Ellingworth and Hatton, *First Corinthians*, 180.
7. Fee, *First Corinthians*, 421.
8. D. A. Carson, *When Jesus Confronts the World* (Grand Rapids: Baker, 1987), 125.

Although chapter 9 deals primarily with an apostle's rights, verse 14 allows us to generalize Paul's principles to any one in full-time gospel ministry. Verses 9–11, with their metaphors of sowing and reaping, suggest that such ministry need not even be full time. Nothing in the analogies of farming suggests how long the laborer works, and Paul's tentmaking activity would qualify him for the label of "part-timer." Therefore, it is appropriate at times to pay a wide variety of Christian workers for specialized tasks, just as it is equally appropriate for workers to *volunteer* their "off hours" to meet the needs of the church.

Paul's model of accepting help from other churches but not from the congregation to which he is currently ministering finds a partial parallel in the common practice of itinerant Christians ministering freely in their home congregations but receiving gifts or love offerings elsewhere. A closer parallel emerges with the practice of missionaries receiving support from one or more congregations in one location to enable them to minister full time somewhere else. But none of these models can be absolutized, since the first Christians themselves employed different methods in different places.[9] No one model, therefore, should be mandated as the only legitimate practice for a certain organization or group of believers.

Individuals may derive their authority from charisma, specialized expertise, a particular office, or because they have earned the respect of others who freely assign authority to them. The last of these forms is the most spiritually legitimate and precisely what Paul claims he should have received from the Corinthians (v. 2). Instead, sadly, he is reduced to arguing for his need not to argue for this kind of respect. Still, all ministers can learn from Paul's example. Whatever their office, education, or personality might have already granted them, their faithful work and gracious love for their congregations should reinforce.

Verses 4–6 remind us that provision for those who minister to us need not be purely monetary. Historically, congregations have often provided housing, helped stock food supplies, and offered other material provisions to their pastors and their families. This scheme has its strengths and weaknesses. On the one hand, it can enable the gift givers to know for sure where their help goes; on the other hand it can prevent ministers from choosing the most appropriate ways of disposing of more liquid assets. Verse 5 offers a healthy reminder that itinerant ministry by the married should include family members when possible (recall under 7:35). A "ministry widow" (or widower)

---

9. Cf. further Dean S. Gilliland, *Pauline Theology and Mission Practice* (Grand Rapids: Baker, 1983), 246–56. The one principle that *is* ruled out is that of a church-plant forever remaining financially dependent on those who planted it.

is almost by definition an oxymoron! The adjective "believing" in this verse reinforces 7:39; when given a choice Christians should marry fellow Christians.

The hermeneutic Paul adopts in verses 8–11 has troubled many. How can he maintain that a command about oxen really applies to preachers? Once we understand that Paul is not claiming that the *meaning* of the original text of Deuteronomy 25:4 was about people, much of our discomfort should dissipate. Rabbinic tradition, probably already in existence in Paul's day, regularly applied this passage, and parallel Old Testament imagery elsewhere, to humans. As in verse 12, the logic is "from the lesser to the greater." If God is concerned with rewarding animals for their work, how much more must he be concerned for workers he has made in his own image?[10]

Interestingly, in 1 Timothy 5:18 Paul again links Deuteronomy 25:4 with Luke 10:7 in the explicit context of giving double honor (including financial remuneration) to elders who direct the affairs of the church well in the areas of preaching and teaching. Verse 12a points us to a consistency and even-handedness of treatment that has wide-ranging applications. Treating all leaders, indeed all people, without favoritism or partiality (cf. James 2:1–4), is a key element in preserving the unity and vitality of any Christian gathering.

Verse 12b provides the clue to knowing when to refuse pay for spiritual work, though the principle must be applied sensitively. The criticism of a small minority of believers about how a person is handling his or her money may not outweigh the potential damage done by not having funds for crucially needed ministries. On the other hand, widespread ridicule by unbelievers when Christians appeal for money in certain ways should cause great alarm and almost instant application of Paul's principle of voluntarily relinquishing our rights.

The theme of an inherent spiritual reward for spiritual service, which permeates verses 13–18, meshes with the experiences of countless volunteers and underpaid Christian workers over the centuries. Occasionally, Christian ministry has elicited an unusual amount of prestige and financial reward, usually when the gospel has been compromised by political entanglements (see above, p. 57). But for the most part, believers who have chosen paid ministry as a career have foregone higher salaries and more comfortable lifestyles that other occupations or careers could have afforded them. Yet those who are truly called with the compulsion Paul felt will confess that no other line of work could have proved so satisfying, notwithstanding all of the obstacles they may have encountered.

---

10. See esp. D. Instone Brewer, "1 Corinthians 9:9–11: A Literal Interpretation of 'Do Not Muzzle the Ox,'" *NTS* 38 (1992): 554–65.

A good test for would-be full-time Christian workers is to ask themselves the question if they could imagine being truly happier doing anything else. If the answer is yes, they probably have not been called. Without Paul's sense of compulsion, it will be too easy to give up when the hard times come.[11] Even for laity, if people have identified their spiritual gifts and are living lives of fellowship and obedience to God, they will naturally want to devote a large amount of their free time to utilizing those gifts for the upbuilding of the church and the work of the church in the world. Indeed, they will work hard precisely in order to *create* such free time.

Paul's personal commission (vv. 15–18), of course, does not apply to everyone, even though all believers must be prepared to give an account of the hope within them (1 Peter 3:15). But each of us is called to use our spiritual gifts with diligence, generosity, and earnestness—in short, going above and beyond the call of duty (Rom. 12:3–8). And those in positions of authority do well to obey Peter's words to his fellow elders: "Be shepherds of God's flock that is under your care, serving as overseers—not because you must, but because you are willing, as God wants you to be; not greedy for money, but eager to serve; not lording it over those entrusted to you, but being examples to the flock" (1 Peter 5:2–3).[12]

OUR WORLD ALTERNATES between heavy doses of rebellion against sentiment and equally putrid servings of authoritarianism. Not surprisingly, the church all too frequently imitates the world in these pendulum swings. Paul's words in 1 Corinthians 9 suggest a third way. Christian ministers retain genuine spiritual authority over those entrusted to their care, notwithstanding the radically egalitarian and democratizing forces of modern society. But that authority must be used for the best interests of others, not self, and used for that which will best promote the gospel in a world quick to ridicule and reject it. The heavy "top-down" hierarchies of many Christian organizations find no support from Paul's (or Jesus') models of servant ministry (recall our discussion above, pp. 92–93).

"Tentmaking," in particular, is making a healthy comeback, especially in missions circles, though it needs to be taken as a serious option by even larger

---

11. Paul's words in verses 15–18 cannot mean that those who are paid for ministry can get no spiritual reward, since verses 13–14 have just insisted that material remuneration *is* apppropriate in certain cirucmstances. One's motive and the response of others are the keys (cf. Matt. 6:1).

12. An excellent resource for these and related issues is James E. Means, *Effective Pastors for a New Century: Helping Leaders Strategize for Success* (Grand Rapids: Baker, 1993).

numbers of Christian workers. There are no countries "closed" to the gospel, notwithstanding the frequent use of this expression to refer to nations with government bans on missionary visas. Rather, Christians prepared to employ their skills overseas in business, industry, or teaching English as a foreign language, may regularly gain entry into those areas otherwise most hostile to professional Christianity. Their witness, in word and deed, can break down barriers that traditional missionary efforts never will. And even in countries that grant missionary visas, people who come first of all to share a practical skill or trade will find their more informal friendship evangelism opens new doors on many fronts.

Given the growing costs of sending a Western family to live abroad, and given the increasing reluctance of churches to support missionaries they do not personally know, it would seem more compassionate and efficient for would-be missionaries and already existing missions organizations to consider the tentmaking model much more often than they do.[13] Not merely 1 Corinthians, but Paul's ministry and message as a whole evidence almost no concern with formal missionary or evangelistic mandates, yet they are permeated with models of individuals who voluntarily proclaim and share in every walk of life how Christ has transformed their lives.[14] In Third-World contexts, of course, many Christians have no choice but to ply a trade and minister "on the side."

Even at "home" in the Western world, bivocational ministry is increasingly needed. In many instances, small congregations of young Christians in working-class or impoverished neighborhoods should not be asked to try to support their ministers. Even when they are asked, they often cannot do so. With more and more people taking early retirement and/or enjoying years of good health after retirement, churches are hiring and should increasingly continue to hire senior citizens, for nominal remuneration, to engage in ministries of visitation, outreach, care, and the like. Where pensions are meager, the church may supplement them, but many times older people have the means to donate large amounts of time freely.

Affluent suburbia does not as easily motivate people to substantial volunteer ministries, but here verse 12 comes into play. Large segments of the well-to-do, non-Christian world, highly influenced by secular education

---

13. Important suggestions for implementation appear in Don Hamilton, *Tentmakers Speak: Practical Advice from Over 400 Missionary Tentmakers* (Ventura: Regal, 1987). Cf. the alarming statistics of the cost of traditional missionary work and the questions of stewardship raised by Roger S. Greenway, *Discipling the City* (Grand Rapids: Baker, 1992), 216–18.

14. On which, see esp. Paul Bowers, "Church and Mission in Paul," *JSNT* 44 (1991): 89–111.

and media, remain convinced that most conservative Christians are racketeers, seeking to bilk the rich out of their money for self-serving ends. Radio and television ministries that constantly harangue their audiences for donations do little to dispel this stereotype. Numerous televangelists keep phone numbers constantly on their viewers' screens, distracting from any message they might be trying to preach other than "we want your money." Questionable spending practices of the money they do receive often add fuel to the fire.

If such techniques are genuinely necessary just to "stay afloat," then rigorous financial disclosure and accountability remains crucial. Even then, one wonders just how many of the largely overlapping parachurch ministries currently competing for the same donors' dollars are really necessary. Why not work together and strive for one (and only one) quality Christian radio or television station per audience market? Why not consolidate the proliferation of missions organizations into a few vibrant, healthy ones? Why can't Christian publishers jointly decide what their markets need, rather than constantly duplicating efforts to produce yet another profitable but overpriced product?

Tentmaking, nevertheless, has substantial weaknesses, not least of which is the amount of time available to devote to evangelism, discipleship, preaching, teaching, and so on. The paid professional minister is not likely to disappear from the horizon in the near future. In some circles, old myths still persist, such as the philosophy of congregations that keep their pastors poor in hopes that they will depend more on God. Where possible, both the extremes of poverty and of riches (as defined locally) should be avoided (Prov. 30:8), but when this is not possible, the minister must accept his or her lot graciously and with contentment (Phil. 4:11–13). Some churches have adopted the partially helpful policy of paying their pastors the median salary of their congregation or community. While better than setting such people up on financial pedestals, this policy nevertheless discourages outreach to anyone who earns less than the median, lest one's salary be lowered for the next year!

A better guideline, perhaps, is to give enough so that basic needs are always covered but never so much that leaders are tempted to enter or remain in ministry because of how much they can make. The amounts commanded by the senior pastors of many megachurches, well-established Christian counselors in private practice, and Christian celebrities in particular, often seem substantially out of sync with this guideline. Seminarians are often heard discussing how much a church has to offer them before they will consider it. Not surprisingly, small or less affluent parishes have a difficult time finding pastors. Some pastoral search committees of local churches have committed to never hiring any candidate who raises the question of money too early in the interviewing process or who makes inappropriate requests for salary or fringe benefits. Such caution seems wise.[15]

---

15. For the biblical foundations for many of the thoughts of pp. 179–82, see Jouette M. Bassler, *God and Mammon: Asking for Money in the New Testament* (Nashville: Abingdon, 1991), esp. 65–69. For contemporary insights into "how God liberates us from the false promises of wealth," see David Neff, ed., *The Midas Trap* (Wheaton: Victor, 1990).

1 Corinthians 9:19–27

T HOUGH I AM FREE and belong to no man, I make myself a slave to everyone, to win as many as possible. ²⁰To the Jews I became like a Jew, to win the Jews. To those under the law I became like one under the law (though I myself am not under the law), so as to win those under the law. ²¹To those not having the law I became like one not having the law (though I am not free from God's law but am under Christ's law), so as to win those not having the law. ²²To the weak I became weak, to win the weak. I have become all things to all men so that by all possible means I might save some. ²³I do all this for the sake of the gospel, that I may share in its blessings.

²⁴Do you not know that in a race all the runners run, but only one gets the prize? Run in such a way as to get the prize. ²⁵Everyone who competes in the games goes into strict training. They do it to get a crown that will not last; but we do it to get a crown that will last forever. ²⁶Therefore I do not run like a man running aimlessly; I do not fight like a man beating the air. ²⁷No, I beat my body and make it my slave so that after I have preached to others, I myself will not be disqualified for the prize.

IN VERSES 19–27, Paul makes plain the evangelistic principle underlying his attitude to both idol meat and money for ministry. Whatever he does, he wants to clear the ground of unnecessary obstacles that might hinder unbelievers from coming to Christ. Verses 19–23 enunciate this principle in terms of "all things to all people." Verses 24–27 describe the spiritual discipline involved in adapting oneself to diverse cultural and moral situations.

The main thought of verses 19–23 is essentially stated six times: to win or save "as many as possible" (v. 19), "the Jews" (v. 20a), "those under the law" (v. 20b), "those not having the law" (v. 21), "the weak" (v. 22a), and "some" (v. 22b). Freedom from human "strings" or entanglements allows Paul to give the best possible service to the widest range of people (v. 19).

The four specific examples of verses 20–22a are closely parallel. "Those under the law" probably include Gentile God-fearers and proselytes to Judaism as well as ethnic Jews. "Those not having the law" obviously refers to Gentiles apart from any Jewish influence. It is less clear who "the weak" are. In chapter 8 they referred to Christians, but here Paul seems to be talking about those who need salvation. Is he using the term as in 1:27 or Romans 5:6 for the powerless of society? Yet this meaning seems out of place in this context. Given the explicit sequence of 10:32, with which Paul concludes his discussion of idol meat ("Do not cause anyone to stumble, whether *Jews, Greeks or the church of God*"), he probably is referring to the same three groups here, in the same order. After mentioning those under the Law and those not having the Law, the "weak" most likely refer to Christians with weak consciences, that is, those with mildly legalistic scruples. Paul must therefore be using "win" in the broader sense of winning to a more mature form of Christian faith.[1]

Paul understands that with the death of Christ the age of the Law has come to an end (Gal. 3:19–4:7). Scripture itself is still relevant for followers of Jesus (2 Tim. 3:16) but only as it is interpreted in light of what Christ has done (Rom. 10:4). Nevertheless, to Jews and others under the Law, Paul at times acts as if he is still subject to all of the laws of Moses (cf. Acts 16:1–3; 21:20–26), so long as it is clear that his actions are not a proof of salvation or spiritual maturity in any way. Hence he is not really "under the law" as non-Christian Jews believe they are. With the Gentiles he does not impose his Jewish scruples or follow Jewish ritual, but he avoids becoming antinomian and is careful not to transgress God's timeless moral principles.

For Christians, God's will is now summed up as Christ's law (v. 21; cf. Gal. 6:2), which probably includes both Jesus' explicit teachings as well as the laws of the Old Testament as they now apply in light of the work of Christ.[2] Verses 22b–23 summarize the paragraph, repeating Paul's principle of flexibility one last time and noting an additional rationale for his behavior. As in verses 15–18, there is inherent blessing in fulfilling his commission and seeing the results—people saved from their sins.

Verses 24–27 have been taken as belonging more with 10:1–13 than with 9:19–23. But the theme of sharing in the gospel's blessings continues, and the analogies of strict discipline fit the single-minded passion Paul has

---

1. See esp. Kenneth V. Neller, "1 Corinthians 9:19–23: A Model for Those Who Seek to Win Souls," *RestQ* 29 (1987): 129–42.

2. Paul's theology of the Law is a highly controversial topic. Probably the most exegetically valid study, which also surveys most of the recent discussion, is Thomas R. Schreiner, *The Law and Its Fulfillment: A Pauline Theology of Law* (Grand Rapids: Baker, 1993).

articulated in verses 15–18. So Paul is probably not thinking of the Christian life in general as a race or boxing match (as he does, for example, in 2 Tim. 4:7) but is referring instead to these particular tasks of being all things to all people and voluntarily relinquishing his rights. The Corinthians would have been familiar with all of these analogies from the regular athletic training and competition that surrounded the Isthmian games the city hosted every other year.[3]

In verses 24–26a, Paul reminds the Corinthians that not all who run in a race receive the prize for first-place—a "crown" (actually a pine wreath) that "will not last" (literally, "corruptible"). He does not want any of the members of his church to fail to get their spiritual and incorruptible crowns. Because this is an analogy, we must not press the correspondence too far. Paul scarcely imagines that there will be only one faithful Christian on Judgment Day! But he is aware that some who begin the race of fulfilling their commission may not complete it and thereby be disqualified (v. 27). So too he likens his struggle to a boxer who dare not shadow box or miss too many punches if he intends to knock out his opponent (v. 26b).

Verse 27 then spells out the spiritual import of these two analogies. Verse 27a does not imply that Paul is promoting asceticism after all; rather he is now referring to the spiritual training and self-discipline that he exercises so that his ministry will not become futile. Verse 27b has been taken as Paul's concern that he might lose his salvation (a remarkable thought in view of Rom. 8:31–38) or that "the prize" refers to some kind of rewards above and beyond eternal life itself (an idea for which there is no shred of contextual support). More probably, "disqualified" (*adokimos*) should be interpreted in light of the other reference to testing in the context of Judgment Day in 1 Corinthians (3:12–15). There Paul says God will "test" (*dokimasei;* v. 13) believers' works and give out corresponding praise or censure (see the discussion above, pp. 74, 80). But neither one's salvation nor eternal status in heaven is at stake.[4]

Bridging Contexts

THE KEY TO applying verses 19–27 is to keep Paul's evangelistic principle clearly in focus. Verses 19–23 have massive implications for strategies of outreach and friendships with unbelievers,

---

3. For elaboration of the details of this paragraph, see Victor C. Pfitzner, *Paul and the Agon Motif* (Leiden: Brill, 1967), 82–98.

4. Cf. Prior, *1 Corinthians,* 164; Morris, *1 Corinthians,* 138; Judith M. GundryVolf, *Paul and Perseverance: Staying in and Falling Away* (Louisville: Westminster/John Knox, 1991), 233–47.

though they can be exaggerated. Paul is not promoting pure situation ethics. These verses form part of his larger discussion of morally neutral matters (8:1–11:1). So we dare not apply his strategy of "all things to all people" to issues of fundamental morality or immorality. Paul would never have said "to the thief I become like a thief," or "to the adulterer I become an adulterer." Conversely, he would never have stopped practicing those virtues that are always right, for example, the fruit of the spirit: love, joy, peace, patience, kindness, goodness, faithfulness, gentleness, self-control (Gal. 5:22–23).

But in the morally gray areas of life, such as eating food sacrificed to idols, and their numerous cultural equivalents in any era, Paul bends over backwards to be sensitive to the *non-Christian* mores of society around him so as not to hinder people from accepting the gospel. He does not assume that all aspects of culture are inherently evil but practices what has come to be called the contextualization of the gospel—changing the *forms* of the message precisely in order to *preserve* its content. Then Christianity stands the best chance of being understood and even accepted.[5] Sadly, Christians of many eras have instead tended to be more sensitive to the legalism of fellow church members and have too quickly censured contemporary social customs, alienating themselves from the very people they should have been trying to win to Christ.

A comparison with Galatians 2:11–21 also proves instructive. Some have found Paul's approach to Peter at Antioch hopelessly at odds with 1 Corinthians 9:19–23. How can he rebuke Peter so harshly for shrinking back from table fellowship with Gentiles in the presence of Judaizers, when here he himself admits that to the Jews he became like a Jew? A little probing, however, discloses the answer fairly quickly. At Antioch, the Judaizers were insisting that the ritual law was necessary for salvation (Acts 15:1). Giving in to their scruples at this point would have sent the wrong signal to the Gentile believers and therefore would have jeopardized the very foundation of the gospel—salvation by grace rather than works. But in Corinth the people to whom Paul is accommodating himself are neither believers nor individuals promoting works-righteousness. In fact, Paul's "evangelistic principle"—his desire that as many people be saved as possible—is the unifying motive that accounts for his diametrically opposite behavior in Antioch and Corinth. Here he accommodates himself to Corinthian pagans on

---

5. One of the most balanced and helpful studies of this process is David J. Hesselgrave and Edward Rommen, *Contextualization: Meanings, Methods, and Models* (Grand Rapids: Baker, 1989). Cf. also John R. W. Stott and Robert Coote, eds., *Down to Earth: Studies in Christianity and Culture* (London: Hodder & Stoughton, 1981).

morally neutral matters precisely in the hopes that more of them will come to faith in Christ that way.[6]

The world's religions and cultures include many such practices that at times may be intertwined with anti-Christian spirituality but that in many settings are not. These include ceremonial foods, days, festivals, dress and grooming, forms of recreation, social functions, and so on. Where participating in any one of these would inherently compromise the gospel, Christians must refrain. Where abstaining would inappropriately distance believers from their non-Christian friends and neighbors, they should participate. Overcoming non-Christian misconceptions about the nature of Christianity, misconceptions that more often than not involve legalism rather than license, forms a crucial part of the evangelistic process and makes the Christian claims of freedom and joy more credible.

As noted above, verses 24–27 are not immediately applicable to all aspects of Christianity. They appear in this context of Paul's voluntarily adopted patterns of flexibility and accommodation for the sake of gaining a greater hearing for the gospel. Still, in 11:1 he will encourage all believers to imitate him in these patterns. So we may generalize and apply these verses to the discipline of evaluating life's circumstances on a situation-by-situation basis to know when it is important to assert our freedoms and when voluntarily to relinquish our rights.

It is of course far easier and requires far less thought to adopt one of these options consistently—either pure separatism or pure indulgence. But neither of these courses of action is in the gospel's best interests. Paul's athletic metaphors of self-discipline make plain that he is calling us to the far more rigorous approach of proceeding on a case-by-case basis with morally neutral matters.

The sacrifices that athletes in training make call to mind as well that Paul's "evangelistic principle" should permeate all of our lives and order all of our priorities. From time to time we verbally share our faith and explain our moral commitments, but all of life involves modeling for a fallen world the balance of freedom and restraint that Paul articulates here. Whether at work or at play, at church or in the world, we are never "off-duty" with respect to the tasks of exhibiting the values of a balanced Christian life or of identifying with our culture for the sake of redeeming it.[7] Verse 27 closes this section

---

6. On the contrast between 1 Corinthians 9 and Galatians 2, see esp. David [sic] Carson, "Pauline Inconsistency: Reflections on 1 Corinthians 9.19–23 and Galatians 2.11–14," *Churchman* 100 (1986): 6–45.

7. For an excellent example of this approach with respect to the arts, an area often most neglected by evangelicals, see Leland Ryken, *Culture in Christian Perspective: A Door to Understanding and Enjoying the Arts* (Portland: Multnomah, 1986).

with a fitting reminder. We should never take our success in any of these areas for granted nor "retire" from diligent, self-controlled Christian living as long as God extends our days on this earth.

IN LIGHT OF verses 19–23, it is hard to justify the prevailing patterns of evangelism by formula: using identical tracts, sets of questions, or pre-packaged approaches on everyone with whom we want to share Christ. Paul's model far more closely approximates "friend-ship evangelism"—coming along side and getting to know unbelievers, valu-ing them as God's creation in his image in and of themselves, and not just as potential objects of conversion.[8] Then as we become familiar with each per-son's unique hopes and fears, we may contextualize the gospel in such a way as to speak most directly to those concerns.

Contextualization, of course, has become a buzz word among missiolo-gists and missionaries. When a person tries to reach people of different cul-tures, the need for doing more than dumping a canned condensation of gospel truths becomes both apparent and acute. Contemporary Jewish Christianity helpfully incorporates Sabbath (Saturday) worship, Christian-ized versions of the major Jewish festivals, folk music and dance, use of key Hebrew terms, and so on, in ways designed to make Christianity seem less Gentile and more true to its Jewish roots. Occasionally it lapses into legal-ism, insisting that various Jewish rituals *must* be observed, but usually this is avoided. Contemporary Palestinian and Arab Christianity increasingly rec-ognize the legitimacy of praying at times and in postures common to Islam, using houses of worship that resemble mosques in appearance, and stressing regular times of reflection and devotion over against the frenetic activity that so often characterizes Western faith and missions. Yet these Christians must be careful not to so resemble the distinctive features of Islam that they un-wittingly communicate the notion that they have converted to the faith of their Muslim neighbors![9]

For many Western Christians living and working in relatively homoge-neous secular settings, the most important lesson from verses 19–27 may re-late to their choices of companions, whom they spend significant time with, cultivating friendships and engaging in recreation or leisure-time pursuits. Many Christians barely know any non-Christians well enough to share their

---

8. Aldrich, *Evangelism*, is again helpful throughout on this model.

9. For evangelical contextualization in Muslim lands, see esp. Phil Parshall, *New Paths in Muslim Evangelism* (Grand Rapids: Baker, 1980).

faith in less than superficial fashion. Many congregations so insist on their members attending countless church functions that faithful followers have no time left for a fallen world. Better to spend less time in church and more in the world, so long as that does not reflect a lack of commitment to Christ and mature Christian living.[10]

In addition, as Michael Green says pointedly, "[Paul] would not . . . have tolerated the middle-class captivity of the church in the Western world. He would have been as active in evangelizing skinheads as undergraduates. He would have been as much at home talking of Christ in the bar or the open air as at the supper party."[11] Ministries to the outcasts and marginalized of our day—the unwed mothers, inner city and ethnic minorities, prisoners, prostitutes, homosexuals, and AIDS victims—begin to implement the vision of "all things to all people" that Paul presents so challengingly.

Verses 24–27 fall on deaf ears in an age of hedonism, entertainment, and leisure. Almost every church competes each Sunday with television, local or national sporting events, and outdoor recreation, as pastors wonder who will show up that week. Getting believers to commit to activities, particularly ministries of visitation and outreach, at times other than Sunday morning, often defies the creativity of even the most innovative of leaders.

Yet Paul compares the evangelistic lifestyle of believers to athletes who sacrifice normal pursuits for the sake of strict training and a competitive edge. In a day when fewer and fewer Christians commit themselves to long-term pastorates, career missions, lifetime service as elders or deacons, or other multi-year ministries, we need people who will make such commitments to Christ and to a particular local body of believers. The same is true of personal spiritual discipline and holy obedience to all God's commands.

10. Cf. Prior, _1 Corinthians_, 162: "Paul's versatility in seeking to win men of all backgrounds to Christ challenges us to cross the culture-gap between the Christian sub-culture of cozy meetings and holy talk and the pagan culture of our local community. The task of identification with and incarnation into our contemporary paganism, of all kinds, is one of the biggest tasks confronting the church."

11. Green, _Corinth_, 96.

1 Corinthians 10:1–22

FOR I do not want you to be ignorant of the fact, brothers, that our forefathers were all under the cloud and that they all passed through the sea. [2]They were all baptized into Moses in the cloud and in the sea. [3]They all ate the same spiritual food [4]and drank the same spiritual drink; for they drank from the spiritual rock that accompanied them, and that rock was Christ.

[5]Nevertheless, God was not pleased with most of them; their bodies were scattered over the desert. [6]Now these things occurred as examples to keep us from setting our hearts on evil things as they did. [7]Do not be idolaters, as some of them were; as it is written: "The people sat down to eat and drink and got up to indulge in pagan revelry." [8]We should not commit sexual immorality, as some of them did—and in one day twenty-three thousand of them died. [9]We should not test the Lord, as some of them did—and were killed by snakes. [10]And do not grumble, as some of them did—and were killed by the destroying angel.

[11]These things happened to them as examples and were written down as warnings for us, on whom the fulfillment of the ages has come. [12]So, if you think you are standing firm, be careful that you don't fall! [13]No temptation has seized you except what is common to man. And God is faithful; he will not let you be tempted beyond what you can bear. But when you are tempted, he will also provide a way out so that you can stand up under it.

[14]Therefore, my dear friends, flee from idolatry. [15]I speak to sensible people; judge for yourselves what I say. [16]Is not the cup of thanksgiving for which we give thanks a participation in the blood of Christ? And is not the bread that we break a participation in the body of Christ? [17]Because there is one loaf, we, who are many, are one body, for we all partake of the one loaf.

[18]Consider the people of Israel: Do not those who eat the sacrifices participate in the altar? [19]Do I mean then that a sacrifice offered to an idol is anything, or that an idol is anything? [20]No, but the sacrifices of pagans are offered to demons, not

to God, and I do not want you to be participants with demons. ²¹You cannot drink the cup of the Lord and the cup of demons too; you cannot have a part in both the Lord's table and the table of demons. ²²Are we trying to arouse the Lord's jealousy? Are we stronger than he?

THE DANGER OF failing to exercise strict self-control in the Christian life (9:24–27) is now illustrated. First Corinthians 10:1–13 uses numerous examples of the sins of the Israelites during their wilderness wanderings to warn against Corinthian participation in idolatrous idol feasts (10:14–22). The parallels prove particularly intriguing, not least because the Israelites demanded *meat* from Moses (Exod. 16:3; Num. 11:4). Verses 1–5 describe four privileges the Israelites received which did not guarantee subsequent blessings: (a) guidance by God in the cloud, (b) crossing the Red Sea, (c) eating manna and quail in the desert, and (d) supernaturally provided water. Verses 7–10 recall four ways in which many of those same Israelites proved faithless and suffered for their sins: idolatry, immorality, testing the Lord, and grumbling. Verses 6 and 11 punctuate these two sections with parallel reminders that the Israelites' experience should caution the Corinthians against behaving similarly. Verses 12–13 close off this section by balancing a summary warning (v. 12) with a promise that history need not repeat itself (v. 13).

In verse 1, Paul casts perhaps another subtle aspersion at the Corinthians' claims to *gnosis* (knowledge) by suggesting that they may in fact be "ignorant" after all. To correct this oversight, he reminds them of the behavior of their spiritual predecessors. After Israel departed from Egypt, God led them with a cloud by day and a pillar of fire by night (Ex. 13:21–22). He parted the waters of the Red Sea, enabling the people to walk across on dry ground (14:22–29). The association of water with both cloud and sea prompts Paul to conceive of this deliverance as a kind of baptism "into Moses" (v. 2). Obviously the Israelites were not immersed in literal water; baptism here suggests identification with and allegiance to the leader of a spiritual community. Paul uses the preposition "into" to match the idea of baptism "into Christ" (Gal. 3:27; Rom. 6:3), a reminder of the fact that both "baptisms" initiated people into the fellowship of a body of believers.

The Israelites experienced further supernatural blessing when God gave them manna from heaven to eat (e.g., Ex. 16:4, 35) and water from a cleft rock to drink (Ex. 17:6; Num. 20:11) on occasions in which they otherwise would have died from hunger and thirst. From a Christian perspective, Paul recognizes Christ as the pre-existent Son of God, active with God the Father in creation and redemption, and hence the agent of both physical and spiritual nourishment for his people in the desert (v. 4b).[1] Yet none of these miracles guaranteed that the children of Israel would reach the Promised Land. In fact, of the adults only Joshua and Caleb ever did. Disobedience caused people to forfeit the promise and die in the wilderness (v. 5).

In verse 6 Paul exhorts the Corinthians to learn from this example. "To keep us from setting our hearts on evil things" reads literally "to keep us from lusting after evil." The four additional examples of verses 7–10 illustrate more specific forms of this improper lust. First, Paul cites Exodus 32:6, part of the story of the Israelites' idolatrous worship of the golden calf while Moses was receiving the Law on Mt. Sinai (v. 7). Second, he refers to the episode in Numbers 25:1–9, in which Israelite men engaged in immoral sexual activity with Moabite women (v. 8).[2] Third, he alludes to Numbers 21:4–9, when the people complained against Moses and God about the hardships of the desert (v. 9).[3] Fourth, he recalls the characteristic grumblings and murmurings of the people, most notably in Numbers 16:41–50, when their opposition to God's judgment of Korah's rebellion led to an additional 14,700 deaths (v. 10). But Numbers 14:26–35 may also be in view, because there the grumbling leads to the prediction of the death of almost everyone over the age of twenty during the wilderness wanderings. No "destroying angel" is mentioned in either passage, but Paul's inference is natural, given the language of Exodus 12:23 in which God struck down the firstborn of the Egyptians.[4]

---

1. Because God provided water from the rock both near the beginning and near the end of the Israelites' wanderings, Jewish traditions developed that streams of water or a well of water actually followed God's people during their travels. It is a short jump from this belief to the concept of a traveling rock that can provide streams of water (E. Earle Ellis, *Prophecy and Hermeneutic* [Tübingen: Mohr, 1978], 209–12). But more likely, Paul is contrasting these legends with his belief "that Christ accompanied his people as a spiritual source of refreshment throughout this period" (Bruce, *1 and 2 Corinthians*, 91).

2. Numbers 25:9 refers to 24,000 dying; Paul to 23,000. Morris, *1 Corinthians*, 141, explains: "Both are obviously round numbers, and in addition Paul may be making some allowance for those slain by the judges (Nu. 25:5)."

3. Significant early manuscripts read, "We should not test *Christ*, as some of them did." If this reading is accepted as the original (so, e.g., NRSV), then we have another example like verse 4 of Paul seeing Christ as present in God's activity in Old Tesrtament times.

4. For a discussion of the possibility that all of the illustrations in verses 6–10 refer to the role of idolatry in the Israelites' rebellion, corresponding to the danger of Corinthian participation in idol feasts, see Wayne A. Meeks, "'And Rose Up to Play': Midrash and Paraenesis in 1 Corinthians 10:1–22," *JSNT* 16 (1982): 64–78.

Verse 11 repeats the warning of verse 6, all the more crucial since Christians live in the climactic era of human history for which all previous ages were preparing.

Verse 12 summarizes the significance of these warnings for the Corinthians—even those who think they stand securely should take care, like Paul in 9:27, lest they fall and be disqualified. After all, the pagan temple feasts in Corinth involved similar idolatry, sexual sin, and trying God's patience. And the Corinthian quarrels could certainly qualify as grumbling against one another. Nevertheless, verses 1–12 are all balanced by the marvelous promise of verse 13. The circumstances that tempt us to sin are never qualitatively different from those which God's people of every era have experienced, and we never have to give in to them. There is always an escape-hatch, which is defined as a way to persevere without sinning in whatever difficult situation we find ourselves.[5]

Verses 14–22 now return explicitly to the topic of idol meat in Corinth, with which chapter 8 began. Although the food itself is morally neutral, Paul does make one absolute prohibition: eating it in the context of explicitly pagan worship services is always wrong. In such cases eating is idolatry (v. 14). Sexual immorality often accompanied such worship, making the parallel with verse 7 even clearer. Paul appeals to the Corinthian Christians to come to the same conclusion. Notwithstanding their divisions, he trusts that common sense will win out in this instance (v. 15).

To cement his position, Paul offers two further analogies, from the sacred meals of Christianity (vv. 16–17) and Judaism (v. 18). Partaking of the elements of the Lord's Supper—the bread and the wine—involves a "participation" (Gk. *koinonia*—"fellowship") with the risen Lord and an appropriation of the benefits of his shed blood and broken body. "Participation" in verses 15–16 includes both communion with fellow believers and partnership in Christ. The common loaf reminds the Corinthians of their unity in Christ, which should also separate them from false religion. So too in ancient Judaism, those who ate sacrificial meat in the temple communed with Yahweh and appropriated the temporary forgiveness associated with those animal sacrifices.[6]

---

5. A helpful philosophical study of the implications of this verse for the Calvinist-Arminian dispute is David M. Ciocchi, "Understanding Our Ability to Endure Temptation: A Theological Watershed," *JETS* 35 (1992): 463–79. He also gives a clear summary of the verse's meaning: "The faithfulness of God guarantees that no superhuman temptation will enter the life of any believer and that each believer's temptations will be commensurate with his own ability to endure them" (p. 471).

6. On the meaning of verses 16–18 in this context, see esp. W. A. Sebothoma, "Κοινωνία in 1 Corinthians 10:16," *Neot* 24 (1990): 63–69.

The application to religious temple feasts in Corinth follows naturally (vv. 19–22). Pagans too commune with the spiritual beings they worship, in ways that make it ghastly to think of Christians participating. In drawing this parallel, Paul anticipates an objection. He is not now contradicting his earlier claims that idols have no objective, spiritual existence (8:4). But he knows from the Law that demons—fallen angels—are the true objects of pagan ritual, however unwittingly they may be worshiped (cf. Deut. 32:17). As with the Old Testament examples previously cited, Christian involvement in this kind of idolatry risks incurring God's severe judgment.[7]

Bridging Contexts

FIRST CORINTHIANS 10:1–22 is the passage from which Protestants derive the idea that baptism and the Lord's Supper are the two distinctive "sacraments" or "ordinances" of Christian worship. Incidental evidence appears for the corporate meaning and practice of these two rites. Baptism is fundamentally an initiatory rite into a covenant *community*, based on one's allegiance to Christ.[8] Early Christians followed Jesus' practices of breaking pieces of bread off a common loaf and passing around a common cup to stress the corporate significance of Communion as well, though no text anywhere commands that it must always be so. But in general, 10:1–22 is not about the sacraments or ordinances at all. Paul is not arguing from Jewish and pagan practices to draw conclusions about these Christian rituals, but from the aspect of *fellowship* inherent in the Christian and Jewish rites to demonstrate the communion with demons that takes place in the pagan idol feasts.[9]

Doctrinal conclusions about the significance of the Lord's Supper, therefore, must be derived from 11:17–34 or from the three texts in the Synoptic Gospels that describe Jesus' Last Supper (Matt. 26:17–30; Mark 14:12–26; and Luke 22:7–38). What probably can be inferred from verses

---

7. Brian S. Rosner, "'Stronger than He?' The Strength of 1 Corinthians 10:22b," *TynB* 43 (1992): 171–79, notes that both Numbers 14:13–19 and Deuteronomy 32:36–38 allude to God's and Israel's respective strengths. And given that these texts lie behind Paul's earlier examples, his final rhetorical question in verse 22 follows naturally. Do we think we are stronger than God, and can try his patience with impunity? Surely not!

8. See esp. William B. Badke, "Baptised into Moses—Baptised into Christ: A Study in Doctrinal Development," *EvQ* 60 (1988): 23–29.

9. Hence, traditional Roman Catholic inferences about the need to pray a blessing over the physical cup of wine or about the Eucharist as an ongoing sacrifice of Christ's body and blood entirely invert the direction of Paul's reasoning (and flounder exegetically on other grounds).

1–22 here is something of the nature of the Corinthians' misguided beliefs about the Lord's Supper and baptism. Most likely, the "strong" Christians among them maintained that participation in these rituals guaranteed them immunity from spiritual danger so that they could freely partake in idol feasts. Quite the opposite, Paul declares, by his elaborate Old Testament analogies: "Participation in spectacular spiritual experiences does not relieve the people of God from ethical responsibility."[10]

Nor does it guarantee freedom from grave moral failure and God's judgment. The meaning of disqualification in 9:27 should probably determine the nature of falling in verse 12.[11] There it seemed unlikely that Paul feared loss of salvation. The Old Testament examples in verses 1–11 confirm this suspicion. No passage of Scripture ever teaches that Joshua and Caleb were the only Israelites for forty years who were ever "saved," spiritually speaking.

Rather, physical death and loss of blessing in this life are consistently in view. So too chapter 11 will describe how some Corinthians have become sick or have died from profaning the Lord's Supper (v. 30), without necessarily implying they were damned. At the same time, 3:16–17 reminds us that Paul does not take for granted that everyone in his church is necessarily saved, so some who fall under God's temporal judgment may incur his eternal wrath as well.

Verses 6 and 11 point to one of the key functions of Old Testament narrative (cf. Rom. 15:14). Although "character studies" can be abused by squeezing too much doctrine out of minor actions and incidental details, one of the important purposes of all of the stories of the Bible is to illustrate desirable and undesirable behavior. Most of the principal characters in major narratives can be classified in literary terms as heroic or tragic—examples to be imitated or to be avoided.[12] Because the word translated "example" in these two verses could also mean "type," some have understood Paul to be employing a kind of typology that sees Old Testament events as deliberately designed to foreshadow corresponding New Testament events. But that would imply a kind of fatalism that the Corinthians *had* to fall into these same errors, whereas verse 13 specifically promises them that they need not. So "exemplary warnings" remains a better way to describe the analogies.

Readers have long puzzled over Paul's meaning in verse 4. Is he using some kind of Jewish hermeneutic that we do not readily accept? Does he be-

---

10. Richard B. Hays, *Echoes of Scripture in the Epistles of Paul* (New Haven: Yale, 1989), 91.

11. Robertson and Plummer, *First Corinthians*, 208.

12. Particularly helpful in this respect are the numerous works of Leland Ryken, not least of which is one of his earliest: *The Literature of the Bible* (Grand Rapids: Zondervan, 1974), 45–78, 95–106.

lieve extracanonical legendary material? In light of the uncertainty, it is best to err on the side of caution. New Testament writers regularly use the Old Testament in "creative ways." One of the most common is to see Christ at work where the Old Testament speaks only of God. But once one believes that Christ formed part of the Godhead from all eternity past, this equation becomes natural, particularly in contexts where God provides salvation for his people, which was precisely the heart of Jesus' first-century mission. Paul himself regularly responds to and revises common Jewish interpretive methods and traditions. Here he may well be turning some story of a literal "traveling rock" (or stream or well) into an affirmation of the spiritual power behind God's miraculous provision.[13]

Verse 7 is particularly well known from its renderings in the KJV, "sat down to eat and drink and rose up to play," and in the Living Bible, where instead of "play" we find "dance." The NIV has better captured the sense: "indulge in pagan revelry." Neither playing nor dancing is inherently immoral, anymore than eating or drinking is, but all are wrong in the context of idolatrous worship services.

Though short compared to the more immediately needed warnings of verses 1–12, verse 13 provides a crucial balance to the previous verses, especially for those who fear they will be unfaithful during tough times. Given the severity and general nature of the preceding examples, this verse too should be applied universally. No matter how unique our temptations seem externally, we face the same spiritual struggles God's people have endured throughout history. God won't give us anything we can't handle, so long as we rely on his strength, yielding ourselves to the power of his indwelling Holy Spirit, rather than trying to resist temptation on our own.

Tolerance to temptation varies widely from one person to the next. Clearly we can also choose to reject the "way out" and yield to temptation, but it is precisely that freedom which makes us accountable before God when we do sin. And it is important to stress that the way out is not necessarily the removal of the difficult circumstances but the ability to "stand up under" them. Other key theological truths are reflected here as well. God tempts no one (James 1:13), but he does allow trials and temptations (Luke 4:1) in order to help us to mature (James 1:2–4), even as he encourages us to pray for the strength not to give in and sin (Matt. 6:13).

---

13. For an overview of New Testament uses of the Old Testament, with evaluative remarks and suggestions for how believers today can or cannot treat the Old Testament similarly, see William W. Klein, Robert L. Hubbard, Jr., and Craig L. Blomberg, *Introduction to Biblical Interpretation* (Dallas: Word, 1993), 120–32.

In view of verses 1–13, verses 14–22 then express the one central truth that Christian and pagan worship are fundamentally incompatible with each other because of the diametrically opposite spiritual beings worshiped in each setting. "Strong" Christians who defiantly ignore this truth risk God's harsh punishment. Weaker believers who feel unable to resist the lure of the pagan can count on God to help them overcome temptation. The world of demons is best known in the New Testament from Jesus' exorcisms of demon-possessed individuals. Yet here is a second and perhaps more characteristic example of demonic influence, which is the true spiritual force behind all anti-Christian religions (cf. 2 Cor. 4:4, in which Satan as "the god of this world" has blinded the hearts of all unbelievers).

FIRST CORINTHIANS 10:2 IS one of the most crucial verses in Scripture to combat the persistent heresy of baptismal regeneration; that is, the view that baptism into a religious community is a requirement of or guarantees salvation. In evangelical circles, this view persists in certain branches of the Church of Christ and various independent Baptist groups. In mainline Roman Catholic, Episcopal, and Lutheran churches, official dogma usually maintains that subsequent confirmation is necessary to make one's baptism as an infant effective, but less precise language in such circles often equates "baptized" with "Christian."

Questions about the salvation of children too young to be confirmed often hinge on whether or not they have been baptized. And confirmation itself can at times become a meaningless ritual that adolescents are expected to go through to please their parents, but without genuinely experiencing saving faith. In baptistic circles, some churches offer prebaptismal instruction classes for children in ways that put subtle pressure on them to go ahead with the rite whether or not they are ready to be serious about professions of faith. Even baby dedications have sometimes arisen as a kind of baptist alternative to infant baptism to placate family members who think some kind of ceremony is what counts the most. Care must be exercised in each branch of the church to insure that baptism or confirmation is undertaken voluntarily as a public affirmation of genuine, saving faith in Christ, which those undergoing the rite have sincerely professed.[14]

---

14. One of the most bizarre practices, reflecting a serious misunderstanding of the ritual, is the baptism of dead bodies in funeral homes as a way of placating the anxieties of relatives. At best, this leaves those requesting the procedure thoroughly misled about the meaning of baptism; at worst, it gives them false hopes that they or others can go to heaven without having trusted in Christ.

The Lord's Supper has also come to be viewed as quasi-magical in numerous Christian traditions, so that members of liturgical churches often stress the need to partake frequently, especially as one is dying, to appropriate forgiveness for the most recent round of sins in one's life.

Nominalism in Christianity can aptly be characterized by the priority of church over Christ, of ritual over a relationship with the living Jesus. Millions of Americans weekly attend worship services in buildings with the label *Christian* attached to them, thinking that in so doing they are or are becoming right with God, without ever having been truly born again. Some share a spirituality more akin to paganism, particularly in the New Age movement and in the fascination with the afterlife, that is devoid of anything like the biblical doctrine of hell.

Against all of these practices, 1 Corinthians 10:1–22 speaks worlds. What counts are inward spiritual realities. External rituals or even experiences of the supernatural prove no guarantee either of salvation or of Christian maturity (vv. 3–5). Compare the growing number of near-death or out-of-the-body experiences "demonstrating" the pleasant nature of the world to come irrespective of one's decisions in this life.[15]

Our discussion of 5:10–11 has already focused on numerous contemporary idolatries that are similar to the Old Testament examples in verses 7–10 here. These practices reject God's unique revelation to humanity in favor of sexually oriented substitutes. And, as with the Israelites worshipping the golden calf, they continue to revolve around materialism and tenets of false religion.

Contemporary idolatries infiltrate the church as well as the world, as large numbers of Christians buy into each of the latest secular fads for church growth, fund-raising, marketing, and so on. Polls of Americans, including American Christians, have shown that the two things we long for the most are more money and better bodies, precisely what the counterfeit "health-wealth" gospel claims to be able to deliver.[16] If only more people could pray with the apostle John for friends' physical health to match their spiritual health, knowing that the latter has a higher priority in their lives (3 John 2).

We can scarcely read verse 12 without thinking of the fallen leaders that dot the Christian landscape today, particularly as a result of sexual sin. But Paul's warning extends far more broadly. A smug complacency and ethno-

---

15. One thinks esp. of the experiences first discussed in Elisabeth Kübler-Ross, *On Death and Dying* (New York: Macmillan, 1969), a work that in turn spawned an entire discipline of pseudo-scientific literature of a similar genre.

16. James Patterson and Peter Kim, *The Day America Told the Truth* (New York: Prentice Hall, 1991), 53.

centric arrogance tends to characterize middle-class Western Christianity. Yet urban poor and Third-World congregations at times exhibit much deeper loyalty and devotion to Christ, even if their external circumstances make them more impoverished. We must guard against the formula-mentality to sanctification, as if filling in the blanks in a booklet of Bible studies on "Ten Basic Steps to Christian Maturity" will somehow enable us to arrive quickly at our spiritual destination.

Yet lest we become too cynical, verse 13 should offer great hope for those painfully aware of their fragile spiritual status. We live in an age with unparalleled developments of technology, unprecedented amounts of information, new physical and emotional diseases, natural disasters, and human warfare. When we realize that these factors cause suffering on a scale never before known in human history, it is reassuring to know that the temptations believers face are not new. The external circumstances may differ, but the spiritual dynamics remain unchanged. The human propensity to see "my problem" as different or worse than what anyone else has experienced is decisively debunked. The contemporary trend to blame the way I am on God, parents, society, or the devil, rather than acknowledging that our own sinful natures are the most direct causes of our disobedience (James 1:14), also runs counter to this text.

We never have to give in to temptation; no one "makes" us sin. Certain factors may generate greater temptations for some individuals than for others, as with the exponential increase in dysfunctional families in our day, but ultimately we are accountable for our own free choices. And for believers, one of those choices remains to accept God's escape-hatch from sin. Our culture would rewrite the end of verse 13 so that it said, "But when you are tempted, he will also provide a way out so that you don't have to stand up under it any longer," but that of course is the opposite of what God actually inspired Paul to write.

It is ironic too that the very meal intended to demonstrate the unity of believers (vv. 16–17) has become one of the most divisive ceremonies of the Christian church throughout its history.[17] The irony increases when we recognize that even when congregations can agree to put aside doctrinal differences so fundamental that unbelievers (though church members) can partake of the Lord's Supper, still genuine Christians in other denominations may be excluded (cf. further, below, pp. 236–39).

If the Lord's table symbolizes and promotes fellowship and unity with the risen Christ, then it should be open to *all* believers but to believers *only*.

---

17. See esp. David Bridge and David Phypers, *Communion: The Meal That Unites?* (Wheaton: Harold Shaw, 1983).

Where hygiene permits, the practice of sharing a common loaf and common cup should probably be preserved as an important symbol of the unity the church can offer, especially in our fractured, compartmentalized, individualistic society. Where health concerns make this risky, having all participants partake simultaneously can preserve some of the symbolism. Least helpful of all are services in which each person eats and drinks separately, in splendid isolation, at best communing solely with God, and with no thought for fellow-Christians present.

Paul's absolute prohibition in verses 19–22 against that which is inherently idolatrous finds contemporary analogies for virtually every one of the otherwise neutral practices discussed under chapter 8 (see above, pp. 167–71). Of course, overtly pagan rituals remain off-limits to believers, as do other practices that are inherently immoral, illegal, or destructive.

Yet even that which is amoral can often give way to the immoral. Indeed those links usually account for why even morally neutral practices were first forbidden. Drinking can turn into drunkenness, working long hours can lead to workaholism, association with gang members can tend to make one join in their criminal activities or be victimized by them, respect for one's parents can border on ancestor worship, excessive patriotism can produce idolatry of the state, watching television can displace more meaningful activities, a desire for material goods can lead to materialism, taking medication can result in addiction, and on and on. Situation ethics must not prevail at these points. At the same time, we must keep the emphases of 8:1–13 and 10:23–11:1 close at hand, so that the legalism that banned all drinking, movies, card games, and so on, does not return.

The syncretism reflected in verse 21 finds parallels in numerous contemporary contexts. Some entire faiths have been spawned, most notably the Ba'hai, by trying to combine together the "best" of all the world's ideologies. More pervasive is the belief that all or most religions contain at least some salvific truth, in other words, that it is possible to know the true God of the universe and experience eternity with him through many different religious paths.[18] Both of these approaches fail to observe that fundamentally incompatible or logically contradictory claims lay at the very foundation of most any two major world religions when they are compared side-by-side. If the Qu'ran is a true revelation from God, then the transmission of the New Testament has been so corrupted that Jesus has been transformed from a prophet into the Son of God and Allah from an indivisible oneness into a

---

18. The classic contemporary exposition of this perspective is John Hick and Paul Knitter, eds., *The Myth of Christian Uniqueness: Toward a Pluralistic Theology of Religions* (Maryknoll, N.Y.: Orbis, 1987).

Trinity. If Hinduism or Buddhism is true, then perfect bliss involves dissolution into nothingness rather than personal, conscious existence for eternity. To hold a coherent worldview, one must choose among conflicting claims.

Verses 14–22 also challenge the popular view in modern culture that we must recover the devalued spiritualities of ancient paganism—Native American religions, goddess worship, earth worship, white witchcraft, and the like. Though it would be politically incorrect, were Paul alive today he would say that these spiritualities had been properly devalued. Whereas we admire ancient civilizations for their culture and cultural artifacts (large percentages of which were overtly religious) and devote countless museums and exhibitions to honor them, Paul went to Athens and grieved over the monuments to false gods he saw everywhere (Acts 17:16). While seeking points of common ground, he clearly felt responsible to move the Athenians far beyond their polytheistic beliefs into a knowledge of the one true and living God uniquely revealed in Jesus Christ (vv. 21–33).[19]

---

19. A responsible evangelical discussion of this problem appears in Terry Muck, *Alien Gods on American Turf* (Wheaton: Victor, 1990), esp. pp. 89–114.

1 Corinthians 10:23–11:1

"EVERYTHING IS PERMISSIBLE"—but not everything is beneficial. "Everything is permissible"—but not everything is constructive. ²⁴Nobody should seek his own good, but the good of others.

²⁵Eat anything sold in the meat market without raising questions of conscience, ²⁶for, "The earth is the Lord's, and everything in it."

²⁷If some unbeliever invites you to a meal and you want to go, eat whatever is put before you without raising questions of conscience. ²⁸But if anyone says to you, "This has been offered in sacrifice," then do not eat it, both for the sake of the man who told you and for conscience' sake—²⁹the other man's conscience, I mean, not yours. For why should my freedom be judged by another's conscience? ³⁰If I take part in the meal with thankfulness, why am I denounced because of something I thank God for?

³¹So whether you eat or drink or whatever you do, do it all for the glory of God. ³²Do not cause anyone to stumble, whether Jews, Greeks or the church of God—³³even as I try to please everybody in every way. For I am not seeking my own good but the good of many, so that they may be saved. ¹¹:¹Follow my example, as I follow the example of Christ.

Original Meaning

AT LAST PAUL RETURNS to where he began this discussion of idol meat. Apart from the unique instance of eating during pagan worship, believers have the freedom to partake so long as it is for God's glory and others' well-being. Verse 23 restates 6:12 almost verbatim ("Everything is permissible . . ."), except that here Paul substitutes "but not everything is *constructive*" at the end. Now he is thinking more of the corporate than of the individual effects of exercising freedom in Christ. Still, his "Yes, but" approach to the Corinthian slogans remains unchanged. Verse 24 amplifies the qualification. Christians are free to serve others above self. Verses 25–30 apply Paul's principles to the two specific contexts of purchasing and consuming meat sold in the Corinthian marketplace (vv. 25–26) and eating it in a friends' home (vv. 27–30). In each instance, the likelihood was great that the meat would have been sacrificed to idols.

In the case of marketplace food, Paul's command is unqualified: feel free to buy it and eat it. Food and drink are part of God's good creation (Ps. 24:1) and have been given to his people to be enjoyed (vv. 25–26). No food is unclean in itself (cf. Rom. 14:14). In the case of a friend's home, even that of an unbeliever not likely to have any scruples about what is eaten, Paul is only slightly less enthusiastic. His general affirmation is equally sweeping—go if you like, eat, and don't ask any questions (v. 27). Only if someone else present makes an issue of the food having been sacrificed to idols should abstention even be considered (v. 28a). Presumably this person is a "weaker" fellow-Christian (recall 8:7), since unbelievers would not likely have any scruples about eating idol meat.[1] In this situation, one might decide to refrain so as not to risk leading the other person into sin or confusing his or her conscience (vv. 28b–29a).

Verses 28–29a should probably be punctuated as a parenthesis, as in the old RSV. Verses 29–30 then resume Paul's primary line of thought. He defends his freedom to partake of food for which he is grateful to God and not to be paranoid about what the unspoken thoughts of others present might be.[2]

First Corinthians 10:31–11:1 restates the twin principles of freedom and restraint one last time, now in the context of God's glory—that which conforms to his standards and priorities (v. 31). Paul tries to lead as few into sin as possible, both outside and inside the church, but his most basic underlying motive is the salvation of as many as possible (vv. 32–33; recall 9:19–23). And he has included this somewhat lengthy discussion of his actions and motives precisely so that the Corinthians might imitate him carefully, at least to the extent that he successfully models Christ-like behavior (11:1).

Bridging Contexts

MOST OF THE PRINCIPLES behind 10:23–11:1 have been discussed under chapter 8. Clearly the two fundamental principles remain unaltered. Christians have essential freedom in morally neutral matters, but their behavior must be tempered with concern for

---

1. Kistemaker, *First Corinthians*, 355, protests: "But would a Christian first inquire about the food and then stay for dinner? Of course not." Unfortunately, it is not at all that clear cut. It is quite conceivable that such a Christian might well stay for dinner but simply refrain from eating the offending item on the menu.

2. For this interpretation of the interrelatedness of the three main parts of verses 25–30 (vv. 25–27, 28–29a, 29b–30), see Bruce, *1 and 2 Corinthians*, 99–100. For a survey of approaches to the structure of this paragraph, see Duane F. Watson, "1 Corinthians 10:23–11:1 in the Light of Greco-Roman Rhetoric: The Role of Rhetorical Questions," *JBL* 108 (1989): 301–18. Probably the most common solution, which Watson defends with a

others. The twin emphases of the summary paragraph (10:31–11:1) call to mind Jesus' twofold summary of the Law: love God with all your heart and your neighbor as yourself (Matt. 22:37–40). Only here Paul phrases it in terms of giving God the glory and trying to please fellow human beings. As before, the permission implied in verses 25–26 may not be generalized to inherently immoral or destructive actions.

The major new item in this section is Paul's tipping of the scales in verses 25–30 in favor of freedom over abstinence.[3] God has created the material world for human enjoyment, though we must not abuse it (Gen. 1:28). All creation remains under his sovereignty, with potentially useful purposes for believers (v. 26). Above all else, Paul wants as many men and women as possible to come to a saving knowledge of the Lord Jesus (v. 33b). There are stumbling-blocks in the gospel message that dare not be removed, most centrally the cross of Christ (1:18–2:5). But the path must be cleared of all unnecessary obstacles, and a legalistic lifestyle that depicts Christianity as submission to a long list of dos and don'ts has been one of the major hindrances to faith for unbelievers in most periods of church history.

Ideally, Paul will never offend anyone (v. 33a), but Abraham Lincoln would correctly remark centuries later that "you can't please all of the people all of the time."[4] So if someone will be offended no matter what Paul does, he would rather it be a fellow Christian, already secure in his or her Savior's hand, than an unbeliever who might turn away from Christ for entirely the wrong reasons. This preference is completely consistent with Paul's tirades elsewhere against more severe forms of legalism (Gal. 2; Phil. 3) and with the lifestyle of Jesus himself, who consistently mingled with "tax-collectors and sinners" in ways that angered the conservative religious establishment.

First Corinthians 11:1 also offers a challenging model, which we addressed in connection with 4:16. It is as if Paul says, "Do you want to know what it means to live a consistent Christian life, properly balancing freedom

---

new twist, is that verses 29–30 reflect another Corinthian slogan to which verses 31–33 then indirectly respond. But the connections are meager at best. Watson rejects the parenthetical view I favor because he thinks Paul's concern for the "weak" seems stronger in 8:13; 9:19–23 and 10:24. But, as I argue below, Paul is in fact here tipping the scales in favor of freedom over restraint, precisely because of its evangelistic potential in mixed companies of believers and unbelievers.

3. On this theme in Paul's writings more generally, see esp. Peter Richardson, *Paul's Ethic of Freedom* (Philadelphia: Westminster, 1979).

4. What is more, Paul's principle here must not be confused with his denial in Gal. 1:10 of trying to please people. There "pleasing men" is evil because "it is done with a view to currying favour with them, or so as to avoid persecution;" here it is good because "it is done so as to lead them to the faith" (Barrett, *First Corinthians*, 245).

and restraint? Then watch me, follow me, and live with me. I may not be perfect, but I try to imitate the selfless life Christ lived, and to the extent that I succeed, you should do the same." Little wonder that ancient Christian behavior often stood out among the pagans of the day. Early believers often drew from 10:32 the concept that in Christ one was no longer Jewish or Gentile but a member of a "third race," qualitatively distinct from the other two.

AGAIN I WOULD refer readers to the applications of chapter 8. But a little more can be said here. Verse 25 contains implications for ecology and stewardship of the environment that go beyond the original issue of acceptable food to eat. As with biblical teaching on the subject more generally, Paul recognizes that the created world is categorically distinct from humanity, which alone was fashioned in God's image. So we have the right and the responsibility to use creation for good purposes (Gen. 1:28). Mandating vegetarianism or elevating animal rights to the level of human rights blurs this distinction between humanity and the rest of creation, but the more common modern malady of a cavalier rape of the environment proves even more heinous in God's eyes.[5]

More central to this section is Paul's preference for freedom over restraint when commending the gospel to unbelievers. Non-Christian stereotypes of conservative Christianity consistently characterize us as dour, legalistic joy-killers. And at least part of this caricature is deserved. Evangelicals often do argue over where to draw the boundaries in morally gray areas. Fee correctly observes that "conservatives on these issues simply fail to reckon with how 'liberal' Paul's own view really is. Hence Paul is seldom heard for the sake of traditional regulations."[6]

Pleasant exceptions to this trend often occur in creative church youth groups and parachurch campus ministries that defy the stereotype, organize lots of fun activities, usually attract good crowds, bring many to genuine faith, and weather the criticisms of the "professional weaker brothers" in their communities. Unfortunately, there are not as many models of similar exuberance, creativity, and freedom among older adults either inside or outside the church. Service projects and "target group ministries"[7] may prove effec-

---

5. A generally balanced perspective on Christian ecological responsibilities may be found in Richard D. Land and Louis Moore, eds., *The Earth is the Lord's: Christians and the Environment* (Nashville: Broadman, 1992).

6. Fee, *First Corinthians*, 491.

7. See Frank R. Tillapaugh, *The Church Unleashed* (Ventura: Regal, 1982).

tive alternate approaches to reaching adults from a wide variety of walks of life. Our outreach can be even more effective if we adopt attitudes and lifestyles that are quicker to affirm the truth and goodness that appear in unbelievers' lives than to condemn their sins.[8]

Once again, modeling at all levels is clearly needed. Happily, some Christians are bucking the prevailing trends of individualism and isolationism. There are families who open their homes to guests or renters, leaders who take younger Christians along with them in their ministry, teachers and counselors who make generous amounts of time available for their students and clients during off-hours, and business people who practice ethical behavior in the workplace and at home. But such people remain in a minority. Many more mentors and spiritual directors are needed throughout the Christian world.[9]

---

8. For an excellent, popular exposition of the exuberance of Christian freedom, with suggestions for implementing the ideas suggested here, see Charles R. Swindoll, *The Grace Awakening* (Dallas: Word, 1990).

9. Cf. further Paul D. Stanley and J. Robert Clinton, *Connecting: The Mentoring Relationships You Need to Succeed in Life* (Colorado Springs: NavPress, 1992); Ron C. Davis with James D. Denney, *Mentoring: The Strategy of the Master* (Nashville: Thomas Nelson, 1991).

1 Corinthians 11:2–16

I PRAISE YOU for remembering me in everything and for holding to the teachings, just as I passed them on to you.

³Now I want you to realize that the head of every man is Christ, and the head of the woman is man, and the head of Christ is God. ⁴Every man who prays or prophesies with his head covered dishonors his head. ⁵And every woman who prays or prophesies with her head uncovered dishonors her head—it is just as though her head were shaved. ⁶If a woman does not cover her head, she should have her hair cut off; and if it is a disgrace for a woman to have her hair cut or shaved off, she should cover her head. ⁷A man ought not to cover his head, since he is the image and glory of God; but the woman is the glory of man. ⁸For man did not come from woman, but woman from man; ⁹neither was man created for woman, but woman for man. ¹⁰For this reason, and because of the angels, the woman ought to have a sign of authority on her head.

¹¹In the Lord, however, woman is not independent of man, nor is man independent of woman. ¹²For as woman came from man, so also man is born of woman. But everything comes from God. ¹³Judge for yourselves: Is it proper for a woman to pray to God with her head uncovered? ¹⁴Does not the very nature of things teach you that if a man has long hair, it is a disgrace to him, ¹⁵but that if a woman has long hair, it is her glory? For long hair is given to her as a covering. ¹⁶If anyone wants to be contentious about this, we have no other practice—nor do the churches of God.

THE NEXT THREE TOPICS Paul addresses all deal with behavior in worship. They include what men and women should or should not wear on their heads (11:2–16), proper conduct during the Lord's Supper (11:17–34), and the use and abuse of spiritual gifts (chaps. 12–14). Only the last of these is introduced with the "now about" phrase that suggests a direct reply to an item in the letter from Corinth. Yet 11:2 seems abrupt and awkwardly placed unless it reflects Paul's response to some affirmation by the Corinthians that they were "remembering [Paul] in everything and holding to [his] teachings" (literally, "traditions"). It may well be that they went on to specify faithfulness to his teaching on male and female equality (cf. Gal. 3:28) and to the tradition of regularly practicing the Lord's Supper (cf. v. 23).[1] Whether or not these two issues had been specified, Paul has information (if not at least partly from their letter, then clearly from other personal reports—v. 18) that suggests all is not well.

In the case of head coverings, Paul continues his "yes, but" logic. Yes, he praises them for their faithfulness to his teaching—probably about freedom (v. 2), but they have carried things too far ("now" in v. 3 should probably be translated "but"). Yes, it is true that men and women are equal in Christ before God, but that does not mean that all differences between the sexes may be blurred.

The events that lie behind verses 3–16 seem to proceed as follows. Because of their new found freedom in Christ, women in the Corinthian church were praying and prophesying (v. 5a). Christian tradition from Pentecost on had approved of such practice (Acts 2:18), and it readily fit Paul's own emphasis on freedom. But these women were not merely speaking in worship but doing it in a way that unnecessarily flaunted social convention and the order of creation. So Paul has to encourage them to exercise restraint. As in chapters 8–10, knowledge must be tempered with love.[2]

One of the keys to understanding verses 3–10 is to recognize Paul's play on the word "head." The main point of this paragraph is the claim that what one does or doesn't put on one's physical head either honors or dishonors one's spiritual head. Verse 3 establishes three such relationships of spiritual headship, but what the term for head (Gk. *kephale*) means here is hotly debated. The word was not often used figuratively (i.e., to refer to something other than a part of one's anatomy); when it was it seems that its two main meanings were either "source" or "authority."[3] Paul appears to use both meanings elsewhere (e.g., Eph. 4:15 more readily yields "source"; Eph. 1:22, "authority"), so a decision will ultimately depend on the immediate context. But even here Paul sends mixed signals, supplying an argument from the ori-

---

1. Cf. Gail P. Corrington, "The 'Headless Woman': Paul and the Language of the Body in 1 Cor 11:2–16," *PRS* 18 (1991): 225.

2. The most detailed reconstruction of events in Corinth, generally persuasive in its broad contours though often speculative in its particulars, is Antoinette Wire, *The Corinthian Women Prophets* (Minneapolis: Fortress, 1990).

3. Good brief presentations of the data appear in Joseph A. Fitzmyer, "Another Look at ΚΕΦΑΛΗ in 1 Corinthians 11.3," *NTS* 35 (1989): 503–11; and idem, "*Kephale* in 1 Corinthians 11.3," *Int* 47 (1993): 52–59. Those interested in pursuing the debate at greater length may consult Wayne Grudem, "The Meaning of *Kephale* ('Head'): A Response to Recent Studies," in *Recovering Biblical Manhood and Womanhood*, ed. John Piper and Wayne Grudem (Wheaton: Crossway, 1991), 425–68, and the literature there reviewed.

gin of men and women in verses 8–9, 12 but speaking explicitly of authority (Gk. *exousia*) in verse 10. The other passage in which Paul calls a man "head" over a woman refers as well to wives' subordination to their husbands (Eph. 5:22–24), so "authority" seems somewhat more likely here too.

The order of the three parts of verse 3 also proves significant. Some commentators stress that the sequence does not set up a chain of command, as if Paul had written, "The head of the woman is man, the head of every man is Christ, and the head of Christ is God." On the other hand, since the problem in Corinth involved men and women (but not Christ) dishonoring their heads, it is natural that he should refer to the heads of the man and of the woman first. The rationale for placing Christ's relationship to God last is most likely to draw attention to it as an analogy for the relationship between men, women, and their heads (the same sequence in v. 12).

There are at least three additional problems with an interpretation that denies any sense of "authority" to the word "head" in verse 3. First, if "head" is taken merely as "source," it would require interpreting "the head of Christ is God" as a reference to the incarnation, in order to avoid the ancient Arian heresy of claiming that God created Christ. But nothing else in the passage deals with Jesus coming to earth from heaven, while Paul's theological arguments in both verses 8–9 and 10–11 explicitly appeal to the way God fashioned things at the time of creation. Second, the vast majority of all church history has understood "head" as "authority." Traditional consensus, of course, is not inspired, but weighty arguments are needed to overthrow it. Third, up until the last few years, almost everybody who argued for "source" still did so within a hierarchical framework. That is to say, even if Paul is talking only about origins in verse 3, he does so to set up his subsequent commands about honoring those in authority over us.[4] Fortunately, however, the overall thrust of this passage remains clear even if one cannot agree on the precise meaning of "head."

Another disputed issue in verses 3–10 involves the translation of the words the NIV consistently renders as "man" (*aner*) and "woman" (*gune*). In every other place in Paul where they are paired, with the possible exception of 1 Timothy 2:8–15, they refer to husband and wife. It is much harder to un-

---

4. The most widely cited article in support of κεφαλή as "source" (Stephen Bedale, "The Meaning of κεφαλή in the Pauline Epistles," *JTS* n.s. 5 [1984]: 211–15) makes this point explicit ("That is to say, the male is κεφαλή in the sense of ἀρχή [beginning] relative to the female; and, in St. Paul's view, the female in consequence is 'subordinate' [cf. Eph. v.23]," 214), but Bedale's view is consistently misrepresented by feminist writers who omit his conclusions. Cf. also Elisabeth Schüssler Fiorenza, *In Memory of Her* (New York: Crossroad, 1983), 229, who explains Paul's perspective as "a descending hierarchy, God—Christ—Man—Woman, in which each preceding member as 'head' or 'source,' stands above the other 'in the sense that he established the other's being.'"

derstand how Paul could have claimed that every man is an authority over every woman and much easier to interpret the passage if husbands and wives are meant throughout (e.g., v. 5). References to the creation of man and woman (vv. 8–9) have understandably given rise to the former translation, but Adam and Eve were not only the prototypical male and female but also the first "married" couple. Given that Paul addresses the problems of singleness and widowhood in chapter 7, we may not deduce that every woman in the Corinthian church, even in a patriarchal society, necessarily had one specific male authority living—that is, a husband or father. The NRSV, therefore, may well be justified in translating the middle clause of verse 3 as "The husband is the head of his wife."

Verses 4–5a proceed with Paul's play on words. In each verse, the first use of "head" refers to the physical anatomy; the second to the spiritual authority or originator (depending on how one interprets *kephale*). The reference to praying and prophesying shows that the context is public worship; the latter in particular required an audience to be effective! Chapters 12–14 will explain Paul's understanding of prophecy. For now it must suffice to define it broadly as the proclamation of a message given by God to a Christian speaker for the benefit of a particular congregation. It may include both spontaneous utterances and carefully thought-out communication, so long as the prophet is convinced that God has led him or her to preach a certain message (cf. below, pp. 244–45).

"With his head covered" in verse 4 reads literally, "having down from the head." As the NIV footnote makes plain,[5] this might refer to long hair rather than to some external covering like a veil or shawl. In verses 14–15 Paul is definitely talking about relative lengths of hair for men and women, so it is somewhat more natural to assume that he has been talking about hairstyles all along. Long hair on Greek men might well have led to suspicions of homosexual behavior.[6] If an external covering is meant, then Paul is probably objecting to a practice which resembled that of Roman priests pulling their togas up over their heads while offering sacrifice or performing religious rituals.[7]

---

5. "Every man who prays or prophesies with long hair dishonors his head. And every woman who prays or prophesies with no covering of hair on her head dishonors her head—she is just like one of the 'shorn women.' If a woman has no covering, let her be for now with short hair, but since it is a disgrace for a woman to have her hair shorn or shaved, she should grow it again. A man ought not to have long hair."

6. See esp. Jerome Murphy-O'Connor, "Sex and Logic in 1 Corinthians 11:2–16," *CBQ* 42 (1980): 482–500.

7. See esp. Richard E. Oster, "When Men Wore Veils to Worship: The Historical Context of 1 Corinthians 11.4," *NTS* 34 (1988): 481–505.

Still another possibility is that long hair on men made their appearance resemble the elaborate hairdos of the sophists.[8]

Wives, however, should keep their heads covered (v. 5a). Again, the covering could refer to long hair. It could be that Paul wants them to keep it "done up," as was the custom among married women, rather than loose and flowing—a sign in some circles of being unmarried or, worse still, of suspected adultery (among Jews) or pagan, prophetic frenzy (among Greeks). Or it could be that they are simply wearing their hair too short, perilously close to the shaven heads of a convicted adulteress in Jewish circles or of the more "masculine" partner in a lesbian relationship in the Greek world. Alternately, if an external head covering is meant, Paul probably wants married women to wear a shawl over their hair and shoulders, as many Greek women still did in public, and not to resemble those who discarded their hair coverings during pagan worship in order to demonstrate their temporary transcendence of human sexuality.[9]

In verses 5b–6, Paul remarks ironically that if women are going to send ambiguous signals about their sexuality or religious commitments through inappropriate hairstyles or lack of headdress, then they might as well go all the way and become bald (or discard all head coverings) and unequivocally send the wrong signals! Verses 7–10, however, state Paul's true preference— that the Corinthian husbands and their wives revert back to the culturally appropriate signs of marital fidelity and worship of the one true God. Verse 7 makes this point by referring to the husbands as the "glory and image of God" and the wives as the "glory of their husbands." In verses 14–15 "glory" is the opposite of "disgrace," so in both places it probably carries the sense of "honor." For a Christian man to appear gay or pagan dishonors God; for a woman to appear lesbian or unfaithful dishonors her husband. Obviously husbands also dishonor their wives and wives dishonor God when they act in these inappropriate ways, but if an authority structure is implicit in this passage, Paul's less inclusive wording becomes understandable. One should be particularly concerned not to dishonor one's immediate spiritual head.

---

8. See Stanley K. Stowers, "Social Status, Public Speaking and Private Teaching: The Circumstances of Paul's Preaching Activity," *NovT* 26 (1984): 75.

9. For the possible Jewish backgrounds in each of these cases, see esp. James B. Hurley, *Man and Woman in Biblical Perspective* (Leicester: InterVarsity Press; Grand Rapids: Zondervan, 1981), 162–84, 254–71; for Greco-Roman backgrounds, cf. Fee, *First Corinthians*, 508–12; with Dennis R. MacDonald, "Corinthian Veils and Gnostic Androgynes," in *Images of the Feminine in Gnosticism*, ed. Karen L. King (Philadelphia: Fortress, 1988), 276–92.

Verses 8–9 ground the commands of verses 4–7 in a two-fold argument from creation:[10] (1) Adam was created first and then Eve (v. 8); (2) woman was created to be a helper suitable for man (Gen. 2:18) and not the reverse (v. 9). Verse 10 brings the first part of Paul's argument to a climax, but with a notoriously obscure statement. "For this reason" suggests that this sentence is giving a further rationale for women keeping their heads covered (either with lots of hair or with a shawl). The NIV therefore translates *exousia echein epi* (literally, "have authority on") as "have a *sign* of authority on." But there is no word for "sign" in the Greek, and "to have authority" most naturally means something the woman would actively exercise. So a popular recent view has been that the woman's head covering indicates *her* authority to pray and prophesy.[11] Yet every other use of this three-word construction in the New Testament means "to have authority (or control) *over*" (Matt. 9:6 [par. Mark 2:10; Luke 5:24]; Rev. 11:6; 14:18; 16:9; 20:6; and cf. the similar constructions with *epano* for *epi* in Luke 19:17, and with *peri* for *epi* in 1 Cor. 7:37). This suggests a translation more along the lines of "For this reason . . . a wife should exercise control over her head [i.e., keep the appropriate covering on it]."[12]

"Because of the angels" proves equally perplexing. The suggestions that these are fallen angels who might be sexually seduced or human messengers or church leaders go against the consistent meaning of *angeloi* used without qualification elsewhere in the New Testament. It is better to see them as the angels who remain God's servants, watching over creation and protecting the worship of his people. They in particular would want to see services proceed with appropriate dignity and decorum.[13]

Verses 11–12 introduce an important qualification into Paul's discussion. Beginning with a strong contrast (*plen*—"however"), Paul reminds the Corinthians that as Christians, notwithstanding creation, husbands and wives (or perhaps men and women more generally) are fundamentally interdependent. The order of creation is reversed in subsequent procreation, and whatever hierarchies remain are significantly tempered by the fact that

---

10. On which, see esp. L. Ann Jervis, "'But I Want You to Know. . . .': Paul's Midrashic Intertextual Response to the Corinthian Worshipers (1 Cor 11:2–16)," *JBL* 112 (1993): 231–46.

11. Beginning esp. with Morna D. Hooker, "Authority on Her Head: An Examination of 1 Cor. xi.10," *NTS* 10 (1966): 410–16.

12. See esp. Jerome Murphy-O'Connor, "1 Corinthians 11:2–16 Once Again," *CBQ* 50 (1988): 271.

13. See esp. Joseph A. Fitzmyer, "A Feature of Qumran Angelology and the Angels of 1 Cor. xi.10," *NTS* 4 (1957): 48–58.

God is the origin of everything that belongs to redemption. He is therefore our ultimate and most important authority.

Verses 13–16 return to the specific problem of head coverings, this time explicitly referring to long hair on men and women, with three further arguments. After appealing to the Corinthians to conclude that what Paul is saying is true ("Judge for yourselves"—v. 13a; cf. 10:15), he argues further from propriety (v. 13b), nature (vv. 14–15), and the widespread first-century custom (NIV "practice") of all believers (v. 16).[14] The first and third of these clearly refer to the "status quo" in Paul's day. "Nature" sounds like an appeal to the way God created things, but Paul the Jew would have known of the Nazirites whom God blessed precisely because they did not cut their hair (of whom Samson was the most famous example; Judg. 13:5). In the Greek world, the Spartan men were known for their shoulder-length hair. But it was true, then as now, that most cultures maintained a relative difference in hair length between men and women. So "nature" is probably best understood here as that which is "almost instinctive because of long habit," a "long-established custom."[15]

Verse 15b also supports the idea that hair length or style has been the issue throughout verses 2–16. "As a covering" might more literally be rendered "instead of a wrap-around garment." That is, rather than wearing the customary hair shawl as Greek women did, long hair, perhaps done up in a bun, will suffice for Christian women. On the other hand, if an external garment is in view in verses 3–10, then Paul will be drawing an analogy here. Just as "nature" teaches that women should wear long hair as a head covering, so it is appropriate for women to further cover their heads according to the established custom of the day. But the transition is abrupt, and it would seem slightly better to follow the NIV footnote for verses 4–7 and see hair as the primary topic of this entire section. Grammatically, the least probable portions of this alternate rendering are the phrases, "let her be for now with short hair" and "she should grow it again" in verse 6. But the translation prob-

---

14. Verse 16 literally reads, "We have no *such* custom, nor do the churches of God." Some have therefore argued that Paul is claiming that first-century Christians have *no* established pattern of behavior regarding hairstyles, exactly the opposite of the meaning suggested by the NIV's "we have no *other* practice . . ." But this translation makes no sense in light of verses 13–15, in which Paul *is* arguing for a particular practice. "The practice of certain Corinthian women who *refuse to wear head coverings* is what Paul refers to when he says 'we have no such practice.'"—Thomas R. Schreiner, "Head Coverings, Prophecies and the Trinity: 1 Corinthians 11:2–16," in *Recovering Biblical Manhood and Womanhood*, 138.

15. John T. Bristow, *What Paul Really Said About Women* (San Francisco: Harper and Row, 1988), 84.

lems are solved if we adopt the interpretation that women were not keeping their hair "done up" properly. Then this verse would convey the sense, "If a woman will not do her hair properly, she might as well cut it off. But if it is disgraceful for a woman to be shorn or shaven as men are, she should do her hair in a womanly fashion." Verse 15 might then be translated, "For long hair is given her so that she may wind it around her head."[16]

THIS PASSAGE IS probably the most complex, controversial, and opaque of any text of comparable length in the New Testament. A survey of the history of interpretation reveals how many different exegetical options there are for a myriad of questions[17] and should inspire a fair measure of tentativeness on the part of the interpreter. Still, there are several points about which we can remain relatively confident. Very little evidence supports the suggestions that Paul did not write this passage or that the most objectionable parts for many modern interpreters (vv. 3–7 or verses 3–10) are in fact a Corinthian position that Paul goes on to refute in verses 11–16.[18] The former position founders on the complete lack of manuscript evidence for verses 2–16 as a later addition; the latter neglects the fact that verses 13–16 also support the position outlined in verses 3–10.

More positively, most interpreters agree that one timeless principle that may be deduced from this passage is that Christians should not try to blur all distinctions between the sexes. Gnosticism may have valued the androgynous human being as the return to some pristine ideal, but Christianity recognizes that God created men and women as sexual beings, with sexual differences. So we must not try to efface these distinctives by dressing or grooming in ways that make it impossible to recognize a person's gender or, worse still, by changing our sexual appearance through transvestite behavior. There is also general agreement that there is nothing inherently moral or immoral about head coverings, whether veils, shawls, hats, or whatever.

---

16. Murphy-O'Connor, "Sex and Logic," 499.

17. A selective overview of interpretation from Calvin to the late 1970s appears in Linda Mercadante, *From Hierarchy to Equality* (Vancouver: G-M-H, 1978). Wire briefly updates the survey in "Women's Head Covering," in *Prophets*, 220–23. A helpful list of the key issues, with representatives of all of the major exegetical options for each, is provided by Sanford D. Hull, "Exegetical Difficulties in the 'Hard Passages,'" in Gretchen G. Hull, *Equal to Serve* (Old Tappan, N.J.: Revell, 1989), 252–57.

18. See, respectively, William O. Walker, Jr., "The Vocabulary of 1 Corinthians 11.3–16: Pauline or Non-Pauline," *JSNT* 35 (1989): 75–88; and Thomas P. Shoemaker, "Unveiling of Equality: 1 Corinthians 11:2–16," *BTB* 17 (1987): 60–63.

The same is essentially true for hairstyles, but one must be sensitive in certain cultures to the social connotations that may be present with certain fashions of men's or women's hair and even, occasionally, with other kinds of head coverings.

Careful attention to the nature of Paul's argumentation in this passage supports these consensus views. When he speaks explicitly of length of hair, he grounds his arguments in what is proper (v. 13), normal practice (vv. 14–15) and contemporary custom (v. 16). None of these verses, as we have seen in the discussion of original meaning (see pp. 213–14), implies a timeless, transcultural mandate, even if the customs were widespread in the first century and have often been imitated in other cultures and eras. When Paul does ground his commands in the order and purpose of creation (vv. 8–9), he does so to support his statements that husbands are the image and glory of God and that wives are the glory of their husbands (v. 7). When in a particular culture, appropriate honor to God and husband cannot be maintained without certain head coverings, such coverings must be used. When covered or uncovered heads and long or short hair imply nothing about one's religious commitment or marital faithfulness, worrying about the appearance of one's physical head in these ways becomes unnecessary.

This last remark leads us to another important historical-cultural observation. Even though we cannot be sure if shawls or hair are the main problem, and even though there are numerous possibilities for what the use or non-use of these head coverings would have implied, all of the options boil down to one of two issues: what the Corinthians did with their heads mattered because of either the *sexual* or the *religious* implications of their appearance (or both).

In any culture, believers must strenuously avoid whatever forms of dress or grooming potentially communicate to the non-Christian world sexual misconduct or idolatrous worship. Indeed, Romans 1:21–27 identifies the theological core of unbelief as idolatry and the ethical core as sexual sin. Behavior, mannerisms, clothing, or hairstyles that suggest that a person is sexually unfaithful to his or her spouse, promiscuous, homosexual, or the devotee of some non-Christian religion or cultic or occult sect are entirely inappropriate for Christians, particularly in church.

Beyond this, the consensus among interpreters begins to break down. It is still widely acknowledged, irrespective of the meaning of "head," that verses 8–9 present an argument based on the subordination of women (or at least of wives) to support Paul's command that they ought not to disgrace their men (husbands).

It is not at all agreed as to how verses 11–12 relate to verses 8–9. Some treat verses 11–12 as a mere parenthesis, so that the mutuality they stress is barely heard. Others take them as canceling out everything else Paul has said, even though they account for only two of the fifteen verses in the passage.

A mediating view seems preferable. "In the Lord," that is among Christians, the nature of creation is substantially qualified but never erased altogether.[19] This view follows from several observations: (1) "Creation ordinances" (arguments based on how God set things up before the Fall of Gen. 3) are regularly used throughout the New Testament as desirable, timeless principles that all Christians should follow (e.g., Jesus' arguments on the permanence of marriage in Matt. 19:4–9). (2) Paul himself supplies verses 8–9 as a rationale for behavior he is commanding of *Christians*, not unredeemed people. (3) Verses 8–9 would be meaningless and unnecessary if verses 11–12 entirely canceled them out. (4) Attempts to translate *plen* ("however," in v. 11) as "the point is" (so that vv. 11–12 become the point Paul has been building to all along) rely on an extremely rare use of the adverb. (5) The interdependence that verses 11–12 stress actually reinforces Paul's insistence in the first half of the passage that wives not dishonor their husbands.

Some object that verse 8 supplies an argument from creation that is nonsensical. The order of creation has no logical connection to any hierarchy of authority; if it did, animals ought to be above people, since in Genesis 1 they were created before humanity. But Paul is not arguing from Genesis 1 but from Genesis 2. He is not claiming that order *always* implies rank, merely that it does in the one part of the one creation account to which he refers. People in the ancient world familiar with the privileges that firstborn sons retained (of dynastic succession, inheritance, etc.) would not have found Paul's argument unusual.

This argument must also be considered together with the second (v. 9— that Eve was created to be Adam's helper). The fact that the Hebrew word for "helper" is often used for God, as he helps humans out of many difficult circumstances throughout the pages of the Old Testament, proves that the term itself does not inherently imply subordination, but it does not prove that it *cannot* imply subordination. Some helpers are authority figures, others are peers, many others are subordinates. And in the context of verses 3–7, it is hard to escape the feeling that Paul intended to speak of a hierarchy in verse 9 too.

---

19. Cf. esp. Talbert, *Corinthians*, 70.

On the other hand, verses 3 and 11–12 radically redefine that hierarchy in ways that should render it unobjectionable. If verse 3 suggests that the authority of a husband over his wife parallels that of God over Christ, then certainly one is struck by the mutuality of the relationship far more than by any act of subordination. Still, both are present. The historic, orthodox view of the Trinity, supported by the New Testament, involves ontological equality (equality of essence or being) combined with functional subordination (submission within role differentiation).[20] Christ emptied himself of the independent exercise of his divine attributes in the incarnation (Phil 2:6–8). But even before he took on human flesh, the Father had to send him. (No Scripture ever speaks of the Son sending or commanding the Father.) And even after Christ's resurrection and exaltation, Paul speaks of the day when "the Son himself will be made subject to him who put everything under him, so that God may be all in all" (1 Cor. 15:28). Jesus himself can declare without any sense of contradiction that "the Father is greater than I" (John 14:28) and "I and the Father are one" (John 10:30). And there is no evidence that any human society or any Christian community has ever functioned successfully without *de facto* if not duly recognized authorities to whom others submit. Most Christians regularly experience situations in which they submit to authorities with whom they believe they are essentially equal.

Still, there is a legitimate objection to this perspective. The most acceptable subordination in society does not rely on forever barring certain categories of people from certain functions simply because of innate features such as gender. Here is where the interpretation of *aner* and *gune* as "husband" and "wife" becomes attractive. It does seem unfair if all women are forever subordinate to one or more men in their lives. If, however, authority and subordination in this passage are limited to the institution of marriage, then those who cannot live with this relationship need not enter into it.

Yet even the "hierarchy" of marriage as Paul defines it in Ephesians 5:21–33 seems not only innocuous but wonderful. Here is no authority of extra privilege but one of extra responsibility. No husband may legitimately refer to these verses to support an authoritarian leadership style. Quite the opposite, Paul commands husbands to love their wives sacrificially, with Christ's death for humanity as their ultimate model (v. 25). Unlike children and slaves (6:1, 5), women are *not* commanded to "obey" their husbands but to "submit" (vv. 22–24), a term that in some contexts can be almost as mild as our concept of "deferring."[21] And Paul's hierarchy is qualified even further by the context of mutual submission (v. 21) into which it is introduced.

---

20. Barrett, *First Corinthians*, 249.
21. J. Ramsey Michaels, *1 Peter* (Waco: Word, 1988), 154–58, on 1 Peter 3:1.

Marriages that operate according to Paul's guidelines will appear in real life very similar to the ideal of evangelical feminists—each person concerned to seek the best interests of the other above self and to arrive at decisions through mutual prayer and discussion. But they contain a mechanism for breaking the deadlocks that do at times occur, when two people cannot jointly reach a decision on which both agree. Then it is up to the husband to exercise his authority to resolve the problem—*but on the basis of what is in the best interests of his spouse (and children, if any)*, not merely to please his own interests.[22] Some individuals protest that if two people cannot make a joint decision, equally agreeable to both, then they should make no decision and continue to pray and work it out together. This is good advice, when it is possible, but it is not always possible. Cultures of many kinds impose deadlines on people for decision-making, and often not to make a decision is to opt for one alternative over another.

When men and women in a marriage become "liberated traditionalists" in this sense, then God and husband are properly honored (v. 7). When their appearance or demeanor in church does not distract from this honor, God is glorified.

But why does Paul call the man "the image" as well as the glory of God, while referring to the woman merely as "the glory" of her husband? He knows his Bible too well for us to believe that he did not think woman was also created in God's image (Gen. 1:27). So it must be precisely because women with men jointly reflect the image and likeness of God that Paul does not repeat the word "image," lest he wind up saying women are the images of their husbands. But why then introduce the idea of "image" at all into the discussion? Probably because "image" and "glory" were already closely connected in Jewish thought. Particularly suggestive is Exodus 33:18–34:7, in which God reveals his very nature to Moses, the moral and relational attributes of the image of God, under the auspices of his "glory." It may well be that Paul is thinking of husbands modeling God precisely in the areas that 34:6–7 spell out: "compassionate and gracious, slow to anger, abounding in love and faithfulness, maintaining love, forgiving wickedness, rebellion and sin," though not leaving "the guilty unpunished."[23]

---

22. Cf. further Klyne Snodgrass, *Ephesians* (Grand Rapids: Zondervan, forthcoming) on 5:21–33. One of the most balanced books within the flood of recent literature on Christian marriage, which essentially articulates the position advocated here, is Ronald and Beverly Allen, *Liberated Traditionalism: Men and Women in Balance* (Portland: Multnomah, 1985). Also generally helpful, though at times inconsistent in application, are the articles in the section entitled "Applications and Implications," in *Recovering Biblical Manhood and Womanhood*, 345–99.

23. Cf. further R. Ward Wilson and Craig L. Blomberg, "The Image of God in Humanity: A Biblical-Psychological Perspective," *Themelios* 18 (1993): 8–15.

In all of this discussion, we must not lose sight of verse 5. Paul *does* assume it is appropriate for the women to pray and prophesy in public worship. It is true that the only explicit references to the church gathered come in the next two sections of 11:2–14:40 (e.g., 11:18, 20, 33; 14:26), but 11:3–16 shows every indication of reflecting this identical context: (1) It follows verse 2, which with verse 17 ties 11:3–16 closely together with verses 18–34. (2) While prophecy could be given to an individual, the detailed concern for one's outward appearance does not fit private contexts, in which such customs were irrelevant. (3) The analogies with Jewish and Greco-Roman religious behavior all involve public worship. (4) Paul regularly conceives of the exercise of the spiritual gifts as in the church (see esp. chaps. 12–14). (5) Even in Christian circles, women would probably not have had much occasion to minister to men in "one-on-one" settings, given the misleading impressions such encounters could create. (6) The presence of angels concerned about gender-specific behavior (v. 10) makes best sense when seen as analogous to Jewish beliefs about their role in public worship. (7) Verse 16 refers to the practice of other "churches," which favors a reference to the gathered assembly.

What then of 14:33–38? We will discuss the implications of that text in more detail when we get to that point in the letter, but suffice it for now to say that commentators are almost unanimously agreed that Paul is not silencing all speech by women in the church. Contextual indicators in chapter 14 make that highly unlikely. In fact, recognizing that he permits prayer and prophecy here will help us choose from among the options presented to us when we get to that later passage. And to the extent that prophecy overlaps with what is more commonly called preaching, this passage remains one of the clearest New Testament texts in support of women preachers.

But chapters 12–14 will also make it clear that Paul views prophecy as a spiritual gift, and gifts are not the same as offices. So to say that Paul permits, and perhaps even encourages women to preach—in ways, of course, appropriate to their cultures—does not settle the vexed question of whether they should be elders or overseers. One's exegesis of 1 Timothy (esp. 2:8–15) should be more relevant to that problem. But given Paul's greater interest in gifts than in offices, our point here stands: gifted women must be given abundant opportunity, however formally or informally, to preach God's word to his people as he calls and leads them.

If 14:33–38 sometimes tempts interpreters to apply 11:2–16 too narrowly, Galatians 3:28 often tempts people to apply it too broadly. Though it is often maintained that when Paul wrote, "There is neither . . . male nor female, for you are all one in Christ Jesus," he left no room for role differentiation or hierarchy of any kind, this sweeping claim simply does not follow. Other Jewish and Greco-Roman teachers regularly made similar claims even as they upheld far more chauvinistic distinctions between men and women than anything found in the Bible.

At the same time, Paul probably did mean more than simple equality before God for salvation, since Galatians 3:28 appears in the context of baptism. We often forget what a radically inclusive social statement baptism made in the first century, as the Christian initiatory rite replaced one limited to men—Jewish circumcision. At the very least, the church of Jesus Christ should seek outward, public signs in every culture to affirm the full equality of the sexes—and also of races and classes.[24] Particularly in contexts in which local congregations come to believe that certain ministries or offices are reserved for men, these fellowships must then go out of their way to encourage women to use their gifts to the fullest in every setting that is open to them.

As we move to our discussion of contemporary application, it is worth pondering one additional question. One of Paul's rationales for his commands in this passage is to avoid hindering the spread of the gospel by sending misleading cultural signals. Yet if we restrict women's roles in *any* area of the church or domestic life, don't we erect unnecessary barriers to the expansion of Christianity in democratic and egalitarian cultures? On the other hand, if Paul's logic flows also from creation ordinances, then some of those hindrances may be inescapable and part of the scandal of the cross—the voluntary relinquishing of rights we feel we deserve.

CLEARLY, HEAD COVERINGS SEND virtually no sexual or religious messages in contemporary Western societies. Perhaps the only exception is in those few extremely conservative churches that still insist on women wearing hats, scarves, or hairnets. And the message these churches usually send to the culture at large is that they are hopelessly out of touch with modernity! For them it would be best to abandon the practice at once, so that they could better implement Paul's principle of being all things to all people in order to save as many as possible (9:19–23). In other cultures, however, head coverings often continue to carry great significance. Christian workers in Muslim lands will have to consider seriously whether

---

24. For both of the above, cf. esp. Ben Witherington III, "Rite and Rights for Women—Galatians 3.28," *NTS* 27 (1981): 593–604.

or not it will promote their witness if their women wear some kind of veil. At the very least, they will have to avoid causing the offense that is almost universally created when women's shoulders are not covered with appropriate attire. For many Muslims, bare-shouldered women are sexually promiscuous; the practice is almost tantamount to bare-breasted women in this country.

In Jewish circles, Christian men should be prepared to wear the yarmulke or skull-cap when entering holy places. This does not violate verse 4 precisely because it fulfills the same function that not wearing a head covering did in Corinth—it prevents people from thinking that a person is deliberately worshiping a false god or dishonoring the one true God of Israel. Interestingly, the Jewish practice of covering a man's head during worship did not become widespread before the fourth century A.D., though it "seems to have been innovatively tried in the Jewish synagogues of Paul's time," and may have actually arisen in response to Paul's commands, to differentiate Jews from Christians.[25]

Whenever Christianity enters a new culture, the hermeneutical principles at stake here will need to be discussed. Charles Kraft, for example, tells the story of his missionary work in Nigeria in which new believers could not understand why Western Christians "obeyed the Biblical commands against stealing and not those about head-coverings."[26] That the one practice is inherently immoral and the other not may seem self-evident to us whose laws have been deeply informed by the Judeo-Christian tradition but may not be at all transparent to other, quite different peoples.

Hairstyles too are generally seen as morally neutral these days. Since the 1960s we have watched men's hair grow long and short again, and we have seen teens of both sexes fall in and out of love with punk styles. New generations will doubtless bring still different fashions and resurrect others tried in the past. To the extent that people's grooming or dress deliberately flaunts authority and social convention, such actions cannot be condoned by Christians, because it gives us an unnecessarily bad reputation among non-Christians. No doubt some of this occurred in the 60s and with punk. But wise Christians, like wise parents, will choose their battles carefully. We should not get overly upset by a person's outward appearance when there are more fundamental theological and ethical issues to be concerned about in our society.

Exceptions to this principle involve dress or hairstyle which in certain contexts is likely to communicate misleading sexual signals. Men should not

---

25. Mare, "1 Corinthians," 255–56, and the literature there cited.
26. Charles Kraft, *Christianity in Culture* (Maryknoll, N.Y.: Orbis, 1979), 138.

wear dresses, since this suggests transvestite behavior to most onlookers. Women should not wear the excessive make-up and revealing clothing typical of prostitutes "on their beat." Less dramatically, both men and women should avoid any clothing that would prove unnecessarily seductive, particularly in settings where God is to be worshiped and participants should be free from such distractions. More specifically, husbands and wives should carefully guard against sending signals that suggest they are not married or are disloyal to their spouses. In some contexts, it would be misleading and inappropriate not to wear a wedding ring if one is married. Flirtatious conversation or behavior with someone other than one's spouse also puts one in a position of asking for trouble.

Dress and grooming do not usually send misleading religious signals today. But still there are exceptions. An unwise application of 9:19–23 could actually convince non-Christians that one had converted to a non-Christian religion or sect. It would not be good, for example, for believers to don the garb of the saffron robes and shaved heads of the Hare Krishna, just for the sake of relating to them. Certain combinations of long, disheveled hair, tattoos, and other self-mutilation in certain circles would suggest that one is the member of an occult or even Satanic group. It is even arguable that this passage hints at the inappropriateness of distinctive clerical garb, at least to the extent that it fosters unbiblical notions about clergy and laity as somehow qualitatively distinct.[27] And to the extent that such dress is valid in certain places, it would certainly be inappropriate for one who is not a member of the clergy to wear garments that deceive others into thinking he or she is. In general, one should not seek to defy social fashion and convention merely as an expression of one's own freedom; to do so is to deny Paul's concern to put others above self.

Many contemporary Christians also repudiate this concern in their intransigent positions on one side or the other of the debates about women's roles in home and church. Many today are understandably uncomfortable with any hierarchical interpretation of Paul's words, because modern society is trying to vanquish patriarchal structures on all fronts. Evangelical feminists insist that Paul never intended for male/female relationships of authority and submission to be preserved cross-culturally.[28] But it is hard to believe that Paul was really a modern egalitarian, as entrenched as patriarchy

---

27. Snyder, *First Corinthians*, 162.

28. See esp. Craig S. Keener, *Paul, Women and Wives* (Peabody, Mass.: Hendrickson, 1992), 19–69. Keener's work is currently by far the most persuasive of the various evangelical feminist treatments of Paul, even if the present writer in places remains "almost persuaded."

was in his society and in the rest of Scripture, and given his arguments from creation in verses 8–9.

Tellingly, non-evangelical feminists regularly agree with more traditional evangelicals that Paul is promoting the subordination of wives here.[29] But they usually deny that we can accept his instruction, because they are not committed to the authority of all parts Scripture in the same ways evangelicals are. Yet they admit that *Paul* would have wanted his patriarchy to be preserved cross-culturally. Those who are bound by a higher view of Scripture, therefore, should at least be considerably wary of rejecting all forms of hierarchy in this passage.

Part of our problem lies in our inability to see submission and equality as simultaneously possible. Earle Ellis agrees, and his words merit extensive citation precisely because they reflect insights not widely recognized today:

> The mind-set that places "equality and subordination" in opposition and that views distinctions of class and rank as evil per se is largely a modern phenomenon. It may reflect a justifiable resentment toward attitudes of disdain and elitism that often (and in a sinful society always) flow from such distinctions, but it seems to be less aware of the egoistic and antisocial evils inherent in egalitarianism itself and sometimes expressed in programs for economic or social conformity, in a libertarian rejection of authority, and in a despisal of servanthood as a "demeaning" role.
>
> In any case Paul, like the New Testament generally, holds together quite harmoniously an equality of value and diversity of rank and resolves the problems of diversity in a manner entirely different from modern egalitarianism. In this issue, as in others, the Apostle finds the key to the problem in his Christology. . . . That is, Jesus the Son of God manifested his equality with God the Father precisely in fulfilling a role of subordination to him.[30]

There is an acute need for a balanced application of this "liberated traditionalism" to contemporary Christian marriages. On the one hand, there are far too many authoritarian relationships in which husbands continue to abuse their wives physically, emotionally, or verbally, all in the name of

---

29. And consistently in his writings. See esp. Clark H. Pinnock, "Biblical Authority and the Issues in Question," in *Women, Authority and the Bible*, ed. Alvera Mickelsen (Downers Grove, Ill.: InterVarsity Press, 1986), 55, on Col. 3:18: "The radical feminists and the traditionalists both argue that such texts are not feminist in content, and I suspect that their view, agreeing as it does with the 'plain sense' reading so widely held, will prevail and not be successfully refuted by biblical feminists."

30. Ellis, *Pauline Theology*, 57.

Christian headship. More tragic still are the numbers of churches and pastors who call women to continue to submit to and tolerate such abuse. Scripture makes it plain that God's people must not submit to authorities when they are transgressing God's laws (Dan. 1, 3; Acts 5:29), and mistreatment of one's wife surely qualifies as such transgression, given Ephesians 5:25–29. Sadly, much of the literature in conservative circles about men's and women's roles in marriage teaches precisely the opposite.[31] On the other hand, the more liberal wings of Christian feminism consistently promote the assertion of one's rights and self-realization in ways that play down or deny altogether the dominant biblical theme of servanthood as the model for all Christians of either gender.[32]

In between these ends of the spectrum there is much room for individual diversity. Male headship, even when defined as "authority," implies nothing about whether or not a woman should work outside the home, who should perform various domestic chores, or which parent should be the primary caregiver for young children. Rather it speaks volumes about a husband's responsibility to see that his entire family is involved in activities that promote their mutual spiritual growth and in harmonious agreement (when possible!) about the major decisions that affect each individual. And, of course, wives should work toward these ends too, not leaving all responsibility to their husbands. Again the Allens seem to have captured the correct balance: "In our day, without wishing to risk the excess of some feminist writers, we may do well to emphasize the element of equality this passage represents. In a context that depends on hierarchy for the apostle's argument to work, we are most impressed by his stress on mutuality."[33]

In the same vein, many churches must come to grips with this passage's implied mandate to allow and even to encourage women to participate publicly in worship services, particularly in praying and preaching. Many gifted but frustrated Christian women have lamented that they'd be happy to keep

---

31. An extreme, but unfortunately very popular, example is the teaching of Bill Gothard in his numerous seminars and in his unpublished notes distributed at those seminars. Less extreme, but sometimes equally stereotypic are some of the viewpoints emanating from the so-called "men's movement." An excellent resource that *does* reflect biblical values is Bill McCartney, et al., *What Makes a Man?* (Colorado Springs: NavPress, 1992).

32. A theme that also pervades the writings (and even the titles) of some evangelical or biblical feminists—e.g., Letha Scanzoni and Nancy Hardesty, *All We're Meant to Be: A Biblical Approach to Women's Liberation* (Waco: Word, 1970); Patricia Gundry, *Woman Be Free!* (Grand Rapids: Zondervan, 1977). Many more recent biblical feminist authors, however, are more humble in tone (and in titles). Two notable examples are Hull, *Equal to Serve*; and Mary S. van Leuween, *Gender and Grace* (Downers Grove: InterVarsity Press, 1990).

33. Allen and Allen, *Liberated Traditionalism*, 146.

their heads covered, as Paul said, if other Christians would just let them prophesy or preach!

Of course, once we understand these verses rightly, we probably shouldn't ask women to worry about head coverings as they preach. And even churches that believe women shouldn't hold certain leadership offices ought at the very least to encourage them to be ushers, serve Communion, pray, read Scripture, lead hymn-singing, and fill a variety of other roles generally reserved in such churches for men, even though those roles have nothing to do with teaching or exercising authority over men (1 Tim. 2:12).

On the other hand, against the prevailing feminization of certain parts of our society and of our Christian community, it is at least arguable that Paul would have seen the church built along the lines of the family, so that male headship should be modeled in both contexts. If women can and should preach, it does not necessarily follow that they can or should be appointed to the office of elder or to the role of senior pastor (see further under 14:33–38). Or if Paul has exclusively husbands and wives in view, then perhaps he would perceive a problem only if married women were given offices of authority in the church that placed them in positions "over" their husbands.[34]

One of the most compelling models of ministry today, balancing the concerns of hierarchicalists and egalitarians is that practiced by John Stott, in which church leaders function as a "team" of equals, including both men and women, but the team leader remains male. Yet even then his leadership is one of empowering others on the team for ministry rather than "lording it over" them.[35]

Far more common, sadly, are models that forbid all pastoral roles to women or ones that assume women should do anything men can do.[36] The issue is usually compounded by beginning the debate with the question "Should women be ordained?" This question can only be answered, however, once one replies to a counterquestion, "Ordained to what?" And it is unnecessarily digressive even then, since there is little biblical support for a very developed concept of ordination in the first place.[37] Better to ask what roles are appropriate for husbands and wives in light of Paul's principle of male headship.

---

34. Again, see Ellis, *Pauline Theology,* 71–77.

35. John Stott, *Involvement: Social and Sexual Relationships in the Modern World,* vol. 2 (Old Tappan, N.J.: Fleming Revell, 1985), 248–56.

36. Again, this confuses gift with office (cf. Eph. 4:11 with 1 Cor. 12:11). Pastoring is a gift that the Spirit gives to whomever he wills.

37. See esp. E. Margaret Howe, *Women and Church Leadership* (Grand Rapids: Zondervan, 1982).

A passage such as 1 Corinthians 11:2–16 reveals the need for all believers to have a relatively sophisticated grasp of principles of biblical hermeneutics, so that they can sift through historical-cultural background, understand the meaning of key terms and grammatical interrelationships within a passage, and fit this passage in with Paul's other teaching on the topic. Even then, interpreters who show great exegetical common sense elsewhere often say downright silly or irresponsible things when issues as emotional or volatile as this one come into play.

We all need regular reminders of the role presuppositions play in our interpretation, and we must moderate our opinions with healthy doses of humility. We must study all of the Scriptures relevant to a topic like men's and women's roles and affirm a position that we believe does adequate justice to all of the biblical data. In short, we must agree to disagree at times.

Biblical feminists and moderate traditionalists are generally closer to each other in practice than the rhetoric of their theoretical disagreements might suggest. We must leave room for one another's models in case we ourselves are wrong. But we also must draw the line to exclude more strident or more dangerous forms of hierarchicalism and egalitarianism. When most of a certain hierarchicalist's arguments sound indistinguishable from the arguments used to support slavery in pre-abolition days, we must beware.[38] When most of a certain egalitarian's arguments closely resemble those used to support homosexual behavior, we must shrink back.[39] But in between there is a wide berth in which we can continue to study the relevant texts together in love, trusting that none of us has yet received ultimate illumination.

---

38. See the helpful exposé in Willard Swartley, *Slavery, Sabbath, War and Women* (Scottdale, Pa.: Herald, 1983), 198–202.

39. As with the Evangelical Woman's Caucus, which very fact in part led to the withdrawal of the more conservative participants and the founding of the Christians for Biblical Equality.

1 Corinthians 11:17–34

I N THE FOLLOWING directives I have no praise for you, for your meetings do more harm than good. [18] In the first place, I hear that when you come together as a church, there are divisions among you, and to some extent I believe it. [19] No doubt there have to be differences among you to show which of you have God's approval. [20] When you come together, it is not the Lord's Supper you eat, [21] for as you eat, each of you goes ahead without waiting for anybody else. One remains hungry, another gets drunk. [22] Don't you have homes to eat and drink in? Or do you despise the church of God and humiliate those who have nothing? What shall I say to you? Shall I praise you for this? Certainly not!

[23] For I received from the Lord what I also passed on to you: The Lord Jesus, on the night he was betrayed, took bread, [24] and when he had given thanks, he broke it and said, "This is my body, which is for you; do this in remembrance of me." [25] In the same way, after supper he took the cup, saying, "This cup is the new covenant in my blood; do this, whenever you drink it, in remembrance of me." [26] For whenever you eat this bread and drink this cup, you proclaim the Lord's death until he comes.

[27] Therefore, whoever eats the bread or drinks the cup of the Lord in an unworthy manner will be guilty of sinning against the body and blood of the Lord. [28] A man ought to examine himself before he eats of the bread and drinks of the cup. [29] For anyone who eats and drinks without recognizing the body of the Lord eats and drinks judgment on himself. [30] That is why many among you are weak and sick, and a number of you have fallen asleep. [31] But if we judged ourselves, we would not come under judgment. [32] When we are judged by the Lord, we are being disciplined so that we will not be condemned with the world.

[33] So then, my brothers, when you come together to eat, wait for each other. [34] If anyone is hungry, he should eat at home, so that when you meet together it may not result in judgment.

And when I come I will give further directions.

Original Meaning

FOR ONCE PAUL abandons his "Yes, but" logic. Whatever the Corinthians may have claimed in their letter about faithfully celebrating the Lord's Supper (vv. 2, 22c), Paul has heard additional news that horrifies him (v. 18—from Chloe's people or others). His comments are overwhelmingly critical, underlining the severity of their "malpractice." Verse 17b reads literally, "For you come together not for the better but for the worse." Verses 18–22 explain what the problem involves. Verses 23–26 appeal to foundational Christian tradition that teaches a quite different attitude to the Lord's Table. Verses 27–34 explain the resulting implications for the church in Corinth.

Once again Paul refers to "divisions" (Gk. *schismata*, as in 1:10). But here he is not thinking of the rival parties that possibly separate various congregations but of the gulf between the rich and poor within a given house-church. The minority of well-to-do believers (1:26), including the major financial supporters and owners of the homes in which the believers met, would have had the leisure-time and resources to arrive earlier and bring larger quantities and finer food than the rest of the congregation. Following the practice of hosting festive gatherings in ancient Corinth, they would have quickly filled the small private dining room. Latecomers (the majority, who probably had to finish work before coming on Saturday or Sunday evening—there was as of yet no legalized day off in the Roman empire) would be seated separately in the adjacent atrium or courtyard. Those that could not afford to bring a full meal, or a very good one, did not have the opportunity to share with the rest in the way that Christian unity demanded.[1]

The clients of the wealthy patrons were probably accustomed to being treated unequally. The house churches in part resembled other religious associations and fraternal organizations in Corinth, where knowing one's place in the hierarchy of fellowship meals was important.[2] "No doubt there were affluent Christians in the church at Corinth who took it for granted that such differentiations were part of the nature of things."[3] Although Paul allows for a measure of bias or exaggeration in the reports he has received, he recognizes that they fit well enough with the rest of the Corinthian problems to be generally credible (v. 18).

Ironically, Paul laments that if some have deviated so far from the intention of the ceremony, then the divisions will at least magnify the authentic-

---

1. For the details, cf. further Gerd Theissen, *The Social Setting of Pauline Christianity* (Philadelphia: Fortress, 1982), 145–74 .

2. See esp. Wayne A. Meeks, *The First Urban Christians* (New Haven: Yale University Press, 1983), 77–80.

3. Watson, *First Corinthians*, 118.

ity of those who have remained faithful (v. 19). The word for "differences" is that which later developed into the concept of "heresies," but here it simply means "factions." The result of the lack of consideration by the wealthy for the less well-to-do implies that they are not celebrating the *Lord's* Supper at all, merely "*their own* supper." (The NIV "Each of you goes ahead without waiting for anybody else" in verse 21 is unusually paraphrastic. It reads literally, "Each goes ahead with his own supper.")

Instead of sharing in a kind of "potluck" and ensuring that all get plenty to eat and drink, some gorge themselves and get drunk at the expense of those who come later or have less. Jude 12 seems to reflect and address a similar problem, and it uses the popular early Christian term "love feasts" for these communal meals. They would have probably culminated in the Lord's Supper, based on Jesus' model from the final Passover festival he celebrated with his disciples (Matt. 26:26–29; Mark 14:22–25; Luke 22:14–20). Paul doesn't object to the well-to-do enjoying a reasonable quantity or quality of food in the privacy of their own families (v. 22a). But in this church setting, their satiating themselves at the expense of the "have-nots" proves singularly inappropriate (vv. 22b).

The account of Jesus' Last Supper stands in striking contrast to the report of the Corinthians' behavior. Verses 23b–26 run closely parallel to the passages noted above in the Synoptic Gospels, especially to Luke's version (Luke 22:17–20). "Receive" and "pass on" in verse 23 reflect standard terminology for the transmission of oral tradition. So when Paul says he received this information from the Lord, we must not think of some kind of direct revelation. Rather he is referring to that which the Lord Jesus spoke while he was alive, words remembered by the disciples and widely repeated and perhaps even memorized in the early Christian community (recall the similar phenomenon in 7:10). "Betrayed" and "pass on" in this verse both come from the verb "to deliver." By this deliberate play on words, Paul thinks back to Jesus' subsequent arrest and crucifixion, an appropriate introduction for reflections on a rite that commemorates Christ's death.

The focus of those reflections centers on Jesus' so-called "words of institution" about the significance of the bread and the wine (vv. 24–26). During the Passover, Jews ate unleavened bread to recall their hasty departure from Egypt when God rescued them from the hands of Pharaoh (Ex. 12). The head of the household would open the meal in prayer and then distribute pieces of the bread broken from a common loaf (recall 10:17).[4] This histor-

---

4. Hence, several ancient manuscripts actually read, "This is my body, which is *broken* for you," a reading well-known from the KJV. But there is not enough textual evidence to make it likely that this reading is the original one.

ical setting makes any literal rendering of "is" in Jesus' statement "this is my body" incoherent. No one sitting with Christ at table would have thought he was saying that the bread was somehow a literal extension of his flesh or spirit. Rather the bread *symbolized* or *represented* his coming bodily death, an atoning sacrifice for the sake of all who would accept the forgiveness of sins it made available.[5] Each time the Corinthians ate the bread of the Lord's Supper, they should have recalled this death and acted in ways consistent with Christ's immeasurable self-giving and grace on their behalf. The last line of verse 24 (and v. 25) is probably best translated, "Do this as my memorial."[6]

The cup that was drunk after supper would probably have been the third of four cups of wine consumed during the Passover meal, again with redemptive implications. This was the point in the ceremony at which the words "I redeem you" from Exodus 6:6 were read. There is no chance that unfermented beverage was poured into the cup, since some who drank excessively were getting drunk (v. 21). The reason Paul, like the gospel writers, calls it the "cup" rather than using the word *wine* is because the expression would evoke Old Testament associations of suffering the "cup" of God's wrath (e.g., Ps. 75:8; Isa. 51:17). Christ's shed blood demonstrated that he accepted the wrath we deserved to experience and so made possible for us peace with God. In so doing he inaugurated the new covenant that had been prophesied (see esp. Jer. 31:31–34). "Whenever you drink it," in verse 25, may hint at the fact that wine was not present with every meal. Or it may mean that bread and wine should form the center of the Lord's Supper whenever it is celebrated. The message about the significance of Christ's death which this ceremony re-enacts should be proclaimed throughout church history. Only when the Lord returns (v. 26) will cross-centered Christianity become redundant, a fact that the Corinthians clearly had yet to learn (recall under 1:18–2:5).

In verses 27–34 Paul draws out the implications for the Corinthians of his appeal to tradition. Jesus' self-giving love for them makes their behavior (as described in verse 21) that much more shameful. "In an unworthy manner" in verse 27a translates the Greek adverb *anaxios* ("unworthily"). Paul does not use the adjective "unworthy," which would have referred to a person's char-

---

5. Cf. Morris, *First Corinthians*, 158, who notes three additional reasons for this interpretation: (1) "this" is neuter, whereas "bread" is masculine, so the former cannot modify the latter, rather it must refer to the entire action of blessing, breaking, and distributing the bread; (2) "Is" in 10:4 clearly means something like "represents" (and in the Aramaic Jesus originally spoke, it would have been entirely absent from the sentence); (3) the "cup" is equated with the new covenant, not with the blood directly.

6. Fritz Chenderlin, *"Do This As My Memorial"* (Rome: BIP, 1982).

acter, but highlights instead the nature of their *actions*. Thus his "warning was not to those who were leading unworthy lives and longed for forgiveness but to those who were making a mockery of that which should have been most sacred and solemn by their behaviour at the meal."[7] "The body and blood of the Lord" in verse 27b again refer to Jesus' crucifixion and its significance. Instead of eating and drinking without consideration of others, the Corinthians ought to share with each other and partake in moderation. "Examine" (v. 28) means "test and find approved." If their behavior towards their fellow-Christians is appropriate, then they qualify to participate themselves.

Verse 29 ("not recognizing the body of the Lord"[8]) seems to reflect the same problem described in verse 27 (eating unworthily), which in turn looked back to verse 21 (overeating and overdrinking). So "the body" in verse 29 probably refers to the corporate body of Christ, the church, particularly since Paul does not refer to both body and blood as in verse 26.[9] Those who eat and drink in flagrant disregard of the physical needs of others in their fellowship risk incurring punishment from God. Alternately, "body" may be an abbreviation for "body and blood" and again refer to Christ's atoning death. In neither instance, however, is there any contextual support for interpreting "recognizing the body" to mean "recognizing that Christ is actually present in the bread or wine."

Verse 30 unpacks what was involved in God's punishing the Corinthians for their profaning his holy table. "Weak" and "sick" are two relatively synonymous words for physical illness. "Sleep" was a common euphemism for death. In the latter case, one thinks of the tragic end of Ananias and Sapphira in Acts 5:1–11. The way to avoid such tragedy is to monitor one's own behavior (v. 31). And Paul ends on a somewhat upbeat note by reminding his readers that even those who have died for their actions are not damned (*contra* the original KJV rendering of "judgment" in verse 29 as "damnation"). Rather God disciplines those he loves (cf. Heb. 12:5–11) to protect them from further damaging themselves or others (v. 32).

---

7. I. Howard Marshall, *Last Supper and Lord's Supper* (Grand Rapids: Eerdmans, 1980), 116. Marshall's book in general contains the best overview of the historical background of the Lord's Supper, exegesis of the biblical texts which refer to it, and suggestions for contemporary application.

8. Significant early manuscripts omit "of the Lord." These words may be a later copyist's addition to clarify the meaning of "the body."

9. Cf. Talbert, *Corinthians*, 79: "Failure to discern the body can mean only inability to perceive the Christian unity rooted in the sacrifice of Christ and actualized in the sacred meal (1 Cor 10:16–17; cf. Didache 14.2, 'Let none who has a quarrel with his fellow join in your meeting until they are reconciled, lest your sacrifice be defiled.')."

Verses 33–34 bring this chapter to a close by restating and summarizing Paul's solution to the Corinthians' unholy activity during Communion. "Wait for" (v. 33) might also be translated "welcome." Anyone's genuine hunger pangs can be satisfied privately (v. 34a), so that the main point of the public Christian meal is to share with one another rather than to satisfy one's own needs. This is the core of Paul's instructions; other matters can wait until he personally arrives in Corinth (v. 34b).

Bridging Contexts

THE LORD'S SUPPER, designed precisely to foster Christian unity, not only divided the Corinthians but has divided believers ever since. Early and medieval Roman Catholicism developed elaborate doctrines of transubstantiation (the bread and wine literally, though invisibly, turn into Christ's body and blood) and incomplete sacrifice (the Eucharist or mass completes the atoning work that Christ left incomplete), which went far beyond and even contradicted the explicit teaching of Scripture. Whereas the Protestant Reformers sharply broke with many Catholic practices, Lutheran and Anglican traditions at least remained quite similar with respect to Communion. Luther's doctrine of consubstantiation saw Christ's body and blood "really present in, with and under the wine." Zwingli and the so-called radical Reformers swung the pendulum to the opposite extreme, seeing nothing but the memorializing aspect of the Lord's Supper. Calvinism and Methodism may have captured the best balance by perceiving a special spiritual presence evoked by the powerful symbolism of the elements, but even they often carried the debate far beyond terrain that the Scriptures clearly cover.[10]

Yet the controversial issues go well beyond those of the relationship of the bread and wine to Christ's body and blood and of a complete or incomplete atonement, though those have certainly been the most crucial. Almost every denomination has its distinctive traditions for how to perform the ritual: what if any liturgy to use in accompaniment, who may participate, who may distribute the elements, what form of food and drink is used, and so on. Often Paul's threats of judgment have been unleashed on anyone who disagrees with one denomination's unique traditions. In so doing, many Christians have entirely missed the real meaning of these threats, which, as we

---

10. For good, brief histories of the varying strands of thought on the Lord's Supper in Christian tradition, see Donald Bridge and David Phypers, *Communion: The Meal That Unites?* (Wheaton: Harold Shaw, 1983); and Gary Macy, *The Banquet's Wisdom: A Short History of the Theologies of the Lord's Supper* (New York: Paulist, 1992).

have seen, are directed against those who are not adequately loving their Christian brothers or sisters and providing for their physical or material needs.

Even when Paul's words are supplemented by the Gospel accounts, there is very little in Scripture that insists that the Lord's Supper must be celebrated a certain way. No text ever restricts who can officiate or distribute the bread and wine. No particular words mandate what must be spoken. Prayers of thanksgiving are appropriate, but this is a far cry from the formal "blessing" of the elements that has become enshrined in certain ecclesial traditions. No specific frequency of celebration is ever commanded, although the references to the "breaking of bread" in Acts 2:42 and 20:7 may suggest that at first Christians partook of the Lord's Supper daily and later weekly. Acts 2:42 also suggests it was one of four central elements in early Christian worship, along with prayer, fellowship, and instruction. There is thus nothing wrong with including communion as a part of every worship service, though there is something to be said for reserving it for certain announced occasions, so that what was intended to be special runs less of a risk of becoming mere routine. On the other hand, churches that celebrate the Eucharist only quarterly or semiannually, and even then often with little fanfare, run the risk of so minimizing its role that its centrality to worship may be lost.

First Corinthians 5:8 has already clarified that Christians remove yeast from their bread not literally but spiritually, as they purge all kinds of evil from their lives. So there is no need to insist that Communion bread be unleavened, though the link with the Passover meal of the Jews may be heightened in so doing. Hence some churches use wafers, others crackers, others full-fledged bread that has risen. All are acceptable. The common loaf, however, provides powerful symbolism in most all cultures of the unity the rite intends to signify, and there is much to be said for preserving that specific symbol. Where health concerns prevent people from actually passing a loaf and each breaking a piece off it, eating simultaneously, perhaps accompanied by some outward expression of friendship for those nearby, can serve as an adequate substitute.

There is no theological reason why the "wine" must be fermented. Grape juice or other red drinks, preserving the symbolism of Christ's blood, may be substituted. Again a common cup is desirable, perhaps with a cloth for wiping the lip of the cup after each person has drunk, but simultaneous drinking of individual glasses may prove more sanitary. Neither is there any reason why small cups of actual wine may not be used; no one will get drunk on a tiny sip. But for the sake of those who prefer total abstinence, perhaps the ideal compromise is the use of trays that contain two separate sections for cups of wine and others of grape juice, each clearly distinguished. Then individual celebrants can choose what is best for them.

Can other food or drink be used? If part of the purpose of both Passover and the Last Supper was to use that which best symbolized daily sustenance and ordinary drink in the ancient world, then perhaps the answer is yes. In some cultures, other food may be the staple (for example, rice) or other drink more common (for example, tea).[11] But the further removed one gets from that which can be broken, like bread, or is red, like wine, the less the fullness of the original symbolism is preserved. Perhaps asking how far we can go away from literal bread and wine is asking the question backwards. Instead it would seem we should ask how close we can get to preserving what the first Christians themselves did, without exorbitant cost to others and without losing the actual meaning for the sake of preserving the original form.

Early in the church's history, the inclusion of the Lord's Supper as part of a full meal disappeared. Again, such inclusion was never commanded, but there are strong arguments for reinstating the practice, at least part if not all of the time.[12] Most cultures have considered eating meals a significant time of intimate, interpersonal fellowship, even if not always to the degree that biblical societies did. When Christian communities contain needy people in their midst, serving meals can be an opportunity to share with those less fortunate a quantity and quality of food not always otherwise available to them. Some churches have served weekly meals for their members apart from the Lord's Supper; how much more meaningful when the two are combined.

Taking up collections for the poor is also very appropriate in the context of the Lord's table. Paul's words in verses 22 and 34 distance him from both socialist and capitalist ideals. On the one hand, he does not condemn the wealthy from enjoying extra material benefits in private. On the other hand, he sets limits on public Christian behavior that leave no room for hoarding and indulgence at the expense of the needy.

The Eucharist should be a time of self-examination, not so much for past sins, though repentance from them is always appropriate. Rather, Christians should consider their present attitudes toward those more needy than themselves. This would lead to a radically different group of people who ought to refrain from the Lord's Supper than usually appears. All repentant sinners are welcome, no matter how far away from God they may have recently felt.

---

11. Cf. the similar discussion in Eugene E. Uzukwu, "Food and Drink in Africa, and the Christian Eucharist," *African Ecclesial Review* 22 (1980): 370–85, who proposes millet and palm-wine as the elements for one particular African subculture.

12. See esp. J. Timothy Coyle, "The Agape/Eucharist Relationship in 1 Corinthians 11," *GTJ* 6 (1985): 411–24.

All professing believers who are unprepared to give generously of their wealth to help the poor in their midst, or who treat people of lower classes as second-class citizens, or who simply remain unreconciled with fellow celebrants, should refrain. Jesus' words concerning a somewhat analogous situation remain remarkably relevant here too: "If you are offering your gift at the altar and there remember that your brother has something against you, leave your gift there in front of the altar. First go and be reconciled to your brother; then come and offer your gift" (Matt. 5:23–24). Above all, whatever individual introspection is involved should not overwhelm the dominant symbolism of unity.

Either of the interpretations of verse 29 that we have noted supports the restriction of participants in the Lord's Supper to those who are true believers. Those who partake must recognize "the body of the Lord," referring either to the church or to his atoning death. Unbelievers, by definition, do not accept the biblical meaning of Christ's death nor do they adequately care for his people.

On the other hand, Paul's words include no restrictions that limit celebration to members of one local church, denomination, or theological tradition. Children old enough to profess faith should be welcomed, so that they do not feel like outsiders to the table. No Scripture suggests any link between baptism and communion so as to exclude unbaptized believers from partaking. Even less is there any suggestion that one must first be catechized or confirmed, though instruction on the significance of the ritual, whether formal or informal, is obviously important. Children too young to participate might receive a blessing, perhaps accompanied by the laying on of hands, after the manner of Jesus' welcoming the children (Matt. 19:13–15). This would make them feel accepted, while guarding the integrity of the Lord's Supper itself.

Verse 18 may not be applied as a rationale for deliberately dividing the church. Paul's whole point in the larger context is to call those who have been behaving badly to change their ways and restore proper fellowship with one another. Yet, after a group has left a church, Paul's words may at times help explain theologically what has happened. But frequently churches divide into two or more separate groups, not because one is clearly preserving right doctrine or practice and the other is not. Commonly, as with the Corinthian divisions in chapter 1, peripheral issues and powerful personalities in each group provide the major impetus for division.

Verses 24–26 suggest a theology of the Lord's Supper that balances past and future. Debates as to which is dominant prove futile—both remain crucial. We commemorate the crucifixion, looking back to Christ's Last Supper even as we anticipate his return, looking forward to the Messianic banquet (cf. Isa. 25:6–9; 65:13–14; Matt. 22:1–14; Rev. 19). Meanwhile we should revel in our present fellowship with each other and with the risen Lord (see under 10:16–17) and seek to incorporate ever larger numbers into that fellowship by the evangelistic function of the Lord's Table. Verse 26b makes an explicit message of explanation and evangelism accompanying Communion very appropriate. But the word of proclamation need not be verbalized all the time. Paul's language suggests that the ritual itself "proclaims the Lord's death."[13]

The threat of God's judgment as a response to inconsiderate behavior among his people is unusual even within the New Testament and is rarely acknowledged as an option when sickness and death occur within the church. Perhaps if we were more open to the possibility that personal or corporate suffering was a response to Christian lovelessness, we would see the link more often. But God is gracious and usually does not respond in a tit-for-tat fashion.

The question most believers of most eras tend to ask is "Why does God treat his people this harshly, even if only rarely?" Verse 32, of course, provides Paul's answer in this context: they are being disciplined. But the question itself is misguided. All human beings deserve discipline for all of their sins. What Christians ought instead to ask is "Why aren't we punished more directly more often?" In so doing, God's grace—his undeserved favor lavished on his people—becomes greatly magnified.

Michael Green gives an excellent sixfold summary of the theology of the Lord's Supper that Paul stresses in verses 17–34: look back (to Christ's death), look in (in self-examination), look up (fellowship with God), look around (fellowship with each other), look forward (to Christ's return), and look outward (to proclaim God's word to others).[14]

ONE OF THE ironies of the modern ecumenical movement is that many denominations or branches of the church have been willing to abandon fundamental doctrines of the faith (the deity of Christ, belief in the biblical miracles, the historical trustworthiness of Scripture, and so on) and hence achieve a measure of unity around liberal theological perspectives, while balking at agreement on issues that stem

---

13. See esp. Beverly R. Gaventa, "'You Proclaim the Lord's Death': 1 Corinthians 11:26 and Paul's Understanding of Worship," *RevExp* 80 (1983): 377–87.

14. Green, *Corinth*, 46–49.

from purely human traditions that divide them. One of these divisive issues is the significance of the Lord's Supper and how it is to be celebrated. The most significant ecumenical document on the topic in recent years notes that areas of agreement have yet to be reached on the matters of the Eucharist as a sacrifice, the real presence of Christ in the elements, the *epiklesis* (calling upon the Lord to come and be present), the relation between communion and baptism, and whether or not the elements are changeable.[15] Yet not one of these issues is demonstrably addressed in Scripture!

In other arenas, significant progress has been made. Protestants are now sometimes welcome to participate in Catholic or Eastern Orthodox communion services, particularly in the West. And the theological reinterpretations that some Catholics and Orthodox have given make it possible at times for Protestants to partake in good conscience. Most evangelicals invite all "born-again" Christians to participate irrespective of denomination. There is a growing realization in both conservative and liberal churches that ordained clergy are not the only persons who can preside over the Lord's Supper. A number of theological traditions are increasingly willing to leave the nature of Christ's presence at the table somewhat undefined,[16] or to express it merely by analogy.[17] But, sadly, there remain widespread exceptions to each of these trends.

Debates still rage as to whether the Lord's Supper should be called an ordinance or a sacrament. The latter historically has suggested the unbiblical notion of a quasi-mechanical "means of grace." The former seems to limit the ritual to an act of obedience to Christ. Our culture is one of the few in the history of the world that has lost respect for the immense value of tradition, ritual, symbolism, and religious drama. Not surprisingly, evangelical liturgical churches thus prove very appealing to many who are more and more frustrated with this loss. Some evangelicals, unable to find such churches within their own traditions have increasingly turned to Anglicanism, Catholicism, and even Greek Orthodoxy to recover those emphases. What we need are balances between liturgy and spontaneity in the Eucharist and in worship more generally. We also need balances between planned sameness to stress our link with the past and opportunities for creativity to keep services fresh

---

15. *Baptism, Eucharist and Ministry*, Faith and Order Paper #111 (Geneva: World Council of Churches, 1982), 10–17.

16. Cf. already Robertson and Plummer, *First Corinthians*, 245: "Happily, no theory of the manner of Christ's Presence in the Eucharist is necessary for the fruitful reception of it."

17. Cf. esp. Marshall, *Supper*, 152, who notes that Christ is always present among his people but present in a special way at Communion, much like a parent who always loves his or her children but at times picks them up and gives them special hugs.

and meaningful for different subcultures within our society. We must simultaneously avoid the error of very formal churches that restrict God's grace to ceremonies performed in duly authorized fashion and the error of very informal fellowships that measure God's grace by "exotic experience."[18] The former seems most pronounced today in very conservative or traditional Catholic, Episcopal, and Lutheran contexts; the latter is most notable in charismatic circles. But to one degree or another, both problems usually appear sooner or later in all traditions.

As for the temporal emphases of the Lord's Supper, the church in general today seems best at stressing the backward look to the cross. Most neglected is our anticipation of the heavenly banquet. Somewhere in between falls our focus on present fellowship with God and others. Celebration in homes and house churches could improve the last of these, and it is increasing, especially in charismatic circles. Other churches helpfully seat communicants in small groups around numerous tables in a fellowship hall. This format can easily be combined with a dinner or potluck, giving time for informal conversation as well as the more formal ritual. Christian Passover services, especially when led by Messianic Jewish congregations, can prove particularly significant in enhancing appreciation of the original setting of the Lord's Supper.[19]

Many churches today appropriately include an offering for a "deacon's fund" or similar account reserved for the financially needy within a congregation. This emphasis could be stressed considerably without risking the danger of "extreme obedience." Messages that accompany the Eucharist, and that often tend to be unnecessarily repetitive in content, could emphasize the desperate plight of poor Christians around the world and the need for most Western Christians to be far more generous in giving their money and other aid to the marginalized both at home and abroad.

One way of modeling this concern within the communion service itself is to include women (and other minorities) intentionally among those who pray and distribute the elements. Even the most conservative interpretations of the "problem passages on women" in the Bible cannot logically preclude them functioning in this role. Culturally appropriate symbols of Christian fellowship—the kiss of peace, warm hugs or handshakes, and the like, also prove desirable.

Paul's warnings against profaning the Lord's Supper and incurring God's judgment are consistently applied to all the wrong situations. People are made to feel they should abstain if they have not felt close to God recently,

---

18. Bridge and Phypers, *Meal*, 181.

19. For modest suggestions regarding variety and creativity in the celebration of the Lord's Supper, see Roger Lovette, *Come to Worship* (Nashville: Broadman, 1990), 128–41.

or if they have been particularly disobedient, or if they have not achieved a certain level of Christian maturity, no matter how much they are prepared to repent or grow. Instead, pastors should caution their congregations against partaking if they are unwilling to be generous in helping the poor in their midst, or if they remain unreconciled with a fellow-Christian over some interpersonal dispute or squabble.

In churches that limit communion to those who have been baptized or confirmed, stress should be shifted instead to limiting it to those who have truly accepted Christ as Lord and Savior. The closest analogy to the Corinthian problem, of course, rests with those who are the most factious. These are the believers who are least qualified to partake of the table. Ironically, these are the persons who when they refuse to change their ways should be most vulnerable to excommunication (Tit. 3:10). Yet today the most factious people in many congregations are also the power brokers, who intimidate or run-off dissenting members rather than being properly disciplined themselves.[20]

The link between sin and sickness or death is also usually ignored, except in certain charismatic circles, where it often runs the risk of being overly exploited. Paul knows that suffering often is not the result of one's personal sin at all (2 Cor. 4:7–12; 6:4–10; 12:7–10). But the average noncharismatic church these days would do well to consider that perhaps *sometimes* such links are present. Weakness and illness can be "part of the wise, loving, painful, but productive, discipline of a perfect Father."[21]

Paul's vision of a church united across sociological divisions also calls into questions certain wings of the church-growth movement that overemphasize the value of homogeneous grouping. The Corinthians were doubtless preserving this kind of grouping during the Lord's Supper, and it is precisely this which Paul condemns! Today we often go beyond separate seating for different socioeconomic groups and form entirely separate congregations— along ethnic, linguistic, or geographical lines. No wonder it is hard for worship to demonstrate sharing between the rich and the poor. Urban congregations tend to have too few rich to have many material resources to share. Suburban congregations tend to have too few poor for the rich to share with. Both models are an affront to Christ.

---

20. Cf. Otfried Hofius, "The Lord's Supper and the Lord's Supper Tradition: Reflections on 1 Corinthians 11:23b–25," in *One Loaf, One Cup: Ecumenical Studies of 1 Corinthians 11 and Other Eucharistic Texts*, ed. Ben F. Meyer (Macon, Ga.: Mercer, 1993), 113–14: "Inconsiderateness, indifference, and lovelessness towards the 'brother for whom Christ died' are consequently nothing short of a denial of the ὑπὲρ ὑμῶν [on behalf of you] . . . whoever acts in this way makes it plain that he does not know or grasp what these acts mean."

21. Prior, *1 Corinthians*, 190.

One contemporary Catholic writer notes that both in Scripture and in the early church, the Eucharist often functioned as a time of preparation for going back into a harsh, persecuting world during the week.[22] We too live in a world in which social justice and basic human rights are increasingly denied to large numbers of people. At this point the words of the ecumenical commission referred to earlier prove highly relevant:

> The Eucharist celebration demands reconciliation and sharing among all those regarded as brothers and sisters in the one family of God and is a constant challenge in the search for appropriate relationships in social, economic and political life. All kinds of injustice, racism, separation and lack of freedom are radically challenged when we share in the body and blood of Christ. . . . As participants in the Eucharist, therefore, we prove inconsistent if we are not actively participating in this ongoing restoration of the world's situation and the human condition . . . and above all, the obstinacy of unjustifiable confessional oppositions within the body of Christ.[23]

22. Xavier León-Dufour, *Sharing the Eucharistic Bread: The Witness of the New Testament* (New York: Paulist, 1987), 301.

23. *Baptism, Eucharist and Ministry*, p. 14.

1 Corinthians 12:1-31a

🌿

NOW ABOUT SPIRITUAL GIFTS, brothers, I do not want you to be ignorant. ²You know that when you were pagans, somehow or other you were influenced and led astray to mute idols. ³Therefore I tell you that no one who is speaking by the Spirit of God says, "Jesus be cursed," and no one can say, "Jesus is Lord," except by the Holy Spirit.

⁴There are different kinds of gifts, but the same Spirit. ⁵There are different kinds of service, but the same Lord. ⁶There are different kinds of working, but the same God works all of them in all men.

⁷Now to each one the manifestation of the Spirit is given for the common good. ⁸To one there is given through the Spirit the message of wisdom, to another the message of knowledge by means of the same Spirit, ⁹to another faith by the same Spirit, to another gifts of healing by that one Spirit, ¹⁰to another miraculous powers, to another prophecy, to another distinguishing between spirits, to another speaking in different kinds of tongues, and to still another the interpretation of tongues.

¹¹All these are the work of one and the same Spirit, and he gives them to each one, just as he determines. ¹²The body is a unit, though it is made up of many parts; and though all its parts are many, they form one body. So it is with Christ. ¹³For we were all baptized by one Spirit into one body—whether Jews or Greeks, slave or free—and we were all given the one Spirit to drink.

¹⁴Now the body is not made up of one part but of many. ¹⁵If the foot should say, "Because I am not a hand, I do not belong to the body," it would not for that reason cease to be part of the body. ¹⁶And if the ear should say, "Because I am not an eye, I do not belong to the body," it would not for that reason cease to be part of the body. ¹⁷If the whole body were an eye, where would the sense of hearing be? If the whole body were an ear, where would the sense of smell be? ¹⁸But in fact God has arranged the parts in the body, every one of them, just as he wanted them to be. ¹⁹If they were all one part,

where would the body be? ²⁰As it is, there are many parts, but one body.

²¹The eye cannot say to the hand, "I don't need you!" And the head cannot say to the feet, "I don't need you!" ²²On the contrary, those parts of the body that seem to be weaker are indispensable, ²³and the parts that we think are less honorable we treat with special honor. And the parts that are unpresentable are treated with special modesty, ²⁴while our presentable parts need no special treatment. But God has combined the members of the body and has given greater honor to the parts that lacked it, ²⁵so that there should be no division in the body, but that its parts should have equal concern for each other. ²⁶If one part suffers, every part suffers with it; if one part is honored, every part rejoices with it.

²⁷Now you are the body of Christ, and each one of you is a part of it. ²⁸And in the church God has appointed first of all apostles, second prophets, third teachers, then workers of miracles, also those having gifts of healing, those able to help others, those with gifts of administration, and those speaking in different kinds of tongues. ²⁹Are all apostles? Are all prophets? Are all teachers? Do all work miracles? ³⁰Do all have gifts of healing? Do all speak in tongues? Do all interpret? ³¹But eagerly desire the greater gifts.

PAUL NOW RESUMES addressing issues clearly raised by the Corinthians in their letter to him, but the theme of behavior in worship carries over from chapter 11. The Corinthian services were somewhat chaotic, and the more libertine wing was apparently equating spirituality with the exercise of the more spectacular gifts. Chapter 12 thus insists on the need for diversity of gifts within the unity of the body. Chapter 13 stresses that without love the gifts are worthless. Chapter 14 then focuses on two of the more controversial gifts—prophecy and tongues—telling the Corinthians to prefer the former to the latter because of its more immediate intelligibility (vv. 1–25) and giving guidelines for the use of each so as to promote order in the church (vv. 26–40).

Within chapter 12, Paul begins with an introduction highlighting the basic criterion for distinguishing the work of the Holy Spirit from that of other spirits (vv. 1–3). Verses 4–6 then ground the diversity of spiritual gifts within the unity of the Triune Godhead. Verses 7–11 offer samples of the diverse gifts, while stressing that each comes from the same sovereign Spirit. Verses 12–26 develop in more detail the metaphor of the body of Christ, while verses 27–31 bring the chapter to a close with a second representative list of gifts which stresses that not one of them is given to all Christians. "The successive waves of Paul's argument may be summed up as follows: (1) not disunity, but (2) unity; yet unity (3) not uniformity, but (4) of mutual concern and love."[1]

"Spiritual gifts" in verse 1 is either the neuter or masculine gender of the adjective *spiritual* and so could also be translated "spiritual things" or "spiritual people." In 14:1 it is definitely neuter, but "things" may include "people." The term probably reflects the prideful way the Corinthian leaders referred to themselves. So too Paul picks up on their claims to knowledge and with a tinge of irony fears that he actually needs to dispel their "ignorance" (recall 10:1).

Part of their problem is that they have not made a radical enough break from their pagan backgrounds, which employed counterparts to many of the controversial gifts discussed here, especially tongues and prophecy. Some of them had doubtless spoken seemingly inspired utterances during various Greco-Roman religious rituals (v. 2).[2] But in those settings, participants who had heard of Christ's claims might well have cursed him, so Paul notes that no one can sincerely declare Jesus to be *anathema* who is a true believer (v. 3a). Conversely, only Christians—those indwelt by the Spirit—can acknowledge Jesus as Lord (v. 3b). Here is the fundamental early Christian confession of faith (cf. Rom. 10:9–10), flying both in the face of pagan affirmations of some other deity or emperor as god and master and in the face of Jewish insistence that Yahweh alone merited the title.

Verses 4–6 continue with three closely parallel statements. Paul elucidates spiritual gifts from three different angles: They are bestowed freely by the Spirit's grace (v. 4), are intended to be used in a Christ-like attitude of servanthood (v. 5), and are the result of God's powerful working in a person's life (v. 6). Verse 7 employs yet a fourth term, "manifestations," and stresses that all the Corinthian Christians have at least one such gift, which is to be used for mutual edification (cf. Eph. 4:11–13).[3]

---

1. Ellingworth and Hatton, *First Corinthians*, 252.

2. Terence Paige, "1 Corinthians 12.2: A Pagan *Pompe?*" *JSNT* 44 (1991): 57–65, thinks that vocal participation in religious parades is particularly in view and translates "Whenever you were led [in the processions] you were [really] being carried away captive."

3. Barrett, *First Corinthians*, 284: Verse 7 "sums up the argument so far," which is that "each member of the church has a gift; none is excluded." "Manifestation," therefore, should be seen as just another synonym for "gift."

The words for "another" in verses 8–10 switch in the Greek from *allos* ("another of the same kind") to *heteros* ("another of a different kind"), so that these verses divide into three sections: wisdom and knowledge (v. 8); faith, healings, miracles, prophecy, and distinguishing spirits (vv. 9–10a); and tongues and their interpretations (v. 10b). This suggests an ABA structure that shifts from gifts of word to those of deed and back again, though prophecy perhaps falls in both categories.[4] Peter recognizes a similar twofold classification of the gifts: speaking and serving (1 Peter 4:11). All nine represent the more miraculous gifts, precisely because these were what the Corinthians were overly stressing in divisive ways. Paul, on the other hand, repeatedly states that they all come from the same Spirit. And because it is the Holy Spirit, and not individual merit, who determines who gets what gifts (v. 11), they cannot be used to mark out any one for special status within the church in Corinth.

A "message" (literally, "word") of wisdom or knowledge (v. 8) reflects the ability to bring spiritual insight to bear in a timely, helpful fashion in a specific Christian context. If Paul intends any difference between the word of wisdom and the word of knowledge, it may be that wisdom is knowledge applied, particularly in moral contexts (see Prov. 1:7). In 13:2, knowledge is linked with understanding mysteries, so it may involve an element of explaining the inscrutable as well. "Faith" in verse 9 is not the trust in Christ that all persons must have in order to be saved, but a special measure of faith that God can work miracles (again cf. 13:2) or to sustain a person when he chooses not to work them. "Gifts of healings" (the Greek is plural) refer to supernatural cures of physical maladies. The plurals suggest either that the gift may come and go for various occasions or, perhaps more likely, that there are different gifts for different kinds of illnesses. "Miraculous powers" (v. 10—Gk., "the workings of powers") include additional kinds of miracles, such as the apostles and other early Christians were enabled to perform, including, most notably, exorcisms.

New Testament prophecy builds on the background of prophetic activity in both the Old Testament and Greco-Roman religions, while differing in crucial ways from each. Both inside and outside of the canon, prophecy consistently included both "foretelling" (predicting future events) and, more predominantly, "forthtelling" (exhorting God's people, and occasionally his enemies, about his will for their present circumstances). It shares the common feature of a sense of declaring a message one believes one has received

---

4. Cf. Ellis, *Pauline Theology*, 36. *Allos* and *heteros* do not always differ from each other in the New Testament, but here and in 15:39–41 the distinction seems to hold up well.

relatively directly from God (cf. 14:30).[5] New Testament prophecy therefore included both conventional preaching, when the preacher had the sense of being gripped and convicted by the Spirit about his or her message, and more spontaneous, unpremeditated utterances. Hill captures both of these concepts in his definition: Christian prophets are "those who have grasped the meaning of Scripture, perceived its powerful relevance to the life of the individual, the Church and society, and declare that message fearlessly."[6] Their prophecy is not on a par with Scripture and their exercise of the gift, like that of all other spiritual gifts, is subject to error and misinterpretation (cf. esp. Acts 21:4 with vv. 11, 13–14).[7]

"Distinguishing between spirits" probably refers to the God-given ability to discern if an apparently inspired speaker is ministering by the power of the Holy Spirit or by some counterfeit power. It cannot be the same as evaluating the contents of an alleged prophecy, since 14:29 assigns that responsibility either to other prophets or to the entire congregation.

"Speaking in tongues" (glossolalia) must not be confused with what happened to the disciples at Pentecost. There the audience understood what was being proclaimed without benefit of an interpreter (Acts 2:1–13); here an interpretation is required. Various Greco-Roman religions had comparable phenomena, so it is best to understand the Corinthian experience as involving some kind of initially unintelligible verbal utterance. It may or may not have had a discernible linguistic structure; the word for "tongue" is broad enough in meaning to cover any audible vocalization.[8]

"Interpreting" tongues then refers to putting the otherwise unintelligible message into words which are understood by those present.[9] Chapter 14 will elaborate in more detail on both prophecy and tongues and on appropriate responses to each.

In verses 12–26, Paul develops the extended metaphor of the church as the body of Christ. An ABBA pattern is discernible as he follows up an

---

5. See esp. David E. Aune, *Prophecy in Early Christianity and the Ancient Mediterranean World* (Grand Rapids: Eerdmans, 1983), whose study is also by far the most thorough of this phenomenon in antiquity.

6. David Hill, *New Testament Prophecy* (London: Marshall, Morgan & Scott, 1979), 213.

7. See esp. Wayne A. Grudem, *The Gift of Prophecy in 1 Corinthians* (Washington, D.C.: University Press of America, 1982); cf. idem, *The Gift of Prophecy in the New Testament and Today* (Westchester, Ill.: Crossway, 1988).

8. A well-balanced treatment of the phenomenon appears in Watson E. Mills, *A Theological/Exegetical Approach to Glossolalia* (Grand Rapids: Eerdmans, 1986). A guide to additional research is found in idem, ed., *Speaking in Tongues* (Lanham, Md.: University Press of America, 1985).

9. Anthony C. Thiselton, "The 'Interpretation' of Tongues: A New Suggestion in the Light of Greek Usage in Philo and Josephus," *JTS* 30 (1979): 15–36.

initial statement of the metaphor (v. 12) by moving from the theme of unity (v. 13) to diversity (v. 14), and then describes in more detail first diversity (vv. 15–21) and then unity (vv. 22–26).[10]

Verses 13–14 give a twofold rationale for permitting diversity within unity: (1) those who are being saved come from all ethnic and socioeconomic brackets of the ancient world; and (2) that is how a human body works. Verse 13 refers to incorporation into the body of Christ as "baptism in one Spirit" (the NIV footnote—"Or *with*, or *in*"—is better than the "by" of the text, because it preserves the analogy with "baptism *in* water"). Spirit-baptism is not identical to water baptism but occurs at the moment of conversion (cf. Rom. 8:9). However, Paul probably associated the concepts closely together, inasmuch as water baptism in the early church regularly followed quickly on the heels of belief. "Given the one Spirit to drink" could also be rendered "watered with the one Spirit" (cf. Paul's use of the same verb in 3:6–7). Either way, both clauses of verse 13 refer to the same spiritual action of being incorporated into the company of the redeemed and suggest that the Spirit both indwells and surrounds us.

Verses 15–20 underline what is demonstrable with respect to a human body: all the parts serve an important function, regardless of any claims to the contrary. Without the diversity that comes from specialization of function, one no longer has an organism, merely one giant organ, unable to do anything.

Verses 21–26 continue the analogy but begin to apply it to the church. Where there is seemingly less value, power, or honor in the body, compensation occurs to preserve relative equality. In fact, the true value of a particular body part is often inversely proportional to its outward appearance. When Paul speaks of weaker body parts (v. 22) he may be thinking of fingers or toes, or the less protected organs such as one's eyes. The "less honorable" parts (v. 23a) may refer to internal organs, usually covered by clothing, since the verb for "treat" can also mean "clothe." The "unpresentable" parts (v. 23b) most naturally refer to genitalia and the excretory tracts. Paul's fundamental concern is that the gifts and/or people the Corinthians are demeaning should be affirmed, while those they are overly exalting should be put in more balanced perspective. Presumably, he has in mind the more visible and dramatic gifts, but he may also be thinking of the more wealthy power brokers in the church—recall 11:17–34. So verse 26 rounds out Paul's discussion of the body with another reminder of mutuality and interdependence. What modern medicine has recently come to under-

---

10. Cf. Thomas A. Jackson, "Concerning Spiritual Gifts: A Study of 1 Corinthians 12," *Faith and Mission* 7 (1989): 61–69.

stand even better than did the ancients—that the body is a psychosomatic whole—should apply that much more to the fellowship of believers. One individual's joy or suffering should prove contagious.[11]

Verses 27–31 complete this chapter with one final restatement of the body metaphor and another listing of sample gifts. But this time Paul's main point is that not one of the gifts is intended for all believers. The rhetorical questions in verses 29–30 all employ the Greek word *me*, which demonstrates that the implied answer to each question is, "No."

This list includes some of the same and some different gifts as in verses 8–10. "Apostles" in Paul's usage include not merely the Twelve but himself (1:1), Titus (2 Cor. 8:23), Epaphroditus (Phil. 2:25), James, the Lord's brother (Gal. 1:19), and Andronicus and Junia (Rom. 16:7), the latter probably a woman's name. Clearly he is using the term in its root sense of those sent out on a mission, in this case a divinely commissioned one. Christians would later come to call such people missionaries or church-planters. "Teachers" in the ancient world limited themselves largely to the communication of a fixed body of information to their students, often solely by rote memory work. "Those able to help others" is as vague in the Greek as in English but would have included special acts of assistance to the poor and needy. "Administration" may also be translated "oversight" or "guidance" and encompasses the governing aspect of church leadership.

To take "first," "second," and "third" in verse 28 as a ranking in significance would clearly violate the whole point of Paul's discussion thus far. So it is best to see in this enumeration a chronological priority (cf. Eph. 2:20).[12] To establish a local congregation requires a church-planter. Then the regular proclamation of God's Word must ensue. Next teachers must supplement evangelism with discipleship and the passing on of the cardinal truths of the faith. Only at this point does a viable Christian fellowship exist to enable all the other gifts to come into play. Tongues may be last on the list because the Corinthians were overestimating their value, but it cannot be demonstrated that Paul assigned them any inherent inferiority.

After all this, verse 31a seems out of place. How can Paul now encourage people to desire *greater* gifts? Some have therefore translated his words as a statement ("But you are eagerly desiring the [so-called] greater gifts") or as a question ("But are you eagerly desiring greater gifts?"). But these translations are not possible with Paul's parallel statement in 14:1, and they require an ironic reading of this verse for which there is no contextual evidence. So

---

11. On the "body of Christ" in Paul's thought more generally, cf. Andrew Perriman, "'His body, which is the church . . .': Coming to Terms with Metaphor," *EvQ* 62 (1988): 123–42.

12. Cf. Talbert, *Corinthians*, 85; Watson, *First Corinthians*, 137.

it is better to translate it as the NIV does and understand "greater" as referring to the less visible gifts given special honor and treatment (v. 23) or to prophecy as over against tongues (chap. 14). This verse also reminds the Corinthians that verse 11 need not lead to fatalism. It is entirely proper for them to pray for and even to try to cultivate certain gifts, so long as they leave room for the Spirit to refuse to grant their desires if he so chooses.

THE PRACTICE OF spiritual gifts can prove as divisive in settings outside first-century Corinth as it did there. But that is precisely what we must seek to avoid. In fact, the parallels between the squabbling among the Corinthian Christians and contemporary debates over the charismatic movement are surprisingly close. Most of Paul's instruction, therefore, transfers quite readily to our modern world, if we are willing to listen and follow what he says.

Any study of the spiritual gifts should include not only 1 Corinthians 12–14 but Romans 12:3–8 and Ephesians 4:7–13 as well. None of the various lists of gifts Paul gives in these chapters is identical, suggesting that none of them, individually or together, is intended to be comprehensive. Paul's use of the term *charisma* elsewhere (e.g., for celibacy and marriage in 7:7), like his use of a variety of terms for spiritual gifts in 12:1–6, suggests that the concept is not as fixed or technical an expression as some have made it out to be.[13] The range of functions covered by Paul's various lists of gifts makes it likely that any combination of talents, abilities, and endowments, however suddenly given or leisurely cultivated, may qualify as spiritual gifts, if a believer uses them for God's glory and his work in the world.[14] Certainly Paul's own unique preparation for Christian ministry as a Hellenistic Jew and Roman citizen makes it difficult to believe that he would have viewed all of his spiritual gifts, including preaching and teaching (Acts 13:1), as acquired only after his conversion. But precisely because all of the gifts have non-Christian analogues, a talent or ability becomes a *charisma* only when it is used by a believer for the "common good" (v. 7).

---

13. So, rightly, Enrique Nardoni, "The Concept of Charism in Paul," *CBQ* 55 (1993): 68–80.

14. Cf. Ralph P. Martin, *The Spirit and the Congregation* (Grand Rapids: Eerdmans, 1984), 37: "Any condition of life may *become* a person's *charisma* from God 'only when I recognize that the Lord has given it to me and that I am to accept this gift as his calling and command to me.'" Again, "no 'gift' is inherently charismatic, but it has the possibility of becoming so if it is claimed and utilized under the domain of Christ. Thus the natural order is 'sacralized' by being owned for Christ."

Verse 3 cannot be the only criterion for determining genuine from counterfeit spiritual utterance; in most contexts it will not get us very far! But it remains the most foundational test. Other scriptural helps include checking for further doctrinal orthodoxy, especially concerning the person of Christ (1 John 4:1) and observing the "fruit" or results of the ministry of the speaker (Matt. 7:15–20). If a given prophecy is predictive and truly inspired by God, then it will come true (Deut. 18:22). But even after applying these criteria, there may remain ambiguities, which is one reason why any apparent expression of the Spirit's gifts must never be accorded "divine" or inerrant status.

Verses 4–6 contain important Trinitarian implications, all the more significant because they are not the main point of the paragraph. The primary function of Paul's word here is to argue for a legitimate diversity of gifts, which the Corinthians were not acknowledging, based on the very nature of God himself.

Verse 7a teaches the important principle that all Christians receive at least one spiritual gift. Some may receive more than one, at the same time or at different times in life. It is even possible that individual gifts may be rescinded (e.g., through disuse; but cf. Rom. 11:29, although that is in a different context), but never so as to leave a believer without any. Like 1:7, this verse discourages an approach to the Christian life that is forever looking for some new gift or experience or that claims conversion alone is inadequate to equip believers for immediate service to the church. The repetition of "the same Spirit" throughout verses 8–11 hammers home the point that diversity doesn't necessarily threaten unity. Given the conjunctions of wisdom and knowledge, of healings and other miracles, we must be wary of drawing too fine a distinction between any pair of spiritual gifts. Paul elsewhere closely links prophecy and knowledge (13:2) and pastors and teachers (Eph. 4:11), and Luke similarly conjoins prophets and teachers (Acts 13:1).

In general, there is little to commend either the approach that restricts a particular gift to a uniquely supernatural manifestation or the approach that leaves a gift virtually indistinguishable from a natural talent. Carolyn Osiek's words on prophecy prove particularly helpful: It "is the living word that compels to constructive action, that rends our hearts and pushes us to deeper connectedness with life, so that we dare to reach out to others with greater love and faith." She continues, "If today in many of our contexts, it does not take the same form as it did in the Pauline churches, that is only because the prophetic Spirit is sufficiently agile to adapt to changed cultural assumptions and behavior."[15] What is true of prophecy is true of teaching, of helping, of

---

15. Carolyn Osiek, "Christian Prophecy: Once Upon a Time?" *CTM* 17 (1990): 296–97.

administering, and so on. God may use and cultivate innate abilities or give people brand-new capacities. It is entirely up to him.[16]

Classifications of the gifts also regularly risk imposing artificial categories on the textual data that Paul would not have endorsed. Nevertheless, we may note that certain gifts do seem to require more direct supernatural empowering than others (e.g., tongues, interpretation, healings, miracles). Others appear to grant individuals an extra measure of some virtue commanded to one degree or another of all Christians (e.g., wisdom, knowledge, faith, helping, giving, service, exhortation, mercy). Still others are closely tied with leadership roles in the church (e.g., apostles, teachers, administrators), and some may cut across two or more of these categories (e.g., prophecy, spanning the first and third category; or evangelism, spanning the second and third).

This kind of classification raises the important question of the relationship between gifts and offices. Paul consistently recognizes two established offices of church leaders: overseers, also known as elders, and deacons (cf., e.g., Acts 20:17–28; Phil. 1:1; 1 Tim. 3:1–13). But the criteria for these offices are expressed not in terms of any specific gifts but as spiritual maturity more generally (1 Tim. 3:2–12; Tit. 1:6–9). So while certain gifts are surely more appropriate for certain offices than others (prophecy or teaching for elders; helping for deacons, etc.) the two categories must not be confused. It is possible to exercise the gift of pastoring without becoming the pastor of a particular church. It is possible to exercise the gift of prophecy, including Spirit-led preaching, without necessarily being "the preacher" in a given congregation. Some are enabled to effect miraculous cures by virtue of their gifts. Others are called to lay on hands and pray for the sick by virtue of their office of elder (Jas. 5:14). God gives gifts indiscriminately and irrespective of gender (cf. Acts 2:17–18), but each local congregation should determine who its officers are going to be according to their understanding of the biblical criteria.[17]

Romans 12:3–8 suggests that determining and then faithfully using one's spiritual gifts is the next most important task in a Christian's life after the fundamental cognitive and moral transformation that accompanies conversion (Rom. 12:1–2). We have already seen how 1 Corinthians 1:7 pointed to gifts

---

16. Cf. Prior, *1 Corinthians*, 198: "It would seem wrong either, on the one hand, to *confine* the gifts of the spirit to natural abilities harnessed and released by God or, on the other hand, to assert that the *real* gifts of the Spirit are only those which are manifestly supra-natural."

17. On the overlap and distinction between gifts and offices, see esp. Ronald Y. K. Fung, "Ministry, Community and Spiritual Gifts," *EvQ* 56 (1984): 3–20.

as the characteristic expression of each Christian's ministry throughout the church age. Surely then a crucial question for believers in every time and culture is how they determine what their individual gifts are. Various diagnostic tools have been developed, from the relatively simple to the quite sophisticated, and these can be helpful in confirming suspicions and suggesting new possibilities.[18] But most of the church down through history has not had access to these tools, and God can overrule the natural desires or abilities that these various diagnostic tests disclose. So all Christians remain responsible for praying, searching their hearts, trying out ministries, and seeking loving but truthful feedback from mature believers to guide them in ascertaining their distinctive gifts.

Once a person is reasonably sure how he or she has been gifted, that person needs an outlet for service. This fact has staggering implications for the way churches must be organized. Opportunities within worship must be made, whether at the level of small or large groups, for every member to participate in ways that the Spirit leads, even if it is not planned for in the order of service (cf. further on 14:26). Leadership must encourage each member to exercise his or her gifts and help each person to find ways of using them within the local body of believers. When it is time to fill the slots of church responsibilities, people should be matched with areas of their strengths and not their weaknesses. And members ought willingly to volunteer for jobs in those areas without waiting to be asked.[19]

Verse 11 provides a crucial caution against the natural human tendency to want or expect everyone else to be gifted in the ways we are. It completely refutes all claims that any one gift is necessary for someone to be a Christian, or to be a mature Christian, or to be in the center of God's activity in some part of the world. Just as "there are no one-member churches," neither "are there any every-member gifts!"[20]

---

18. Cf., e.g., Eddie Gibbs, *I Believe in Church Growth* (Grand Rapids: Eerdmans, 1983), 452–53, for a simple one-page questionnaire. Clyde B. McDowell, *How to Discover Your Spiritual Gifts* (Littleton, Col.: Lay Action Ministry Program, 1988; Elgin, Ill: David C. Cook, 1988), gives a brief cluster of statements to respond to for each of the various gifts. Don and Katie Fortune, *Discover Your God-Given Gifts* (Old Tappan, N.J.: Fleming Revell, 1987) have elaborate inventories for seven major categories of gifts in three different forms, tailor-made for adults, teens, and children. See also the *Network* materials (Grand Rapids: Zondervan, 1994), written by Bruce Bugbee, Bill Hybels, and Don Cousins.

19. For numerous practical suggestions on implementing the ideas of this paragraph, see Paul Stevens, "Equipping for Spiritual Gifts," in George Mallone, ed., *Those Controversial Gifts* (Downers Grove, Ill.: InterVarsity Press, 1983), 121–43.

20. J. W. MacGorman, "Glossolalic Error and Its Correction: 1 Corinthians 12–14," *RevExp* 53 (1983): 394.

Spirit-baptism in verse 13 must not be confused with water-baptism. The expression "baptize with [in/by] the Spirit" occurs seven times in the New Testament. All other six uses are references to John the Baptist's prophecy that Jesus would baptize with or in the Holy Spirit (Matt. 3:11; Mark 1:8; Luke 3:16; John 1:33; Acts 1:5; 11:16), which was fulfilled at Pentecost, as the Acts 1:5 reference clarifies. Both the word and practice of baptism in the ancient world suggests that what Paul has in mind here is an initiation experience that immerses a person into the realm of the Spirit. Given that Paul says all the Corinthian believers have been so baptized, and given the level of immaturity of at least some of them, it is impossible that Spirit-baptism should be any kind of second blessing or subsequent experience of God apart from conversion and the initial arrival of the Spirit into a person's life. Whatever else the stories of the Samaritans in Acts 8 and of John's disciples in Acts 19 mean, it is clear that in each instance Luke describes the first and only arrival of the Spirit, an arrival that Paul equates with becoming a Christian (Rom. 8:9).[21]

Verse 13, like Galatians 3:28, also reminds us of the crucial need in every age for the church to model heterogeneous groupings that cause the world to marvel at our unity within diversity (cf. Eph. 4:4–11). Church should be a place where people gather and get along with each other who have no merely human reason for doing so.

Verses 14–26 remain largely self-explanatory, and their overarching principles are clear. Body parts are interdependent, not independent of each other. The New Testament recognizes no individual or "lone-ranger" Christians who are not attached to some local Christian fellowship. That is not to say it is impossible to be saved and uninvolved, merely that it is unhealthy. In societies where individualism is valued above corporate responsibility, the importance of the metaphor of Christ's church as a body looms large. Paul's emphasis on all of us needing every other believer greatly relativizes any hierarchy of status, rank, or privilege that we might otherwise try to establish. If there is to be any disparity in the amount of honor accorded anyone, then the less visible, less publicly acknowledged gifts, such as helping, service, or giving, merit greater acclaim.

The gift of faith exercised by particularly powerful prayer warriors probably belongs here too. People with these gifts form the glue that holds

---

21. On this theme in both Acts and Paul, see esp. J. D. G. Dunn, *Baptism in the Holy Spirit* (Philadelphia: Westminster, 1970), 38–172. For a Pentecostal response to Dunn, see Howard M. Ervin, *Conversion-Initiation and the Baptism in the Holy Spirit* (Peabody, Mass.: Hendrickson, 1984). Ervin points out certain weaknesses in Dunn's exegesis but in general fails to overturn the main points of his book.

churches and ministries together, even as leaders, programs, and public performances come and go. Encouraging all believers to major in the areas of their strengths, but in a context of intimate interdependence, also makes possible obedience to verse 26. It is difficult for people to weep or rejoice with those to whom they do not feel close.

In verse 28 Paul alters his list of gifts from that of verses 8–10 apparently to broaden the scope of the Corinthians' focus. Instead of concentrating only on the more miraculous gifts, Paul adds samples of gifts for church leaders as well as other less status-filled roles. This categorization, however, remains somewhat anachronistic; the first Christians doubtless thought of all the gifts as miraculous. Nevertheless, everyday acts of service are now set on a par with the recognized, supernatural phenomena of the Spirit.[22] Verses 29–30 reinforce the principles stressed in connection with verse 11: every believer has at least one gift, but no one gift is given to every Christian. Verse 31a concludes Paul's discussion by reminding believers that it is all right and even desirable to seek certain gifts, particularly those less likely to induce pride and more likely to be immediately intelligible. But we dare never presume on God's sovereignty and pretend that he has to give us what we ask.[23]

 PAUL'S DISCUSSION OF spiritual gifts proves highly timely in our day. The gifts, particularly the ones that seem more supernatural, tend to be as controversial and divisive today as in first-century Corinth. After years of neglecting the ministries of the Holy Spirit, and due largely to the impetus of modern Pentecostalism and the subsequent charismatic movement, almost all Christian circles now focus periodically if not regularly on spiritual gifts. There are also promising signs in many quarters that churches are recovering the biblical models of every-member ministry, both by means of an emphasis on small groups within larger congregations and by virtue of small groups that become congregations (i.e., house churches).[24] But much progress is still needed on many fronts.

---

22. Cf. Hans Conzelmann, *First Corinthians* (Philadelphia: Fortress, 1974), 215.

23. On the principles associated with spiritual gifts in these chapters, see further esp. Kenneth Hemphill, *Spiritual Gifts: Empowering the New Testament Church* (Nashville: Broadman, 1988); and Siegfried Schatzmann, *A Pauline Theology of Charismata* (Peabody, Mass.: Hendrickson, 1987).

24. See esp. Robert Banks, *Paul's Idea of Community* (Grand Rapids: Eerdmans, 1980); Christian Smith, *Going to the Root: 9 Proposals for Radical Church Renewal* (Scottdale, Pa.: Herald, 1992).

Verses 2–3 jointly warn against automatically assuming all apparently spiritual gifts are from God, a caution needed especially within the so-called neo-prophetic movement, and against automatically equating the more supernatural gifts with human manufacture or worse, a caution needed especially among cessationists. On the one hand the gifts can be and are counterfeited by many contemporary sects and religions. On the other hand, the devil is not in the habit of bringing people to Christ, promoting faith, sanctification, unity, and evangelical doctrine, as has often occurred in charismatic Christianity in the Third World, in various state churches of Protestant Europe, and in certain branches of the Roman Catholic church worldwide.

All of Paul's emphasis on diversity within unity gives the lie to those extreme wings of the charismatic movement that continue to claim that a person must speak in tongues (or experience prophecy, healing, or whatever) in order to be saved or to be spiritually mature. That same emphasis equally betrays the imbalance among zealous advocates for evangelism or missions as the most fundamental task of the church. Continuing elevation of clergy over laity remains similarly inappropriate.

All of Paul's emphasis on unity within diversity calls into question the behavior of growing numbers of Americans who claim to be religious, believe in God and even Christ, and yet drop out of organized church life or at least fade to its periphery.[25] In a land still heavily influenced by a heritage of rugged individualism, believers need to work ever harder to demonstrate that Christianity is not a merely personal religion but fundamentally corporate. Even evangelical language for conversion betrays this bias: a *"personal* relationship with Jesus Christ."* That is the necessary starting point, but we dare not stop until that relationship leads to intimate *inter*personal relationships with other Christians.

Definitions of individual gifts tend to be polarized along the lines of more supernatural conceptions (among charismatics) and more naturalistic conceptions (among noncharismatics). Both sides need to broaden their definitions and not limit God quite so much. A helpful guide in settling debates about a gift that proves controversial in a particular context is to see if the same principles being applied to it would stand up when assessing a less controversial gift. So, for example, some claim that a contemporary prophet must be one hundred percent accurate, as Old Testament prophets were supposed to be. But who requires that standard of inerrancy from those with the gift of teaching? On the other hand, one who claimed to be gifted as a

---

25. See esp. the trends discussed in Robert Bellah, et al., *Habits of the Heart* (Berkeley: University of California, 1985), esp. 219–49.

teacher who was consistently wrong would quickly be discredited. So too those who claim to bring more direct words from the Lord or to have an ongoing gift of healing, and yet consistently prove unable to use their "gift" accurately and effectively, should be encouraged to realize that they might not have such gifts.[26]

Whether gifts promote unity or division can also help to sift the genuine from the counterfeit. In many contexts, charismatics insist on their own way, elevating the value of their gifts above other less sensational ones, and thus quickly divide congregations. But in many other contexts, they appeal far more politely for their gifts to have some outlet in an otherwise non- or anti-charismatic setting, and division comes because of the intransigence of church leadership or other informal power blocks. In these cases the charismatics are more likely to have found "the real thing," despite the discord that still results. Ideally, a congregation should decide together in love whether it can tolerate the exercise of all the gifts and, if not, agree to refrain from whatever proves divisive for the sake of unity. Better still, it should allow them all but make none a criterion of any kind of status or maturity.[27]

Our analysis of verse 13 has shown that the expression "baptism of the Spirit" should not be applied to any post-conversion, "deeper-life" experience, as it continues to be in classic Pentecostal circles. But this does not mean that Christians cannot or should not seek fresh, invigorating experiences of God, to bring them to new levels of maturity throughout their lives. Noncharismatics need to acknowledge this more often. Yet if we want to be scriptural, we will follow Luke's lead and refer to these events as repeated "fillings" of the Spirit (cf., e.g., Acts 4:8, 31; 9:17).

Diversity within unity seriously challenges those prevailing models of church growth that stress homogeneous grouping principles. Perhaps at certain foundational levels, outreach and fellowship occur best among those most like ourselves. But the most dynamic evangelistic power of the gospel comes when the world is forced to sit up and take notice that people are loving each other in ways it cannot account for with humanistic presuppositions. In America, this is especially true when blacks and whites worship and work together for the Lord.[28] Yet, what Martin Luther King, Jr., often observed still

---

26. For a relatively balanced discussion, see Jack Deere, *Surprised by the Power of the Spirit* (Grand Rapids: Zondervan, 1993), 67 and throughout.

27. Cf. esp. the pastoral reflections in D. A. Carson, *Showing the Spirit* (Grand Rapids: Baker, 1987), 183–88. Overall, Carson's book is probably the best semi-popular exposition and application of 1 Corinthians 12–14 available.

28. A recent, powerful exposition of this theme appears in Spencer Perkins and Chris Rice, *More Than Equals* (Downers Grove, Ill.: InterVarsity Press, 1993). Cf. also Raleigh Washington and Glen Kehrien, *Breaking Down Walls* (Chicago: Moody, 1993).

proves true—11:00 on Sunday morning remains the most segregated hour of American life. Here is one of the most tragic indictments against contemporary Christendom within almost every ethnic group.

Indeed, lack of powerful evangelism more generally afflicts much of current Western Christianity. When Paul encourages believers eagerly to desire the greater gifts, we recognize that he means those that are not being given enough attention in Corinth. Many gatherings of suburban American Christians today disclose few, if any, who rank high in evangelism on spiritual gifts inventories. Surely we too then need to seek to fill this gap by praying that God would give some of us this gift and bring others into our fellowships who already have it.

It is less clear whether God desires every local church to have all the more supernatural gifts. The often-heard slogan in charismatic circles, "seek *all* the gifts," is precisely what Paul never says! But we should at least be open to them. If Christians of all theological stripes could today pray, "God give me tongues (or healing, or whatever the controversial gift is in a given context), *if and only if* you want to," charismatics and noncharismatics alike could bridge a substantial amount of the gap that still separates them.

In an age of increasing specialization in careers and knowledge more generally, it becomes all the more crucial for Christians to view spiritual gifts as broadly as possible. We ought to encourage believers to consider as spiritual gifts many kinds of abilities dedicated to the Lord's work. Surely music fits this category (cf. Eph. 5:18–19); and probably trade skills do as well (cf. Ex. 31:1–5). Barclay rightly remarks, "The mason, the carpenter, the electrician, the painter, the engineer, the plumber all have their special gifts, which are from God and can be used for him."[29] Doubtless, many others could be added to the list. Specialization deserves its place within pastoral staffs as the megachurches are increasingly recognizing. Instead of dividing up the labor merely into preaching, Christian education, youth, music, and evangelism, one may consider also administrative pastors, computer programmers, and even spiritual planning directors who help to identify individuals' gifts and mobilize them for service. The whole target-group ministry movement, first made famous by Frank Tillapaugh, follows logically from encouraging every member to discover his or her personal gifts and passions and "unleash" them for experimental ministries in the areas that most excite them.[30]

In all of this, however, we must beware of continuing to play down the significance of the "behind the scenes" people. Ours is an age that delights

---

29. Barclay, *Corinthians*, 109.
30. Frank R. Tillapaugh, *Unleashing the Church* (Ventura: Regal, 1982).

to exalt Christian celebrities, to demand that our pastors entertain, have charismatic personalities, and display more spiritual gifts than any one Bible character ever had! Little wonder that burn-out from full-time ministry seems to be at an all-time high and that moral failure often results from the stress. We need to relearn the model of servant leadership (recall under chapter 4) and to allow our leaders and ourselves to spend the majority of time doing those things at which we excel.[31]

Implementing verse 26 will require every believer to be regularly and intimately involved with a network of Christian friends who commit to pray for each other and learn how to suffer and rejoice with each other through "thick and thin." These pairs, trios, and small groups, ideally the outgrowth of one larger local church, can then be enabled to look beyond themselves via prayer lists of broader concerns, communication between sister congregations, networks of information about the church of Jesus Christ locally and globally, and active missionary concerns, including regular correspondence, telephoning, fax, and travel from one part of the world to another.[32]

Verse 28 reminds us of the present need to continue to extend the gospel into new areas and among unreached peoples. In an age of mass media and multimedia, many methods prove useful but none can ever supplant the prophetic ministry of the ongoing, Spirit-directed proclamation of the Word in the context of local congregations. Then that proclamation must be supported by consistent teaching of both the content and application of all the different genres of the biblical literature. Growing, healthy churches will spawn daughter congregations that repeat the process.

In a day when more and more "worship services" are being turned into soft-sell evangelism in "seeker-sensitive" styles, the need for accompanying "Sunday School" or its equivalent, with a solid teaching component, becomes all the more acute. More traditional churches that continue to major on "in-house" teaching need to be encouraged to supplement their work with a greater focus on church-planting and evangelistic proclamation.

---

31. See esp. John Bradley and Jay Carty, *Unlocking Your Sixth Suitcase: How to Love What You Do and Do What You Love* (Colorado Springs: NavPress, 1991).

32. See esp. the helpful models suggested in John Ronsvalle and Sylvia Ronsvalle, *The Poor Have Faces: Loving Your Neighbor in the 21st Century* (Grand Rapids: Baker, 1992).

1 Corinthians 12:31b–13:13

🌿

AND NOW I will show you the most excellent way. ^{13:1}If I speak in the tongues of men and of angels, but have not love, I am only a resounding gong or a clanging cymbal. ²If I have the gift of prophecy and can fathom all mysteries and all knowledge, and if I have a faith that can move mountains, but have not love, I am nothing. ³If I give all I possess to the poor and surrender my body to the flames, but have not love, I gain nothing.

⁴Love is patient, love is kind. It does not envy, it does not boast, it is not proud. ⁵It is not rude, it is not self-seeking, it is not easily angered, it keeps no record of wrongs. ⁶Love does not delight in evil but rejoices with the truth. ⁷It always protects, always trusts, always hopes, always perseveres.

⁸Love never fails. But where there are prophecies, they will cease; where there are tongues, they will be stilled; where there is knowledge, it will pass away. ⁹For we know in part and we prophesy in part, ¹⁰but when perfection comes, the imperfect disappears. ¹¹When I was a child, I talked like a child, I thought like a child, I reasoned like a child. When I became a man, I put childish ways behind me. ¹²Now we see but a poor reflection as in a mirror; then we shall see face to face. Now I know in part; then I shall know fully, even as I am fully known.

¹³And now these three remain: faith, hope and love. But the greatest of these is love.

Original Meaning

MORE IMPORTANT than all the gifts is love (12:31b). First Corinthians 13:1–3 makes the point that without love the gifts are worthless. Verses 4–7 describe the nature of love, in language designed to point out how little the Corinthians are measuring up. Verses 8–13 highlight the temporary nature of all the gifts, contrasting with love's permanence. The entire passage is quasi-poetic in nature, with an elaborate structure of symmetry and parallelism.[1]

---

1. For a good display of this structure, see Watson, *First Corinthians*, 140–41. On the overall genre of the chapter as an encomium (rhetorical praise), see James D. Sigountos, "The Genre of 1 Corinthians 13," *NTS* 40 (1994): 246–60.

Verses 1–3 drive home the same truth repeatedly by using five of the spiritual gifts as illustrations of the identical principle: without love the most exemplary use of a particular gift profits a believer nothing. In verse 1, Paul makes the point with reference to glossolalia. "Tongues of angels" probably refers to the Corinthians' estimation of this gift. "A resounding gong" is perhaps better taken to refer to a large "acoustic vase" used for amplification in the Greek theaters. Combined with a "clanging cymbal," Paul graphically highlights that tongues without love leave only a hollow reverberation.[2]

In verse 2, Paul uses the example of gifts of spiritual insight and of a faith to work miracles. Here he may be echoing the tradition of Jesus' own words in Matthew 21:21, although the expression was proverbial for trusting God to perform great deeds. Verse 3 hammers home the point one more time with the most extreme example yet—seemingly total self-abandonment in exercising the gift of giving. The NIV footnote ("surrender my body that I may boast") may actually be the more original reading, instead of "surrender my body to the flames."[3] In that case "giving up one's body" could include self-immolation but might also refer to the ancient practice of selling oneself into slavery to raise funds for distribution to the poor.

The NIV's translations of the various terms in verses 4–7 are generally quite good and self-explanatory. But we may add a few footnotes. "Patience" (v. 4) conveys the sense of "long-suffering." "Boast" refers to the negative sense of "bragging about oneself." "Proud" is more literally "puffed up." "Rude" (v. 5) uses the same word translated as "unpresentable" in 12:23 and refers to activity "in defiance of social and moral standards, with resulting disgrace, embarrassment, and shame."[4] "Easily angered" translates a term from which our English "paroxysm" derives. "Protects" (v. 7) might instead mean "bears" or "puts up with annoyances"; it seems roughly synonymous with "endures." "Trusts" is the common New Testament word for "believes." Verse 7 thus forms a small chiasm (ABBA pattern), with the outside and inside pairs of verbs each meaning approximately the same thing. Taken together, verses 4–7 clearly portray love as selfless, seeking the good of the other first and foremost. "Love is what God in Christ has shown and done for 'others' in their helpless plight and hapless estate as sinners. In love we take God's side, share his outlook and implement his designs; and we treat our neighbors as we know God has treated us (see Rom. 15:1–7)."[5]

---

2. William W. Klein, "Noisy Gong or Acoustic Vase? A Note on 1 Corinthians 13.1," *NTS* 32 (1986): 286–89.

3. See esp. J. H. Petzer, "Contextual Evidence in Favour of καυχήσωμαι in 1 Corinthians 13.3," *NTS* 35 (1989): 229–53.

4. Louw and Nida, *Lexicon*, 759.

5. Martin, *Spirit*, 56. Cf. Chafin, *1 and 2 Corinthians*, 161: Christian love "means that caring, forgiving, spontaneous, redeeming love which is the essence of God's nature."

Verse 8 states the thesis of verses 8–13. Again Paul makes the point with sample gifts that were of particular importance in Corinth. Whereas faith, hope, and love endure, spiritual gifts prove less permanent. The NIV renders the same verb *katargeo* ("to destroy or abolish") four different ways in verses 8–11 ("cease" [v. 8a], "pass away" [v. 8c], "disappears" [v. 10], "put . . . behind" [v. 11]), but each of these captures an important nuance of the term. Paul uses a different verb (*pauomai*) with tongues (NIV "be stilled"—v. 8b) but probably just for stylistic variety (creating an ABA pattern for the three parallel elements of v. 8). Although it is a middle voice (sometimes translated as action done to, by, or for oneself), this particular verb has become a virtual deponent (a verb without active voice endings) in the Greek of the New Testament, so it is dangerous here to read anything much into this specific grammatical form.

Why will the gifts cease? It is because they are imperfect provisions for an imperfect world, rendered unnecessary when perfection comes (vv. 9–10). But to what does "perfection" refer? The other main biblical meaning of the word (Gk. *teleios*) is "maturity" (cf. the metaphor in v. 11), but neither perfection nor consistent maturity has yet come to the church of Jesus Christ.[6] Although later interpreters have at times felt otherwise, nothing in Paul supports any consciousness of his writing near the end of an apostolic age or the close of a biblical canon. And the metaphors in verse 12 fit poorly with such interpretations. After the Bible was completed, Christians did not see God "face to face" (only "face to book"!) or know him to the degree that he knew them. When we recall that 1:7 pointed out the ongoing role of the gifts until the return of Christ, there can be only one possible interpretation of "perfection"—it is the life in the world to come after Jesus reappears on earth.

But love abides on into eternity. So too probably do faith and hope (v. 13a), if faith is taken as belief in Jesus and faithful service to him, and if hope refers to the expectant anticipation of the good things God has in the future for us. Paul adds these other two virtues because the triad "faith, hope, and love" is a favorite of his (cf. 1 Thess. 1:3; 5:8; Col. 1:4–5; Eph. 1:15–18).[7] But love remains the greatest (v. 13b) because it is the most foundational,

---

6. Against those who think otherwise, Fee, *First Corinthians*, 645, n. 23, observes, "It is perhaps an indictment of Western Christianity that we should consider 'mature' our rather totally cerebral and domesticated—but bland—brand of faith, with the concomitant absence of the Spirit in terms of his supernatural gifts! The Spirit, not Western rationalism, marks the turning point of the ages, after all."

7. Wolfgang Weiss, "Glaube—Liebe—Hoffnung: Zu der Trias bei Paulus," *ZNW* 84 (1993): 196–217.

essential and central to Paul's understanding of the Christian ethic (cf., e.g., Gal. 5:6, 14, 22–23).

IF IT IS MORE EXCELLENT than even the greater gifts, then love itself cannot be a spiritual gift. Rather it represents the cardinal Christian virtue, the first on the list of the "fruit" of the Spirit (Gal. 5:22), which must be present with all the gifts if they are to be used in ways that will please God and have eternal value. The key to understanding chapter 13, then, is to keep it in its context. Whatever inspiration it may have as a self-contained poem or hymn to love, Paul intended it to be used to help solve the specific problem of the destructive manner in which the Corinthians were using their spiritual gifts. So it is perfectly legitimate to substitute other gifts for tongues, prophecy, faith, and so on, in verses 1–3 and 8–9. So too there are no doubt other facets of love that could be added to the description of verses 4–7, but these appear because they were precisely the areas in which the Corinthians were most lacking.

To say that certain gifts benefit the people exercising them only when they do so in love does not mean that we wait to use them until we can do so flawlessly! Communicating messages to God's people instructs them even if the manner in which that knowledge is imparted is less than perfect. Giving our goods to the needy certainly helps *them* regardless of our attitude! But this chapter presents the ideal for which we should always strive, even as we are painfully aware of how far we still have to go to measure up.

The term for love throughout 1 Corinthians 13, of course, is *agape*. But we must beware of overexegeting this term. It is not the word itself that conveys the sense of divine love but the context. In first-century Greek, *agape* was coming more and more into use, as the *philia* word-group (often used of "brotherly" or "friendship" love) increasingly came to mean "kiss" in certain contexts. Thus the verb *agapao* can be used interchangeably with *phileo* (e.g., in John 21:15–17), while in the LXX *agapao* can even refer to Amnon's incestuous love/lust for his sister Tamar (2 Sam. 13:1)![8] But the way Paul unpacks the concept in 1 Corinthians is obviously quite different. We must also be careful not to divorce "love" from its larger theological context. It is the outgrowth of faith in Jesus (Gal. 5:6). In other settings (such as Galatians), Paul is equally concerned to stress that love, as the summary of the Law, is worthless without faith.

---

8. Cf. further D. A. Carson, *Exegetical Fallacies* (Grand Rapids: Baker, 1984), 30, 51–54.

It has often been observed that one could substitute the word "Jesus" for "love" throughout verses 4–7. Indeed, as the only sinless person in human history, he provides the perfect model for helping us to understand what patience, kindness, lack of envy, and so on, are. In so doing, we also guard against misinterpreting these attributes. If Jesus was all-loving, but could clear the temple in righteous indignation (Mark 11:15–18) or unleash a torrential invective against the hypocrisy of the conservative religious leaders of his day (Matt. 23), then our concept of love must leave room for similar actions.

Lewis Smedes outlines this approach in his excellent study of this chapter. Among other insights, he notes that God has limits to his patience, and so must we, but "when I turn off suffering for the sake of *my* pleasure, I turn it off too soon."[9] Neither does patience include the toleration of evil. Kindness is both intelligent and tough; "without wisdom and honesty," it "easily becomes mere pity, bound to hurt more people than it helps."[10] *Agape* transcends jealousy without destroying it; it is right, for example, to be upset when someone runs off with your spouse! "Love does not move us to seek justice for ourselves," but it should "drive us to move heaven and earth to seek justice for others."[11] *Agape* does not disguise or unleash anger; it does not remove irritants from our lives or reduce irritability by forbidding anger. Rather it meets our deepest needs, enabling us to respond differently to enraging circumstances, reduces the potential for frustration, gives us the power to communicate anger appropriately, and increases our gratitude for the way God has worked in our lives.[12]

The antithesis in verse 6 between evil and truth is striking. One would have expected evil and good to be paired, or truth and falsehood. But Christian truth and goodness are each both cognitive and volitional. Much lovelessness is based on the loss of one or the other of these aspects. In Ephesians 4:15, Paul commands us to speak the truth in love. Christians do no one a favor if they remain pleasant but fail to communicate important truths which others neglect at their peril. But all the truth in the world, when not transmitted in a spirit of sensitivity and compassion, is likely to fall on deaf ears.

A major theological error that follows from the misinterpretation of verses 8–13 is the belief that any or all of the gifts of the Spirit have already ceased. As we have already seen, this violates every sensible reading of verse

---

9. Lewis B. Smedes, *Love Within Limits* (Grand Rapids: Eerdmans, 1978), 6.
10. Ibid., 18.
11. Ibid., 37.
12. Ibid., 61–65.

12, and it has to distort the actual record of events throughout church history. Neither tongues nor prophecy nor miracles ceased at the end of the first-century; they continued at least into the third century and have recurred sporadically if not consistently ever since. The relative disappearance of these gifts during the later Patristic period can be attributed largely to their abuse in certain sectarian circles.[13] Worse still, the cessationist view of the gifts is forced to attribute many apparently powerful works of the Spirit during the past century to human manufacture at best and diabolical counterfeit at worst.

It remains equally inappropriate, however, to see the "resumption" of these gifts during the last hundred years as the sign of anything having to do with the end times. If the gifts never entirely ceased, and if they were squelched for centuries by an overpowering and unbiblical institutionalization of the church, then their revival may in general be a sign that a certain health and balance is returning to Christianity, but not that some final generation or period of history prior to Christ's return is necessarily present. In every era of church history, "we see but a poor reflection as in a mirror"; only when Christ returns will we "see face to face." This reminder should inspire humility in our personal relationships, our intellectual endeavors, and the spiritual claims that we make for ourselves.

Love as the centerpiece of the Christian ethic must remain believers' focus in every era and culture. But it must be taken in conjunction with other major biblical themes. A correct reading of Old and New Testaments does not permit a radical contrast between law in the Old and love in the New. The double love-command (Deut. 6:4–5; Lev. 19:18) is Jesus' own summary of the Law (see Mark 12:29–31 and parallels), while Paul himself echoes the second half of Jesus' words in Galatians 5:14. And in this letter, we have already been reminded that the Christian ethic is not without its own "law of Christ" (9:21).

Similarly, John enunciates three parallel tests of life, each defined in terms of the other two: belief in Jesus as the God-man, obedience to the commandments, and love (1 John 3:23–24, and throughout the letter). Theologians have rightly stressed that love and justice jointly sum up God's "communicable attributes," that is, those in which his people should strive to be like him. But ultimately there remains an asymmetry even here, as love,

---

13. A good history of glossolalia appears in Morton Kelsey, *Tongue Speaking: The History and Meaning of Charismatic Experience* (New York: Crossroad, 1981). A good study of prophecy in an influential part of the third-century church is Cecil M. Robeck, Jr., *Prophecy in Carthage: Perpetua, Tertullian, Cyprian* (Cleveland: Pilgrim, 1992). More briefly but more generally, cf. the catalogues of references to the ongoing presence of the more supernatural gifts in the early centuries of the church's history in Talbert, *Corinthians*, 82–83, 88–90.

like mercy, triumphs over judgment (James 2:13). If that were not true, none of us could ever be saved.

THE NEED FOR GENUINE, Christ-like love remains as great today as ever. Yet one of our greatest problems is defining love. Popular culture—in literature, music, advertising, and the visual arts—uses the word to mean just about everything *except* what the Bible means by it. So even Christians are easily misled into thinking love is primarily a feeling, something you fall in or out of. We equate it with lust or sexual intercourse itself, speaking of one's "lover" (unless one is properly married, when the term actually *would* be appropriate) or of "making love." But in this chapter, as throughout Scripture, love is first of all an action, an unconditional commitment, a promise that is never broken.[14]

We too face the problems against which Paul warns in verses 1–3. Some tongues-speakers insist that everyone must imitate them, a most unloving action toward those whom God has not so gifted. Many who proclaim God's Word seem to think that preaching requires a change of tone and volume which shouts more than exuding compassion. Many intellectuals, including Christians, destroy their opponents' arguments in person and in print, in a style indistinguishable from that of the hardened cynic. Some of our greatest philanthropists substitute giving for faith, as do civic and fraternal organizations that pride themselves on charitable causes into which they often throw money without the costly, loving personal involvement of the majority of their members. Liberal and liberationist "Christians" sometimes substitute social action for the authentic Christian love that flows from the assurance of salvation. Modern-day warfare has seen thousands of young people sacrifice their lives in battle and in terrorism, often in the name of religion, and sometimes, as in Islam, in hopes of quick passage to heaven. Tragically, without the foundation of genuine Christian love, any such martyrs only speed up their trip to hell.

In an age in which demanding one's rights is considered a virtue, we must read again and again that love "is not self-seeking" (v. 5). At the same time, when we understand love's limits, we will avoid co-dependency. The most loving thing to do for the repeatedly abusive, perennially alcoholic husband is not to cover-up for him or to believe his empty promises of reform, but to insist that he seek professional help and to refuse to carry on with "business as usual" if he does not.[15]

---

14. Cf. further Josh McDowell, *The Secret of Loving* (San Bernardino: Here's Life, 1985).

15. Cf. esp. Margaret J. Rinck, *Can Christians Love Too Much?* (Grand Rapids: Zondervan, 1989).

"Love" without an objective grounding in the living, Triune God of the universe runs rampant. John's affirmation that God is love (1 John 4:16) has been inverted in the popular slogan, "Where there is love, there is God." Whereas Paul insists that love "rejoices with the truth" (v. 6), contemporary pluralism avoids discussing the competing truth claims of incompatible religions and ideologies, in the name of preserving "love." Modern people "delight in evil" in all kinds of ways. Smedes notes four in particular—monistic philosophies that have to redefine evil as actually good within some larger framework, theological systems that blur the distinction between God tolerating evil and actually causing it (*contra* James 1:13), civil religion that accords the state (or a particular region, culture, or ethnic group) honor due to God alone, often in the name of patriotism or loyalty to kin, and the widespread personal glee that we exhibit when enemies suffer, leaders fall, and others in general fare worse than ourselves.[16] Other examples could be added, particularly in the sexual arena, as the media portrays as desirable virtually every conceivable form of homosexual and heterosexual sin, while regularly refusing to portray or even acknowledge the existence of positive married life and family relationships, particularly those based on Christian convictions.

Verses 8–12 caution us against ever rashly labeling apparent manifestations of the Spirit as something other than that, on the basis that certain gifts are no longer with us. This is particularly sobering when we recall that the one sin Christ identified as unforgivable was the allegation by certain Jewish leaders that signs of the Spirit's presence were actually the work of the devil (Mark 3:29–30). But these verses also make plain the imperfection of all current exercise of the gifts. So we should be quick to reject all claims that exalt alleged prophecy, tongues, and the like, above Scripture, or which give them even equal value. The so-called neo-prophetic movement often seems in danger of crossing these boundaries, even while occasionally offering disclaimers. The contemporary signs and wonders movement seldom exceeds a five percent success rate in attempted healings.[17] So it would seem that its claims to spiritual giftedness are at least exceedingly inflated.

As Paul ends his chapter by associating love with faith and hope, so it is appropriate to conclude this discussion with a comment on love's role in the future, as believers today wonder what the coming days will hold in store.

---

16. Smedes, *Love,* 74–79.

17. John Wimber with Kevin Springer, *Power Healing* (San Francisco: Harper & Row, 1989), 158, believes that "the most fundamental reason—why people are not healed when prayed for today" is that "we do not seek God as wholeheartedly as we should." The Risen Lord gave Paul a diametrically opposite reason in 2 Corinthians 12:8–9.

So long as we live between Christ's first and second comings, between the inauguration and the consummation of God's kingdom or reign, we should maintain a realistic optimism about our potential, through the Spirit, to love our neighbors and create good in our world. We can believe that history is going somewhere, whether or not the pundits who constantly revise their interpretations of prophecy to fit current events are right that this is the final generation. We can believe that the bleak events of our contemporary world—warfare, famine, ecological disaster or anti-Christian hostility—have their God-ordained limits. We can cautiously hope, pray, and work for the implementing of God's standards in society, realizing that sometimes we will fail and other times we will succeed. Neither the overly optimistic triumphalism of certain forms of postmillennialism (most notably, reconstructionism) nor the overly pessimistic defeatism of certain forms of premillennialism (most notably, classic dispensationalism) are justified. God is at work in history, through fallen human beings and governments. Our generation has seen the unthinkable in the fall of much of communism throughout the world and of apartheid in South Africa, but we have also seen the horrors of ancient ethnic rivalries revive attempted genocide in Eastern Europe and Eastern Africa. Neither should be quite so surprising when we understand the power of God and the depths of evil, but we look forward to the ultimate triumph, after Christ's return, of the power of God in the love of Christ.[18]

---

18. For a good application of these principles to contemporary Hong Kong as it awaits reunification with China in 1997, see Emily Wong, "1 Corinthians 13.7 and Christian Hope," *LouvStud* 17 (1992): 232–42.

1 Corinthians 14:1–25

FOLLOW THE WAY of love and eagerly desire spiritual gifts, especially the gift of prophecy. ²For anyone who speaks in a tongue does not speak to men but to God. Indeed, no one understands him; he utters mysteries with his spirit. ³But everyone who prophesies speaks to men for their strengthening, encouragement and comfort. ⁴He who speaks in a tongue edifies himself, but he who prophesies edifies the church. ⁵I would like every one of you to speak in tongues, but I would rather have you prophesy. He who prophesies is greater than one who speaks in tongues, unless he interprets, so that the church may be edified.

⁶Now, brothers, if I come to you and speak in tongues, what good will I be to you, unless I bring you some revelation or knowledge or prophecy or word of instruction? ⁷Even in the case of lifeless things that make sounds, such as the flute or harp, how will anyone know what tune is being played unless there is a distinction in the notes? ⁸Again, if the trumpet does not sound a clear call, who will get ready for battle? ⁹So it is with you. Unless you speak intelligible words with your tongue, how will anyone know what you are saying? You will just be speaking into the air. ¹⁰Undoubtedly there are all sorts of languages in the world, yet none of them is without meaning. ¹¹If then I do not grasp the meaning of what someone is saying, I am a foreigner to the speaker, and he is a foreigner to me. ¹²So it is with you. Since you are eager to have spiritual gifts, try to excel in gifts that build up the church.

¹³For this reason anyone who speaks in a tongue should pray that he may interpret what he says. ¹⁴For if I pray in a tongue, my spirit prays, but my mind is unfruitful. ¹⁵So what shall I do? I will pray with my spirit, but I will also pray with my mind; I will sing with my spirit, but I will also sing with my mind. ¹⁶If you are praising God with your spirit, how can one who finds himself among those who do not understand say "Amen" to your thanksgiving, since he does not know what you are saying? ¹⁷You may be giving thanks well enough, but the other man is not edified.

¹⁸I thank God that I speak in tongues more than all of you. ¹⁹But in the church I would rather speak five intelligible words to instruct others than ten thousand words in a tongue.

²⁰Brothers, stop thinking like children. In regard to evil be infants, but in your thinking be adults. ²¹In the Law it is written:

> "Through men of strange tongues
>   and through the lips of foreigners
> I will speak to this people,
>   but even then they will not listen to me,"

says the Lord.

²²Tongues, then, are a sign, not for believers but for unbelievers; prophecy, however, is for believers, not for unbelievers. ²³So if the whole church comes together and everyone speaks in tongues, and some who do not understand or some unbelievers come in, will they not say that you are out of your mind? ²⁴But if an unbeliever or someone who does not understand comes in while everybody is prophesying, he will be convinced by all that he is a sinner and will be judged by all, ²⁵and the secrets of his heart will be laid bare. So he will fall down and worship God, exclaiming, "God is really among you!"

IN CHAPTER 14 Paul climaxes his discussion of spiritual gifts by encouraging the Corinthians to prefer prophecy to tongues. But he acknowledges a place for both, and for the other gifts, if they are made intelligible (vv. 1–25) and exercised in an orderly fashion (vv. 26–40). Verses 1–25 fall into an ABBA pattern. Verses 1–6 supply reasons for preferring prophecy, verses 6–12 outline some of the problems with tongues, verses 13–19 address a solution to those problems, and verses 20–25 return to reasons for preferring prophecy.

Verse 1 resumes the thread of 12:31, picking up the two themes of that verse (love and desiring the greater gifts) in reverse order. Paul now specifies one of those "greater" gifts, namely, prophecy. Verse 2 makes it reasonably certain that the misuse of tongues was one of the Corinthians' major problems in the exercise of their spiritual gifts during worship. Apparently they were manifesting glossolalia without interpretation. Verse 5b demonstrates that all of verses 2–5a must be understood as Paul's criticisms of tongues *when they are not interpreted*. When they *are* interpreted, they, like

prophecy, contain a fundamentally instructional and exhortational component (vv. 3, 4b, 5b). For more on the nature of prophecy and tongues, see the
discussions under 12:8–10 and 27–31 (pp. 244–45, 247 above).

"Mysteries" (v. 2) simply refer to that which "no one understands." Grammatically, the NIV footnote ("by the Spirit") is somewhat more likely than the
text ("with his spirit"), since there is no word in Greek corresponding to "his."

Unlike uninterpreted tongues, prophecy edifies the whole assembly, not
just the individual speaker (vv. 3–4). Paul thus isolates two reasons why
prophecy is greater: people, not just God, are addressed, and they can be
more positively affected. Verse 5 does not contradict 12:30. Paul is not clan-
destinely commanding all the Corinthians to seek tongues, merely admitting
that it would be nice if all could speak in them. But given their abuse, he is
"dramatically contrasting the importance of seeking gifts which are better
suited to edification (like prophecy)" with "those which are more dramatic
but less edifying (like tongues)."[1]

Verse 6 presents the thesis of the next paragraph (vv. 6–12), repeating the
need for intelligibility. The four elements of verse 6b ("revelation or knowledge or prophecy or word of instruction") all share this attribute, as over
against uninterpreted tongues. "Word of instruction" is literally "teaching," so
it seems that Paul is lumping more and less miraculous gifts together here to
stress the importance of clear communication.

Verses 7–11 then give three illustrations of this principle. In order to be
understood or appreciated, musical instruments must play a discernible
melody (v. 7). Trumpet calls to battle must be clear enough for soldiers to distinguish "Advance!" from "Retreat!" (v. 8). And foreign languages remain unintelligible to those who have not learned them (vv. 9–11). "Foreigner" in
verse 11 is *barbaros* (from which we get "barbarian"), originally a scornful term
for someone who was not a Greek or Roman, and it may carry a pejorative
connotation here too.

Verse 12 concludes by repeating the point with which the first paragraph
of this chapter ended (v. 5). The NIV misleads us here; "Excel in gifts that
build up the church" reads as if some gifts do not build up the church! But
the Greek merely says, "Seek that you abound towards the edification of the
church."

So what must a person do if God *has* given him or her the gift of tongues?
Verses 13–19 address this problem. Verse 13 applies to this situation the encouragement of 12:31 on seeking certain gifts. The tongues speaker should
pray for the ability to interpret his or her tongue. Verses 14–15 show that

---

1. Hemphill, *Spiritual Gifts*, 97.

receiving the gift of interpretation benefits oneself first of all. Without it, the tongues-speaker has no way of personally knowing the meaning of the message he or she has just uttered (v. 14). Praying with one's spirit versus praying with one's mind (v. 15a) is probably equivalent to the distinction in verses 13–14 of speaking in tongues versus interpretation. Tongues and their interpretation might also come in song form too (v. 15b). It is also possible that praying and singing "with my mind" include more ordinary worship as well.

In verses 16–17, Paul turns to the effect on others present. Again, interpretation is crucial if the rest of the congregation is to be able to agree. "Amen" (v. 16) is a Hebrew interjection roughly equivalent to "this is most certainly true." "Those who do not understand" translates one Greek word that refers to someone who is not an expert or not initiated into a given sphere of activity; hence, the alternate translation in the NIV footnote ("inquirer"). In some pagan circles, such a person was a "catechumen," one being instructed in a given religion or philosophy prior to fully committing to it. But in this context, the NIV text makes more sense (cf. the REB's "ordinary person"). Even mature Christians play the role of the uninitiated when they hear uninterpreted tongues. They have no idea what the message means.[2]

Verses 18–19 probably surprised Paul's original readers, who may even have been criticizing him for not using glossolalia. If Paul refrains almost entirely from its public exercise, these verses surely substantiate his extensive private use of tongues as a "prayer language." "Intelligible" (v. 19) is more literally "with my mind." "Ten thousand" could also be translated "a myriad"; 5/10,000 does not represent a precise ratio! In verse 27 Paul certainly permits a few tongues in each service, which shows that he doesn't expect every one to refrain quite as much as he does.

Verse 20 forms the transition to the last paragraph of this first section of chapter 14. A preoccupation with tongues without concern for their effect on oneself and others is childish. There are ways Christians should be childlike (e.g., being innocent of evil—cf. Matt. 10:16) but not in their use of spiritual gifts. Mature faith never stresses the noncognitive at the expense of the cognitive. "Thinking" translates a word (*phren*) which means "the psychological faculty of thoughtful planning, often with the implication of being wise and provident."[3]

Verses 21–25 proceed further to justify Paul's appeal to prefer prophecy to tongues. Paul begins by citing parts of Isaiah 28:11–12, a passage in

---

2. Cf. F. W. Grosheide, *Commentary on the First Epistle to the Corinthians* (Grand Rapids; Eerdmans, 1953), 326–27.

3. Louw and Nida, *Lexicon*, 325.

which God pronounces judgment against rebellious Israel at the hands of the foreign empire of Assyria (v. 21). The verses that bracket this quotation in Isaiah use Hebrew syllables that resemble nonsense sounds (vv. 10, 13— Hebrew: *sav lasav sav lasav; kav lakav kav lakav*). So Paul may have been inspired by that context to apply Isaiah's prophecy to the similar impression that glossolalia created.

To make any sense of verse 22, the sign to which Paul refers must again be a sign *of judgment*. Verse 23 thus explains verse 22a: tongues are a sign of judgment for unbelievers. Like the unbelieving Israelites, non-Christians in Corinth will wind up being condemned (even if inadvertently) by those who speak in undecipherable languages. They will remain lost in their sins because they will reject the gospel as the product of insane babblers.

Verses 24–25 go on to elucidate verse 22b. Prophecy is a sign of judgment for believers in the positive sense that it creates Christians by convicting unbelievers of their sins and bringing them to repentance (v. 25b echoes Isa. 45:14). Verses 23–24 again use the term that some would translate as "inquirer" (see NIV footnote), and it makes a bit more sense in this context. But in light of its use in verse 16, it is probably best to translate it consistently, as the NIV text does. Non-Christians are certainly one important class of people who do not understand tongues.[4] "All" in the expressions "convinced by all" and "judged by all" (v. 24) more naturally refers to "all that is said," not "all the people." And verses 24–25 do not guarantee that all who hear prophecy rather than tongues will be saved. They simply stress that an intelligible proclamation of the gospel stands a far better chance of convicting unsaved people and regenerating their hearts.[5]

AS IN CHAPTER 11, successful application of the more controversial parts of chapter 14 hinges in large measure on successfully defining terms and choosing from a wealth of competing interpretations. If prophecy referred only to expository preaching or only to sudden

---

4. A few, of course, would have regarded tongues as they did comparable phenomena in paganism. But the closest parallels to Christian glossolalia come mostly from a later date than that of this letter; see Christopher Forbes, "Early Christian Inspired Speech and Hellenistic Popular Religion," *NovT* 28 (1986): 257–70.

5. On verses 21–25 and the line of interpretation adopted here, see further David E. Lanier, "With Stammering Lips and Another Tongue: 1 Cor 14:20–22 and Isa 28:11–12," *CTR* 5 (1991): 259–85. The view that verse 22 is the position of Paul's opponents in Corinth, which verses 23–25 reject (B. C. Johanson, "Tongues, A Sign for Unbelievers," *NTS* 25 [1979]: 180–203) fails to account adequately for the connection ("so," or "thus") between verses 22 and 23. This is no "Yes, but" logic here, but rather "A and therefore B."

spontaneous revelation, then churches that do not regularly experience one or the other of those practices would have little to heed here. If tongues were the same phenomenon as at Pentecost, then all Paul's talk about interpretation would be rendered superfluous. But if prophecy and tongues are the types of spiritual gifts that we have described, then contemporary applications abound.

If prophecy is the proclamation of a message given by God, irrespective of the amount of prayer or preparation preceding it, then chapter 14 applies in significant ways to both charismatic and non-charismatic circles. Those who typically preach only after extensive study and preparation should also make sure that they preach only that which God has first applied to themselves.[6] Those accustomed to speaking on the sudden impulse of the Spirit should concentrate on communicating their message in the clearest possible way to benefit those present. Neither kind of preacher should assume that their words automatically constitute prophecy, unless these guidelines are followed. Both should take great pains to see that their messages "strengthen, encourage, and comfort" (v. 3).

Verse 6 supports the conclusion that Paul is concerned with intelligibility of Spirit-inspired utterances, however they are obtained. Thus he can combine supernatural "revelation" with more ordinary "teaching," tossing in prophecy and knowledge, to span the spectrum in between. The illustrations concerning music and foreign languages in verses 7–11 reinforce this call for clarity. Indeed, many Christian speakers will attest that the boundaries are very fluid between saying what one has planned to say in advance and deviating from one's prepared speech on the basis of the actual audience present and one's flow of thought as one speaks.

Charismatics and noncharismatics alike can and should consider thoughtfully what God wants to say to a particular congregation at a particular time but be sensitive enough to the Spirit to say what seems most appropriate and lucid for that audience as they speak. In fact, preparation can actually function to aid spontaneity, as one chooses "on the spot" from a wealth of previously considered thoughts. Lack of preparation, conversely, can often hinder successful articulation of a message, as one simply becomes at a loss for words or a logical flow of thought and lapses into a disconnected "stream of consciousness."

---

6. Cf. Barclay, *Corinthians*, 129–30: "No man can speak to others unless God has first spoken to him," and "We never give to men or to scholars truth which we have produced, or even discovered; we transmit truth which has been given to us." Cf. John R. W. Stott, *I Believe in Preaching* (London: Hodder & Stoughton, 1982), 220–24 .

Verse 5b provides an important qualification for Paul's disparaging of tongues. When an interpretation is given,[7] then tongues plus their interpretation closely resemble prophecy in function. Why then does Paul still relativize tongues so much, particularly in his own practice, which is not limited to the troubled context of Corinth (vv. 18–19)? Presumably verse 23 answers this question. Even with an interpretation, the phenomenon of tongues seems so bizarre to some that it prevents them from giving the gospel a serious hearing. Yet even with this observation, Paul refuses to prohibit tongues, but only regulates them so that they do not get out of hand (vv. 27–28).

Verse 10 does not imply that Paul recognized glossolalia as actual foreign languages spoken by people somewhere on earth, or even that they have a comparable linguistic structure, any more than verses 7–8 imply that tongues actually sounded like or employed flutes, harps, or trumpets. Rather, in both instances, he is using an analogy to make one central point of comparison which may not be pressed to include subordinate details. Like musical instruments and human languages, glossolalia must be understandable to be effective. Various Greco-Roman religions were well-known for their outbursts of ecstatic speech and unintelligible repetition of "nonsense" syllables.[8] This is precisely what Paul wanted to avoid.

As noted above (pp. 269–70), verses 14–19 highlight a key role for tongues in prayer and praise, rather than instructing the congregation in the way prophecy does. These verses do not preclude tongues communicating a more didactic message, but Paul does not emphasize that aspect of their use. Verses 18–19 stress the value of tongues as a private prayer language, in which instruction of others by definition cannot come into play. It is not clear whether Paul would distinguish this use of tongues from the "spiritual gift" of glossolalia. One suspects he might, since the gifts must be used for public edification of the church.

Yet, under whatever label, a private prayer language can prove very beneficial and therapeutic to those who use it. Indeed using tongues in this manner may provide one illustration of the way in which "the Spirit helps us in our weakness," when "we do not know what we ought to pray for, but the Spirit himself intercedes for us with groans that words cannot express"

---

7. The most natural translation is that of the NIV, in which the interpreter is the same person as the speaker. But it is just possible to take the clause as the NRSV does: "unless some-one interprets . . ."

8. On prophecy, see Terrence Callan, "Prophecy and Ecstasy in Greco-Roman Religion and 1 Corinthians," *NovT* 27 (1985): 125–40. On tongues, cf. H. Wayne House, "Tongues and the Mystery Religions of Corinth," *BSac* 140 (1983): 134–50.

(Rom. 8:26).[9] Throughout history, and especially in the last hundred years, where Christians have spoken in tongues in prayer, they have consistently testified to the sense of a spiritual "breakthrough," as God has overcome their growing frustration with the confines of merely cognitive worship.

Verse 20 balances this emphasis, however, by reminding believers that the cognitive aspect always must continue to play an important role in the Christian life, even if it must also be supplemented by more affective elements. One thinks of Romans 12:2 with its foundational command for Christians to "be transformed by the renewing of their mind," and of Paul's later words to the Corinthians that "we demolish arguments and every pretension that sets itself up against the knowledge of God, and we take captive every thought to make it obedient to Christ" (2 Cor. 10:4c–5).

Cognitive psychology has since recovered Paul's emphasis on the mind: dysfunctional behavior often stems from warped thinking. If one learns to think correctly, godly behavior often follows. If this is the case, then one can scarcely overestimate the value of thoughtful prayer, study, and Christian education, both formal and informal, in conversation with wise and mature believers, past and present. A lesson thus comes through this first half of chapter 14 "with startling force. Whatever the place for profound, personal experience and corporate emotional experience, the assembled church is a place for intelligibility. Our God is a thinking, speaking God; and if we will know him, we must learn to think his thoughts after him."[10]

Verses 21–25 remind us that Christian worship must at least periodically relate directly to the unbeliever. This in turn presupposes that non-Christians will regularly be present at Christian worship, most commonly no doubt because Christian friends have invited them. Without denying the central scandal of the cross (1:18–2:5), worship leaders and participants must reflect on how they can best "package" their ministry and message so as to make Christianity attractive rather than repulsive to interested outsiders. Then they can expect people to come to Christ as a result of their services, though how many and how often depends entirely on the Spirit's sovereign hand in convicting men and women and regenerating human hearts. And if tongues are signs *of judgment* for unbelievers (v. 22), then we cannot apply this paragraph, as some Pentecostals do, to claim that tongues-speaking is designed to convert unbelievers.

---

9. But the Romans passage cannot be limited to this type of experience. See esp. Emmanuel A. Obeng, "The Origins of the Spirit Intercession Motif in Romans 8:26," *NTS* 32 (1986): 621–32.

10. Carson, *Spirit*, 106.

CHRISTIANS SOMETIMES STRUGGLE to find relevant passages of Scripture that speak directly and in detail to contemporary problems. Such is the case, for example, with abortion, ecology, and nuclear war. In chapter 14, however, we find remarkably clear and detailed teaching that bears directly on one of the most divisive issues in the church today—the debate over the so-called charismatic or more supernatural gifts.

The charismatic movement is known for emphasizing the value of speaking in tongues. To many in that movement, Paul would surely say today that greater emphasis is needed on the more immediately intelligible and more cognitive gifts. Many sermons in charismatic or Pentecostal circles lack consistent, clear exposition of texts of Scripture. The recent neo-prophetic movement has heralded something of a shift away from tongues to prophecy. But it tends to conceive of the latter in a very narrow, highly supernatural sense and often does not submit its revelations from the Lord to the evaluation of a congregation and a duly recognized group of church leaders. Decision-making in the charismatic world often seems highly subjective, as people explain their actions with little more than the rationale, "The Lord told me to do such-and-such." But how do they know for sure what they heard was from the Lord or, if it was, that they interpreted it entirely correctly? Authoritarian leaders within this movement can at times rule ruthlessly and without fear of contradiction because those under them believe everything spoken "in the name of the Lord." It would probably be good if no Christian today ever said, "The Lord told me . . ." lest God get blamed for human error, but rather preface their remarks with, "I *believe* the Lord has told me . . ."[11]

Noncharismatic churches too are increasingly moving away from solid instructional messages based on biblical content. Many favor a more entertainment-oriented style of worship, and "seeker-sensitive" messages, often with the worthy motive of attracting the unbeliever or church-hopper who judges local congregations on the value of many services they provide other than preaching.[12] Such churches recognize the need to avoid Christian "jargon," in-house or theological language that outsiders find strange and difficult to comprehend. But if large-group worship services take this form, then

---

11. For a balanced perspective from within one influential wing of the modern charismatic movement, see Wayne Grudem, *Power and Truth* (Anaheim, Calif.: The Association of Vineyard Churches, 1993).

12. See esp. Bruce Shelley and Marshall Shelley, *Consumer Church* (Downers Grove, Ill.: InterVarsity Press, 1992).

it becomes crucial that the church stress that its members become involved in additional activities that provide detailed instruction in the Bible, Christian doctrine, ethics, and the like. These can take the form of Sunday School, special seminars, or small groups.

The value in both charismatic and noncharismatic circles of a clear proclamation of God's Word over and above more unusual phenomena like tongues remains indisputable. In Paul's world, at least the more exotic phenomena reminded people of analogous practices in other religions, so that they were not entirely foreign. In our modern day, many unbelievers seeing glossolalia for the first time will be all the more convinced that Christians are "out of their mind" (v. 23). Indeed, the excesses of the charismatic movement, especially through televangelism, are one of the major reasons all conservative Christianity has been caricatured, stereotyped, and rejected as weird and out-of-touch with reality by many contemporary Westerners, especially in the media.[13]

When the charismatic church experiences large numbers trusting in Christ, it is more often in spite of their more exotic phenomena than because of them, since, to its credit, this movement has done more than any other wing of the church in modern times to recover the patterns of worship and fellowship outlined in 14:26, often accompanied by sincerely warm and loving interpersonal relationships. Some of the fastest-growing charismatic churches today have caught on and play down the role of tongues to such an extent that most services do not contain them, and a majority of members have never spoken in tongues in public.

A much more positive use of tongues continues to appear in Christians discovering a private prayer language. Testimony after testimony describes how the Spirit intervened to liberate some frustrated individual from his or her fruitless quiet time, lifeless worship, or inconsistent walk with the Lord. Indeed, the winds of the charismatic movement seem to have blown freshest and most purely in the middle of dead, formal, traditional churches, where it has given to congregations such "radical" ideas, by no means distinctively charismatic, as singing choruses, using musical instruments besides piano or organ, clapping or raising hands, sharing praise items and prayer requests, and conversational prayer.

---

13. On televangelism and modern culture, see esp. Quentin J. Schultze, *Televangelism and American Culture* (Grand Rapids: Baker, 1991).

1 Corinthians 14:26–40

🔥

WHAT THEN SHALL we say, brothers? When you come together, everyone has a hymn, or a word of instruction, a revelation, a tongue or an interpretation. All of these must be done for the strengthening of the church. ²⁷If anyone speaks in a tongue, two—or at the most three—should speak, one at a time, and someone must interpret. ²⁸If there is no interpreter, the speaker should keep quiet in the church and speak to himself and God.

²⁹Two or three prophets should speak, and the others should weigh carefully what is said. ³⁰And if a revelation comes to someone who is sitting down, the first speaker should stop. ³¹For you can all prophesy in turn so that everyone may be instructed and encouraged. ³²The spirits of prophets are subject to the control of prophets. ³³For God is not a God of disorder but of peace.

As in all the congregations of the saints, ³⁴women should remain silent in the churches. They are not allowed to speak, but must be in submission, as the Law says. ³⁵If they want to inquire about something, they should ask their own husbands at home; for it is disgraceful for a woman to speak in the church.

³⁶Did the word of God originate with you? Or are you the only people it has reached? ³⁷If anybody thinks he is a prophet or spiritually gifted, let him acknowledge that what I am writing to you is the Lord's command. ³⁸If he ignores this, he himself will be ignored.

³⁹Therefore, my brothers, be eager to prophesy, and do not forbid speaking in tongues. ⁴⁰But everything should be done in a fitting and orderly way.

IF INTELLIGIBILITY IS A PRIORITY for the gathered community, how then should worship proceed? Verses 26–40 answer this question and subdivide into three parts: a description of orderly spontaneity in verses 26–33a, the silence of women during the evaluation of prophecy in verses 33b-38, and a concluding summary in verses 39–40.

Verse 26 insists that the Corinthians continue to worship in highly participatory and spontaneous fashion: "Everyone has a hymn, or a word of instruction, a revelation, a tongue, or an interpretation." This does not mean
that every person present exercises all of the gifts, nor even that all exercise
at least one in every service. But opportunity is made available for all whom
the Spirit leads on any given occasion to contribute.

This list gives sample contributions; other standard elements of early
Christian worship are itemized in Acts 2:42–47: apostolic instruction, fellowship, the Lord's Supper, prayer, miracles, sharing of finances, praising
God, and evangelism. Yet once again Paul stresses the need for everything
to be done so as to build up fellow believers. It is just possible that the shift
in focus from evangelizing non-Christians in verses 22–25 to edifying believers in verse 26, together with the more informal and highly participatory
model of verse 26, indicates that this is the pattern for the regular small
home-fellowship gatherings, whereas the earlier verses reflect periodic
larger, more public assemblies of multiple house-churches.[1]

Verses 27–32 again narrow the focus to the two key gifts of tongues and
prophecy. In closely parallel fashion, verses 27–28 and 29–32 temper the
spontaneity described in verse 26 by regulating the exercise of these two particular gifts. No more than two or three may speak in tongues in any given
service (or, less likely, before someone interprets), they must do so sequen-
tially not simultaneously, and there must be an interpretation (vv. 27–28). If
this is not possible, then the would-be tongues-speaker should remain silent
or say his or her prayer inaudibly to God.

Verses 29–32 regulate prophecy in similar fashion, lest it too be abused,
however inherently more valuable it may be. Again only two or three should
speak, one at a time, and their messages should be evaluated. This last con-
straint probably applies to the interpretations of tongues as well, since
tongues plus interpretation closely resembles prophecy in function.

The "others" of verse 29 are more naturally taken to refer to the rest of the
congregation, not merely the other prophets.[2] If "weigh carefully" meant exercising the gift of discernment (12:10), then there would be clearly no
guarantee that those who had the gift of prophecy necessarily had the gift
of discernment too. But even if, as we have suggested, exercising the gift of
discernment is not what Paul means by carefully weighing prophecy, it is still

---

1. Prior, 1 Corinthians, 249–50. This view, along with an analysis of the early Christian
house-church movement more generally, is elucidated in detail in Vincent Branick, The
House Church in the Writings of Paul (Wilmington: Glazier, 1989).

2. Carson, Spirit, 120: "If Paul had wanted to say 'the rest (of the prophets),' the Greek
more plausibly should have been οἱ λοιποί (hoi loipoi) rather than οἱ ἄλλοι (hoi alloi)."

unlikely that the prophets were the best persons to evaluate each others' messages. Certainly, when prophecy is taken to include Spirit-filled preaching, it seems clear that the ordinary "layperson" is often in a better position to determine how well or accurately the preacher has communicated than are fellow-preachers, who are absorbed in the fine points of the theology or technique of the message.[3]

Verse 30 parallels verse 27 in insisting that prophets, like tongues-speakers, exercise their gifts in turn. Verse 31 parallels verse 5 in illustrating Paul's desire that all might exercise these gifts, without implying that all can or will. Paul merely leaves the door open for the Spirit to empower whomever he chooses on any given occasion. Verse 32 proves that Christian prophecy (and presumably also tongues and their interpretation) is not "ecstatic" in the technical sense of that term. In other words, believers in the process of exercising their spiritual gifts are never so "out of control" as to be unable to stop or regulate their behavior. Verse 33a concludes the unit of thought begun in verse 26 by giving the rationale for the regulations of tongues and prophecy just stipulated: orderliness and peace.

Verses 34–35 seem quite intrusive at this juncture. Why does Paul seemingly interrupt his discussion of these two spiritual gifts in order to silence women? In verses 37 and 39–40, he is clearly still addressing the topic of tongues and prophecy. A few late manuscripts, probably for this very reason, place verses 34–35 after verse 40 instead. At least in that position, they could appear as the beginning of a brand new discussion. A popular view in more liberal circles today is that Paul did not write these words; rather, they were added later by some scribe who was far more conservative than Paul himself.[4] But there is not one existing manuscript in which these verses are lacking, and the textual relocation that occurred in a few manuscripts is readily explainable along the lines noted above, without resorting to the conjecture that verses 34–35 were not what Paul originally wrote.

Another popular recent proposal is that these two verses represent another Corinthian slogan which Paul quotes only to refute in verses 36–38.[5]

---

3. Cf. further Grudem, *Prophecy*, 58–67.

4. See, e.g., Winsome Munro, "Women, Text and the Canon: The Strange Case of 1 Corinthians 14:33–35," *BTB* 18 (1988): 26–31. Few evangelicals have lingered long in considering this view, though remarkably Fee, an excellent textual critic, actually adopts it and argues for it at some length (*First Corinthians*, 699–708).

5. Two important early explications of this approach were Neal M. Flanagan and Edwina H. Snyder, "Did Paul Put Down Women in 1 Cor 14:34–36?" *BTB* 11 (1981): 10–12; and David W. Odell-Scott, "Let the Women Speak in Church: An Egalitarian Interpretation of 1 Cor 14:33b–36," *BTB* 13 (1983): 90–93. Cf. in more detail Robert W. Allison, "Let Women Be Silent in the Churches (1 Cor. 14.33b–36)," *JSNT* 32 (1988): 27–60.

This view too proves highly implausible, for no fewer than seven reasons: Unlike all the other widely acknowledged slogans in 1 Corinthians, these verses (1) are not concise or proverbial in form; (2) do not reflect the libertine wing of the church; (3) require the assumption that there was a significant Judaizing element in the church, which little else in the letter supports; (4) are not qualified by Paul but rejected outright; and (5) as best as we can tell represent an explanation that was never proposed in the history of the church until the twentieth century. In addition, (6) this view requires taking the Greek conjunction *e* ("or," left untranslated in the NIV) at the beginning of verse 36 as a complete repudiation of what has gone before, even though no other use of *e* in Paul functions in that way. Finally, (7) it assumes that "the only people" in verse 36, a masculine plural adjective (*monous*), refers just to men rather than to both men and women, even though no other plural reference to the Corinthians ever singles out the men in this way without explicitly saying so.

Equally implausible is the older, extremely conservative perspective that verses 34–35 are absolute commands silencing women in every way during the Corinthian worship service. This view has to assume that 11:5 was in fact not implying Paul's approval of women praying or prophesying publicly, but surely if that were the case he would have had to say so. Or else one has to assume, without any contextual support, that two different kinds of Christian assemblies are in view in the two passages. Or, if one has an extremely low view of Paul, not only as uninspired but also as unable to remember what he has recently written, one can simply admit a contradiction. But these approaches surely reflect last-ditch resorts to support a highly chauvinistic interpretation of 14:34–35.

Another cluster of interpretations seems more probable, though none is without its problems. Factors of cultural background may have explained Paul's commands.[6] Perhaps the largely uneducated women of that day were interrupting proceedings with irrelevant questions that would be better dealt with in their homes. This would explain the language of verse 35.[7] Perhaps they were "chattering," or even gossiping, as some Jewish women sitting in their segregated synagogue balconies reputedly liked to do. Or perhaps they were caught up in subtly promoting false teaching. But while historically and contextually plausible, each of these views fails to explain why Paul si-

---

6. For a thorough sampling of attitudes toward and customs concerning women, reflected in the primary documents of the ancient Greco-Roman world, see Mary R. Lefkowitz and Maureen B. Fant, *Women's Life in Greece and Rome* (Baltimore: Johns Hopkins, 1982).

7. This view is ably defended in what is probably the best egalitarian treatment of Paul on women which has thus far appeared (Keener, *Paul, Women, and Wives*, 70–100).

lenced *all* women and *no* men, when presumably there were at least a few well-educated, courteous, or orthodox women and at least a few uneducated, less than polite, or doctrinally aberrant men![8]

Still others think Paul is excluding women from speaking not in general but in tongues. This perspective has the advantage of recognizing that the verb "speak" in verse 34 is regularly used throughout this chapter for charismatic speech. But if tongues is a spiritual gift, then surely the Spirit gives it to whomever he chooses irrespective of gender (cf. 12:11; 11:15).

Perhaps the best perspective, therefore, is to take Paul's commands as prohibiting women from participating in the final church decisions about the legitimacy of any given prophecy. To begin with, "speak," in twenty of the twenty-one appearances of this verb in this chapter outside of vv 34–35, refers either directly or by analogy to one of four very particular kinds of speech: tongues, their interpretation, prophecy or its evaluation. But the first three of these are spiritual gifts, distributed regardless of gender. An authoritative evaluation of prophecy, however, while requiring input from the whole congregation, would ultimately have been the responsibility of the church leadership (what Paul elsewhere calls elders or overseers), who, at least in the first century, seem to have been exclusively male. This interpretation also explains why these verses come where they do. The sequence of topics from verses 27–33 has been precisely: tongues, their intepretation, prophecy, and its evaluation, in that order. The obvious drawback of this approach is that it must infer a meaning for "speaking" which Paul never spells out. But that problem afflicts all of the views that take Paul's words as less than absolute at this point, and this view seems to have the least number of additional difficulties.[9]

What then do we do with verse 33b? It is awkward whether we take it as concluding the sentence begun in verse 33a or as introducing verses 34–35. The NIV's approach seems slightly more probable. "It is difficult to think that such a far-reaching principle" as that of God's orderliness "should be qualified as no more than the custom of the churches."[10] The awkward repetition created by taking it with verse 34 (literally, "as in all the churches of the saints, let the women in the churches be silent") can be plausibly explained

---

8. D. A. Carson puts it more strongly when he calls the interpretations surveyed in this paragraph "unbearably sexist" ("'Silent in the Churches': On the Role of Women in 1 Corinthians 14:33b–36," in John Piper and Wayne Grudem, eds., *Recovering Biblical Manhood and Womanhood* [Wheaton: Crossway, 1991], 147).

9. Cf. further Grudem, *Prophecy*, 239–55; Hurley, *Man and Woman*, 185–94; Kistemaker, *First Corinthians*, 511–15.

10. Morris, *First Corinthians*, 196.

by understanding Paul to be moving from the non-Corinthian congregations to the different Corinthian house-churches. They seemingly think they have a corner on the truth with respect to a practice that no one else has adopted (v. 36), so Paul reminds them that what is done everywhere else should be observed in *their* assemblies as well.[11]

As in 11:2–16, the women whom Paul silences may be only wives. This would explain why they must not publicly challenge the church's prophecies but consult "their own men" at home (v. 35, surely a reference to husbands, as in the NIV). To do otherwise might be to challenge their husbands in church in ways that would contradict their God-ordained submission to them (v. 34).[12] The "Law" cannot refer to a specific Old Testament passage telling women to be silent in public worship, since no such passage exists. Neither does it likely refer to Genesis 3:16, since Paul does not elsewhere cite the results of the Fall as a rationale for desirable *Christian* behavior.[13] Rather he probably alludes to the order and purpose of creation in Genesis 2, just as he did in 11:8–9 with respect to women's honoring their heads.

Verses 36–38 thus challenge the Corinthians not to reject Paul's counsel lightly. If every other Christian church practiced what Paul preached on this matter, who are they to be the sole exceptions (v. 36)? Those who contested Paul's teaching undoubtedly justified their rebellion by claiming the Spirit's direction (v. 37a). So Paul adds that if they are truly Spirit-led they will come to acknowledge his views as from the Lord (v. 37b). If they continue to go their own way, they demonstrate that they are out of touch with the Spirit, and the Lord will continue to ignore them and to accomplish his work without them (v. 38). (The NIV footnote ["If he is ignorant of this, let him be ignorant"] reflects a less well-attested textual variant that was probably trying to smooth out the text.)

Finally, verses 39–40 bring all three chapters (12–14), but especially this last one, to a fitting conclusion, as they balance Paul's twin concerns for freedom and structure. Every gift has its place, but each must be used to build up the church in unity and love.

---

11. Cf. Bruce, *1 and 2 Corinthians*, 135.

12. Cf. E. Earle Ellis, "The Silenced Wives of Corinth (1 Cor. 14:34–5)," in *New Testament Textual Criticism*, ed. Eldon J. Epp and Gordon D. Fee (Oxford: Clarendon, 1981), 213–20.

13. 1 Timothy 2:14 is no exception, despite common interpretations to the contrary. See Craig L. Blomberg, "Not Beyond What Is Written: A Review of Aída Spencer's *Beyond the Curse: Women Called to Ministry*," CTR 2 (1988): 413–14.

Bridging Contexts

THE DIFFERENCES BETWEEN most contemporary church services and the picture of Corinthian worship in verse 26 makes application of this verse difficult. The vexed question of why Paul silences women in verses 34–35 should make our applications tentative there. Nevertheless, there are numerous important principles that emerge from the passage as a whole that have cross-cultural value.

Verses 26–33a illustrate key facets of Christian worship. As in chapter 12, Paul strongly encourages every member's participation or use of his or her gifts. Little wonder that the church historically has usually grown the fastest, and evangelism has proved the most effective, in small, informal fellowships. These may be fledgling "church plants," or small groups within larger, more established congregations.[14] Even the exceptions to this trend, as with mass response to large crusades, tend not to bear lasting fruit unless newly converted individuals are linked up with local congregations for ongoing nurture and discipleship.[15] Crucial to that nurture is involving new believers in the exercise of their gifts. As the "headline" to this half-chapter, verse 26 reminds us that Paul's principles for prophecy and tongues in verses 27–38 apply to all the gifts. And preeminent among them is the principle that God gives gifts to prepare *all* church members to contribute to the growth of the body (v. 12).

Verses 27–33a balance verse 26 by stressing the need for order in worship. The fact that Paul never mentions church leaders does not mean they are not present. Acts 14:23 describes Paul and Barnabas appointing elders in all the churches they evangelized. Our reconstruction of the role of patrons in Corinth suggests that the church had powerful leaders indeed (see Introduction, p. 20). Although Christianity, like new religious groups in general, experienced a growing institutionalization over its first few centuries, the evidence suggests that there was a built-in structure from the beginning. The discussion of the offices of overseer and deacon, with the criteria for selecting people to hold these offices (1 Tim. 3:1–13; Tit. 1:6–9), cannot be relegated merely to a late, post-Pauline date, on the presupposition that Paul did not write the Pastoral Letters. After all, Paul's indisputably authentic letter to the Philippians begins with a greeting to precisely these two categories of church officials (Phil. 1:1), no later than A.D. 62, only seven years after the writing of 1 Corinthians.[16]

---

14. Cf. Gibbs, *Church Growth*, 234–74.

15. Christopher Catherwood, *Five Evangelical Leaders* (Wheaton: Harold Shaw, 1985), 201–2.

16. For a good discussion of the compatibility of authority structures with the spontaneous exercise of the charismata in the Pauline churches, see Ellis, *Pauline Theology*, 87–121.

Verse 27 combines with verse 13 to show us two ways in which inter-pretation of tongues can take place. If certain believers know they have the latter gift, they can proceed to speak in tongues with greater confidence, trusting that they will subsequently be able to provide the interpretation. It is interesting that verse 13 introduces a paragraph on glossolalia, in which tongues function not to communicate a message to God's people, but to pray and give praise to God. Perhaps in such a situation it is more natural to ex-pect the tongues-speaker to be able to interpret his or her own message. That way, such people could speak in tongues privately as well, while still under-standing the meaning of what they are saying. Verse 28, on the other hand, acknowledges the truth of 12:30, that not all tongues-speakers will neces-sarily be able to interpret. If such people find themselves in Christian as-semblies where they do not know if anyone else has the gift of interpretation, they should proceed more cautiously.

It is probably appropriate, in settings in which glossolalia has never be-fore been experienced, for persons who believe God is leading them to speak in tongues to "float a trial balloon" and go ahead and speak at a timely moment that does not interrupt someone else. They might want to proceed cautiously, however, unless they sense some openness to tongues in that par-ticular assembly. But if no interpretation is forthcoming, they should refrain from continuing to speak in tongues in that congregation until they have rea-son to believe an interpreter is present. This might occur, for example, when another member of the church admits to feeling that he or she understood the message but was simply too fearful or shy to speak up.

Given our interpretation of verses 5a and 31, we must continue to insist that believers never try to make any one gift a criterion of any kind of spir-ituality. It is illegitimate to insist that all Christians prophesy or speak in tongues, or experience any other particular spiritual gift. These verses do show, however, that all believers can potentially receive any specific gift, in-cluding these two. So it remains appropriate for us to pray for a gift that we earnestly feel would benefit the church, but we may never claim that God has to give it to us.

These verses almost certainly imply as well that Paul anticipates the Spirit's sovereign distribution of his gifts irrespective of gender, as in 12:11. Nor is there any need to try to distinguish between these verses and 12:29 by arguing that all believers may occasionally prophesy or speak in tongues, whereas only some do so often enough for others to consider that they are actually gifted in these areas. There is no indication in Scripture that gift-edness is based on frequency of use. It is true that the same terminology can in some cases be used to refer to both gifts and offices (teaching/teacher, pastoring/pastor, and perhaps prophecy/prophet), but there is no hint in 1 Corinthians 12–14 that Paul has any offices in view.[17]

Verses 27–32 also refute all claims to "ecstasy" in the practice of tongues, interpretation, and prophecy. If a person is genuinely "out of control" in the exercise of such behavior, he or she is not being controlled by the Holy Spirit! These verses also demonstrate that even the more supernatural gifts do not carry the same authority as Scripture, since it is conceivable that a particular revelation might never get spoken if the guidelines Paul lays down are carefully followed. "Truth is not arrived at by quantity."[18] What is more, believers dare not assume that even genuine tongues or prophecy is necessarily communicated or interpreted inerrantly, otherwise there would be no reason for the congregation to "weigh carefully what is said" (v. 29).

A good example of this problem appears in Acts 21:4. There Luke describes how Christians in Tyre urged Paul "through the Spirit" (the identical expression used for Agabus' prophetic speech in Acts 11:28) not to go on to Jerusalem. In 21:11, Agabus himself arrives in Caesarea and declares in the name of the Spirit how Paul will be imprisoned if he goes ahead with his travel plans. But he remains unpersuaded, and when he decides to continue on his journey anyway, Paul's fellow Christians reply, "The Lord's will be done." Someone has misunderstood the Lord's will, and it doesn't seem likely that it was Paul! More probably, the Christians in Tyre had received the same message as Agabus did but mistakenly interpreted the prediction of Paul's fate as a command to him not to go on. But they presented their word from the Lord as if the Spirit himself had told Paul not to continue.[19] Clearly, Christians must have the freedom to test and reject what other believers tell them God has privately revealed, if it does not match up to the ways they believe God is personally guiding them.

What criteria can be deduced, then, for evaluating Christian prophecy? Michael Green gives seven suggestions: (1) Does it glorify God rather than the speaker, church, or denomination? (2) Does it accord with Scripture? (3) Does it build up the church? (4) Is it spoken in love? (5) Does the speaker submit him- or herself to the judgment and consensus of others in spiritual humility? (6) Is the speaker in control of him- or herself? (7) Is there a reasonable amount of instruction, or does the message seem excessive in detail?[20] Even after using criteria such as these, there will often remain ambiguities,

---

17. Cf. further Grudem, *The Gift of Prophecy*, 234–38.

18. Harrisville, *1 Corinthians*, 242.

19. On this example, see esp. Murray J. Harris, "Appendix: Prepositions and Theology in the Greek New Testament," in *NIDNTT*, vol. 3, 1183.

20. Green, *Corinth*, 77–78.

further reinforcing our conviction that such messages cannot be trusted perfectly. But where several of these principles are clearly violated, the church should lovingly but firmly insist that the speaker stop claiming gifts of inspired utterance, or at the very least work with a mentor in smaller, less public settings to cultivate his or her gifts so as to be able to use them more accurately or appropriately.

A valid application of verses 34–35 obviously depends on the option adopted as to the original meaning of these verses. If Paul did not write them or if they reflect a Corinthian slogan that he refutes, then clearly we can ignore the commands that they contain and even work to combat a similar mentality in contemporary Christianity. But if they do reflect Paul's perspective, as seems highly likely, then we ignore them at our own peril (vv. 36–38). That still would not necessarily mean that they remain normative today, at least not in every detail. If one of the cultural explanations for Paul's silencing the women is accepted, then contemporary Christians will silence women in church only where comparable problems—lack of education, interfering chatter, or the promotion of false teaching—still exist. And they will impose silence on men who fall victim to one of these problems as well.

If the evaluation of prophecy is in view, several more options come into play. For interpreters who limit prophecy to its more spontaneous manifestations, the application of verses 34–35 will be limited to more charismatic congregations, where such manifestations occur. Those who adopt a broader understanding of prophecy will raise again the question of women in the highest levels of Christian leadership. If the elder/overseer was the office that was uniquely responsible for teaching and exercising authority over the congregation (1 Tim. 3:2; 5:17), then perhaps Paul is precluding women from holding this (and only this) office. This interpretation, incidentally, stands a good chance of explaining the combination of verbs ("teach" and "exercise authority") in 1 Timothy 2:12. There Paul is referring to the office of overseer, which he immediately elucidates in the opening verses of chapter 3.[21] But if "women" is better interpreted as "wives," then these restrictions would not bar single women from the eldership, nor husbands and wives from positions of joint leadership, nor wives from offices of oversight in churches in which their husbands are not members (though the last of these arrangements is less than desirable on other grounds).[22] And, as noted in dis-

---

21. See Blomberg, "Not Beyond," 411–13.

22. Cf. Craig L. Blomberg, "The Globalization of Biblical Understanding," in *The Globalization of Theological Education*, ed. Robert A. Evans, Alice F. Evans and David Roozen (Maryknoll: Orbis, 1993), 219.

cussing 11:2–16, our understanding of sensitive topics such as women in ministry will ultimately have to be governed by our synthesis of all the biblical material relevant to the issue.

Interestingly, Paul gives the same threefold rationale for his commands in verses 33b–35 as he did for honoring one's head in 11:2–16. These include cultural disgrace (v. 35), the universal practice of the churches in Paul's day (v. 33b), and an appeal to creation order (v. 34). As in chapter 11, the specific injunction is supported by situation-specific arguments, while the broader principle of submission is supported by an appeal to a timeless mandate.[23] So married women in other times and places should feel free to participate even in the evaluation of prophecy, and even beyond the general level already implied in verse 29, so long as they do not do so from the vantage point of an office of leadership that jeopardizes their God-ordained deference to their husbands.

Verses 39–40 round out Paul's discussion with remarkably balanced conclusions. We dare not rule out any of the spiritual gifts as limited to some previous age or as a sign of the immaturity of particular believers or congregations. But we dare not make any gift, especially tongues and prophecy, a criterion of anything. Unity and mutual edification always remain the overriding goals. Everything must be done decently and in order. But Paul's last word here does not endorse a dead formalism. Decorum itself is highly culture-specific. The thrust of chapter 14 still highlights spontaneity and freedom.[24] Church should be a place that exudes joy and life, but never to such a degree that outsiders are repelled or insiders alienated from each other.

Contemporary Significance

SIGNIFICANT SECTORS OF the Christian world continue to insist that all who really want to be at the center of God's activity must experience one or another of the seemingly more supernatural gifts, an insistence that flatly contradicts Paul's theology in this half-chapter. In other cases, churches stop short of this demand but continue to violate, week in and week out, Paul's rules for regulating tongues and prophecy. Repeatedly, alleged words of the Lord are never tested or challenged; indeed no mechanism is in place for doing so. Far more than two or

---

23. Cf. Stephen Clark, *Man and Woman in Christ* (Ann Arbor: Servant, 1980), 183–89.

24. William Richardson, "Liturgical Order and Glossolalia in 1 Corinthians 14.26c–33a," *NTS* 32 (1986): 150: "Paul says little that would inhibit the enthusiastic element; his directives have only to do with the manner of sharing that experience with the group."

three individuals speak in tongues at any given service. People are taught to pray, or have had hands laid on them while they are told to pray, in order to claim by faith that they will receive a certain gift, even though Paul makes it clear they can have no assurance that God will choose to grant that particular gift.

More subtly, some churches have a regular period of time in which large numbers of people simultaneously pray out loud in tongues, justifying this practice as the mass exercise of a private prayer language. But unbelievers can have the identical reaction to this behavior as to regular tongues (recall verse 23), so this theological sleight of hand seems indefensible. When Paul says "two or three," and "one at a time" (v. 27), he means precisely that. And private prayer language is for personal, private edification. "The building up of the community is the basic reason for corporate settings of worship. They should probably not be turned into a corporate gathering for a thousand individual experiences of worship."[25]

The noncharismatic church, on the other hand, has a large number of lessons to learn from verse 26. If gifts are given to every believer for the corporate edification of the gathered community, then there must be opportunities for church members to exercise those gifts in public worship. One of the few modern churches to capture this emphasis has been the Plymouth Brethren, but even their "spontaneous" sharing can become quite predictable.

> If Paul were writing the average congregation today, his advice would have to work the other side of the street. Rather than an unstructured spontaneity that creates bedlam, he would be confronted with a well-regulated order of worship that often creates boredom. The smallest of churches often prints or mimeographs for its members a program of everything that is going to happen during the hour and the sequence in which it will take place, and once it has been printed it becomes a sacred thing to those who planned it. And the likelihood of the Spirit's leading anyone to say or do something that was not anticipated on Tuesday when the stencil was cut is very remote.[26]

Orders of service are not necessarily bad, but if they are to be used there must be consistent, built-in opportunities for congregants to share more spontaneously how the Lord has been guiding them to contribute to worship. Some churches do this effectively by including a time for anyone to request or lead in a hymn, share a brief message, offer a prayer, share an

---

25. Fee, *First Corinthians*, 667.
26. Chafin, *1 and 2 Corinthians*, 173.

answer to prayer, and so on. If Sunday morning worship services are too large for most people to feel comfortable entering into this process, other settings must be found where they can—for example, in Sunday School, during other worship services, or in small groups meeting in members' homes. Even more significant may be the resurgence of the house-church movement, both in charismatic and increasingly in noncharismatic circles as well. Where there are several like-minded house-churches in reasonably close geographical proximity, they may choose to unite periodically for larger group worship and instruction and enjoy together the resources to which none of them has access on its own.[27]

Verses 27–33 remind us, at the same time, that however creative or flexible the structure of worship may be, duly recognized leaders must have the authority to intervene and correct when Scripture is contradicted or disobeyed. When someone speaks out loud in a tongue, if no one proceeds to give an interpretation, the worship leader should call for one. If one still does not emerge, the leader should request that no further tongues be manifested at that particular service. This in fact is the procedure that many churches do follow today, though at times uninterpreted tongues are tolerated without response.

In other instances, if no one answers the call for an interpretation, the worship leader himself or herself often supplies one. In such instances, it is hard not to suspect that the "interpretation" is fabricated. If God had given the interpretation to that individual in the first place, he or she should have spoken it at once. Giving it after no one else is willing to do so unfortunately looks more like a "face-saving" device.

A somewhat daring but certainly reliable way to test the authenticity of the practice of interpreting tongues in a given context is for a speaker who knows a *bona fide* foreign language that no one else in the congregation knows to speak a brief message in that language. If an interpretation follows that bears no relationship to the meaning of the words, as has at times happened when such a test has been conducted, we can be sure it is not the Spirit supplying the "interpretation."[28]

Comparing verses 1–33a with contemporary Christian practice suggests two sweeping generalizations to which there are many exceptions. First,

---

27. The latter are increasingly called "cell-churches;" the former, "metachurches." For more on cell-churches, see now the journal *Cell Church Magazine*, begun in 1992. For a detailed description of the metachurch, see Carl F. George, *Prepare Your Church for the Future* (Old Tappan, N.J.: Fleming Revell, 1991).

28. Cf. Carson, *Spirit*, 87. One wonders, however, if "faking" a tongue is any less objectionable than "faking" an interpretation!

large segments of charismatic Christianity so dwell on alleged words of the Lord, under various labels, that are so trite, repetitive, and predictable in nature that one cannot help but suspect that most of them come from human manufacture. God is not in the business of using miraculous means consistently to call attention to the obvious or ordinary. Probably a few people in each of these circles experienced the genuine gift, others wanted or were encouraged to get on the "bandwagon," and so they have imitated the genuine gifts in their own strength. Second, large segments of noncharismatic Christianity are so enslaved to traditional patterns of worship that the Spirit could not break through without substantial disruption. A considerable majority of the church members are convinced that their gifts don't count. Not surprisingly, they remain relatively uninvolved. Both groups typically recreate worship after the models of their immediate spiritual predecessors rather than genuinely seeking to overhaul their worship and bring it into conformity with 1 Corinthians 14.[29]

When we turn to verses 33b–38, we enter another maze of competing applications. Not surprisingly, many egalitarians quickly jump to endorse one or the other of the two least probable interpretations—that verses 34–35 are an interpolation or a Corinthian slogan. Equally predictably, some hierarchicalists continue to try to defend an absolutist interpretation of these verses, notwithstanding 11:5, and they too throw aside exegetical common sense in the process. One can maintain greater credibility, and still be either egalitarian or hierarchical, by supporting one of the other positions surveyed earlier (see pp. 280–82). If Paul is responding to a lack of education or a problem with chattering or false teaching, then one must look for contemporary analogies. Where believers remain so uneducated that their questions would overly distract from the proceedings of a service or time of instruction, they must be given extra teaching privately. Many churches effectively meet this need with special classes for prospective or new members and with "graded" curricula for adults who need to be taught the basics of the faith before entering into more advanced discussions. Some congregations unfortunately tolerate adults and teenagers incessantly talking during the worship service, or coming and going at will, in ways that hinder those around them from entering into or remaining fully concentrated on actual worship. Words from the pulpit to discourage such behavior can prove very helpful.

If the issue in verses 34–35 is the evaluation of prophecy by an all male eldership at Corinth, then we must ask what are the functional equivalents

---

29. For a good beginning, see Ronald Allen and Gordon Borror, *Worship: Rediscovering the Missing Jewel* (Portland: Multnomah, 1982).

to elders today? That office is usually most closely approximated, at least in congregationally run churches, by the senior pastor, except in those rare instances in which a body of elders is made up of individuals who are genuinely equal in responsibility for teaching and directing the affairs of the congregation. In presbyterian or episcopalian forms of church government, even senior pastors submit to larger structures of authorities over them, so presumably women's subordination could be preserved even with a female senior pastor at the congregational level. And women's contributions to the leadership of the church in general, and to the evaluation of reputed messages from God in particular, dare not be stifled in ways that prevent them from a full exercise of their spiritual gifts.

Men and women alike need to evaluate with greater consistency and acumen the messages their leaders proclaim to them week in and week out . Ours is the age of professional Christian leadership. Sermons are swallowed by a gullible laity even though they promote rank heresy in many liberal churches, racism and other forms of discrimination in many conservative churches, and less serious mistakes and banalities in both contexts. Better are the models in which Sunday-morning messages are discussed in question and answer or dialogical format on Sunday evenings (or at some other time), or in which pastors consult with a group of trained laity before and/or after sermons to aid in preparation and debriefing.[30]

Equally troubling is the phenomenon of church members trusting some itinerant Christian celebrity over their own local pastors. It is good occasionally to invite guest speakers to a church to bring a fresh perspective and energy, but many churches rely on outsiders to bring a level of expertise that they should be cultivating among their own members. A seminary professor, for example, can offer a breadth of biblical and theological learning to which few in any local congregation have had access, but with the wealth of commentaries and other Bible study tools available in the Western world today, we ought to be encouraging all church members to use these resources on a regular basis.

Verses 36–38 call into question the continued attachment to denominational distinctions that prevent the contemporary evangelical church from achieving powerful, visible unity. If only one small branch of contemporary Christianity holds to a particular doctrine or practice, it is probably not clearly mandated in Scripture and therefore not important enough to divide believers. The main exception to this principle lies in matters of racism, sexism, ageism, and the like, precisely because the groups that are discriminated

---

30. Cf., e.g., Roger E. van Harn, *Pew Rights* (Grand Rapids: Eerdmans, 1992), 149–59.

against are by definition minorities! But the broad-based consensus on the fundamentals of the faith achieved by many organizations in the parachurch movement needs to be imitated by church folk too.[31] Then views on baptism, church polity, eschatology, and so on would no longer hinder churches from working in cooperative ventures for the promotion of kingdom priorities. And surely views on women's roles come under this category.

We desperately need to allow one another the freedom to agree to disagree, to set up alternate models, to encourage local fellowships to determine for themselves, according to their best understanding of Scripture, what men and women should and should not do in home and in church. Egalitarians and hierarchicalists alike need to stop accusing each other of being unbiblical and instead acknowledge more humbly that the biblical data simply aren't clear enough to permit dogmatism on either side.

The same is also most certainly true for charismatics and noncharismatics. Verses 39–40 end with strikingly plain words that are nevertheless disobeyed by large sections of the contemporary church. Many noncharismatics flatly forbid tongues, while many charismatics seldom come close to worshiping decently and in order. As Fee comments,

> It is of some interest that people who believe so strongly in the Bible as the Word of God should at the same time spend so much energy getting around the plain sense of verses 39–40. Surely there is irony in that. What Paul writes in these chapters he claims to be the command of the Lord; one wonders how he might have applied verse 38 to those who completely reject this command.[32]

On the other hand, if a majority of Christians obeyed Paul's commands, most of the divisiveness of the charismatic phenomena could be prevented and Paul's dominant concern for the mutual strengthening of believers enhanced. In some circles, the best illustration of the balance Paul commands appears in the charismatic renewal movement within liturgical churches. But where they may achieve an exemplary combination of structure and freedom, other problems sometimes intrude, not least of which is the danger of authoritarian charismatic leaders compounding their heavy-handedness with the weight of an elaborate denominational hierarchy above them. A combination of true congregational governance, with a balance between spontaneity and structure in worship, would seem to reflect Paul's ideal. But such churches remain few and far between.

---

31. One thinks especially of the widely recognized doctrinal statements of the National Association of Evangelicals, the International Fellowship of Evangelical Students, and the various documents of the Lausanne Committee for World Evangelization.

32. Fee, *First Corinthians*, 713.

1 Corinthians 15:1–34

〰

NOW, BROTHERS, I want to remind you of the gospel I preached to you, which you received and on which you have taken your stand. ²By this gospel you are saved, if you hold firmly to the word I preached to you. Otherwise, you have believed in vain.

³For what I received I passed on to you as of first importance: that Christ died for our sins according to the Scriptures, ⁴that he was buried, that he was raised on the third day according to the Scriptures, ⁵and that he appeared to Peter, and then to the Twelve. ⁶After that, he appeared to more than five hundred of the brothers at the same time, most of whom are still living, though some have fallen asleep. ⁷Then he appeared to James, then to all the apostles, ⁸and last of all he appeared to me also, as to one abnormally born.

⁹For I am the least of the apostles and do not even deserve to be called an apostle, because I persecuted the church of God. ¹⁰But by the grace of God I am what I am, and his grace to me was not without effect. No, I worked harder than all of them—yet not I, but the grace of God that was with me. ¹¹Whether, then, it was I or they, this is what we preach, and this is what you believed.

¹²But if it is preached that Christ has been raised from the dead, how can some of you say that there is no resurrection of the dead? ¹³If there is no resurrection of the dead, then not even Christ has been raised. ¹⁴And if Christ has not been raised, our preaching is useless and so is your faith. ¹⁵More than that, we are then found to be false witnesses about God, for we have testified about God that he raised Christ from the dead. But he did not raise him if in fact the dead are not raised. ¹⁶For if the dead are not raised, then Christ has not been raised either. ¹⁷And if Christ has not been raised, your faith is futile; you are still in your sins. ¹⁸Then those also who have fallen asleep in Christ are lost. ¹⁹If only for this life we have hope in Christ, we are to be pitied more than all men.

²⁰But Christ has indeed been raised from the dead, the first-fruits of those who have fallen asleep. ²¹For since death came through a man, the resurrection of the dead comes also

through a man. ²²For as in Adam all die, so in Christ all will be made alive. ²³But each in his own turn: Christ, the firstfruits; then, when he comes, those who belong to him. ²⁴Then the end will come, when he hands over the kingdom to God the Father after he has destroyed all dominion, authority and power. ²⁵For he must reign until he has put all his enemies under his feet. ²⁶The last enemy to be destroyed is death. ²⁷For he "has put everything under his feet." Now when it says that "everything" has been put under him, it is clear that this does not include God himself, who put everything under Christ. ²⁸When he has done this, then the Son himself will be made subject to him who put everything under him, so that God may be all in all.

²⁹Now if there is no resurrection, what will those do who are baptized for the dead? If the dead are not raised at all, why are people baptized for them? ³⁰And as for us, why do we endanger ourselves every hour? ³¹I die every day—I mean that, brothers—just as surely as I glory over you in Christ Jesus our Lord. ³²If I fought wild beasts in Ephesus for merely human reasons, what have I gained? If the dead are not raised,

"Let us eat and drink,
for tomorrow we die."

³³Do not be misled: "Bad company corrupts good character." ³⁴Come back to your senses as you ought, and stop sinning; for there are some who are ignorant of God—I say this to your shame.

THIS IS THE FIRST major topic in the second half of Paul's letter, dealing with issues arising from the Corinthians' correspondence (7:1–16:4), that does not contain any hint of what the Corinthians wrote. Nor does it begin with "now about," as do 7:1; 8:1, and 12:1. First Corinthians 16:1 will use that phrase again, so perhaps Paul simply omits it here for variety's sake. Or maybe this section is meant to be more closely connected with chapters 12–14, reflecting some of what the Corinthian prophets and tongues-speakers were proclaiming. A third possibility is that chapter 15 may be addressing the otherwise unstated issue at the root of all the other problems the Corinthians faced.

At any rate, the position of some in the Corinthian church is specified in verse 12 ("How can some of you say that there is no resurrection from the dead?"), and it is to this challenge that Paul responds. By denying the resurrection, the Corinthians were almost certainly not denying life after death; virtually everyone in the ancient world believed in that. Rather, they would have been disputing the Jewish and Christian doctrine of *bodily* resurrection and endorsing one of the more Greek forms of belief that limited the afterlife to disembodied immortality of the soul (cf. 2 Tim. 2:17–18). In keeping with their overly realized eschatology (see p. 25), and like some later Gnostics, they may have applied the language of resurrection to the state of spiritual transformation they believed they had already achieved in this life.[1]

Chapter 15 falls into two main sections. Verses 1–34 present Paul's arguments for the certainty of the bodily resurrection, while verses 35–58 discuss the nature of resurrection bodies. The first section also divides into two parts. Verses 1–11 reiterate the fact of Christ's bodily resurrection. Verses 12–34 outline the consequences of disbelief and belief in this fact. The first of these parts in turn has three components. Verses 1–2 provide an introduction to Paul's treatment of resurrection. Verses 3–8 rehearse the early Christian creed or confession about Christ's death and resurrection. And verses 9–11 highlight Paul's unique role as an "untimely" witness to the risen Lord.

Paul begins by reminding the Corinthians what they should have remembered. With a twinge of irony, he actually says "I make known to you," using their favorite language about knowledge (*gnosis*), as if they had never heard of this central doctrine before (v. 1). But this was what they believed when they first became Christians, and only by continuing to believe in a bodily resurrected Jesus can they demonstrate the reality of their faith and persevere until the end (v. 2). "In vain" at the end of verse 2 could also be translated "heedlessly" or "rashly."[2]

In verses 3–7 Paul repeats the foundational tradition that he had first taught the Corinthians. Although he became a Christian and therefore revised his thinking on basic doctrine, including Christ's resurrection, as a result of his direct encounter with the risen Lord on the Damascus road (Gal. 1:12), he would not yet have known of all the eyewitnesses to whom he refers here until later discussion with two of them, Peter and James (Gal. 1:18–24).[3] The early tradition would certainly have included reference to Christ's death, burial, resurrection, and one or more appearances. Its inclu-

---

1. For more details on this background, see esp. Richard A. Horsley, "'How Can Some of You Say That There Is No Resurrection of the Dead?': Spiritual Elitism in Corinth," *NovT* 20 (1978): 203–11.

2. Robertson and Plummer, *First Corinthians*, 332.

3. On a harmonization of Galatians 1 and 1 Corinthians 15, see esp. Ronald Y. K. Fung, "Revelation and Tradition: The Origin of Paul's Gospel," *EvQ* 57 (1985): 23–41. Considerable scholarly discussion has surrounded the question of how much of verses 3–7 reflect

sion here makes it the earliest recorded oral or written testimony to the resurrection, tradition which is "of first importance" (v. 3; a more likely translation than the NIV footnote, "at the first").

"That Christ died" (v. 3) refutes those docetists who believed that Christ only seemed to be human (because they also believed that matter was inherently evil). That it was "for our sins" points to a vicarious atonement—paying the penalty we deserved to pay on our behalf. "According to the Scriptures" probably has in mind passages such as those in Isaiah 52–53 that speak of God's suffering servant. Jesus' burial (v. 4) again certifies that he really died and also points forward to the empty tomb and the reality of the resurrection. "On the third day" uses inclusive reckoning: Good Friday is day one, Saturday is day two, and Easter morning is day three. It is less clear which Scriptures point to the *resurrection* on the third day. Perhaps Paul meant only that the Scriptures testified to Christ's resurrection, with passages like Psalms 16:8–11 and 110:1–4 in view (cf. Acts 2:24–36). In that case, "according to the Scriptures" would modify only the verb "raised" and not the phrase "on the third day." But he may also have found some typological significance in the third-day references to God's vindication of his people in such texts as Genesis 42:18, Exodus 19:16, Joshua 2:22, Ezra 8:32, Esther 5:1, Jonah 1:17 (cf. Matt. 12:40), and especially Hosea 6:2.[4]

Verses 5–7 proceed to supply a list of key witnesses to certify the truth of Jesus' resurrection. Jesus appeared to Peter by himself on that first Easter Sunday (Luke 24:34). "The Twelve" (v. 5) probably refers to the original apostolic band, even when Judas and Thomas were missing (John 20:19–23). No other reference to an appearance to five hundred (v. 6) is found in Scripture, but that many of these people were still alive to be interviewed provided strong corroboration of Paul's claims. Neither is the appearance to James (v. 7—referring to the Lord's brother) described elsewhere, but it probably caused his conversion (contrast his attitude to Jesus in John 7:5). The appearance to all the apostles could refer to any of several occasions: the Sunday night following Easter (John 20:24–29), the occasion of the Great Commission (Matt. 28:16–20) or the day of Christ's ascension (Acts 1:1–11).

After his ascension, which signaled the end of the resurrection appearances, no one expected to see Jesus in this way again. So Paul's "private

---

what Paul received from tradition, with little consensus. For a survey, see John Kloppenborg, "An Analysis of the Pre-Pauline Formula in 1 Cor 15:3b–5 in Light of Some Recent Literature," *CBQ* 40 (1978): 351–67.

4. B. de Margerie, "Le troisième jour, selon les Ecritures, il est ressuscité," *RSR* 60 (1986): 158–88, who also demonstrates how the ancient rabbis linked such texts together in an early midrash on Genesis 22:4.

viewing" (v. 8; cf. Acts 9:1–31) came as a shock. "One abnormally born" translates the Greek word for "miscarriage." But of course a miscarriage is a premature birth; here Jesus' resurrection appearance to Paul was unusually late. Hence the NIV takes the point of the comparison to be something that was simply abnormal. But it may be that Paul had in mind that when Christ appeared to him, God's purposes for his life were so far unfulfilled. Moreover, "in comparison with the other apostles who had accompanied Jesus during his ministry he had been born without the due period of gestation."[5]

In verses 9–11, Paul acknowledges his inferiority as an apostle because he had persecuted the first Christians (v. 9; cf. Acts 8:1; 9:1–2). But he turns this admission of weakness into an opportunity to magnify God's grace. And that grace did not lead to sloth but to greater effort and substantial accomplishment (v. 10). Yet lest his remarks be seen as prideful or competitive, he closes this paragraph by stressing that all the apostles agree on the message of the resurrection and that this belief is what initially led to the Corinthians' salvation as well (v. 11). Verse 11b repeats the thoughts of verse 1 to bring this first section of chapter 15 to a close.

Verses 12–34 form an ABA pattern. Verses 12–19 and 29–34 both argue for the absurdity of Christian belief and practice if the bodily resurrection is not true. In between, verses 20–28 gloriously reaffirm that it *is* true and point to some of the consequences of this grand doctrine. The main point of verses 12–19 is that if there is no coming bodily resurrection of all Christians, then Jesus himself was not bodily raised, and that makes Christianity futile. Paul continuously repeats this thought from several different angles in these verses. The upshot is that all of the following result if there is no bodily resurrection: both the apostolic preaching and the Corinthians' faith are useless (v. 14); Paul and his companions are liars (v. 15); all humanity stands condemned because of their sins (v. 17); and those who have already died, including believers, are eternally lost (v. 18). As a result, Christians are most deserving of others' pity or compassion, since they have given up creaturely comforts and endured persecution (vv. 30–32) for the sake of an empty promise (v. 19).[6]

---

5. See, respectively, George W. E. Nickelsburg, "An Ἔκτρωμα, though Appointed from the Womb: Paul's Apostolic Self-Description in 1 Corinthians 15 and Galatians 1," *HTR* 79 (1986): 198–205; Barrett, *First Corinthians*, 344.

6. The Greek word "only" in verse 19 either modifies the whole sentence (as in the NIV) or the verb "we have hope." In the latter instance, the contrast in verse 19 would be "between having faith [i.e., hope] *only* and having faith supported by the reality of Christ's present risen life."—Nigel Turner, *Grammatical Insights into the New Testament* (Edinburgh: T & T Clark, 1965), 113.

But wonderfully none of this is true, Paul retorts. Christ *has* been raised bodily and has thus set into motion an inexorable chain of events that will culminate in the universal demonstration of the absolute sovereignty of God (vv. 20–28). Verses 20–22 describe how Christ's bodily resurrection guarantees the future bodily resurrection of all believers, just as the "firstfruits" of a harvest (v. 20) heralded a much larger crop to follow (cf. Lev. 23:9–14). Paul points out the parallel between Adam's sin leading to the sinfulness of all humanity (cf. Rom. 5:12–21) and Christ's resurrection leading to the resurrection of all his followers (vv. 21–22). Because Adam represented the entire human race that would descend from him, sin spread throughout the whole world. Because Christ, as fully human, represented the entire human race in bearing its sins, he is able to apply the benefits of his death and resurrection to all who will accept them (cf. Heb. 2:5–9, appealing to Psalm 8, just as Paul will do in v. 26 here). "All" in the statement "all die" (v. 22a) means "all who are related to Adam." "All" in the declaration "all will be made alive" (v. 22b) refers to "all who are related to Christ," as verse 23 makes clear ("those who belong to him").

But the general resurrection of believers at the time of Christ's return is just the beginning (v. 23). Verses 24–28 go on to explain what will subsequently occur. After some unspecified interval of time, "the end" or goal of human history will arrive. By this time, Christ will have destroyed all opposition to his reign in the universe—both human and angelic (i.e., demonic—vv. 24–25). Finally, death itself will be destroyed, so that God's people will never again have anything to fear for all eternity (v. 26).[7] But the last word is not Christ's but God's (vv. 27–28).

The "he" in verse 27a refers to God; the "his" to Christ, as verse 27b clarifies. As a representative of humanity, and doing what humans were supposed to have done but failed to do (i.e., exercise dominion over the cosmos—Gen. 1:28), Jesus remains ultimately subordinate to God. Compare Psalm 8:5, in which humanity, including Jesus in his incarnation (Heb. 2:9), was made "a little lower than the angels." Here Paul quotes Psalm 8:6 to stress Christ's corresponding conquests as well. The result is that God is "all in all," that is, "pervasively sovereign."[8] Although God the Son is *essentially* equal to the Father, he remains *functionally* subordinate, just as his glorified humanity keeps him distinct from what he was prior to the incarnation.[9]

---

7. For a thorough study of this theme, see Martinus C. de Boer, *The Defeat of Death: Apocalyptic Eschatology in 1 Corinthians 15 and Romans 5* (Sheffield: JSOT, 1988).

8. Martin, *Spirit*, 107.

9. On this theme in the history of theology, which goes beyond Paul's explicit discussion here, see John F. Jensen, "1 Cor. 15.24–28 and the Future of Jesus Christ," *SJT* 40 (1987): 543–70.

In verses 29–34 Paul goes back to arguing the absurdity of denying the bodily resurrection. Here he uses three *ad hominem* and *ad hoc* arguments[10] based on what he and the Corinthians were experiencing (note the references to "they" [NIV "those" and "people"] in v. 29, "us," "we," and "I" in vv. 30–32, and "you" as the implied subject of the commands in vv. 33–34).

The most puzzling of these is the first. Despite all sorts of ingenious alternatives that have been suggested, the plain meaning of verse 29 remains that of some sort of proxy baptism. Early church fathers allude to such a practice among second-century Gnostic and Gnostic-like groups, in which living believers were baptized on behalf of those in their sect or group who had died without being baptized (cf. Tertullian, *Against Marcion* 5.10; Chrysostom's *Homily on 1 Cor.* 40.1; Epiphanius, *Heresies* 28; and Philaster, *Heresies* 49). Given the Corinthians' tendencies toward early Gnostic belief and practice, it is not difficult to imagine something similar having begun among at least a few in Corinth already in the first century. Paul neither condemns nor condones such a practice but argues for its irrelevance if Christ is not raised. In other words, those who are baptizing people on behalf of the dead contradict their own theology that denies the resurrection. The Corinthians might well have replied that they performed such baptisms for the sake of disembodied souls, but Paul is convinced that without a body there is no further life at all.

In verses 30–32 Paul turns to a parallel pair of arguments from his own experience. Why should he continue to tolerate hostility from others and risk his life for the sake of the gospel if there is no hope of resurrection? Second Corinthians 11:23b–29 sheds light on the kinds of trials he has had to endure. In verse 31, "I mean that" translates a Greek word used to introduce an oath or solemn declaration of the truth of a particular statement. "Just as surely as I glory over you" translates the three Greek words, "by your boast," and more naturally refers to the Corinthians boasting in Paul. But since there was little evidence that they were doing that, the NIV may be correct.[11]

Verse 32 is almost certainly not to be taken literally. Roman citizens were exempt from being thrown to animals in the gladiator's ring, and Paul would not have easily survived such an encounter. In fact, language about fighting wild beasts was regularly used metaphorically for human opposition

---

10. An *ad hominem* argument appeals to a person's emotions and does not necessarily use strict, logical reasoning. An *ad hoc* argument is one composed only for a specific occasion and not generalizable to all situations.

11. In technical terms, this would then be the use of the possessive pronoun as a substitute for an objective genitive. Cf. further Donald S. Deer, "Whose Pride (Rejoicing/Glorying) in 1 Corinthians 15.31?" *BT* 38 (1987): 126–28.

(cf. esp. Ignatius, *Romans* 5:1). Some think he is referring to the riot in Ephesus (Acts 19:23–41), but that seems to have occurred just before he left town (Acts 20:1) and therefore after writing this letter (cf. 1 Cor. 16:8). Paul may be alluding to some otherwise unknown personal attack or persecution that threatened his life. Second Corinthians 1:8–11 seems to look back on such an event. One early tradition claims that Paul was temporarily imprisoned in Ephesus, and some modern scholars believe that he wrote Philippians and/or the other Prison Letters (Colossians, Ephesians, and Philemon) during such an imprisonment. We simply do not have enough evidence to know for sure what danger he was recalling here.

Verse 32b reflects the flip side of the logic of verse 19. If this life is all there is, then people ought to "live it up," as the Epicureans did. Paul cites their most famous slogan, as the prophet Isaiah and the author of Ecclesiastes had done centuries earlier (Isa. 22:13; Eccl. 2:24). But he immediately proceeds to reject such logic, since Christ has in fact been raised. Instead he quotes another popular Greek proverb, this one first attributed to the fourth-century B.C. comic playwright Menander (v. 33). Those who deny the resurrection make for "bad company," and their dualistic presuppositions ("matter doesn't matter") foster immoral behavior (as in chaps. 5–6). Paul appeals to the Corinthians to reject this route (v. 34) by again chiding them for their lack of *gnosis* and by trying to shame them into repentance (cf. 6:5).

Bridging Contexts

THE RESURRECTION BRINGS us to the very center of the Christian faith. When Paul was on trial for his life before the Jewish leaders, he summed up the charge against him as his "hope in the resurrection of the dead" (Acts 23:6; cf. 24:21; 26:6–8). When he clothed the gospel for the Athenians in almost entirely different garb, he nevertheless still focused on "Jesus and the resurrection" (Acts 17:18). His emphasis on the resurrection in 1 Corinthians 15 in no way contradicts 2:2—Christ's death and resurrection are inseparable. Without the latter, the former has no eternal significance. To counteract those who play down the weakness and servanthood of Jesus, Paul must stress the crucifixion, but to refute those who deny a future material hope for believers and the cosmos, he must stress Jesus' bodily resurrection. Historically, the Eastern Orthodox have best highlighted the resurrection; the Roman Catholics, the crucifixion. Protestants have alternately magnified elements of each. Both remain crucial.

Although emphases may vary from culture to culture, particularly according to the objections to belief in the resurrection that emerge in each, this doctrine must remain at the core of Christian theology. Applying this chapter requires a comparison between first-century beliefs about life after death and similar beliefs in other cultures. Then the uniqueness of the Christian doctrine of resurrection and its significance can appear more clearly. In Paul's day, almost everyone held to a supernatural worldview that encouraged belief at least in life after death. Most Greeks and Romans, however, did not see that this entailed bodily resurrection. In modern cultures influenced by the skepticism of the Enlightenment, this supernatural worldview is not shared, so we have to defend both the *possibility* and the *need* for bodily resurrection.[12]

Verses 1–2 stress what this chapter will continually repeat, most notably in verses 12–19 and 29–32, that Christian belief without the doctrine of bodily resurrection proves worthless. Verses 3–7 offer a strong apologetic for the reality of Christ's being raised. Given the early date of 1 Corinthians (ca. A.D. 55) and the likelihood of Paul relying on formalized oral tradition that substantially predates the letter, we are indeed in touch with very early testimony.[13] Paul, of course, used this tradition to call wayward believers back to that which they once firmly maintained. But we may also use these verses to argue the case for the resurrection with unbelievers. So too we are reminded of what must remain central doctrine even for mature believers, tempted to move away to peripheral matters. The absolute fundamentals of the faith include the genuine humanity and deity of Christ (making real death and real resurrection possible, respectively), his vicarious atonement, his bodily resurrection, and the authority of the Scriptures, which are twice appealed to in verses 3–4 to corroborate the significance of the historical events described.

These appeals to the Old Testament, as elsewhere in the New Testament, raise questions for us and remind us that the first Christian writers saw all of Scripture pointing to Christ. Indeed, Jesus himself during his resurrection appearances solidified such a hermeneutic in his disciples' minds (Luke 24:25–27). This involved use of such well-known Jewish techniques as typology, midrash, pesher and so on. As we grope today to find specific Scriptures that "predict" the resurrection, we recognize that we have entered a world in which prophecy did much more than provide straightforward

---

12. On which, see esp. Gary Habermas, *The Resurrection of Jesus* (Grand Rapids: Baker, 1980).

13. E.g., Peter J. Kearney ("He Appeared to 500 Brothers [1 Cor. xv 6]," *NovT* 22 [1980]: 264–84) reconstructs a core confession which he traces to Hellenistic Jewish tradition in Jerusalem prior to Stephen's martyrdom. This would probably put us within two years of the very events that the confession recounts.

predictions that were literally fulfilled at a later date in history.[14] At the same time, we must not overlook the significance of Acts 2:30–31, in which Peter claims that at least David understood more directly the prediction of the Messiah's resurrection. Because David was told that one of his descendants would always sit on his throne (2 Sam. 7:13–14), he may have received a clearer understanding than most of his contemporaries of the ministry of the coming Christ.[15]

The contents of the early Christian "creed" embedded in verses 3–7 also refute all the classic suggestions that have been made down through the centuries to account for the origin of resurrection faith apart from a literal bodily resurrection. That "Christ died" disputes the claim that he merely swooned and recovered in the tomb. "That he was buried" renders implausible the views that the disciples stole his body or that the women went to the wrong tomb. Eventually a body could have been produced and the disciples' story laid to rest.[16] The verb *ophthe* ("appeared") refers more naturally to an objective reality that the disciples saw rather than to some subjective vision (as might more plausibly be the case with the word *horama*—"vision"). The number of witnesses and numerous occasions on which Christ appeared seem to rule out mass hallucination.[17] By mentioning Jesus' appearance to two people who did not previously believe in him (Paul and James), Paul refutes the contention that the appearances were the projections of individuals who had so much personally invested in Christ that they simply couldn't imagine him remaining dead.

We do not have enough data to demonstrate how the various resurrection appearances cited here fit in with all of the accounts of the four Gospels, but it is important to stress that none of these data necessarily contradicts any other. Plausible harmonizations have been offered.[18] Charges that the New Testament writers cannot agree on the details remain highly misleading.

---

14. A standard introductory survey to the NT writers' use of the OT, growing out of their Jewish context, is Richard N. Longenecker, *Biblical Exegesis in the Apostolic Period* (Grand Rapids: Eerdmans, 1975).

15. Cf. further Walter C. Kaiser, Jr., *The Uses of the Old Testament in the New* (Chicago: Moody, 1985), 25–41.

16. On the apologetic value of this clause more generally, see esp. William L. Craig, "The Empty Tomb of Jesus," in *Gospel Perspectives*, vol. 2, ed. R. T. France and David Wenham (Sheffield: JSOT, 1981), 173–200.

17. For more details and for the best overall treatment of the reality and meaning of the resurrection, see George E. Ladd, *I Believe in the Resurrection* (Grand Rapids: Eerdmans, 1975).

18. See esp. John Wenham, *Easter Enigma: Do the Resurrection Stories Contradict One Another?* (Grand Rapids: Zondervan, 1984).

Paul's primary purpose in his list of witnesses, however, is to prepare the way for a reference to his own encounter with the risen Christ. He omits mention of the women to whom Jesus appeared (Matt. 28:8–10; John 20:10–18), probably because they were not considered authoritative or valid legal witnesses in much of the ancient world. By singling out the private appearances to Peter and James in verses 5 and 7a, he anticipates his own personal experience in verse 7b. Whatever authority their witness to the resurrection confers on them (or on any of the other apostles), he can lay a legitimate claim to equal authority. That his experience of Jesus on the Damascus road may have been somewhat more subjective (cf. the different experience of his companions in Acts 9:7) does not render the pre-ascension appearances more subjective too. Rather Paul is claiming that, notwithstanding these distinctive elements, his experience was as objective as the earlier apostles' encounters.

Verse 10 reminds us that Paul does not dislike good works! As in Ephesians 2:10, he agrees with James that faith without works is dead (cf. James 2:14–26). Or to use Paul's language, faith necessarily works itself out through love (Gal. 5:6). Here is no cheap grace; rather God's mercy produces more diligent effort on Paul's part than had he merely merited God's favor.

Verses 12–19 return to the theme of the absolute necessity of bodily resurrection, both for Christ and for believers, in order for Christian faith to be genuine or valid. Paul does not permit a perspective on Jesus that views him merely as a good, moral teacher or on Christianity that considers it simply an admirable collection of proverbial truths about how to live. If the resurrection is false, Christianity is worthless. If Christ was not raised, death, the penalty for sin, is not conquered. And his death in particular could not provide forgiveness of our sins, since it would not have eradicated death (cf. Rom. 3:23–25; 4:25). Above all, Paul did not experience enough natural enjoyment or "self-realization" in his life of constant turmoil and persecution to see any point in continuing the struggle if it were based on a myth.

But the reality of the resurrection gives him great hope (vv. 20–28). This life is not all that there is, nor is life after death mere immortality of the soul, though it does include that (cf. verse 53).[19] Though the word "sleep" (vv. 18, 20) was used widely in the ancient world, it is an especially appropriate euphemism for death in Christian circles, since we look forward to "awakening" one day to our new bodies. But the metaphor does not necessarily imply the doctrine of "soul-sleep"—that is, a lack of conscious awareness of

---

19. A particularly well-balanced treatment of the resurrection as involving both immortality and bodily transformation is Murray J. Harris, *Raised Immortal* (Grand Rapids: Eerdmans, 1985).

the presence of God in between death and resurrection. And 2 Corinthians 5:8 and Philippians 1:23 are more naturally interpreted as referring to an intermediate state between these two events that involves conscious, disembodied existence.[20]

Neither may verse 22 be taken to support any doctrine of universalism (that eventually all people will be saved). Our previous discussion has already noted that "all will be made alive" must refer to "all who are in Christ," that is, believers. Paul simply does not address the question of the fate of unbelievers in this passage. Other Scriptures, however, point to a bodily resurrection for them as well, not for glorification but for eternal punishment (e.g., Dan. 12:2; Matt. 25:46; John 5:29; 2 Thess 1:9; Rev. 20:11–15). Verse 23 does not necessarily support a doctrine of the millennium, but it at least allows for it. The adverbs in verses 23b–24a, "then . . . then" (Gk. *epeita . . . eita*), often but not always refer to a sequence of events with a period of time in between. Given the substantial gap between Christ's resurrection and his return (v. 23b), it is natural to assume a similar gap prior to the final destruction of all his enemies (v. 24a), as Revelation 20 seems to teach. But we cannot be sure, and one's views on numerous other parts of Scripture must be considered before arriving at a position on the millennium.[21]

Verses 24–28 remind us of our discussion of women's issues under 11:2–16. Clearly, Paul teaches here an ultimate subordination of the Son to the Father (in function, not essence). Therefore, to the extent that he bases relationships between men and women or husbands and wives on the analogy of the Godhead (11:3), functional subordination remains appropriate in the spheres of home and ministry too. Perhaps Paul is not drawing the analogy that tightly, but if he is, it will not do to dismiss Christ's subordination to the Father as limited just to his time on earth. On the other hand, we dare not jettison his equality of essence or we revert to Arianism and leave the door open for Christ to be viewed as a created being. Neither may verse 28 be interpreted in a pantheistic light, as if God's being "all in all" meant that he was indistinguishable from the created order. Rather, as we have already observed (p. 298), this text makes an absolute claim for God's ultimate sovereignty and lordship.

Given the plethora of suggestions for interpreting verse 29,[22] we dare not be dogmatic in upholding any one of them. But given Paul's parallel reason-

---

20. See esp. Joseph Osei-Bonsu, "The Intermediate State in the New Testament," *SJT* 44 (1991): 169–94.

21. See the helpful surveys in Robert G. Clouse, ed., *The Meaning of the Millennium: Four Views* (Downers Grove: InterVarsity Press, 1977); and Stanley J. Grenz, *The Millennial Maze* (Downers Grove: InterVarsity Press, 1992).

22. For a brief survey, see Fee, *First Corinthians*, 763–67.

ing in verses 30–32, an *ad hoc* understanding seems best. Paul points out the logical implications of the Corinthians' behavior without passing judgment on it one way or the other. We need not shrink from admitting that some of the Corinthians, along with all their other problems, were baptizing people on behalf of unbaptized, deceased believers or inquirers into the faith. *We must simply insist that Paul is in no way condoning the practice*, any more than he approves of the fact that he daily suffers hardships (vv. 30–31) or that he "fought wild beasts in Ephesus" (v. 32). These are simply unfortunate realities that Paul uses as a springboard for furthering his contention for the truth of resurrection. Why continue with them if there is no hope beyond the grave? So there remains no justification for making any of these practices prescriptive rather than descriptive, and certainly no evidence that Christians ever considered proxy baptism valid for total unbelievers. Both of these observations, therefore, contradict historic Mormon belief and practice, despite their appeal to verse 29 for support. What is more, no Scripture ever suggests that salvation is transferable from one individual to another apart from their personal belief in this life, and Matthew 25:9 most likely rules out such transfer.

Some readers are surprised that Paul uses an oath in verse 31, after Christ's apparent prohibition of all oaths in Matthew 5:33–37. But that prohibition is not so sweeping as at first glance it appears. Paul uses oaths elsewhere too (2 Cor. 1:18 and Gal. 1:20), while Jesus is concerned to abolish the elaborate casuistry that encumbered typical first-century Jewish practice. His followers should be people whose words are so characterized by integrity that others need no formal assurance of their truthfulness in order to trust them.[23] But in writing the Corinthians (as with the Galatians), Paul has to resort to extreme measures to counter their growing mistrust of him.

Verse 32b points out how self-indulgence is the consistent outgrowth of a material philosophy that denies the resurrection life. The Epicureans of old did not usually interpret their slogan as a call to sheer gluttony and drunkenness. Rather they sought the "good life," cultivating the arts of fine dining, music and theater, and treasured friendships. Yet ultimately all of this was self-centered, since they did not look to continuing any pleasures beyond the grave. Self-interest may even lead to humanitarian and altruistic concerns, but ultimately it produces nothing permanently satisfying if this life is all that exists.

Christians must have a radically different mind-set. Recognizing that a far better life awaits them, they can risk their lives or well-being for the gospel in ways other people would not be willing to emulate. In Christian ethics,

---

23. Cf. Craig L. Blomberg, *Matthew* (Nashville: Broadman, 1992), 112, 345.

physical death cannot be the greatest tragedy that determines correct human behavior. Rather one must ask what is likely to lead to the spiritual salvation of the most number of people and to avoid the physical (and therefore spiritual) deaths of the greatest number of unbelievers. Snyder puts it well:

> The resurrection addresses those who insist on protection and security of the individual, institutions, and country. Such persons set up mechanisms of defense along economic, racial, and national lines. . . .
>
> In sharp contrast, the life of the Spirit, with its hope in the resurrection, does not, indeed, cannot, dwell on preservation of the flesh (personhood, institutions, nations). Rather the corporate life of the Christian becomes one of risk. A Christian hospital can accept more welfare patients than economically advisable because it knows God's love for the poor does not depend on its continued existence. . . . Christians can call for total disarmament in the midst of a cold war because they know the future of the world does not depend on the survival of their nation. A Christian can risk his or her life because a Christian knows this life is not the end.[24]

Verse 33 proves widely applicable and reminds us that Christians do not become the salt of the earth and the light of the world (Matt. 5:13–16) automatically. Our persistent sinful nature continues to try to corrupt us when we are surrounded by people engaged in sinful practices, unless we take deliberate, conscious action to the contrary. Verse 34a highlights how immorality often flows from false theology. We recall the sexual sin that stemmed from the Corinthians' divorce of body and spirit (chaps. 5–6). Verse 34b reminds us again that shame or guilt can be an appropriate motivation to corrective action when we are objectively guilty and engaged in shameful behavior. But it can be overdone and misapplied as well.

Finally, an important objection to Paul's line of thought throughout this half-chapter must be considered. Many Greeks and Romans in Corinth, like many people today, might well have asked, "Why isn't immortality of the soul enough?" Why not merely affirm that Christ's spirit lives on and that our spirits can also live forever with his? First Corinthians does not directly answer this question. Paul apparently relied on his audience to understand his Jewish background or recall his previous teaching on the topic.

But Scripture's teaching elsewhere points us in the direction of an answer. Against the Greco-Roman dualism that treated matter as inherently evil, the Bible declares that God created the material world, including human bodies,

---

24. Snyder, *First Corinthians*, 211.

as good (Gen. 1:10, 12, 18, 21, 25, 31). Humans were intended to live in bodily form in a material world. Revelation 21–22 describes God's ultimate re-creation of new heavens *and a new earth* in equally material terms. In other words, God intends to see that his original creative purposes are not thwarted. Anything less than full bodily resurrection and full re-creation of the cosmos might still give believers an enjoyable experience but would not vindicate God against all his enemies or provide the absolute perfection that he intends for his people.[25]

DENYING THE REALITY of the resurrection remains a central problem in contemporary culture. Atheism usually rejects the possibility of the existence of all supernatural powers, often claiming support in the "findings" of modern science. But with revolutions in modern physics associated with Einstein and Heisenberg, scientists who understand their discipline are often more reluctant to rule out God and the supernatural on scientific grounds than are students of the humanities and even of world religions![26] Historians usually recognize the absurdity of most of the proposed alternatives to the resurrection—the swoon theory, the stolen body or wrong tomb, mass hallucination, and so on, though that does not stop more popular writers from continuing to perpetuate such nonsense.[27]

Far more common in scholarly circles, however, is the view that resurrection language expresses theological truths in mythological garb, and that some kind of subjective experience of the disciples' faith was transformed over time into the biblical narratives that claim to describe more objective realities. There are numerous problems with this approach,[28] but the most important are these: (1) The disciples were nowhere close to being in a psychological mood favorable to belief in a resurrection (John 20:19). (2) Without a genuinely empty tomb, it is incredible that Christians never came to venerate a holy site in which their founder was supposedly buried, as did most other world religions. (3) Early on, Jesus' disciples stopped worshiping on the Sabbath (Saturday) in favor of Sunday, the first day of the

25. Cf. the helpful discussion in Eugene H. Peterson, *Reversed Thunder* (San Francisco: HarperCollins, 1988), 168–85.

26. See esp. Peter Carnley, *The Structure of Resurrection Belief* (Oxford: Clarendon, 1987).

27. Doubtless the most famous and influential example from the second half of the twentieth century has been Hugh J. Schonfield, *Passover Plot* (New York: Bantam, 1965).

28. For a more detailed presentation and examination, see Craig L. Blomberg, *The Historical Reliability of the Gospels* (Downers Grove, Ill.: InterVarsity Press, 1987), 100–110, and the literature there cited.

week (e.g., Acts 20:7). But why should they abandon one of the very Ten Commandments so central to Judaism unless some genuinely historical event like the resurrection had occurred on that other day as a powerful stimulus for change? (4) The development from spiritual to bodily resurrection makes sense had Christianity moved from Greek to Jewish circles, but not when it in fact progressed in the opposite direction.

Christ's death and resurrection in space and time, as bona fide historical events, actually set Christianity apart from all its major rivals. Later Western religions that developed in part in reaction to Christianity do not claim deity or resurrections for their originators, merely prophetic status (e.g., Mohammed in Islam or Joseph Smith in Mormonism). Older Eastern religions do not even require the actual historical existence of their founders for their beliefs and practices to make sense. In some ways they are more akin to philosophies than to historical truth-claims (e.g., Hinduism, Buddhism, Confucianism).[29] But Christianity lives or dies with the claim of Christ's resurrection. To be sure, it is possible to believe in Jesus' resurrection and not become a Christian,[30] but without the bodily resurrection Christianity crumbles. Finding the bones of Jesus would assuredly disprove our religion!

So it is appropriate to insist on the resurrection not only as the center of contemporary faith but also of contemporary apologetics.[31] But recent evangelical apologetics has at times been one-sidedly rationalistic. Paul's appeal to his own personal experience of the risen Christ (v. 8) to balance the historical facts he had learned (vv. 3–7) means that we too may consider our personal encounters with Jesus as an equally legitimate part of the defense of our faith. On the other hand, without the appeal to historical facts, we have no way of mediating between the competing claims of largely parallel personal experiences. Mormons, Buddhists, and Christians alike often testify today to some strong feeling or spiritual encounter that "confirmed" the truth of their faith. But since these three religions contradict each other at important points, all cannot be simultaneously true. Christians must appeal to more than a personal testimony; they must recognize the historical evidence that is on their side.

---

29. Cf. further Norman Anderson, *Christianity and World Religions* (Downers Grove: InterVarsity Press, 1984).

30. As in the famous modern case of the German rabbi Pinchas Lapide (*The Resurrection of Jesus* [Minneapolis: Augsburg, 1983]), who points out that Jesus still has not fulfilled all of the prophecies associated with being Messiah.

31. As, e.g., on the scholarly level in William L. Craig, *Assessing the New Testament Evidence for the Historicity of the Resurrection* (Lewiston, N.Y.: Mellen, 1989); or on the popular level in Josh McDowell, *The Resurrection Factor* (San Bernardino: Here's Life, 1981).

Saddest of all are the examples of professing Christians, particularly within liberalism, who think they are bolstering the faith in a scientific age by relegating the resurrection to outmoded mythology. In so doing, they turn out to be most misguided of all, because they undermine the very core of what they seek to support.[32] But evangelicalism has its counterparts, as with those who so stress the earthly benefits of belief that Christianity would seem to be a desirable lifestyle irrespective of what happens after death.[33] People who promote such perspectives have never walked in Paul's shoes or, for that matter, in the footsteps of a sizable number of Christians and martyrs throughout church history, who would have quickly abandoned their faith if it were not for hope of eternal reward for the misery experienced in the here and now (cf. vv 19, 30–32).

The non-Christian West today is increasingly implementing the Epicureanism of verse 32b. In more Christian societies, unbelievers at least outwardly have often imitated Christian lifestyles or have felt social pressure to curb their most excessively immoral behavior. But increasingly, we are seeing a culture that refuses to put on the brakes at all. The "Baby Boomers," including many professing Christians, are in debt up to their eyeballs. Advertisements bombard us daily with what we *have* to have immediately. Sexual morals continue to deteriorate, so that what was unthinkable for most non-Christians in another era—addiction to pornography, repeated acts of adultery, or incestuous behavior—is now widely practiced, even at times among those who profess to be born again. Worldwide, consistent indulgence in self-interest has given rise to tribalism and ethnic wars that atheistic Communism once held in check and that humanistic evolution cannot explain.

But even where industrialism and technological advance give rise to the concept of "developed" nations, materialist philosophy fails to satisfy.[34] So we are seeing the rise of the New Age movement, in many respects a reversion to pantheism or ancient Gnostic and earth-mother religions. Reincarnation

---

32. The lasting power of this approach is probably due more to Rudolf Bultmann (see, e.g., his "New Testament and Mythology," in *Kerygma and Myth*, ed. H.–W. Bartsch [London: SPCK, 1953], 4, 7) than to any other single twentieth-century scholar or theologian.

33. One thinks, for example, of the so-called power of positive (or possibility) thinking associated with the ministries of Norman Vincent Peale and Robert Schuller.

34. Cf. Kôshi Usami, "'How Are the Dead Raised?' (1 Cor 15, 35–58)," *Bib* 57 (1976): 493: "Modern industrialized society may be in danger of imprisoning our body in an artificial cage of promised fulfillment and accomplishment of all bodily desires. Our 'body' will rebel. Our whole being will rebel against the excessive dominance of cold reason. In 1 Cor 15, 35–58 Paul explains faith in bodily resurrection by means of experiences that are not foreign to religious experience in many parts of the world."

is in vogue. Interest in the cults and the occult is booming. As authentic Christian spirituality is rejected, counterfeits will take their place to fill the "God-shaped vacuum" in each human heart, to use Pascal's famous expression. Popular culture and media have an intense fascination with life after death, initiated particularly by Kübler-Ross's studies of near-death experiences.[35] Blockbuster movies invent fictitious accounts of those who die and yet live on, or come back to interact in various ways with those still living on earth.

Yet almost without exception, this fascination for the afterlife resembles more the Corinthians' false teaching than orthodox Christianity. Seldom are persons depicted as having fully human bodies in their next life. Rarely does that next life seem incomparably more desirable than the present one. And virtually never are the destinies of Christians and non-Christians appropriately distinguished. Either all people are seen as going to "heaven," or else they are distinguished on the basis of how good or bad they were during their time on earth.

A faulty theology of the resurrection plagues competing world religions in other respects too. Millions of young Muslims have tragically allowed themselves to be killed in war and terrorism, believing that martyrdom speeds their way to heaven. Mormons try to work their way up the ladder of extra-terrestrial privilege and power. Jehovah's Witnesses hope that sufficient obedience will enable them to be one of the 144,000 who get to enjoy the new heavens as well as the new earth. Eastern religionists hope for *nirvana*—to be absorbed into the cosmic consciousness, which is all that there really is. Against all of these perspectives Paul's absolute dogmatism challenges the prevailing tolerance of a pluralistic age. If Christianity is right, Paul would virtually shout, then these perspectives are damning, and people should be warned against them in the most forthright language. But if the Christian hope of resurrection is wrong, then all these other perspectives *are still wrong*, for the only other consistent alternative is total annihilation at death. Then we should eat, drink, and be merry, for tomorrow we may die. The proliferation of alternate worldviews shows how the human instinct recoils at such nihilism. But that in itself is backhanded testimony to the Christian truths that humans are created in God's image, yet have sinned and so distorted that image that they consistently look for inadequate substitutes.

Evangelical Christians must shoulder some of the blame, however, for the unpopularity of biblical teaching about the life to come. Too many pew sitters in contemporary conservative churches think of and represent heaven as an "airy-fairy," ethereal kind of existence to which they do not really look

---

35. Elisabeth Kübler-Ross, *On Death and Dying* (New York: Macmillan, 1969).

forward. Even referring to the life to come simply as "heaven" points out a serious misconception. The biblical hope is for believers to experience all of the wonders and glories of a fully re-created heavens *and earth* (Rev. 21–22). We will enjoy one another's fellowship as well as God's presence in perfect happiness. We will not sit on our private clouds with wings and harps periodically to dispel our eternal boredom! The new earth is centered in the new Jerusalem, a *city* of bustling activity.

Not only have Christians tended to make the life to come unattractive, but our generation in the West is one of few in human history that has so consistently tried to create Paradise on earth in this life. Previous generations often lampooned certain kinds of Christians for being so heavenly-minded that they were no earthly good. It is doubtful if many such people under the age of fifty currently exist in our country. Instead, ours is a generation in which many Christians are so earthly minded that they are no heavenly good. Our society, and Christians often as much as anyone else in that society, has become preoccupied with physical health, dieting, recreation, and fitness, all at the expense of anything close to a comparable concern for spiritual health and salvation.

Yet incurable diseases, unexpected accidents, and periodic exposure to the horrors of the less affluent parts of our world continue to point out the sheer inadequacy of such preoccupations. Sooner or later we will die, and some of us will suffer quite a bit before we do. We need to recapture the longing for the life to come, which enabled Paul to declare confidently even in his most difficult moments: "I consider that our present sufferings are not worth comparing with the glory that will be revealed in us" (Rom. 8:18). Or again, "For our light and momentary troubles are achieving for us an eternal glory that far outweighs them all" (2 Cor. 4:17). Most of us consider our truly minor physical afflictions far more serious than Paul's catalogues of horrible sufferings, and yet he could call *them* "light and momentary"!

An appropriate perspective on the life to come will further enable us to risk our lives for the sake of boldly testifying to Christ in dangerous situations at home and abroad. It will also give us a balanced perspective on the gospel we boldly preach. With much contemporary liberation theology, it is crucial to see our task as including social activism that works to eradicate poverty and liberate the physically oppressed throughout our world today. But many are dying daily before we can get to them, and some will continue to do so until Christ returns. So, against much liberation theology, we dare never truncate our gospel so that we do not simultaneously offer the spiritual deliverance that only Jesus can give and that alone can spare humans from an eternity far more unpleasant than anything they have experienced in this life.[36]

In more modest ways, understanding Paul's theology of resurrection should affect our personal and corporate prayer life. How often do our lists of requests involve almost exclusively physical or material needs? How many of us could commend one another as John did Gaius in praying that his circumstances in this life might find him as healthy physically and materially as he already was spiritually (3 John 2)?

The resurrection hope gives purpose and meaning to all of human history. Christians need not fear that the world will end in a nuclear holocaust, because Scripture teaches that the end of this age comes with Christ's return. And although the world's armies are depicted as amassing for a final battle, Christ intervenes before his people suffer a single casualty (Rev. 19:17–19). This does not mean, however, that we should not take every precaution to guard against a limited nuclear accident that could still inflict more damage and suffering on the earth than it has ever experienced. Nor may we ever consider abortion or euthanasia as a way out of human suffering. God always has a purpose for humans whom he keeps alive.

On the other hand, God's ultimate purposes will be realized only after Jesus comes again. So we must not delude ourselves with the naive optimism that counts on us gradually Christianizing the earth this side of Christ's return. Rather we look forward to the world ending with neither a whimper nor a bang, but with Christ's universal, public, visible return to inaugurate the series of events that will culminate with God's absolute sovereignty being acknowledged throughout the cosmos (vv. 24–28).

In this vein, however, we must beware of a growing evangelical fascination with universalism and other unlikely alternatives concerning the fate of unbelievers (e.g., a second chance after death, annihilationism, or conditional immortality).[37] People will not be saved irrespective of their attitude toward Jesus. Still, evangelicals have perhaps been too narrow or myopic in the last few generations when it comes to the question of the fate of the unevangelized. Orthodox Christianity has historically held a greater diversity of perspectives on the destiny of those who have never heard the gospel than has

---

36. In short, we need an "evangelical liberation theology." Cf. further Craig L. Blomberg, "'Your Faith Has Made You Whole': The Evangelical Liberation Theology of Jesus," in *Jesus of Nazareth: Lord and Christ*, ed. Joel B. Green and Max Turner (Grand Rapids: Eerdmans, 1994), 75–93.

37. Cf. the divergent perspectives reflected in William V. Crockett, ed., *Four Views on Hell* (Grand Rapids: Zondervan, 1992).

recent conservative theology.[38] The real dividing point may not be whether a person has ever heard of the name of Jesus or not but whether he or she is relying solely on God's grace, to whatever extent it is understood, or trusting in his or her own self-righteousness.[39] Such a principle might conceivably let a few who have never heard into the kingdom (and the assumption must be that if they had heard they would have responded positively). It almost certainly means that many who *think* they are in are not—including some professing Christians!

38. See the thorough survey in John Sanders, *No Other Name* (Grand Rapids: Eerdmans, 1992).

39. See esp. Norman Anderson, *The World's Religions* (Grand Rapids: Eerdmans, 1976), 234–35.

1 Corinthians 15:35–58

UT SOMEONE may ask, "How are the dead raised? With what kind of body will they come?" [36]How foolish! What you sow does not come to life unless it dies. [37]When you sow, you do not plant the body that will be, but just a seed, perhaps of wheat or of something else. [38]But God gives it a body as he has determined, and to each kind of seed he gives its own body. [39]All flesh is not the same: Men have one kind of flesh, animals have another, birds another and fish another. [40]There are also heavenly bodies and there are earthly bodies; but the splendor of the heavenly bodies is one kind, and the splendor of the earthly bodies is another. [41]The sun has one kind of splendor, the moon another and the stars another; and star differs from star in splendor.

[42]So will it be with the resurrection of the dead. The body that is sown is perishable, it is raised imperishable; [43]it is sown in dishonor, it is raised in glory; it is sown in weakness, it is raised in power; [44]it is sown a natural body, it is raised a spiritual body.

If there is a natural body, there is also a spiritual body. [45]So it is written: "The first man Adam became a living being"; the last Adam, a life-giving spirit. [46]The spiritual did not come first, but the natural, and after that the spiritual. [47]The first man was of the dust of the earth, the second man from heaven. [48]As was the earthly man, so are those who are of the earth; and as is the man from heaven, so also are those who are of heaven. [49]And just as we have borne the likeness of the earthly man, so shall we bear the likeness of the man from heaven.

[50]I declare to you, brothers, that flesh and blood cannot inherit the kingdom of God, nor does the perishable inherit the imperishable. [51]Listen, I tell you a mystery: We will not all sleep, but we will all be changed— [52]in a flash, in the twinkling of an eye, at the last trumpet. For the trumpet will sound, the dead will be raised imperishable, and we will be changed. [53]For the perishable must clothe itself with the imperishable, and the mortal with immortality. [54]When the perishable has been clothed with the imperishable, and the mortal with immortal-

ity, then the saying that is written will come true: "Death has been swallowed up in victory."

> [55]"Where, O death, is your victory?
> Where, O death, is your sting?"

[56]The sting of death is sin, and the power of sin is the law. [57]But thanks be to God! He gives us the victory through our Lord Jesus Christ.

[58]Therefore, my dear brothers, stand firm. Let nothing move you. Always give yourselves fully to the work of the Lord, because you know that your labor in the Lord is not in vain.

VERSES 35–58 RESPOND to the potential objection that verse 35 notes. "How are the dead raised?" was probably not so much a genuine question but a way of mocking the whole notion of bodily resurrection. Paul's reply again falls into three parts. Verses 36–44a provide analogies from the created world to describe the resurrection body. Verses 44b–49 argue for the need of a heavenly body from the existence of an earthly body. Verses 50–57 describe why such transformation is necessary. Paul then closes the chapter with commands to stand firm in true belief and action (v. 58).

The first analogy Paul uses to illustrate the resurrection body is that of seed and plant (cf. John 12:24, though Jesus' point there is somewhat different). By being buried in the ground, the seed seemingly dies, and it certainly decomposes. Yet on that very spot new life emerges, totally different in appearance from the seed, and yet somehow the mature plant remains the same living entity (vv. 36–38). In fact, the world is filled with different kinds of bodies (v. 39—"flesh" here does not mean "sinful nature") that God has created. So why should it be thought incredible that he could create still one more kind—a resurrected human body? So too the heavenly bodies—sun, moon, and stars—differ in nature and brilliance (v. 41). And an even greater gap exists between the earthly bodies, which all have certain identifiable features in common, and the heavenly bodies, which also resemble each other in certain aspects (v. 40).[1]

---

1. Here is a good illustration of the preservation of the classic Greek distinction between *allos* ("another of the same kind") and *heteros* ("another of a different kind"). Paul uses the former throughout verses 39 and 41 to distinguish earthly bodies from each other and heavenly bodies from each other. But he uses the latter in verse 40 to distinguish heavenly bodies from earthly bodies.

Verses 42–44a make clear where Paul is going with all of these analogies. There yet await for the Corinthians resurrection bodies that will be far more glorious than their present ones. Unlike their current bodies, these new ones will be fitted for eternity, never again to die or be limited by sin or impotence (vv. 42–43). Whereas humans in this world are animated by merely physical life, believers will one day be fully empowered by the Spirit (v. 44a). The terms "natural" and "spiritual" in verse 44 use the identical language Paul has already used in 2:6–16 to indicate the difference between Christians and non-Christians. In this context, the contrast might better be indicated by translating the adjectives as "natural" and "supernatural."[2]

Verses 44b–49 pick up on widespread ancient speculation, in both Jewish and Greek circles, that there were two primal human beings, an earthly one and a heavenly one. Plato, for example, thought of all creation as a pale shadow of heavenly archetypes. Philo interpreted Genesis 1–3 allegorically and thought that God originally created two human men, one who lived on earth and rebelled (chaps. 2–3) and his perfect, heavenly counterpart (chap. 1). Paul agrees that there are two progenitors of humanity (v. 44b). But he makes Jesus the perfect "Adam" (using the Hebrew play on words in which Adam means "man") and stresses that he came *after* the first Adam (i.e., in Christ's incarnation), not before (vv. 46–47).

So too believers who have shared in the finite, fallen likeness of the first Adam can look forward to sharing in the kind of perfect humanity Jesus embodied, but only after this life, when Jesus comes back again (vv. 48–49; the NIV footnote here ["so let us"] is less likely than the text ["so shall we"]). To make this point, Paul cites Genesis 2:7 and then uses it as a springboard for comparing the far more glorious humanity of Jesus, who not only has the breath of human life but is able to give eternal, spiritual sustenance to others (v. 45).[3]

Verses 50–57 further unpack the need for bodily transformation. Frail, mortal humanity cannot survive in God's eternal and perfectly holy presence. "Flesh and blood" in verse 50 was a stock idiom in Jewish circles for "a mere mortal" and does not contradict what Paul has already stressed, that resurrection experience is a bodily one (cf. Jesus' reference to having "flesh and bones" in Luke 24:39). But it must be a body that is "imperishable" and "immortal" (vv. 52b-54a).

---

2. William L. Craig, "The Bodily Resurrection of Jesus," in *Gospel Perspectives*, vol. 1, ed. R. T. France and David Wenham (Sheffield: JSOT, 1980), 58–59.

3. On the admittedly intricate logic of verses 44b–49, see esp. James D. G. Dunn, "1 Corinthians 15:45—Last Adam, Life-Giving Spirit," in *Christ and Spirit in the New Testament*, ed. Barnabas Lindars and Stephen S. Smalley (Cambridge: Cambridge University Press, 1973), 127–41.

Verse 51 supplies more information about the time at which this transformation will take place. On the term "mystery," see under 2:7 (pp. 63–64). The secret that Paul is revealing here is that believers' bodily resurrections will occur when Christ returns. Not all Christians will die first, since some will be alive when he comes back. But all will undergo whatever transformation is necessary to give them their glorified bodies. This change will take place instantaneously not gradually. The trumpet (v. 52a) was a stock metaphor in biblical literature to herald the end (cf. Joel 2:1; Zech. 9:14; Matt. 24:31; 1 Thess. 4:16; and the seven trumpets of Rev. 8:2–9:14).

When all this has happened, then the way will be paved for the events of verses 24–28 to unfold. The climax of this series of events for believers is the destruction of death itself, as Isaiah had predicted (v. 54b, quoting Isa. 25:8). Paul breaks out into a rhapsody at the thought of this marvelous prospect, quoting and slightly adapting Hosea 13:14 (v. 55). And, as in Romans 6–8, he recalls that sin is the primary culprit that has led to both physical and spiritual death, while the law, apart from pointing people to Christ, serves only to promote sin, as it increases conscious rebellion against God's standards (v. 56; cf. Gal. 3:19–24).[4] But praise God that this deadly sequence has been interrupted by the victory over death God has wrought through the death and resurrection of Jesus (v. 57)!

Appropriately, Paul returns from these lofty flights of theological reflection to the practical implications for the Corinthians (v. 58). Since Christ has been raised bodily, they too will one day be physically transformed. Therefore they should remain unswervingly committed to orthodox theology and totally dedicated to the work of the gospel—the purity of living and the faithful exercise of their distinctive avenues of service. No matter what the cost in this life, they can count on the ultimate triumph of all God's people and all his purposes.

Bridging Contexts

THE KEY THEME that permeates verses 35–58 is the simultaneous continuity and discontinuity between believers' earthly bodies and their resurrection bodies. Clearly, though, the stress remains on the latter. There is molecular continuity between seed and plant, but who would have guessed it were it not for the recurring cause and effect relationship between planting a seed and seeing new life sprout in the very place the seed was planted? So one may speak of some kind of ongoing per-

---

4. On the logic of verse 56 in this context, see esp. H. W. Hollander and J. Holleman, "The Relationship of Death, Sin, and Law in 1 Cor 15:56," *NovT* 35 (1993): 270–91.

sonal identity between natural and spiritual bodies but anticipate substantial physical change.[5]

Beyond this, Scripture offers few clues to answer our more detailed questions about what these new bodies will be like. We may hazard some guesses from what we know of Christ's resurrected body—it was tangible, it could eat but didn't have to, but it could also appear and disappear and pass through locked doors (Luke 24; John 20–21). Yet precisely because he had not yet ascended and been fully exalted and glorified, even Jesus' body as the Gospels describe it may not have been exactly what he ended up with. One could assume, for example, that he eventually no longer had any scars in his hands and side.[6]

Some see the references to earthly and heavenly bodies in verse 40 as different from the examples given in verses 39 and 41. In that event, Paul may be giving additional analogies, thinking, for example, of the differences among the various earthly terrains (mountains, rivers, canyons, oceans) and among various kinds of supernatural creatures (angels, demons). But this seems unlikely in view of the framing verses that are surely meant to explain this particular text.

At any rate, there is no support at all here for a view, as in Mormonism, that distinguishes between kinds of heavenly bodies that believers will receive. The whole point in contrasting sun, moon, and stars is not to suggest three different kinds of resurrection bodies but to give further examples of how God can create different kinds of physical entities in general.

Verses 42–44a make plain that Paul is comparing and contrasting only *two* kinds of human bodies—those that live in this world and those that will live in the next. The attributes described in these verses are perhaps best epitomized in Revelation 21:4: "He will wipe every tear from their eyes. There will be no more death or mourning or crying or pain, for the old order of things has passed away."

Verses 44b–49 respond to competing views about the afterlife. They affirm three crucial truths that must be preserved. First, a new body is a necessity for experiencing the world to come. Escape into an *eternally* disembodied state is not an option. Second, that new form of existence does not come until Christ's return. This refutes all claims by believers to having

---

5. Cf. Morris, *First Corinthians*, 220: "It is important that what dies is nothing like what appears;" and Bruce, *1 and 2 Corinthians*, 151: "Personal identity does not require such material reconstitution. . . . All that is necessary for the analogy is the combination of identity with difference."

6. For a valiant attempt to wrestle with these continuities and discontinuities, see Robert Sloan, "Resurrection in 1 Corinthians," *SWJT* 26 (1983): 69–91.

"arrived," spiritually speaking, in this life. Third, this new heavenly body will be far more glorious than anything we currently experience or imagine.

Verse 50 reminds us that our current sinful and mortal bodies are incapable and unworthy of coexisting with an infinite, holy God.

Verses 51–52 contain language and imagery that closely resembles 1 Thessalonians 4:13–18, with its description of death as sleep and resurrection at the last trumpet. The latter passage contains the verse that has given rise to the notion of a "rapture" and spawned countless debates about "pre-," "mid-," or "post-tribulationism" (v. 17). Because of the close correlation between the two passages, and because Paul in 1 Corinthians 15 has been speaking exclusively of transformations occurring at the time of Christ's public return (v. 23), it is unnatural to think of the rapture of 1 Thessalonians as some separate, prior event. The use of trumpet imagery with the Day of the Lord elsewhere in the Bible (see above, p. 317), and in Jewish thought more generally, reinforces this analysis. But again many texts of Scripture must be brought to bear on the debate; exegesis of 1 Corinthians alone will not solve the problems.[7] And since all sides agree that no single passage ever discusses the rapture and the tribulation at the same time, it seems overly restrictive to insist that any one view of the relationship must be held if one is to participate in a certain church or Christian organization.

First Thessalonians 4:15 has also been said to contradict 1 Corinthians 15 by affirming that Paul initially believed that he would live until Christ's return, a view he betrays no knowledge of here and even more explicitly rejects in 2 Corinthians 1:8–11. Others are less certain which group Paul classifies himself with in verse 51. Often elaborate hypotheses about "development" in Paul's theology ensue.[8] But all of this reads far too much into each of the texts. Grammatically, the phrase "we who are still alive, who are left till the coming of the Lord" (1 Thess. 4:15) means simply "whichever Christians are still alive," and nowhere else does Paul unequivocally claim to know if he will be a part of this group of believers.

Verse 56, appearing as incidentally as it does, shows us that Paul's theology of the role of the Law in producing sin and death was not limited to the more polemical contexts of Galatians 3 or Philippians 3 nor merely the product of his later thinking, as in Romans 6–7. The very fact that it emerges so incidentally here testifies to its early, foundational role in Paul's thought. Presumably he has taught on the subject already in Corinth and, for once,

---

7. Cf. further Richard Reiter, Paul D. Feinberg, Gleason L. Archer, and Douglas J. Moo, *The Rapture: Pre-, Mid-, or Post-Tribulational?* (Grand Rapids: Zondervan, 1984).

8. See Klein, Blomberg, and Hubbard, *Biblical Interpretation*, 365–66, and the literature there cited.

can assume they still understand it. Increasing transgressions is not the sole purpose of the Law. Indeed Reformation theology has traditionally recognized three uses of the Law, the other two of which are far more positive— as a deterrent to sin and as a moral instruction for Christians.[9] But the first one is an important use and supports in some measure the classic Lutheran dichotomy between law and gospel.

Given the Corinthians' tendency to divorce theology from ethics, Paul's conclusion (v. 58) remains telling. It is just like him to conclude his discussion with very practical applications. Here he reminds us that it is the resurrection hope, and only this hope, that keeps believers in every place and time from despair and helps them stay faithful in Christian service. In fact, the resurrection demonstrates four sweeping principles that affect all of life: truth is stronger than falsehood, good is stronger than evil, love is stronger than hatred, and life is stronger than death.[10]

THE NATURE OF THE resurrection body remains hotly debated, as Christians continue to try to wrest more detail from the Scriptures than is present in them.

One minority perspective argues that Christ's resurrection body, as the exemplar for our resurrection bodies, was normally invisible and immaterial, since most of the time during his forty days of appearances he was not present with the disciples.[11] In other circles, some Christians still continue to object to cremation,[12] as if God's power in reconstituting and transforming a believer's body were limited to situations in which the corpse was preserved relatively intact! Both debates distract attention from Paul's primary concern, which is to guard against an overly realized eschatology that leads to an overly triumphalist ecclesiology—that is, claiming for the present era too many of the blessings and victories of the age to come (see pp. 25–27 for explanation and illustrations).

---

9. See F. F. Bruce, *Paul: Apostle of the Heart Set Free* (Grand Rapids: Eerdmans, 1977), 191.

10. Barclay, *Corinthians*, 146–48.

11. Murray J. Harris, *Raised Immortal* (Grand Rapids: Eerdmans, 1977), 53. This view in turn spawned a serious overreaction, replete with accusations of heresy and cult-like teaching, esp. in Norman L. Geisler, *The Battle for the Resurrection* (Nashville: Thomas Nelson, 1989), and in the more informal literature of several counter-cult ministries. Harris has more than adequately answered these charges (see idem, *From Grave to Glory* [Grand Rapids: Zondervan, 1990]).

12. John J. Davis (*What About Cremation: A Christian Perspective* [Winona Lake, Ind.: BMH, 1989]) is more sanguine than some but still finds burial preferable wherever possible.

If we are right in suspecting that this triumphalism reflected the attitudes and messages of the Corinthians claiming to speak under the Spirit's inspiration, then the most analogous dangers in our contemporary world surround those, particularly within the charismatic movement, who make overly inflated claims for the degree of spiritual maturity we can achieve in this life. Noncharismatic circles have their counterparts with teaching on Christian perfection and the possibility of going days, months, and even years without sinning. The "prosperity gospel" tricks people into thinking that they can have and deserve excessive health and wealth in this life. Against all of these trends, Paul insists that we haven't yet "arrived," nor will we arrive this side of Christ's return.

Conservative Christians unfortunately continue to debate the different positions on the millennium and rapture in divisive ways, though fortunately much of this is subsiding. Many parachurch organizations have come to recognize that neither doctrine is clear enough in Scripture to merit its inclusion in a statement of faith that their employees are required to affirm. Major exceptions usually involve educational or missionary organizations, whose institutional inertia brings change more slowly. The church can learn a good lesson from the parachurch movement and join in refusing to make pre-, post- or amillennialism, or pre-, mid- or posttribulationism a part of their doctrinal statements, tests of orthodoxy, or criteria of fellowship or of cooperation with other believers. Again, many of the larger, growing churches have already recognized this, but others still have a long way to go.

Although the NIV footnote for verse 49 ("so let us") is not as likely as the text ("so shall we"), it reminds us of the fact that because we will one day fully bear the image of Christ, who is the perfect reflection of God, we should encourage each other to work toward re-creating that image even now. Ephesians 4:24 describes this process as putting "on the new self, created to be like God in true righteousness and holiness."

Contemporary Christianity needs to recover this Reformation emphasis on the image of God as moral and relational. We have been captivated by pop psychologies that tend to define God's image as a trichotomous division of the human psyche, or by the neo-orthodox equation of the image with the creation of male and female, or even by an anti-ecological distortion of the command to exercise dominion over the earth (in the context of the *imago Dei*—Gen. 1:27–28).

Interestingly, Paul here associates God's image ("likeness") with his glory (v. 43), as also in 11:7. And 2 Corinthians 3:7–18 links God's glory with his revelation to Moses on Sinai, a revelation that disclosed that glory in terms of God's communicable attributes (Ex. 33:18–34:7). In many circles eager to preserve God's truth, Christians today need to work equally hard at show-ing his mercy and modeling the facets of God's image that Exodus 34:6–7a recounts: "The LORD, the LORD, the compassionate and gracious God, slow to anger, abounding in love and faithfulness, maintaining love to thousands, and forgiving wickedness, rebellion and sin. Yet he does not leave the guilty unpunished."[13]

The ultimate vanquishing of death, with which 1 Corinthians 15 culmi-nates, surely speaks volumes to those who continue to live in fear of death today. It is not just Sartre who has raised the specter of suicide as the only serious question for humans to debate. Existential and ecological fears per-vade much of the non-Christian world.[14] Christians ought to fear less. They may grieve the loss of loved ones and have a certain anxiety related to the unknown factors surrounding their own death, but neither reaction ought to be "like the rest of men who have no hope" (1 Thess. 4:13). Funerals for Christians ought to be first of all celebrations of their "homegoing." While preserving a culturally appropriate solemnity, a spirit of joy and a message of hope should nevertheless pervade such ceremonies, which may even in-clude a tasteful evangelistic address to unbelievers present. And the hope of resurrection should encourage those of us who remain alive to persevere in a "long obedience in the same direction" (v. 58).[15]

---

13. Cf. further R. Ward Wilson and Craig L. Blomberg, "The Image of God in Hu-manity: A Biblical-Psychological Perspective," *Themelios* 18 (1993): 8–15.

14. Cf. J. Davis McCaughey, "The Death of Death (1 Corinthians 15:26)," in *Reconcili-ation and Hope*, ed. Robert Banks (Grand Rapids: Eerdmans, 1974), 257.

15. Friedrich Nietzche, *Beyond Good and Evil*, tr. R. J. Hollingdale (New York: Penguin, 1973), 109; quoted and reapplied in a Christian context by Eugene Peterson, *A Long Obe-dience in the Same Direction* (Downers Grove, Ill.: InterVarsity Press, 1980).

1 Corinthians 16:1–4

NOW ABOUT THE COLLECTION for God's people: Do what I told the Galatian churches to do. ²On the first day of every week, each one of you should set aside a sum of money in keeping with his income, saving it up, so that when I come no collections will have to be made. ³Then, when I arrive, I will give letters of introduction to the men you approve and send them with your gift to Jerusalem. ⁴If it seems advisable for me to go also, they will accompany me.

PAUL PROCEEDS TO the final topic of the body of his letter. For the next-to-last time he introduces a subject with "now about," probably reflecting the next-to-last question the Corinthians had asked in their letter (cf. 7:1). (The last such issue is not theological but personal; see 16:12.) Because Paul's comments are so brief, much background has to be filled in from additional information supplied in Acts, Romans, and 2 Corinthians.[1]

The collection to which Paul refers in verse 1 formed a major enterprise of his third missionary journey. Significant numbers of Jewish Christians in Jerusalem were impoverished (v. 3; cf. Rom. 15:26), and Paul spent substantial energy raising funds from various Gentile churches in Asia and Europe to help meet their needs (Acts 20:4). But in addition to alleviating physical suffering, Paul undoubtedly saw the collection as an opportunity to bring greater unity within the church across Jewish and Gentile boundaries, to pay off a spiritual debt of sorts that the Gentile congregations owed their "mother church" in Jerusalem (Rom. 15:27), and to demonstrate the genuineness of Gentile Christianity to skeptical Jewish Christians (cf. Acts 24:17). In addition, the offering would be a testimony to the unsaved world and to Christians everywhere of the faith and love of those who participated. More people might well be won to Christ, and others would grow in their faith and give an outpouring of thanks to God (2 Cor. 9:12–15).

---

1. Verlyn D. Verbrugge, *Paul's Style of Church Leadership Illustrated by His Instructions to the Corinthians on the Collection* (San Francisco: Mellen Research University Press, 1992), 25–94, likens verses 1–2 to a "commanding letter," in which an author uses at least one second person imperative form, with no attempt to justify his requests or motivate the recipients beyond an appeal to his own authority.

The rich theological significance of this collection is amply illustrated by the diversity of terms Paul applies to the project: a "gift" (v. 3; the word used here also means "grace"), "fellowship" or "sharing" (2 Cor. 8:4), a "liberal" or "generous" contribution (8:20; 9:5), the presentation of "offerings" (Acts 24:17), and a "service" (2 Cor. 9:1) or even "divine service" (9:12). The Corinthians had themselves taken the initiative to contribute generously and had inspired other churches to imitate them, but now they were lagging behind in keeping their commitments (8:1–12; 9:1–5). Sadly, Paul's brief words here did not adequately motivate them, because he has to return to the topic in much greater detail in 2 Corinthians 8–9.[2] But Romans 15:26 demonstrates that ultimately the Corinthians came through.

"God's people" in verse 1a translates the word for "saints" and refers to Christians in general—in this case in Jerusalem. Despite verse 1b, there is no reference to this collection in the letter to the Galatians, so we must assume that the instructions to which Paul refers here took place after that letter was written in ca. A.D. 49 (six years earlier). But Galatians 2:10 does include "remembering the poor" as an important principle that Paul, Peter, and James all agreed on when they met in Jerusalem to talk about Paul's ministry. Moreover, one of the representatives whom Paul sent with the collection (see Acts 20:4) was Gaius of Derbe, a man from one of the cities of Southern Galatia.

"The first day of every week" (v. 2a) refers to Sunday. It is natural, therefore, to take this verse as the first known reference to a weekly offering as part of Christian worship. Yet the language, "set aside a sum of money . . . saving it up," is more literally rendered "place by himself . . . treasuring," as if each person stored his or her contributions at home. When Paul expresses a desire not to have to make collections upon his arrival in Corinth, what he most likely means, then, is that he hoped "each member would have a prepared sum ready to pay into a central fund."[3] Yet even if the Corinthians did not necessarily bring their monies to a weekly worship service, the fact that this storing was to take place on Sunday strongly suggests that the first day of the week, not the seventh (the Sabbath), had already come to be the most special day of the week for these Christians. This day probably included a time for worship, as with Paul's preaching at Troas in Acts 20:7—an event that should be dated to only a year or two after the writing of this letter.

"In keeping with his income" (v. 2b) translates an expression that might better read, "to whatever extent one is prospered." Paul's instructions about

---

2. The two most important and detailed studies on Paul's collection are Dieter Georgi, *Remembering the Poor: The History of Paul's Collection for Jerusalem* (Nashville: Abingdon, 1992); and Keith F. Nickle, *The Collection* (Naperville, Ill.: Allenson, 1966).

3. Barrett, *First Corinthians*, 387.

representatives and letters of recommendation (v. 3) show his concern for financial integrity and accountability. Acts 20:4 reveals that these representatives came from numerous churches and territories in which Paul had ministered. The lack of any delegate specifically associated with Achaia (the province in which Corinth was located) has been variously interpreted. It probably means nothing more than that Luke's listing, like Paul's elsewhere (Rom. 15:26), was partial. It is possible, though somewhat less probable, to take the "letters" as modifying the verb, "you approve," in which case we should read, "When you arrive, I will send those you approve by letters of introduction with your gift. . . ." What will make it "advisable" (or "fitting") for Paul to go along (v. 4)? Probably he has in mind an adequate sum of money to justify the time and not to embarrass himself before the church leaders in Jerusalem![4]

PAUL PROVIDES POWERFUL principles for Christian giving based on his instructions about the collection for Jerusalem, although many of them are found only in 2 Corinthians 8–9 and must be left to a commentator on that book. Several principles nevertheless emerge from these four verses, as does an important controversy over the background. To begin with the latter, why was the church in Jerusalem poor? There are those who blame it on a supposedly failed experiment with communism (cf. Acts 2:44–47; 4:32–37). To be sure, we do not know how long the early church continued its practice of communal sharing, and silence on the topic may suggest that it had already been abandoned during the twenty-five years between the birth of the church and the writing of 1 Corinthians. On the other hand, Luke indicates that God blessed this "experiment" (2:47; 5:11–16), so we can scarcely play down giving to the poor as merely a second-class alternative to promoting capitalism. Then, as often since, many factors entirely outside the control of Christians can lead to impoverishment. Systemic changes may help, but they are no substitute for generous sharing on the part of God's people who are better off.[5]

Most likely, the Jerusalem church's need was the product of a series of factors that included the famine of the late 40s, the relative poverty level in

---

4. Cf. Robertson and Plummer, *First Corinthians*, 387: "He could not abandon other work in order to present a paltry sum; and an Apostle could not take the lead in so unworthy a mission. It would look like approving niggardliness."

5. See the classic work by Abraham Kuyper, *The Problem of Poverty* (Grand Rapids: Baker, repr. 1991), esp. pp. 59–79.

Jerusalem to begin with, the number of poor people (e.g., the widows of Acts 6:1) who flocked into the early church there, and the fact that these Jews, now turned Christians, would most likely have been cut off from the distribution of food and provisions for the needy that other Jews assiduously practiced. We may take Paul's principles for giving, then, as widely applicable to comparable situations of need and not as a unique response to an idiosyncratic problem that could have been avoided.

Indeed, Paul's two major rationales for this collection have influenced the church's history to such an extent that they provide the two major foci of Christian giving in almost every age—supporting those who are our spiritual parents or authorities over us in full-time ministry and helping to meet the physical and spiritual needs of the world's most dispossessed, particularly within the body of Christ. Other details may be more situation-specific, yet suggest helpful guidelines. Weekly giving, for example, builds in systematic, self-disciplined, consistent generosity. Even if that money is simply set aside privately, its conjunction with the regular worship of the church reminds us that stewardship is as much a part of obedience and devotion to God as prayer, praise, fellowship, instruction, and the like. It also makes it less likely that Christian leaders will have to issue special calls or initiate additional campaigns to reduce regular budget deficits.

Paul's phrase "in keeping with his income" (v. 2) reminds us that neither here nor in any other New Testament text is the tithe taught as incumbent on Christians. Indeed, the only New Testament reference to giving ten percent comes in a passage in which Jesus is instructing Jewish scribes and Pharisees on how they should live *under the old covenant*, and in which he is drastically subordinating the tithe to "the more important matters of the law—justice, mercy and faithfulness" (Matt. 23:23). Paul's ideal appears instead in 2 Corinthians 8:13–15: no one is ever permitted to get too rich or too poor, as more well-to-do Christians share from their surplus with needier ones. The problem with a tithe is that it is too burdensome for many of the poor, while letting most middle- and upper-class Christians off the hook too quickly! So Paul refuses to legislate any percent; indeed, verse 2 here can be taken as support for the concept of a "graduated tithe"—the more one makes, the higher percentage one should normally give.[6] But he does stress that "each" must give; the task may not be restricted to the wealthy patrons, lest they think they are again buying power with their gifts. Paul was also probably well aware of the parallel Jewish and Greco-Roman models of car-

---

6. On this point, see esp. Ronald J. Sider, *Rich Christians in An Age of Hunger* (Downers Grove, Ill.: InterVarsity Press, 1984), 163–77, though without necessarily subscribing to his specific percentages.

ing for the poor and concerned that Christians be perceived as being at least as zealous in caring for their own.[7]

Verse 3 makes plain the importance of accountability in handling money, a concern Paul will take great pains to stress in 2 Corinthians 8:16–24. He wants to be sure the collection is free of any opportunity for mismanagement or even of the accusation of mishandling of funds. Jesus' famous words about not letting "your left hand know what your right hand is doing" (Matt. 6:3) do not contradict Paul's instructions. Rather, they warn metaphorically against parading one's piety in public, in this case by showing off how much one is giving to the needy (vv. 1–2).

ALL KINDS OF objections can be brought to bear as to why believers should not apply Paul's exhortations regarding the collection to Christian giving today—it was a "one-off" event, we have a different economic system in which some of our taxes help pay for welfare, the poor today often have created their own problems, and so on. But none of these objections can withstand careful scrutiny. The plain fact is that the overall standard of living of most Western Christians, even by *contemporary* global standards, is so much superior to that of believers in most other eras and cultures that our excuses for not helping the millions of *Christian* needy, to say nothing of the other poor people in the world, ring exceedingly hollow. We may continue to disagree on the best ways to provide that help,[8] but generous giving must remain a priority.

A better understanding of the principles of stewardship and a more consistent application of them are both acutely needed in the contemporary Western church. The amount of money required annually to relieve the worst suffering of the two-thirds of the world that is desperately poor is far exceeded by the amount Americans spend each year on sports, leisure, recreation, surplus food and clothing, and so on.[9] And a significant percent-

---

7. Cf. Barclay, *Corinthians*, 162: "In the Greek world there were associations called *eranoi*. If a person fell on evil days or was in sudden need, his friends would club together to raise an interest-free loan to help him. The synagogue had officials whose duty it was to collect from those who had and to share out to those who had not. . . . Paul did not want the Christian Church to be behind the Jewish and the heathen world in generosity." For detailed descriptions of this and other models, see Verbrugge, *Church Leadership*, 145–83.

8. See, for example, John A. Bernbaum, ed., *Economic Justice and the State: A Debate Between Ronald H. Nash and Eric H. Beversluis* (Grand Rapids: Baker; Washington, D.C.: Christian College Coalition, 1986).

9. See the sobering statistics presented in John Ronsvalle and Sylvia Ronsvalle, *The Poor Have Faces: Loving Your Neighbor in the 21st Century* (Grand Rapids: Baker, 1992), 45–54.

age of both that impoverished two-thirds of the world and the affluent West are Christian! Obviously, corrupt governments, civil warfare, supply blockades, and various other obstacles would still prevent the alleviation of all human misery, but far more significant progress could be made toward helping the poor than is currently being done. Governments may at times have more resources at their disposal, but they will not usually bring relief in the name of Christ or present the type of holistic antidote to both spiritual and physical maladies that churches and Christians can.

Sadly, however, American Christians give on average about three percent of their income to all charitable causes put together. Some churches still demand and sometimes receive a tithe from a good percentage of their members. One should not object to this, since such donors exceed the average by seven percent! But if most of us were honest, we could afford and would be able to give far more without substantial sacrifice. The list of ideas is almost endless: living in smaller homes, buying less expensive cars, eating less, eating out less, buying fewer clothes, utilizing garage sales, car pooling, conserving water, recycling, watching videos rather than going to movies, avoiding cable television, buying in bulk or wholesale, traveling less by car when bicycling is possible, traveling less by jet when driving is possible, sharing rarely-used household tools and equipment among families on the same block or in the same housing complex, setting up baby-sitting cooperatives, gardening for food, spending less money on pets, conserving energy in our homes and buildings, planning more modest weddings and funerals, giving donations to Christian ministries as birthday or Christmas presents, avoiding disposable diapers, regularly giving away unused clothes, books, toys and other possessions, and on and on.[10]

At times, believers may be able to implement more radical redirection of their funds, freeing them up for use in the Lord's work. Tom Sine describes one church's model of setting up an account from which first-time home owners in their congregation could borrow money at a zero-percent interest rate, in return for which they might contract to work in various ministries for the church or donate the surplus they would have spent on mortgage payments to the kind of holistic ministry Paul envisions here.[11] An individual or

---

10. I have listed here only ideas that my family has at one time or another implemented. Numerous practical suggestions appear in works like Doris J. Longacre, *Living More with Less* (Scottdale, Pa.: Herald, 1980); and Ronald J. Sider, ed., *Living More Simply: Biblical Principles and Practical Models* (Downers Grove, Ill.: InterVarsity Press, 1980). Neither of these works is significantly out of date; if anything the suggestions they contain are *more* relevant today than fifteen years ago!

11. Tom Sine, *Wild Hope* (Dallas: Word, 1991), 274–76.

family who could thus pay $50,000 cash for a home would save approximately $150,000 over thirty years in mortgage payments and have an enormous sum to reinvest in kingdom priorities. Many churches that are starting to outgrow their current facilities should seriously consider the advantages of starting daughter congregations, sending members to infuse new life in nearby struggling churches, meeting in empty parts of shopping malls, and creating numerous other diversions for the huge sums of money that so often get trapped in bigger building programs and the debt services that commonly cling to them.[12]

In short, "baby boomers" and "baby busters" need to be taught to give. If they are not, many churches and Christian organizations will go out of business, as donor bases in this country are currently weighted most heavily in favor of senior citizens.[13] Furthermore, they (and all Christians) must be taught to give to those individuals, organizations, and churches who themselves have their priorities straight, who maximize giving to support a reasonable but not excessive lifestyle for full-time Christian workers and a holistic mission to meet the physical and spiritual needs of hurting people worldwide. Fifty percent of a church's budget given to this kind of holistic mission is not unheard of in Western Europe; our more affluent American churches could do even better if we were willing to significantly reprioritize our church budgets. As Paul was afraid of being shamed by the competing models of his world, we should learn a lesson today from the Mormons who tithe and stockpile goods to take care of their own far more faithfully than most Christians do. Should we permit them to exemplify the principles of the gospel in this area better than we do?

Weekly giving remains a good model, but it need not be imposed legalistically. Good stewardship (less checkwriting, easier bookbalancing, and accountability) may actually be enhanced by monthly or even quarterly giving to Christian work. But we must take care lest the practice become so infrequent that it loses its value as a regular reminder of stewardship as part of worship. In addition, we need to make sure that giving comes "off the top," at the beginning of the pay period, according to what we have determined to give; we should not allow it to fluctuate based on what is leftover after some initial period of spending to meet other needs and desires.

Integrity and accountability in management of funds are as absent today as generous, sacrificial giving. Organizations that hold their member churches and parachurch groups to principles of financial disclosure and

---

12. For these and other practical applications, see pp. 84–89 of my article, "On Wealth and Worry: Matt 6:19–34—Meaning and Significance," *CTR* 6 (1992): 73–89.

13. For an incisive assessment of demographic trends, see Sine, *Wild Hope*, 136–70.

accountability have helped in some circles and should be widely supported. A scrupulous resistance of going into debt for all but the most unavoidable of reasons, by both individuals and churches, needs to be reinculcated. (One legitimate reason might be if one had surplus money that could yield greater interest while being invested than the rate of financing on that debt.) Given the exorbitant rates of credit card interest, there are few legitimate reasons for ever charging purchases unless one pays one's bills interest-free every month.

There are not many situations in which building programs should be financed before most of the money is raised up front. Church budgets should be itemized in detail and open to prayerful examination by all members. Itemization should include pastoral salaries, for even though they may be the most delicate topics of consideration, they can be the most abused areas of our spending, either through paying our leaders too much or too little.

Individual believers need fellow Christians with whom they can share the details of their stewardship so as to hold each other mutually accountable for their lifestyles. Those who are afraid that they will receive too much criticism for these various disclosures more often than not have misguided priorities.[14]

---

14. On financial integrity in churches, cf. Robert R. Thompson and Gerald R. Thompson, *Organizing for Accountability* (Wheaton, Ill.: Harold Shaw, 1991). For numerous biblically based, practical suggestions on personal finance, see Malcolm MacGregor with Stanley G. Baldwin, *Your Money Matters* (Minneapolis: Bethany, 1977); and Howard L. Dayton, Jr., *Your Money: Frustration or Freedom* (Wheaton, Ill.: Tyndale House, 1979).

1 Corinthians 16:5–12

AFTER I GO through Macedonia, I will come to you—for I will be going through Macedonia. ⁶Perhaps I will stay with you awhile, or even spend the winter, so that you can help me on my journey, wherever I go. ⁷I do not want to see you now and make only a passing visit; I hope to spend some time with you, if the Lord permits. ⁸But I will stay on at Ephesus until Pentecost, ⁹because a great door for effective work has opened to me, and there are many who oppose me.

¹⁰If Timothy comes, see to it that he has nothing to fear while he is with you, for he is carrying on the work of the Lord, just as I am. ¹¹No one, then, should refuse to accept him. Send him on his way in peace so that he may return to me. I am expecting him along with the brothers.

¹²Now about our brother Apollos: I strongly urged him to go to you with the brothers. He was quite unwilling to go now, but he will go when he has the opportunity.

THE BODY OF the letter has ended. Paul now concludes his letter with personal remarks (vv. 5–12) and closing greetings (vv. 13–24).

As frequently in his letters, Paul's personal remarks concern his current ministry itinerary (or about those of his representatives, when he was later imprisoned); these serve as a transition to his formal closing (e.g., Rom. 15:14–33; 2 Cor. 13:1–10; Eph. 6:19–22; Col. 4:7–9; Philem. 22). His goal of coming to Corinth after revisiting Macedonia (v. 5) did eventually materialize (Acts 20:1–6), but not as quickly as he had first hoped. The evidence of 2 Corinthians demonstrates that Paul made an intervening visit to Corinth between the two trips described in the book of Acts (2 Cor. 12:14; 13:1) and probably wrote an additional letter between our 1 and 2 Corinthians to deal with a particular antagonist in the church there (2 Cor. 1:15–17; 1:23–2:4).[1] Second Corinthians 8:10 and 9:2 state that

---

1. This may or may not have been the same man as the incestuous offender of 1 Corinthians 5; a good case can be made, however, that it is. For a full reconstruction of events in between the two letters, see esp. Colin Kruse, *The Second Epistle of Paul to the Corinthians* (Grand Rapids; Eerdmans, 1987), 19–24. On Paul's opposition more specifically, see pp. 41–45.

the instructions just surveyed on the collection took place "last year," suggesting that a number of months have intervened since 1 Corinthians. While here he anticipates leaving Ephesus shortly, the trip described in 2 Corinthians 7:5, which finds Paul at last en route to Corinth, must have taken place at least nine months later. If 1 Corinthians was written in the spring of A.D. 55, then Paul would have originally hoped to come during that same calendar year, whereas in fact he did not arrive for his prolonged stay until some time in 56.

His initial desire to spend a full winter in Corinth (vv. 6a, 7a) may still have been fulfilled, however, even if delayed by a year. (His letter to the Romans from neighboring Cenchrea is probably best dated to A.D. 57.) Paul's motivation was at least twofold: (1) He wanted to have a significant period of time with the troubled Corinthians in hopes of substantially improving the situation in the church there; and (2) he hoped to avoid having to travel during that season of the year in which the high seas were generally impassable and travel overland was much more arduous. The verb translated "help . . . on my journey" (v. 6b) means "send me forth" and probably implies material assistance—food, money, and possibly even traveling companions for his trip. "Wherever I go" reflects the same uncertainty as in verse 4; as noted above, later Paul definitely decides to accompany the collection to Jerusalem. Yet in all this planning he knows full well that he must leave the door open for the Lord to change his itinerary (v. 7b).

Verses 8–9 inform us of Paul's current location (Ephesus) and enable us to date the writing of this letter to the time of the events of Acts 19 (see the Introduction, p. 21). There we see ample illustrations of the two principles of verse 9—"a great door for effective work" and "many who oppose me." The former included remarkable conversions and turning away from idols; the latter, occult opposition and town riots. The uprising instigated by Demetrius, however, has probably not yet occurred, since Paul seems to have left town shortly after that event (Acts 20:1), while here he envisions staying on for a while. "Pentecost" (v. 8) was the annual Jewish harvest festival (the Feast of Weeks). On that day the Holy Spirit descended on 120 of Jesus' followers fifty days after his resurrection, to inaugurate the era of the new covenant (see Acts 2). Whether Christians had started to celebrate it as a festival is impossible to determine from this reference; it may simply be Paul's natural way to refer to that time in late spring.

"*If* Timothy comes" in verse 10 is probably too indefinite, in light of Paul's earlier statement that he *is* sending Timothy (4:17). "*Whenever* he comes" would be a better translation.[2] Paul's concern over how Timothy will

---

2. Watson, *First Corinthians*, 184.

be received is certainly related to their conflict with Paul himself, and it is probably heightened by Timothy's youthfulness (1 Tim. 4:12) and possibly even by his personality. Second Timothy 1:7 seems to suggest that Timothy was a naturally timid person, though this may be inferring too much. "Refuse to accept" (v. 11) is literally "despise." "Send him on his way" employs the same verb as "help me on my journey" in verse 6. The unnamed "brothers" probably include Erastus (Acts 19:22), the town clerk of Corinth (Rom. 16:23), and they would have been known to the Corinthians.

Verse 12 appears to respond to the final question the Corinthians had raised in their letter to Paul (cf. 7:1). Not only does Paul again say "now about," but it is unlikely that he alone would have taken the initiative to urge Apollos to return to Corinth in light of the danger of inflaming the sectarian divisiveness there all the more. Did the Corinthians suspect that Paul was hindering Apollos from coming when they really wanted to see him?[3] "Strongly" could also be translated "often." The "brothers" are the same as in verse 11, plus Timothy. Apollos' reluctance to go could reflect his concern to wait for a more opportune time when things had settled down in Corinth. "He was quite unwilling" is more literally, "it was entirely not the will," leading some to suggest that we should think of God's will instead of Apollos'. Presumably Paul would have thought the two coincided in this instance.

Bridging Contexts

PAUL'S DESIRES IN verses 5–7 reflect his concern to spend "quantity" and not just "quality" time with his spiritual children. As he consistently did in his ministry, he wants to revisit this church he has founded, so that he can minister by way of follow-up, training them in discipleship. Paul was never merely content to evangelize, make converts, and move on, even when it meant risking his life to return to the cities in which he previously ministered. Compare, most notably, his ministry in Lystra in Acts 14:19–20; this was a region he visited on each of his three missionary journeys.

Paul's willingness to ask for financial support (implied in verse 6) fits his practice of accepting provisions from Philippi while he was ministering in Corinth (see above under 9:1–18). Although he had offended or upset some Corinthians, most likely including the powerful patrons in the church there, by not accepting money for ministry while in town, he was happy to use their help to minister in other places where "strings" were less likely to be attached.

---

3. So Talbert, *Corinthians*, 106.

"If the Lord permits" (v. 7) is a key proviso that should qualify every Christian's plans and prayers (cf. Matt. 6:10; James 4:13–15), though this does not necessarily mean that we should speak it formally in every situation in which it is applied. People who overly punctuate their conversation with "God willing" often dissolve the meaning of those words into a mere cliché. But neither is there any scriptural warrant for deliberately excluding this qualifier from certain prayers, as if one would be perceived as vacillating in faith.

Paul's twofold rationale for staying in Corinth in verse 9 provides a powerful model for Christians in many times and places trying to decide where to perform ministry or exercise their spiritual gifts. An open door and much opposition often go hand in hand, and they may jointly signify that God's Spirit is mightily at work. To be sure, at times God brings blessing and prosperity for short intervals without significant antagonism. On other occasions, he allows seemingly unmitigated hostility, perhaps even for somewhat longer periods of time. But a prolonged lack of results in ministry more often than not suggests that it is time to move on, while prolonged prosperity without any difficulty should make one question if the full-orbed gospel with all its demands is clearly being preached.

Verses 10–11 further Paul's emphasis on Timothy as his surrogate model (see under 4:16–17 and 11:1). His words here remind us to treat representatives and subordinates of Christian leaders with the same respect and consideration that we give to the leaders themselves.

Verse 12 demonstrates Paul's remarkable willingness to put the unity of the church and the interests of his coworkers above his own personal desires and fears. One is reminded of his equally remarkable concession in Philippians that he rejoiced at those who were preaching the gospel out of rivalry to himself (Phil. 1:15–18), apparently since the word was truly going forth and people were being saved. Apollos' sensitivity reminds us, however, that it is not always in the best interests of our congregations to accede to all their requests, particularly if they stand a good chance of exacerbating factiousness.

Contemporary Significance

DISCIPLESHIP IS A lost art in many Christian circles today. We have numerous prominent evangelists whose messages seemingly bring many to Christ but whose mechanisms for follow-up unfortunately leave a majority to fall by the wayside. The discipleship programs that we do institute often substitute programs and packaging for personal modeling and intimacy. As Christians, we too need quantity as well as quality time with each other, all the more so in our fast-paced, transient, and fractured society. Ours is an age in which the average length of a pastorate is shrinking rather than growing, and in which youth pastors have a short average stay in ministering to an age group that needs long-term modeling the most. Surely we need to recover an emphasis on "hanging in there" in ministry with the same group of fellow believers, through thick and thin and over the long haul. Similarly, church members must resist the inclination to "church hop" when things get tough and should recommit themselves to staying and working in difficult situations for positive resolutions of problems.[4]

The ministry of giving to itinerant Christian workers and providing hospitality for them when they are in our own communities can go a long way to rekindling some of the spirit of familial intimacy that Paul tried to instill in his churches. Giving to churches is good and should be generous, but it should often be supplemented by giving to individuals who have to raise their own support for ministry and by providing lodging and provision for visiting missionaries.

We must find ways to avoid treating church staffs as so hierarchical that the associate and assistant pastors are given less respect than our senior leaders. We must guard against treating those more dynamic or charismatic leaders as somehow inherently better or more worthy of respect than the quieter and less flamboyant ones. It is sad to observe the difficulty that many gifted and dedicated seminary graduates have in finding a job in full-time Christian ministry if they are fairly modest and unassuming. Age too must not necessarily be held up as a criterion of maturity or effectiveness in ministry, though clearly there are certain correlations in certain situations. Sometimes, younger pastors do a better job at certain ministries, most notably in youth work.

The seemingly innocuous caveat, "if the Lord wills," should probably play a more prominent role in most of our thinking and planning than it presently does. Surely we must resist the heresy that demands us simply to "name it and claim it" and at times even declares that adding a clause about God's will actually violates that will![5]

It would be wonderful too if more Christians and churches could see that part of God's will often involves doing the work of ministry through their "rivals." Even if motives for ministry are not always exemplary (consider, e.g.,

---

4. Excellent and timely suggestions for practicing discipleship appear in Billie Hanks, Jr., and William A. Shell, eds., *Discipleship* (Grand Rapids: Zondervan, 1993); and Alice Fryling, ed., *Disciple Makers' Handbook* (Downers Grove, Ill.: InterVarsity Press, 1989).

5. As, e.g., with Kenneth Hagin, cited by Bruce Barron, *The Health and Wealth Gospel* (Downers Grove, Ill.: InterVarsity Press, 1987), 103.

the powerful sway financial remuneration holds for some today), if the genuine gospel is being preached with positive results, we should rejoice. Duplication of ministry, particularly in the West, runs rampant. Churches compete for the same parishioners, publishing houses try to outdo each other with the latest editions of Bibles or commentary series, missionary organizations fight each other for the best footings in newly opened mission fields, and so on. We need to encourage one another not to overlap so much when there is so much of the world largely unreached by each of these spheres of ministry. Then we can rejoice when others succeed, even if they hold slightly different theological perspectives than our own. On the other hand, outright heresy needs to be exposed, in love, as fraudulent, no matter how well-intentioned its practitioners.[6]

---

6. As is done, e.g., by Michael Horton, ed., *The Agony of Deceit* (Chicago: Moody, 1990), though occasionally with a little "overkill."

1 Corinthians 16:13–24

Be on your guard; stand firm in the faith; be men of courage; be strong. ¹⁴Do everything in love.

¹⁵You know that the household of Stephanas were the first converts in Achaia, and they have devoted themselves to the service of the saints. I urge you, brothers, ¹⁶to submit to such as these and to everyone who joins in the work, and labors at it. ¹⁷I was glad when Stephanas, Fortunatus and Achaicus arrived, because they have supplied what was lacking from you. ¹⁸For they refreshed my spirit and yours also. Such men deserve recognition.

¹⁹The churches in the province of Asia send you greetings. Aquila and Priscilla greet you warmly in the Lord, and so does the church that meets at their house. ²⁰All the brothers here send you greetings. Greet one another with a holy kiss.

²¹I, Paul, write this greeting in my own hand.

²²If anyone does not love the Lord—a curse be on him. Come, O Lord!

²³The grace of the Lord Jesus be with you.

²⁴My love to all of you in Christ Jesus. Amen.

Original Meaning

PAUL BEGINS HIS final greetings and "signoff" with two verses of brief exhortation (vv. 13–14). Four parallel commands employ military metaphors to encourage resoluteness in the faith (v. 13). "Be men of courage" should probably be rendered "be adults," that is, "put away the immaturity that has led to so many of your problems and grow up in the Lord." Balancing these commands to be strong is the call to love in verse 14. As with Paul's discussion of spiritual gifts in chapters 12–14, all Christian activity must take place within the sphere of putting others above self.

In verses 15–18, Paul gives thanks for three Corinthian Christians who have come to him in Ephesus and encouraged him. On Stephanas, see under 1:16. Nothing else is known about Fortunatus or Achaicus, although the former was a Hellenistic name often adopted by a freed slave (meaning "fortunate"). It is possible that both of these men, therefore, were part of Stephanas's household, once slaves but now more like "employees," though we have no way of being sure.

"The first converts in Achaia" (v. 15) translates an expression meaning "firstfruits" and raises the question of the apparent contradiction with Acts 17:34, in which several Athenians came to believe after Paul's Mars Hill speech and prior to his arrival in Corinth. There are several possible solutions to this problem: Paul had actually met these men somewhere in the countryside even before arriving in Athens; he is speaking of the first "household" rather than individual converts; or the few who responded in Athens did not seem like "firstfruits," that is, the promise of much more to come.[1] But most likely Paul is simply using the term "Achaia," as certain ancient writers did elsewhere, for the more limited territory of Corinth and its environs (the Peloponnesus), rather than for all of the southern half of Greece.[2]

"Devoted" in verse 15 is literally "appointed." "The saints" are not the believers in Judea, as in verse 1, but refer primarily to the Corinthian Christians (and perhaps others) to whom these three men had ministered. Despite a vigorous debate on the meaning of "submit," its use in verse 16 most likely means to place oneself voluntarily under the authority of someone else.[3] The word-play between verses 15b and 16a is brought out well in the NRSV: "they have devoted themselves *to the service* of the saints; I urge you to put yourselves *at the service* of such people." "Everyone who joins" (v. 16b) translates the Greek noun "coworkers." "Labors" differs from ordinary ministry in that it implies *hard* work. "Supplied what was lacking" (v. 17) refers first of all to the spiritual refreshment and encouragement that Stephanas and his companions gave Paul (v. 18a). These men not only renewed Paul's spirit but also encouraged the rest of the Corinthians. This is more naturally taken as highlighting their previous ministry to fellow believers in Corinth, but it could mean that in the very act of encouraging Paul they were also encouraging like-minded Corinthian believers. "Such men deserve recognition" (v. 18b) tones down the more forceful Greek imperative, "Recognize such people!" Such recognition would include acknowledgment of their service and an accompanying honor of submission as described in verse 16.

Verses 19–20 convey greetings to the Corinthian church from four groups of fellow believers: (1) the various churches in Asia Minor, almost certainly including Colosse and Ephesus, and possibly some of the other seven churches established in the vicinity (cf. Rev. 2–3); (2) Paul's good friends

---

1. For this series of options, see Morris, *First Corinthians*, 239.

2. Fee, *First Corinthians*, 829, n. 19.

3. See, e.g., George W. Knight III, "Husbands and Wives as Analogues of Christ and the Church," in *Recovering Biblical Manhood and Womanhood*, ed. John Piper and Wayne Grudem (Wheaton, Ill.: Crossway, 1991), esp. pp. 166–75. For a balancing perspective, cf. Keener, *Paul, Women and Wives*, 164–72.

Aquila and Priscilla, coworkers with him in Corinth (Acts 18:2–3) and later partners with him in his ministry in Ephesus (18:18–19); (3) the specific house church that met in their home; and (4) Paul's other immediate companions in ministry. The "holy kiss" was probably borrowed from common ancient practice, both sacred and secular, Jewish and Gentile. Customarily, men greeted other men and women other women by embracing each other and kissing one another on the cheek.[4]

After verse 20, Paul stops dictating his letter to his amanuensis (the "secretary" writing down the letter)—was it Sosthenes (1:1)? Paul now picks up pen and papyrus himself to write the closing words in his own hand (v. 21), as was his custom (cf. Gal. 6:11; 2 Thess. 3:17; other ancient letter writers often did the same). The one letter in which we definitely know the name of Paul's amanuensis is Romans, when that individual, Tertius, sent his own greetings at the end (Rom. 16:22).

Both parts of verse 22 follow abruptly. They may reflect conventional liturgical utterances of the early church.[5] Paul's "curse" utilizes the expression *anathema*, as in 12:3 (cf. also Gal. 1:8). "Come, O Lord" is the more likely of two possible translations of the Aramaic *Marana tha* (the other one being, "the Lord has come"). Together the two expressions reflect the profound seriousness with which the early church viewed faithfulness to Christ in view of his imminent return.

Verse 23 substitutes Paul's favorite word for "grace" (*charis*) for the more conventional Greek "good-bye" (*erroso*). And, as in his introductory greeting, Paul makes the Christian perspective of his farewell clear with a reference to the Lord Jesus. Verse 24 ends on an upbeat note with one final reminder of his love for these often exasperating Christians in Corinth. The "Amen" is missing from some of the oldest manuscripts and may well reflect a pious addition by an early scribe.

Bridging Contexts

AS WITH HIS opening, the way to recognize what Paul stresses most in his closing is to see what is most distinctive. Ancient Greco-Roman letters did not have as conventional or formalized endings as they did beginnings, but common elements included "greetings, a health wish, the date, a concluding autograph,

---

4. It is possible, though uncertain, that men and women may have at times kissed each other as well. For more on the practice, see William Klassen, "The Sacred Kiss in the New Testament: An Example of Social Boundary Lines," *NTS* 39 (1993): 122–35.

5. Many scholars have seen the entire sequence of components in Paul's closing as liturgical (e.g., Talbert, *Corinthians*, 106–7, and the references there cited); while possible, this goes beyond anything that can be actually demonstrated.

and postscripts."[6] Almost always there was at least one closing wish of some form. Paul himself usually includes exhortations, a wish for peace, greetings to the church addressed (including some from his various companions), and a benediction. The most striking divergence from this pattern in the closing of 1 Corinthians is the addition of the curse, combined with the call for the Lord's return in verse 22. On the other hand, if Paul is relying here on some preexistent liturgy known to the Corinthians, then the distinctiveness of this verse is somewhat tempered.

The exhortations of verses 13–14 disclose an urgency even in Paul's concluding remarks. The lack of connection between these two verses highlights their striking juxtaposition. Love without strength deteriorates into mere sentimentality; strength without love risks becoming tyrannical.

Verses 15–18 contain key implications for the developing concept of Christian ministry in the early church. We are still a long way from the institutionalization of early catholicism in the second century, but we see hints that Paul envisions certain authorities to whom others are to submit, a hint that we would not have necessarily received from reading 14:26.[7] But the kind of authority Paul endorses is what is usually considered the most legitimate kind; it is an authority that is earned through humble service, not imposed by holding an office or dependent solely on charismatic personality or expert knowledge. One might even speak of mutual submission here; the Corinthians must submit to those who have themselves chosen to serve (or submit to) their fellow Christians.

Paul's generalizing language ("submit to such as these" in v. 16) enables us to apply his principles widely to all similar servant-leaders. "Function, not status, was the important thing in the church's ministry: those who did the work were to receive the appropriate recognition and respect."[8] Hebrews 13:17 generalizes a little further ("Obey your leaders and submit to their authority"), but even that command is dependent on the writer's earlier reference in verse 7: "Remember your leaders. . . . Consider the outcome of their way of life and imitate their faith." Christians in all times and places should cooperate with and defer to church leaders who have earned that respect through faithful service, but no New Testament text enjoins blind subservience to authoritarian or incompetent Christian office-holders. While Paul never totally abolishes hierarchy, he radically redefines its authority in terms of service rather than privilege.

---

6. Fee, *First Corinthians*, 825.

7. Cf. Andrew D. Clarke, *Secular and Christian Leadership in Corinth* (Leiden: Brill, 1993), 132. It is clear that there was leadership in the Corinthian church; indeed, one of Paul's biggest concerns had to do with the way in which it wielded power.

8. Bruce, *1 and 2 Corinthians*, 161.

If Fortunatus and Achaicus once were slaves, then the fact that Paul calls the Corinthians to submit also to them reminds us of the radically equalizing function of the gospel across socioeconomic strata of society. Stephanas' household could well include younger people or even children; this possibility reminds us that youth are often among the most zealous and energetically able to serve. But in lieu of more specific information about these individuals, these suggestions must remain speculative.

Sometimes Paul sends greetings from several individuals by name to a particular church he is addressing; here he mentions only Aquila and Priscilla (v. 19). Perhaps they were the only other immediate companions of his who were known to the Corinthians, besides the three men of verses 15–18. But they play a prominent role throughout the Acts and Paul's letters as his coworkers. Interestingly, in four of the six New Testament references to this husband and wife team, Priscilla is named first (Acts 18:18, 26; Rom. 16:3; 2 Tim. 4:19; the other reference which preserves the order found here is Acts 18:2). To name a wife before her husband would have stood out in ancient letter-writing as unusual, suggesting that Priscilla may have been the more significant partner in some respect. Paul is known for elevating the role of women over against the social background of his day, even if he stops short of demonstrably promoting full-fledged egalitarianism.[9]

For the implications of the house-church model of ancient worship (v. 19), see under 14:26–33a. The holy kiss (v. 20) has remained a liturgical part of some Christian traditions. That it was largely limited to same sex partners in a heterosexual Christian community guarded it against having sexual overtones. Many cultures throughout church history have preserved a close parallel to this practice in public greetings more generally. Where there are dangers of arousing inappropriate desires or behavior, some other cultural analog should be sought. The point was that Christians should demonstrate their affection for one another in warm, interpersonal gestures of nonsexual intimacy, and this can be accomplished in many ways.

The greeting of verse 21 follows a letter-writing convention of antiquity, so that too much should not be read into its presence. But it is probably safe to conclude that Paul saw these words as adding a personal touch, a guarantee of the genuineness of the letter (cf. his concern in 2 Thess. 2:1–2 of a possible forgery circulating in his name), and a reiteration of his apostolic authority.

Verse 22 reminds us how foreign certain aspects of New Testament Christianity are to many other generations of church history. Some of the

---

9. For a particularly balanced study, see Ben Witherington III, *Women in the Earliest Churches* (Cambridge: Cambridge University Press, 1988), 24–127.

harshness of Paul's language against those who do not love the Lord may be attributed to cultural convention; indeed, Paul's anathemas are mild compared to some found among the rabbis, at Qumran, or in Greco-Roman circles.[10] We must also recall that Paul has unique emotions invested in the churches to which he gave birth, and he is talking about people here who demonstrate by their beliefs or actions that they are rank unbelievers despite professing to be Christians. Only here and in Titus 3:15 does Paul use the verb *phileo* (meaning brotherly love) rather than *agapao* (the most common verb for Christian love). His choice may simply have been influenced by the cognate *philema* ("kiss") in verse 20, but he may also be implying, "if anyone does not have even as much affection as φιλεῖν [i.e., the love of ordinary friends or siblings for each other]."[11] Yet having said all this, Paul's anathema still stands out as a reminder of the exclusiveness and zeal that characterized the early church's mission.

Conversely, *Marana tha* in verse 22b (see NIV note, "In Aramaic the expression *Come, O Lord* is *Marana tha*) reflects a strong longing for Christ's return by one of his servants who had experienced enough hostility in his life on this earth not to want to prolong it unnecessarily (cf. Phil. 1:21–24). Paul longed for the coming Day that would make present sufferings pale into insignificance (Rom. 8:18; 2 Cor. 4:17). The term also employs an Aramaic word for "Lord" used in some Jewish circles for Yahweh himself (*mar*), a vivid reminder that high Christology (Jesus as fully God) was not merely the product of a later, more Hellenistic development in the church but was part of the faith of Aramaic-speaking Jewish Christianity from its earliest days.

Despite the strong language of verse 22, Paul must nevertheless close on a positive note of encouragement. In no other letter does he end with this kind of statement of his love, but it was profoundly needed in fractured Corinth. "Paul had been stern with the Corinthian believers, but he closed his letter by assuring them of his love. After all, 'Faithful are the wounds of a friend' (Prov. 27:6)."[12]

THE BALANCE REFLECTED in verses 13–14 between firmness and gentleness, between power and love, surely remains crucial today. Many preach love without judgment; some judgment without love. Scripture consistently holds both together.

---

10. See the references cited in Hans Dieter Betz, *Galatians* (Philadelphia: Fortress, 1979), 50–52.

11. Robertson and Plummer, *First Corinthians*, 400.

12. Warren W. Wiersbe, *Be Wise* (Wheaton, Ill.: Victor, 1983), 172.

Stephanas and his two companions (vv. 15–18) remind us that the most legitimate form of church leadership or authority in our day still remains that which is acknowledged by fellow Christians as stemming from devoted service to the saints (v. 15). While some want to abolish hierarchy and others to employ it in authoritarian fashion, servant leaders guide by loving example, to whom fellow Christians should submit (see further the applications of chap. 4, p. 93). The model of these three men should challenge all Christians today to get involved when they see a need waiting to be met, regardless of whether they hold any formal office or are first invited to participate. We are tearing down today some of the unhealthy barriers between clergy and laity; one helpful principle derivable from this text is to recognize as leaders those who have emerged from within a congregation as its most dedicated servants. Megachurches that are increasingly identifying such commitment among their own membership and then training those persons to be leaders (or sponsoring their training) may well have a good handle on the application of this principle.

The comings and goings of Stephanas, Fortunatus, and Achaicus, like the frequent travels of Aquila and Priscilla to establish home congregations in each community in which they lived, remind us of the ways in which the early church was international and yet interdependent.[13] In our day, when travel and communication make networking and cooperation among various parts of the body of Christ so much easier, it is all the more necessary that we take advantage of this technology. And to the extent that more and more Christians' lives and work revolve around that technology, the need for the uniquely personal touch and for the intimacy possible among believers, so ably modeled by Paul and his coworkers, is growing rapidly.

Both parts of verse 22 call us back to a holy outrage at those who generally try to destroy or corrupt the church today, masquerading as believers. Even as we warn of God's impending judgment against such people (Paul's *anathema*), the cry *Marana tha* reminds us to leave that judgment to God in Christ upon his return. One thinks naturally of the various sects and cults that lead people astray in the name of Jesus; indeed many of these can trace their roots back directly or indirectly to ancient Hellenistic philosophy and even to Gnosticism (particularly the religious sciences—Christian Science, Unity School of Christianity, etc.) But we recall too that Paul's harshest words were consistently reserved for the legalists of his day, particularly among the conservative Judaizing factions (cf. Gal. 1:6–10; Phil. 3:2–4:1). In one instance, he even declares divisiveness itself worthy of excommunication

---

13. Prior, *1 Corinthians*, 279.

(Tit. 3:10–11). So our contemporary applications must range closer to home as well, as we scrupulously ward off and avoid the legalists in our evangelical Christian circles. Those whose long lists of dos and don'ts in their policies on Christian lifestyle go far beyond scriptural commands, like some of the extreme "witch-hunters" in our midst, ironically may be more in need of church discipline themselves than some of those they consistently attack.[14]

Paul's cry of *Marana tha* reminds us of how much our world, even our Christian world, lives in the present without longing for the age to come. We have already spoken of this generation's attempt to create Paradise on earth rather than genuinely longing for Christ's return and the perfect new heavens and new earth that will subsequently be created (see above, pp. 310–11). Little wonder that the 1970s film, *Heaven Can Wait*, about a professional football quarterback who died in a car accident and was disappointed to find himself in heaven because he would miss out on the Super Bowl, proved so popular. Its story line remains as timely and poignant at the end of the century.

Fittingly, Paul closes with one final reminder of the centrality of "grace" and "love" (vv. 23–24). We continue to need both; indeed, we ought to crave them. For detailed application, see under chapter 13. If our generation has sometimes removed God from the concept of love, it has at least correctly captured the centrality of love for any viable human ethic. Love does "make the world go 'round,'" but the only truly life- and world-changing love that will last is that which is founded on a saving relationship with Jesus Christ.

---

14. Cf. the sane discussion and precautions spelled out in Bob and Gretchen Passantino, *Witch Hunt* (Nashville: Thomas Nelson, 1990).

Scripture Index